T0383941

SPIES FOR THE SULTAN

Georgetown Studies in Intelligence History

Series Editors: Christopher Moran, Mark Phythian, and Mark Stout

Editorial Advisory Board: Ioanna Iordanou, Peter Jackson, Tricia Jenkins, Paul Maddrell, Paul McGarr, Kathryn Olmsted, Dina Rezk, Calder Walton, and Michael Warner

Titles in the Series

Canadian Military Intelligence: Operations and Evolution from the October Crisis to the War in Afghanistan
David A. Charters

Crown, Cloak, and Dagger: The British Monarchy and Secret Intelligence from Victoria to Elizabeth II
Richard J. Aldrich and Rory Cormac

SPIES
FOR THE
SULTAN

OTTOMAN INTELLIGENCE IN THE
GREAT RIVALRY WITH SPAIN

EMRAH SAFA GÜRKAN

translated by

JONATHAN M. ROSS AND
İDIL KARACADAĞ

GEORGETOWN UNIVERSITY PRESS / WASHINGTON, DC

This book was originally published in Turkish as *Sultanin Casusları: 16. Yüzyılda İstihbarat, Sabotaj ve Rüşvet Ağları*. The book was translated into English by Jonathan M. Ross, except for Chapter 4, which was translated by İdil Karacadağ.

The publisher is not responsible for third-party websites or their content. URL links were active at time of publication.

Library of Congress Cataloging-in-Publication Data

Names: Gürkan, Emrah Safa, author. | Ross, Jonathan (Jonathan Maurice), translator. | Karacadağ, İdil, 1991– translator.
Title: Spies for the sultan : Ottoman intelligence in the great rivalry with Spain / Emrah Safa Gürkan ; translated by Jonathan M. Ross and İdil Karacadağ.
Other titles: Sultanın casusları. English | Ottoman intelligence in the great rivalry with Spain
Description: First English-language edition. | Washington, DC : Georgetown University Press, [2024] | Series: Georgetown studies in intelligence history | "This book was originally published in Turkish as Sultanin Casuslari: 16. Yüzyılda İstihbarat, Sabotaj ve Rüşvet Ağları." | Includes bibliographical references and index.
Identifiers: LCCN 2023030832 (print) | LCCN 2023030833 (ebook) | ISBN 9781647124410 (hardcover) | ISBN 9781647124427 (ebook)
Subjects: LCSH: Spies—Turkey—History—16th century. | Espionage, Turkish—History—16th century. | Intelligence service—Turkey—History—16th century. | Turkey—History—16th century. | Turkey—History—Ottoman Empire, 1288–1918. | Turkey—Foreign relations—Austria. | Austria—Foreign relations—Turkey. | Mediterranean Region—History—1517–1789.
Classification: LCC UB271.T9 G8713 2024 (print) | LCC UB271.T9 (ebook) | DDC 327.12560182/209031—dc23/eng/20231108
LC record available at https://lccn.loc.gov/2023030832
LC ebook record available at https://lccn.loc.gov/2023030833

♾ This paper meets the requirements of ANSI/NISO Z39.48-1992 (Permanence of Paper).

25 24   9 8 7 6 5 4 3 2   First printing

Printed in the United States of America

Cover design by Brad Norr
Interior design by Robert Kern, TIPS Publishing Services, Carrboro, NC

Dedicated to my beloved daughter, Zeynep,
and our resident corsair, Cap'n Uluc Emre . . .

CONTENTS

TABLES AND MAPS

TABLES

MAPS

FOREWORD

Scholars of Ottoman history have paid relatively little attention to the seemingly marginal topics of intelligence networks and their members. In reality, though, it is worth examining such topics in order to ascertain how the intelligence activities of a state complemented its vision. Indeed, even though the enormous importance of intelligence has not always been recognized, throughout history (and not just during the modern age) intelligence and an intelligence infrastructure have been vital components of any structure endeavoring to acquire the properties of a state. By resorting to undercover sources, the modern state has developed alternative ways of acquiring information and has created the organizational means for doing so. In other words, while the need for intelligence is constant and the goal of obtaining information remains the same, the methods and structures deployed by the modern state differ.

Examples from the very founding years of the Ottoman dynasty suggest that an intelligence network existed even in this early period. Although one might be inclined to attach great significance to such attempts at information gathering, the truth is that they were a practical necessity. This is amply borne out by the sources. For example, there is evidence that, within the Ottoman military organization attached to nomadic tribes, certain measures were taken to acquire information about groups of warriors who may have been inclined to pursue religious goals or who were set on plunder.

A good example is the Battle of Bapheus in 1302, which we know quite a lot about thanks to a contemporary source. When a Byzantine unit under the command of Georgios Mouzalōn crossed over the Gulf of Izmit to Yalova to assist the local Byzantine rulers, who were uneasy about Osman Bey's activities there, the unit was shocked to be suddenly faced with Osman Bey's soldiers. There is no reason to believe that this was just a coincidence and had nothing to do with the Ottomans' system for news gathering or with the dynasty's intelligence network. We should not be surprised to see that, within nomadic communities, there were swift-acting individuals whose duty was to receive and gather news. Indeed, the existence of such people may reflect above all their ability to adapt to the existential threats that they faced, which was possibly their most salient characteristic. This precariousness was a feature of the pastoral way of life. Staying alive and holding on to whatever one had were basic requirements.

Another striking example is Orhan Bey's clash with the Byzantine emperor at the Battle of Pelekanon in 1329. Three days after setting off from Constantinople, the army under the control of the Byzantine emperor reached the area around Gebze, where they were surprised to encounter Ottoman troops waiting for them. Given Orhan Bey's general circumstances and the distance of Gebze from his own powerbase, it is quite remarkable that he and his soldiers arrived at the strategic location before the Byzantines and were in wait there, right under the nose of Constantinople and the Byzantine throne. This would seem to testify to the effectiveness of Orhan Bey's intelligence network. This example also reminds us that, even in this early period, the Ottomans had recourse to a news network that was both well-organized and conscious of its role. There clearly existed people whose responsibility it was to gather news; while they were probably not spies in the modern sense of the word, they did use certain methods to achieve a particular objective. It is possible that the aforementioned cases testify to attempts during the formation of the Ottoman beylik and the establishment of the Ottoman Empire to create a secret apparatus. There may have been a conscious decision to do so, or it might have emerged from the experience of the parties involved. Whatever the case, even if this apparatus was in some sense professional, due to its clandestine nature it has left little traces in the sources. In addition, it would be fair to say that this would not have been a modern, European-style apparatus but would have been made up of different elements; to understand this apparatus, these elements need to be considered in their own right, since they did not exist within an orderly, systematic framework.

Emrah Safa Gürkan has gained eminence for his research on political developments in the Mediterranean and on subjects such as piracy. His present work, which deals with the sixteenth century, generally regarded as the apex of the Ottoman imperial age, draws on authentic domestic and foreign documents, as well as on secondary literature, in attempting to explore the topics of espionage and counterintelligence. As such, it is one of very few serious studies of intelligence-gathering operations in this period and is sure to satisfy the curious mind. Gürkan's general approach is to examine the identities of the members of the Ottoman intelligence service and to investigate whether they operated within a certain system. While his findings are extremely convincing and his approach to the material very systematic, Gürkan's use of interrogation reports offers the reader an insight into what, from the vantage point of Ottoman history, is quite a remarkable world. From a theoretical point of view, the author has mostly managed to steer clear of the generalities that bedevil comparisons with Western states, generalities which can easily lead on to erroneous judgments. In such comparisons of intelligence services and operations in early modern state structures, Western cases have tended to be held up as superior examples of a regular form of organization. In contrast, the Ottoman structure has appeared vague and shrouded in mystery. Gürkan masterfully demonstrates the need for a different approach. For this reason alone, the information provided in this book is invaluable.

Thanks in part to the author's engaging style, this book will appeal not just to experts but also to other educated readers who are curious about the subject. I am sure that for many years ahead this book will retain its status as the first serious study in its field.

—Feridun M. Emecen

ACKNOWLEDGMENTS

I am indebted to all of my professors, who have taught me so much, foremost among them my thesis advisors Gábor Ágoston and the late Halil İnalcık (RIP). Although it is impossible to acknowledge everyone who has assisted me, I should confess that Emilio Sola Castaño, James B. Collins, John McNeill, Faruk Tabak, Claudio Povolo, and Maria Pia Pedani occupy a special place in my heart, as do Feridun M. Emecen, Kemal Beydilli, Ali Akyıldız, Oktay Özel, and Erhan Afyoncu, who never ceased encouraging me to write this book.

Feridun Emecen, Kemal Beydilli, Sadık Müfit Bilge, and Levent Kaya Ocakaçan provided detailed feedback on the book in its entirety, and for this I cannot thank them enough. Special mention should be made of Kemal Beydilli for his scathing criticisms of my translations without exception, foremost among them the Latin ones! Güneş Işıksel, Oğuzhan Göksel, Hüseyin Serdar Tabakoğlu, Martin Rothkegel, Kenan Yıldız, Ekrem Taha Başer, Kahraman Şakul, and Emir Yener were all involved in the genesis of this work by reading individual chapters. Their comments and corrections contributed significantly to the book's content.

I would like to extend my gratitude to colleagues who played a pivotal role in bringing Sultanın Casusları, which first appeared in Turkish seven years ago, to an Anglophone audience: Ioanna Iordanou, herself an expert on Early Modern intelligence in the Mediterranean, for her encouragement; Jonathan Ross for undertaking the tedious task of translating a text replete with myriad historical terminology; and Donald Jacobs for meticulously going through the text and offering changes and additions.

There are numerous friends to whom I remain forever indebted. Among these are my dear friends Cenk Erkan, Bengü Üçüncü, İlker Demir, Özgür Sezer, Polat Safi, Murat Önsoy, Ökkeş Kürşat Karacagil, Harun Yeni, Andrea Chiovenda, Caner Can, Nahide Işık Demirakın, Onur Güneş, Hamid Akın Ünver, Gennaro Varriale, Cengiz Yolcu, Ekin Özbiçer, Barın Kayaoğlu, Erkan Kaderoğlu, Fabio Vicini, Anand Toprani, Kaya Şahin, Serap Mumcu, Fatih Baha Aydın, Alphan Akgün, and Melis Süzer. My immense gratitude is due too to

Michelangelo/Ahmed Guida, the king of the converts, who had the misfortune of sharing an office with me for several years; to my loyal friend and brother-in-law, Ergun; and to my beloved mother-in-law, Işık Ertekin, who has endured no end of strife on account of her blunt-talking son-in-law.

I also thank my dear wife, Elif, who for years has had no alternative but to fall asleep to the sound of the keyboard; my daughter, Zeynep, who, because of her workaholic father, acquired the hobby of filling up Microsoft Word documents when she was just two years old; and my son the master-corsair, Uluc Emre, who reacted by developing an incredible fondness for books and filling his old man with pride. The sacrifices made by these three wonderful people have shown the lie in the belief that an academic who gets married and has children will not be able to find any time to work. In writing this book, I have endeavored to do two things. On the one hand, I have tried to vindicate my father, Doğan, for dragging me from one secondhand bookseller to the next when I was still in shorts. On the other hand, I have tried to prove that my dear mother, Eda, was wrong to dream that I would go into law or engineering but right to swallow my becoming a historian. I hope I have achieved these objectives!

—Emrah Safa Gürkan
August 15, 2023
Moda, Istanbul

ABBREVIATIONS

AGS	Archivo General de Simancas, Valladolid
AK	Istanbul Metropolitan Municipality Atatürk Library
AMP	Archivio Mediceo del Principato, Florence
ASF	Archivio di Stato di Firenze, Florence
ASG	Archivio di Stato di Genoa, Genoa
ASV	Archivio di Stato di Venezia, Venice
BNE	Biblioteca Nacional de España, Madrid
BNM	Biblioteca Nazionale Marciana, Venice
BOA	Başbakanlık Osmanlık Arşivleri (Ottoman Archives of the Office of the Prime Minister), Istanbul
CCX-LettAmb	Capi del consiglio di dieci, Lettere di ambasciatori
CCX-LettRett	Capi del consiglio di dieci, Lettere di rettori et di altre cariche
COSP	Calendar of State Papers
CX-ParSec	Consiglio di dieci, Parti Secrete
DAD	Državni Arhiv u Dubrovniku, Dubrovnik
DocTR	Documenti Turchi
E	Papeles de Estado
HHStA	Österreichisches Staatsarchiv, Haus-, Hof- und Staatsarchiv, Vienna
IS	Inquisitori di Stato
KK	Kamil Kepeci
MD	Mühimme Defterleri (Registers of Important Affairs)
MZD	Mühimme Zeyli Defterleri (Appendixes to Registers of Important Affairs)
SAPC	Senato, Archivio Proprio Costantinopoli
SDC	Senato, Dispacci, Costantinopoli
SDelC	Senato, Secreta, Deliberazioni, Costantinopoli
TSMA	Topkapı Sarayı Müzesi Arşivleri (Topkapı Palace Museum Archives), Istanbul

TSMK	Topkapı Sarayı Müzesi Kütüphanesi (Topkapı Palace Museum Library), Istanbul
b.	born
b.	(It.) *busta*, box
c.	(It.) *carta*, page
c.	circa/approximately
cf.	compare
col.	colon
ed.	edited by
edn	edition
et al.	and others
fil.	(It.) *filza*, file
fn.	footnote
fol.	(It.) *folio*, folio
Fr.	French
Ger.	German
Gr.	Greek
hk.	(Tur.) *hüküm*, decree
It.	Italian
konv.	(Ger.) *konvolut*, bundle
Lat.	Latin
MS	(Lat.) *manuscriptum*, manuscript
no.	number
of.	period in office
Ott.	Ottoman
p./pp.	page/pages
Por.	Portuguese
r.	ruled
r.	(Lat.) *recto*, right/front
reg.	(Lat.) *registro*, record
Sp.	Spanish
v.	(Lat.) *verso*, left/rear
vr.	(Tur.) *varak*, folio
vol.	volume

Note about dates: When citing Ottoman documents, dates are given according to both the Hegira and Gregorian calendars. In the Venetian calendar, because the new year is supposed to begin on March 1, December 31, 1567, would be followed by January 1, 1567, and not January 1, 1568. To alert the reader, in such cases the abbreviation "m.v." (*more Veneto*) has been used; the reader should therefore recognize that reference is being made to the subsequent year.

Greg.	Gregorian calendar
H.	Hegira calendar
Gurre	The first day of the month in the Hegira calendar

Selh	The last day of the month in the Hegira calendar
Eva'il'	The first ten-day period of the month in the Hegira calendar
Evasıt'	The second ten-day period of the month in the Hegira calendar
Evahir	The third ten-day period of the month in the Hegira calendar

INTRODUCTION

Although spread across three continents, the Ottoman Empire managed to survive for centuries. One of the factors critical to this success was the Empire's ability to keep a close eye on the military and political developments taking place around it. Despite all the attempts it made at modernization, the Empire eventually proved incapable of holding its own against the West, which managed to bring the entire world to its knees. The resultant collapse of the Ottoman Empire in 1922 helped to feed a historical narrative that underestimated the military and political capabilities of the Ottomans in earlier years. Within this account of history, which is tied up with the general approach to the Middle East found in Orientalist historiography, the Ottoman Empire is likened to an ostrich with its head stuck in the sand. As a consequence of the revolutionary fervor of the early years of the Turkish Republic, a fixed image came to prevail, that of a country that for six centuries had displayed no interest in its surroundings.

In recent years, however, a number of studies have shown that the Ottomans were not so cut off from the outside world.[1] The purpose of this book is not so much to engage in the debate on this issue as to show how the Ottomans had great success collecting information about other states. On numerous occasions, they managed to outperform their archrivals, the Habsburgs, in the intelligence competition. The fact that this went unnoticed until now was due to the scarcity of documentation related to espionage in the Ottoman archives, a dearth that is itself a product of the decentralized and noninstitutionalized nature of Ottoman espionage. Nonetheless, a comparative reading of documents from different European archives clearly attests to the Ottomans' competence. As will be shown in chapter 4, even in times of acute crises, as was the case in the War of 1570–73, in which Istanbul lost its entire fleet against a united Christian alliance, the Ottomans managed to collect reliable intelligence. Using a variety of sources, ranging from provincial authorities to vassal states, from foreign diplomats to captured soldiers, and from agents in the field to corsairs on reconnaissance missions, they succeeded in sifting accurate information from false information and employing their limited resources based on the intelligence that they received. More impressively, they did so in a timely fashion. A juxtaposition of sources from different European archives allowed a quantifiable comparison between news reaching the Ottoman capital and that reaching Venice, the main center of information in the Early Modern Mediterranean. As will be seen in table 4.3, news of major political and military events reached the Ottoman capital as quickly as it did Venice, allowing Ottoman decision-makers to assess the situation and respond in time.

This book seeks to do more than give a performance test to the Ottoman intelligence. While examining Istanbul's relations with the Western world, it also offers a systematic analysis of the methods and resources that the Ottoman intelligence network employed, as well as the outcomes it achieved. The six-teenth century was both the heyday of the Ottoman Empire and an era that witnessed the emergence of the centralized state and innovations in the fields of military technology, modern diplomacy, and espionage techniques. In this century, when monarchs were chasing dreams of world domination, both the Ottomans and their archrivals the Habsburgs were willing to exploit all their resources and spare no expense in their attempt to found a global empire. In chapter 1, I will explain in more detail how this imperial rivalry created condi-tions that were particularly ripe for espionage.

In this period, what kind of intelligence techniques were used by the Ottoman Empire? While it certainly possessed a military force to be reckoned with, can one even speak of an institutionalized Ottoman intelligence organiza-tion in this period? How did Ottoman spies conduct their operations out in the field? What kinds of backgrounds did these spies have? What kinds of methods did Istanbul develop to prevent enemy spies from operating in the Empire?

These questions may seem simple, but they are questions that Ottoman his-toriography has so far failed to address. Before seeking answers, a brief review of the literature will serve to highlight this book's contribution to Ottoman and European history as well as to place the book's general arguments within their historical and thematic context.

INTELLIGENCE IN THE EARLY MODERN PERIOD

In the sixteenth century, modern states and the apparatuses associated with them had still not taken shape, so intelligence had not been institutionalized either. In fact, the first steps in this institutionalization process are hinted at in this book, but my focus is not so much on intelligence organizations as on the spies themselves. Indeed, in the following pages, you will encounter the fascinating lives of many religious converts, merchants, corsairs, soldiers, and sailors, and you will learn about their intelligence activities.

As I have already mentioned, the sixteenth century was the first golden age of intelligence.[2] There are various reasons for the emergence of intelligence at this point. News (and consequently intelligence) became more important due to factors such as the opening up of new trade routes as a result of geographical discoveries, the Reformation, the spread of the printing press, and the development of postal services. The information boom was epitomized by the emergence of handwritten news bulletins that became widespread during this period and that can be regarded as the precursors of newspapers, which would only appear at the beginning of the seventeenth century (the Italian avvisi).[3] It was also during this period that information stopped being the preserve of the state and became the property of an emerging public sphere. Bankers such as the Fugger family, who to protect their business interests needed to monitor developments across the world, went as far as publishing their own bulletins and—for a certain subscription—sharing with interested parties the news they had managed to collect.[4]

Another key development in the sixteenth century was the emergence of "administrative-bureaucratic structures,"[5] structures that would actually undertake the first steps toward the institutionalization of espionage. These timid steps, however, did not have the desired effect, and it would not be until the end of the nineteenth century that intelligence services would be entirely institutionalized. All the same, it would be fair to say that the aforementioned structures were crucial to the development of intelligence. They enabled the institutionalization of archival and postal services, which are essential for both diplomacy and espionage, and they contributed to the wider use of techniques such as cryptanalysis, cryptology, and steganography (concealed writing).

As will be expanded on in chapter 1, the imperial rivalry between the Ottomans and the Habsburgs, two great empires of their time, raised news-collection and other espionage activities to an unprecedented level. For decision-makers with only a limited military budget, knowing the intention of the enemy is essential when it comes to matching military investments to potential risks. When spring comes, will the enemy's fleet leave port? Will the enemy be able to suppress a rebellion in a remote province? Will the enemy's wheat and barley harvest that year be enough to feed their soldiers, sailors, and oarsmen, not to mention their horses and draft animals? These are just a handful of the questions facing central governments that were constantly beset with financial problems. Decision-makers had no choice but to find answers to such questions in order to choose the correct military strategy and to find a way of distributing their resources rationally. These questions, moreover, did not pertain to just Europe and the Mediterranean. Decision-makers needed to keep track of political and economic affairs across a vast territory, from the Indian Ocean to Russia and from America to Yemen.

Prior to the 1980s, studies on the subject of intelligence in the Early Modern Period had been relatively scant and general in content.[6] From then on, though, a spate of studies emerged that drew on primary sources and tended to focus on a single intelligence organization and a particular period. In 1984 Diplomacia Secreta en Flandes was published, which thematized espionage activities at the time of the Eighty Years' War in the Netherlands (1568–1648),[7] and this was followed by Espionagem e Contra-Espionagem numa Guerra Peninsular, which concentrated on the Portuguese Restoration War (1640–68).[8] However, since works written in Spanish or Portuguese could have only little impact on the world of academia, they remained largely unknown on an international level.

What really stimulated studies of intelligence in the Early Modern age was a French book. In just a short time, Lucien Bély's nine-hundred-page magnum opus examining diplomacy and espionage during the reign of Louis XIV became something of a classic. [9] It was followed by a multitude of works about espionage operations and intelligence apparatuses in France, Britain, Italy, Portugal, and Ragusa.[10] Among these, Paolo Preto's I Servizi Segreti di Venezia, a study of the Venetian intelligence service across three centuries, which drew on thousands of documents, is particularly worthy of mention.[11] It should also be noted that an abundance of articles and monographs were written about the spies operating in the service of the Habsburgs, with the publications of Emilio Sola Castaño particularly outstanding,[12] among others.[13]

A number of well-written works on early modern espionage have appeared since the first publication of this work in Turkish in 2017.[14] Unlike earlier works, mainly focusing on spies, spymasters, and intelligence operations, these innovative studies dealt with hitherto neglected issues such as information flow between political centers,[15] political use of information by nascent central governments and the emerging public,[16] and analysis of concepts such as information[17] and secrecy.[18] Moreover, even when concentrating on spies and intelligence operations, they expanded the field by focusing on women[19] and turncoats,[20] and they divorced intelligence from high politics by studying industrial espionage.[21] A few works entered unchartered waters by concentrating on espionage in the Americas.[22]

The fact that a recently published edited volume on intelligence leaders contains two articles on Ottoman and Venetian espionage is proof of the growing interest in a field dominated by studies focusing on the modern era.[23] This interest is due to a number of impressive works penned by a new generation of young scholars.[24] To mention a few that broke new ground, Gennaro Varriale's book on information gathering in Habsburg Naples testifies to the explicatory potential of sources in Spanish and Italian archives.[25] Ionna Iordanou's comprehensive analysis on Venetian espionage is an indispensable work not only because it sheds light on the complex organization of the era's most sophisticated intelligence mechanism—a task which Preto, lost in detail and plain narrative, failed to undertake—but also because it studies intelligence through a socioeconomic, and not solely political, lens by showing how the Repubblica Serenissima incentivized its ordinary people, otherwise strictly banned from political participation, to gather information for the state, both in Venice and abroad.[26]

Finally, *Pistols! Treason! Murder!* is perhaps the most idiosyncratic work produced by an early modernist, combining illustrated comic strips (in the style of historical woodcuts and engravings), transcripts of the author's dialogues with his friends in Venetian bars (including Caffè Rosso in Campo Santa Margherita, where most historians end up after a tiresome day in the archives), and translations of archival documents. The book's experimental nature, self-styled as "punk history," is by no means a liability. Relying on dili-gent archival research and lacking no academic rigor, Jonathan Walker uses the detective-like story of Venetian spy Gerolamo Vano to recreate the underworld of spies in the seventeenth-century Mediterranean.[27]

In contrast, very little has been produced about intelligence in the Ottoman Empire in the Early Modern Period.[28] With the exception of a twenty-three-page pamphlet,[29] practically all of the publications have been articles. They have either concentrated on the activities of an individual spy acting on behalf of the Ottomans[30] or dwelled on the exchange of information between Istanbul and other capitals.[31] A third group of publications consists of Roman alphabet transliterations of Ottoman archival documents, each accompanied by a short and superficial commentary.[32] There are just three exceptions to this taxonomy. In an article on Ottoman intelligence published in 2003, Haldun Eroğlu devotes five pages to Ottoman spies, which he discusses under subcategories such as voluntary spies, salaried spies, language-learning methods, merchants, and travelers. In addition, Eroğlu presents a chronology of espionage-related inci-dents that he came across in chronicles from the period.[33] Although this article broke new ground, unfortunately it failed to offer deep analysis of the subject. Eroğlu makes rash claims, such as saying that spies were not used during the reign of Alparslan (the Sultan of the Great Seljukids, reigning between 1063 and 1072),[34] and when alleging that foreign agents were operating on Ottoman soil, he is simply stating the obvious.[35] Another study that attempts to offer a general overview of Ottoman intelligence is an article in which Gábor Ágoston sets out how the Ottomans devised a consistent strategy on the basis of the information they obtained through various sources and channels.[36] Although this article could be said to provide a systematic analysis, its aim is not to dis-sect the structure of the Ottoman intelligence apparatus or to offer a compar-ison between the Ottoman intelligence service and those of Venice and the Habsburgs. Finally, Mustafa Dehqan and Vural Genç's article that appeared after the original publication of this book is a good supplement, as it focuses on eastern Anatolia, a region not covered in this work, which mainly deals with the European front.[37]

One of the objectives of the present book is to avoid a shortcoming of the existing literature, namely its reliance on the limited documents in the Ottoman archives, which prevents scholars from fully grasping the subject at hand. To this end, use has been made of documents from various European archives in Spanish, German, French, Italian, Latin, and Portuguese.

ISLAM AND CHRISTIANITY IN THE MEDITERRANEAN BORDERLANDS: A CLASH OF CIVILIZATIONS?

One of the chief debates in the field of Mediterranean history concerns the nature of interactions between religions and cultures. To appreciate the tra-jectory of this debate, it is helpful to draw on Eric Dursteler's reference to the concurrence of "the bifurcated Mediterranean of the battlefield" and "the linked Mediterranean suggested by the region's many bazaars and other places of encounter and exchange,"[38] that is, to acknowledge the coexistence of two competing historical frameworks.

The first scholar to contend that the Mediterranean was divided between the realms of Islam and Christianity was Henri Pirenne, who presented this argument in his posthumously published Mahomet et Charlemagne (1937).[39] According to this Belgian historian, what shattered the unity that the Roman Empire had managed to ensure in the Mediterranean was not the invasion by Germanic tribes, but the emergence of Islam in the seventh century and that religion's expansion along the shores of the Mediterranean. Once this expansion was complete, the Christian West broke its ties with those territories that had come under Islamic sovereignty, and the Mediterranean came to be riven in two by an iron curtain, with one religion on each side.

The school of Middle Eastern historiography associated with Bernard Lewis concurs with the main points of Pirenne's view. Lewis regards Islam as a homogeneous civilization devoid of dynamism.[40] Just as Lewis and his ilk are sometimes quite happy to ignore the geographical, ethnic, and cultural diversity in the Islamic world, they also refrain from recognizing the historical evolution of Islamic religion, culture, and science. According to this doyen of the history of the Middle East, the reasons for the backwardness of Muslim societies should be sought not in external factors such as colonialism and imperialism but in internal factors like zealotry and inertia. Such societies—the argument goes—bank on their political and military superiority while behaving in a "culturally arrogant" manner. This leads them to turn their noses up at the very innovations that enabled Europe to gain global domination. As a consequence, Islamic societies have supposedly lagged behind for centuries, or rather, they have insisted on not advancing. Given Lewis's view of history as being shaped by religions and civilizations that constitute homogenous wholes and function as the main actors in history, it should come as little surprise that Lewis speaks of a "medieval iron curtain," which minimized cultural exchanges between Islam and Christendom "and greatly restricted even commercial and diplomatic intercourse."[41]

In their works, historians like Paolo Preto,[42] Andrew Hess,[43] and Robert C. Davis[44] follow in Pirenne's footsteps and foreground the notion of a holy war being waged between these two religions. This approach, of course, has a great deal in common with the dichotomous view of history peddled by the political scientist Samuel Huntington in his concept of a "clash of civilizations."[45] Although Huntington's argument has not been taken very seriously in academic circles (at least in the realm of early modern history) and appears "analytically bankrupt,"[46] one cannot escape the fact that this reductive and ahistorical paradigm is still remarkably popular.[47]

One of the most important proponents of the notion of a "connected Mediterranean" is Fernand Braudel, the doyen of French historians. In his masterpiece La Méditerranée et le monde Méditerranéen à l'époque de Philippe II, which revolutionized modern historiography, Braudel, "the Pope of New

History," maintained that the Mediterranean should be treated as a whole.[48] According to the French historian, the Mediterranean was not split into two along lines of religion or civilization. Rather, within the Mediterranean space there were "hundreds of borders, some political, some economic and some civilizational."[49] Exchange and contact between religions continued across all these borders and at every level. The civilizations that evolved along the coasts of the Mediterranean were shaped by the same general trends and shared "common destinies" imposed on them by ecological, economic, and social factors.[50] There was no shortage of historians who followed in the footsteps of Braudel in endeavoring to reveal the porousness of religious boundaries in the Mediterranean and to foreground the importance of economic and cultural exchange.

The main purpose of this book, which is closer in approach to the second of the aforementioned schools, is to approach the Mediterranean region as a frontier zone or borderland. As such, this book takes up again a concept that lies at the center of discussions concerning the establishment of the Ottoman Empire; the notion of the borderland, moreover, appears even more valid to this work than it does to the conditions of the fourteenth- and fifteenth-century Balkans. The Mediterranean is a zone of transition between religions and cultures. It is not a space whose everyday complexity can be wished away by resorting to clichéd binary oppositions or by depending on categories that have been forced on us by the works of historiography that derive from the supposed "superior culture." Neither do we gain anything, when considering the Mediterranean, if we think of it as a realm in which Christianity and Islam were engaged in a perpetual holy war. The numerous stories of spies that we encounter in this book give us the opportunity to scratch below the surface of this monotone picture and appreciate the rich historical experience beneath it, complete with all its irregularities and contradictions.

SOURCES CONSULTED

The main reason why Ottoman historians have so far failed to produce a single comprehensive study on intelligence, despite the popularity of this subject, is the inadequacy of the documents in the Ottoman archives. In recent years, it has frequently been maintained with some degree of nationalistic pride that the Ottoman archives are actually rich in content. This, unfortunately, is not entirely true; indeed, such a general label as "rich" should not be applied to any archive. While an archive might contain a wide range of sources on one topic, it may have little to offer a researcher on another subject. When it comes to the sixteenth century, whereas the Ottoman census records and financial documents in some cases prove quite extensive and enlightening, the same cannot be said for materials on political affairs. For reasons that we do not need to go into here, the so-called mühimme defterleri (Registers of Important Affairs) held at the Ottoman Archives of the Prime Ministry, which constitute this book's principal source, do not supply us with sufficient information about the details of intelligence operations, even if they can give us an idea as to how the intelligence system worked. Most of the handful of spies' reports that one comes across at the Topkapı Palace are not related to countries bordering the Mediterranean but to issues closer to home, namely, to struggles for the Ottoman throne.[51] Without access to operational details, a study of intelligence is doomed to remain superficial and merely state the obvious. The handful of articles published prior to this book did not go any further than pointing out that the Ottomans received information about their enemies for intelligence purposes. Given that we are talking about a major empire that lasted six centuries, concluding that the Ottoman Empire gathered information with the aid of spies was hardly a groundbreaking discovery!

It is obviously necessary to dig deeper and take a broader perspective. The sixteenth century was a turning point in the evolution of archives. This period saw the adoption of more systematic methods for storing the considerable quantity of documents that were produced on the one hand by the expansion of chanceries in Venice, Madrid, Ragusa, Florence, Naples, Rome, and Genoa and on the other hand by the increased number of resident ambassadors. Thanks to this increase in documentation, thousands of spies' reports have survived in these archives down to the present. It should also be noted that, as governments became more centralized, they kept a closer eye on intelligence activities, which had previously continued on a local, undocumented basis. States began to keep written records of everything. In European archives, today's lucky historians can find numerous documents from the infancy of modern bureaucracy, documents in Latin, Italian, French, Venetian, Spanish, German, Portuguese, and even Ottoman.

This book attempts to draw on the wealth of documents in the aforementioned archives and the materials in the Ottoman archives to offer an analysis of this rich synthesis. While the Ottoman sources can be said to comprise the indispensable ingredients of this work, the oil and salt as it were, the European documents make up the remainder, lending this book its distinct taste.

CHAPTERS

This book consists of five chapters, four of which are concerned with intelligence. Chapter 1 addresses the imperial rivalry between two great empires of the sixteenth century, the Ottoman and Habsburg Empires, explaining how this rivalry set the context for alliances and diplomatic and military developments.

Without a doubt, in a single chapter one cannot do justice to such an important century as the sixteenth century, a period that saw rapid change in cartography, state formation, and warfare. This was, after all, the century that historians in the mold of Braudel and Wallerstein have identified as the dawn of modern capitalism. It is no less obvious, though, that a brief and concise piece of contextualization is essential for introducing the reader unfamiliar with the subject to the states, individuals, and events that they will encounter in the remainder of the book.

I personally regard chapter 2 as the most interesting chapter of this book. It investigates the backgrounds of the Ottoman spies and presents the fascinating stories of ten different spies, paying special attention to historical context. As well as touching on intelligence-gathering, these stories include details on covert operations such as assassination, bribery, and agitation. They cover a vast geography, from the Low Countries to Spain and from Algeria to Istanbul.

Apart from deploying spies, which other channels did the Ottomans use to gather news and intelligence? This question is addressed in chapter 3, which shifts the focus onto the civilian, military, and diplomatic sources of Ottoman intelligence.

Chapter 4 examines the institutional structure of Ottoman intelligence in an era when central bureaucracies were still in their infancy. On the one hand, it analyzes the intelligence networks under the command of Ottoman grandees and frontier authorities; on the other hand, it evaluates the role of central government in the intelligence system.

Chapter 5 deals with Ottoman counterintelligence, that is, the Ottoman struggle with rival intelligence organizations. At a time when the modern mechanisms of control and public order were not yet in place, what methods did Istanbul and local administrators use to detect enemy spies in their vast "Well-Protected Domains" (Memalik-i Mahrusa)? What would be the fate of spies captured by the Ottomans? How did the Ottomans prevent their enemies from receiving news through other channels?

NOTES

1. Suraiya Faroqhi, *The Ottoman Empire and the World Around It* (New York and London: I.B. Tauris, 2004).
2. Carlos J. Carnicer García and Javier Marcos Rivas, *Espías de Felipe II: Los servicios secretos del Imperio español* (Madrid: La Esfera de Los Libros, 2005), p. 13.
3. Mario Infelise, *Prima dei giornali: Alle origini della pubblica informazione (secoli XVI e XVII)* (Rome: Editori Laterza, 2002).
4. English translations of a selection of these bulletins can be found in Victor von Klarwill, ed., *The Fugger Newsletters: Being a Selection of Unpublished Letters from the Correspondents of the House of Fugger During the Years 1568–1605*, trans. Pauline de Chary (New York and London: The Knickerbocker Press, 1926).
5. Paolo Preto, *I Servizi Segreti di Venezia* (Milan: Il Saggiatore, 1994), pp. 25–38.
6. James Westfall Thompson and Saul K. Padover, *Secret Diplomacy and Cryptography, 1500–1815* (New York: Frederick Ungar Publishing Co., 1937, 1963); Peter Fraser, *The Intelligence of the Secretaries of the State and their Monopoly of Licensed News, 1660–1688* (Cambridge: Cambridge University Press, 1956); Charles Howard Carter, *The Secret Diplomacy of the Habsburgs, 1598–1625* (New York and London: Columbia University Press, 1964); Ionna Iordanou, "The Professionalization of Cryptology in

Sixteenth-Century Venice," *Enterprise & Society* 19, no. 4 (2018): pp. 979–1013.

7. Miguel Angel Echevarría Bacigalupe, *La diplomacia secreta en Flandes, 1598–1643* (Leioa-Vizcaya: Argitarapen Zerbitzua Euskal Herriko Unibertsitatea, 1984).

8. Fernando Cortés, *Espionagem e contra-espionagem numa guerra peninsular 1640–1668* (Lisbon: Livros Horizonte, 1989).

9. Lucien Bély, *Espions et ambassadeurs au temps de Louis XIV* (Paris: Librairie Arthème Fayard, 1990).

10. Romano Canosa and Isabello Colonnello, *Spionaggio a Palermo: Aspetti della guerra secreta turco-spagnola in Mediterraneo nel cinquecento* (Palermo: Sellerio Editore, 1991); Alan Marshall, *Intelligence and Espionage in the Reign of Charles II, 1660–1685* (Cambridge: Cambridge University Press, 1994); John Bossy, *Under the Molehill: An Elizabethan Spy Story* (New Haven, CT: Yale University Press, 2001); Mark Urban, *The Man Who Broke Napoleon's Codes: The Story of George Scovell* (London: Faber and Faber, 2001); Alain Hugon, *Au service du Roi Catholique, "honorables ambassadeurs" et "divins espions": Représentation diplomatique et service secret dans les relations hispano-françaises de 1598 à 1635* (Madrid: Casa de Velázquez, 2004), especially chs. 8–10; Jock Haswell, *The First Respectable Spy: The Life and Times of Colquhoun Grant, Wellington's Head of Intelligence* (Staplehurst: Spellmount, 2005); Stephen Budiansky, *Her Majesty's Spymaster: Queen Elizabeth I, Sir Francis Walsingham, and the Birth of Modern Espionage* (New York: Viking, 2005); Jean-Michel Ribera, *Diplomatie et espionnage: Les ambassadeurs du roi de France auprès de Philippe II du traité du Cateau-Cambresis (1559) à la mort de Henri III (1589)* (Paris: Honoré Champion Editeur, 2007), especially pt. 2; Robert Hutchinson, *Elizabeth's Spy Master: Francis Walsingham and the Secret War that Saved England* (London: Phoenix, 2007); Derek Wilson, *Sir Francis Walsingham: A Courtier in an Age of Terror* (London: Constable, 2007); John Ellis, *To Walk in the Dark: Military Intelligence during the English Civil War (1642–1646)* (Gloucestershire: Spellmount, 2011); Johann Petitjean, "On His Holiness' Secret Service: How Ragusa Became an Intelligence Agency after Lepanto," in *Europe and the 'Ottoman World': Exchanges and Conflicts (Sixteenth to Seventeenth Centuries*, ed. Gábor Karman and Radu G. Păun (Istanbul: The Isis Press, 2013), pp. 83–106; Stéphane Genêt, *Les espions des Lumières: Actions secrètes et espionnage militaire au temps de Louis XV* (Paris: Nouveau Monde Éditions, 2013). For Portuguese intelligence operations in the Indian Ocean and in Ottoman territories, see Vasco Resende, "L'Orient islamique dans la culture portugaise de l'époque moderne, du voyage de Vasco de Gama à la chute d'Ormuz (1498–1622)" (unpublished PhD diss., École Pratique des Haut Études, 2011), ch. 3.

11. Preto, *Servizi Segreti.*

12. Emilio Sola Castaño and José F. de la Peña, *Cervantes y la Berbería: Cervantes, mundo turco-berberisco y servicios secretos en la época de Felipe II* (Madrid: Fondo de Cultura Economica, 1995); Emilio Sola Castaño, *Los que van y vienen: Información y fronteras en el Mediterráneo clásico del siglo XVI* (Alcalá de Henares: Universidad de Alcalá, 2005); Emilio Sola Castaño, *Uchalí: El Calabrés Tiñoso, o el mito del corsario muladí en la frontera* (Barcelona: Edicions Bellaterra, 2011).

13. David Salinas, *Espionaje y gastos secretos en la diplomacia española (1663–1683) en sus documentos* (Valladolid: Ámbito Ediciones, 1994); Carlos J. Carnicer García and Javier Marcos Rivas, *Sebastián de Arbizu, Espía de Felipe II: La diplomacia secreta española y la intervención en Francia* (Madrid: Editorial Nerea S. A., 1998); Javier Marcos Rivas and Carlos J. Carnicer García, *Espionaje y Traición en el Reinado de Felipe II: La historia de vallisoletano Martin de Acuña* (Valladolid: Diputación Provincial de Valladolid, 2001); Carlos J. Carnicer García and Javier Marcos Rivas, *Espías de Felipe II: Los servicios secretos del Imperio español* (Madrid: La Esfera de Los Libros, 2005); Maria José Bertomeu Masiá, ed., *Cartas de un espía de Carlos V: La correspondencia de Jerónimo Bucchia con Antonio Perrenot de Granvela* (Valencia: Universitat de València, 2006); Diego Navarra Bonilla, ed., *Cartas entre espías e inteligencias secretas en el siglo de los stetválidos, Juan de Torres Gaspar-Bonifaz, 1632–1638* (Madrid: Ministerio de Defensa, 2007). For studies of Spanish intelligence from the Middle Ages up to modern times, see Juan R. Goberna Falque, *Inteligencia, espionaje y servicios secretos en España* (Madrid: Ministerio de Defensa, 2007). See also Enrique García Hernán, "The Price of Spying at the Battle of Lepanto," *Eurasian Studies* 2, no. 2 (2003): pp. 227–50; Enrique García Hernán, "Espionaje en la Batalla de Lepanto," *Historia* 16, no. 27 (2003): pp. 8–41; Diego Navarro Bonilla, "Espías honorables, espías necesarios: de la información a la inteligencia en la conducción de la política y la guerra de la monarquía hispánica," in *Ambassadeurs, apprentis espions et maîtres comploteurs: Les systèmes de renseignement en Espagne à l'époque moderne*, ed. Béatrice Perez (Paris: Presses de l'université Paris-Sorbonne, 2010), pp. 31–47; Raphaël Carrasco, "L'espionnage espagnol du Levant au XVIe siècle d'après la correspondance des agents espagnols en poste à Venise," in *Ambassadeurs, apprentis espions*, ed. Beatrice Perez (Paris: Presses de l'universite Paris-Sorbonne, 2010) pp. 203–22; Miguel Ángel de Bunes Ibarra, "Avis du Levant: Le réseau d'espionnage espagnol dans l'empire ottoman à partir du sud de l'Italie, à la charnière des XVIe et XVIIe siècles," in *Ambassadeurs, apprentis espions*, ed. Beatrice Perez (Paris: Presses de l'universite Paris-Sorbonne, 2010) pp. 223–40.

14. See *Journal of Intelligence History*'s vol. 21, no. 3 issue, edited by Tobias P. Graf and Charlotte Backerra and published in 2022, esp. Tobias P. Graf and Charlotte Backerra, "Case Studies in Early Modern European Intelligence"; Ionna Iordanou, "The Secret Service of Renaissance Venice: Intelligence Organisation in the Sixteenth Century;" Tobias P. Graf, "Knowing the 'Hereditary Enemy': Austrian-Habsburg Intelligence on the Ottoman Empire in the Late Sixteenth Century;" and Matthias Pohlig, "The Uses and Utility of Intelligence: The Case of the British Government during the War of the Spanish Succession." Daniel Szechi, ed., *The Dangerous Trade: Spies, Spymasters and the Making of Europe* (Dundee: Dundee University Press, 2010) also contains interesting articles focusing on British, Spanish, and French intelligence from the sixteenth to the eighteenth centuries. Also see Sebastian Sobecki, "'A Man of Curious Enquiry': John Peyton's Grand Tour to Central Europe and Robert Cecil's Intelligence Network, 1596–1601," *Renaissance Studies* 29, no. 3 (2014): pp. 394–410; Santiago González Sánchez, "El espionaje en los reinos de la Península Ibérica a comienzos del siglo XV," *España Medieval* 38 (2015): pp. 135–94; Flora Cassen, "Philip II of

Spain and His Italian Jewish Spy," *Journal of Early Modern History* 21 (2017): pp. 318–42; Stephannie Coeto Coix, "Alexandre Testanegra: An Ottoman Spy in the New World?" (unpublished master's thesis, The University of Texas at Austin, 2018).

15. Ionna Iordanou, "What News on the Rialto? The Trade of Information and Early Modern Venice's Centralized Intelligence Organization," *Intelligence and National Security* 31, no. 3 (2016): pp. 305–26; Johann Petitjean, *L'intelligence des choses: une histoire de l'information entre Italie et Méditerranée (XVIe-XVIIe siècles)* (Rome: École Française de Rome, 2013); John-Paul Ghobrial, *The Whispers of Cities: Information Flows in Istanbul, London, and Paris in the Age of William Trumbull* (Oxford: Oxford University Press, 2013).

16. John Michael Archer, *Sovereignty and Intelligence: Spying and Court Culture in the English Renaissance* (Stanford: Stanford University Press, 1993); Arlette Farge, *Subversive Words: Public Opinion in Eighteenth-Century France*, trans. Rosemary Morris (University Park: The Pennsylvania State University Press, 1994); Jacob Soll, "How to Manage an Information State: Jean-Baptiste Colbert's Archives and the Education of His Son," *Archival Science* 7, no. 4 (2007): pp. 331–42; Filippo de Vivo, *Information and Communication in Venice: Rethinking Early Modern Politics* (Oxford: Oxford University Press, 2007); Jacob Soll, "The Antiquary and the Information State: Colbert's Archives, Secret Histories, and the Affair of the *Régale*, 1663–1682," *French Historical Studies* 31, no. 1 (2008): pp. 3–28; Jacob Soll, *The Information Master: Jean-Baptiste Colbert's Secret State Intelligence System* (Ann Arbor: The University of Michigan Press, 2009); Arndt Brendecke, *Imperium und Empirie: Funktionen des Wissens in der spanischen Kolonialherrschaft* (Köln: Böhlau, 2009); Filippo de Vivo, *Patrizi, Informatori, Barbieri: Politica e communicazione a Venezia nella prima età moderna* (Milano: Feltrinelli, 2012); Filippo de Vivo, "Public Sphere of Communication Triangle? Information and Politics in Early Modern Europe," in *Beyond the Public Sphere: Opinions, Publics, Spaces in Early Modern Europe*, ed. Massimo Rospocher (Bologna: Il Mulino, 2012), pp. 115–36; Adriano Comissoli, "A circulação de informações e o sistema de vigilância portuguesa da fronteira do Rio da Prata (século XIX)," *Revista Eletrônica Documento/Monumento* 13, no. 1 (2014): pp. 23–40; Gregory Dmitrevich Afinogenov, "The Eye of the Tsar: Intelligence-Gathering and Geopolitics in Eighteenth-Century Russia" (unpublished PhD diss., Harvard University, 2016).

17. Johann Petitjean, "Mots et pratiques de l'information: Ce que *aviser* veut dire (XVIe–XVIIe siècles)," *Mélanges de l'École française de Rome* 122, no. 1 (2010): pp. 107–21.

18. Jon R. Snyder, *Dissimulation and the Culture of Secrecy in Early Modern Europe* (Berkeley and Los Angeles: University of California Press, 2009); Daniel Jütte, *The Age of Secrecy: Jews, Christians, and the Economy of Secrets, 1400–1800* (New Haven and London: Yale University Press, 2015).

19. Nadine Akkerman, *Invisible Agents: Women and Espionage in Seventeenth-Century Britain* (Oxford: Oxford University Press, 2018).

20. Andrew Hopper, *Turncoats and Renegades: Changing Sides during the English Civil War* (Oxford: Oxford University Press, 2018).

21. J. R. Harris, *Industrial Espionage and Technology Transfer: Britain and France in the Eighteenth Century* (Aldershot: Ashgate, 1998).

22. Adriano Comissoli, "Bombeiros, espias e vaqueanos: agentes da comunicação política no sul da América portuguesa (Rio Grande de São Pedro, sécs. XVIII–XIX)," *Revista da Indias* 78, no. 272 (2018): pp. 113–46; Adriano Comissoli, "Soberania em território alheio: comandantes e espiões ibéricos nas fronteiras da América, séculos XVIII E XIX," *Almanack* 27 (2021): pp. 1–46.

23. Paul Maddrell et al., *Spy Chiefs, vol. 2, Intelligence Leaders in Europe, the Middle East, and Asia* (Washington, DC: Georgetown University Press, 2018); esp. Ionna Iordanou, "The Spy Chiefs of Renaissance Venice: Intelligence Leadership in the Early Modern World" and Emrah Safa Gürkan, "Laying Hands on *Arcana Imperii*: Venetian Baili as Spymasters in Sixteenth-Century Istanbul." Another edited volume that unites modern and premodern espionage is *Intelligence, Statecraft and International Power— Irish Conference of Historians*, ed. Eunan O'Halpin, Robert Armstrong, and Jane Ohlmeyer (Dublin and Portland: Irish Academic Press, 2006).

24. See Gennaro Varriale, ed., *Si fuera cierto? Espías y agentes en la frontera (siglos XVI–XVII)* (Alcalá de Henares: Universidad de Alcalá, 2018).

25. Gennaro Varriale, *Arrivano li Turchi: guerra navale e spionaggio nel Mediterraneo (1532–1582)* (Novi Ligure: Città del silenzio, 2014).

26. Ionna Iordanou, *Venice's Secret Service: Organising Intelligence in the Renaissance* (Oxford: Oxford University Press, 2019).

27. Jonathan Walker, *Pistols! Treason! Murder!: The Rise and Fall of a Master Spy* (Carlton: Melbourne University Press, 2007).

28. Because this work is concerned with the Early Modern Period, that is, with the years prior to the nineteenth century, this literature review excludes Polat Safi, "The Ottoman Special Organization—Teşkilat-ı Mahsusa: An Inquiry into its Operational and Administrative Characteristics" (unpublished PhD diss., Bilkent University, 2012); Ahmet Yüksel, *II. Mahmud Devrinde Osmanlı İstihbaratı* (Istanbul: Kitap Yayınevi, 2013); Ahmet Yüksel, *Rusların Kafkasya'yı İstilası ve Osmanlı İstihbarat Ağı* (Istanbul: Dergah Yayınları, 2014); Gültekin Yıldız, *Osmanlı İmparatorluğu'nda Askeri İstihbarat (1864–1914)* (Istanbul: Yeditepe Yayınevi, 2019); Ahmet Yüksel, *Sınırdaki Casus: Osmanlı Topraklarında Bir Rus Ajanı: Kafkasyalı Mehdi Kulu Şirvanî* (Istanbul: Kronik, 2019); Polat Safi, *Eşref: Kuşçubaşı'nın Alternatif Biyografisi* (Istanbul: Kronik, 2020); Somer Alp Şimşeker, *Birinci Dünya Savaşı'nda Osmanlı İstihbaratı: İkinci Şube Tarihi* (Istanbul: Kronik, 2022); Mustafa Yeni, "Birinci Dünya Savaşı'nda Başkumandanlık Vekâleti ve Harbiye Nezareti'nin II. Şube (İstihbarat) Faaliyetleri," (unpublished PhD diss., İstanbul University, 2022). That said, all these works are impressively detailed and highly interesting. Also see Servet Afşar, "Birinci Dünya Savaşı'nda Irak Cephesi'nde Aşiretler ve Casusluk Faaliyetleri," *Askerî Tarih Araştırmaları Dergisi* 52 (2002): pp. 129–45; Mehmet Özdemir, "Birinci Dünya Savaşı'nda Propaganda ve Casusluğa Karşı Alınan Tedbirler," *Askerî Tarih Araştırmaları Dergisi* 4 (2004): pp. 55–74; Burhan Sayılır, "Çanakkale Kara Savaşları Sırasında Casusluk Olayları ve Türklerin Aldıkları Tedbirler," *Askerî Tarih Araştırmaları Dergisi* 8 (2006): pp. 100–8; Abdurrahman Bozkurt, "Birinci Dünya Savaşı Başlarında Casusluk Faaliyetleri," *Osmanlı Tarihi Araştırma ve*

Uygulama Merkezi Dergisi 36 (2015): pp. 1–45; Servet Afşar, "Birinci Dünya Savaşı'nda Casusluk Okulları, Casusluk Uygulamaları ve Osmanlı Devleti'nin Casusluğu Önleme Faaliyetleri," *Stratejik ve Sosyal Araştırmalar Dergisi* 3 (2018): pp. 1–46.

29. Robert Anhegger, *Ein angeblicher schweizerischer Agent an der Hohen Pforte im Jahre 1581* (Istanbul: Marmara Basımevi, 1943).

30. Victor L. Ménage, "The Mission of an Ottoman Secret Agent in France in 1486," *Royal Asiatic Society of Great Britain and Ireland* 97, no. 2 (1965): pp. 112–32; S. A. Skilliter, "The Sultan's Messenger, Gabriel Defrens; an Ottoman Master Spy of the Sixteenth Century," in *Wiener Zeitschrift für die Kunde des Morgenlandes* 68 (1976), pp. 47–59; Coix.

31. Nicolaas H. Biegman, "Ragusan Spying for the Ottoman Empire: Some 16th-century Documents from the State Archive at Dubrovnik," *Belleten* 26, no. 106 (1963), pp. 237–55.

32. John E. Woods, "Turco-Iranica I: An Ottoman Intelligence Report on Late Fifteenth/Ninth Century Iranian Foreign Relations," *Journal of Near Eastern Studies* 38, no. 1 (1979): pp. 1–9; Percy Kemp, "An Eighteenth-Century Turkish Intelligence Report," *International Journal of Middle East Studies* 16 (1984): pp. 497–506; Christine Isom-Verhaaren, "An Ottoman Report about Martin Luther and the Emperor: New Evidence of the Ottoman Interest in the Protestant Challenge to the Power of Charles V," *Turcica* 28 (1996): pp. 299–318; Giancarlo Casale, "An Ottoman Intelligence Report from the mid-sixteenth century Indian Ocean," *Journal of Turkish Studies* 31 (2007): pp. 181–88; Géza Dávid and Pál Fodor, "Ottoman Spy Reports from Hungary," in *Turcica et Islamica. Studi in Memoria di Aldo Gallotta, I*, ed. Ugo Marazzi (Naples: Università degli Studi di Napoli "L'Orientale," 2003), pp. 121–31; for the Hungarian-language publications concerning Ottoman intelligence operations in Hungary, see Dávid and Fodor, p. 121, fn. 1.

33. Haldun Eroğlu, "Klasik Dönemde Osmanlı Devletinin İstihbarat Stratejileri," *Ankara Üniversitesi Tarih Araştırmaları Dergisi* 34 (2003): pp. 11–33.

34. Eroğlu, p. 17.

35. Eroğlu, p. 24.

36. Gábor Ágoston, "Information, Ideology, and Limits of Imperial Policy: Ottoman Grand Strategy in the Context of Ottoman-Habsburg Rivalry," in *The Early Modern Ottomans: Remapping the Empire*, ed. Virginia H. Aksan and Daniel Goffman (Cambridge: Cambridge University Press, 2007), pp. 78–92. Ágoston has also published in Hungarian about Ottoman intelligence: "Információszerzés és kémkedés az Oszmán Birodalomban a 15–17 században," in *Információáramlás a magyar ès török végvári rendszerben*, ed. Tivadar Petercsák and Mátyás Berecz (Eger: Heves Megyei Múzeum, 1999), pp. 129–54; "Birodalom és információ: Konstantinápoly, mint a koraújkori Európa információs központja," in *Perjés Géza Emlékkönyv*, ed. Gábor Hausner and László Veszprémi (Budapest: Argumentum, 2005), pp. 31–60.

37. Mustafa Dehqan and Vural Genç, "Kurds as Spies: Information-Gathering on the 16th-Century Ottoman-Safavid Frontier," *Acta Orientalia Academiae Scientiarum Hungaricum* 71, no. 2 (2018): pp. 197–230.

38. Eric R. Dursteler, "On Bazaars and Battlefields: Recent Scholarship on Mediterranean Cultural Contacts," *Journal of Early Modern History* 15 (2011): p. 413.

39. Henri Pirenne, *Mahomet et Charlemagne* (Paris: F. Alcan; Bruxelles: Nouvelle société d'éditions, 1937). Although Pirenne's book was not published until after his death, he also defended the same ideas in an article that came out in 1922: "Mahomet et Charlemagne," *Revue Belge de Philologie et d'histoire* 1 (1922): pp. 77–86.

40. This is especially manifest in Bernard Lewis's *The Muslim Discovery of Europe* (New York and London: W. W. Norton & Company, 1982). However, the first article in which Lewis dealt with the relations between Islam and Christianity in a similar way pre-dated this book by twenty-five years. "The Muslim Discovery of Europe," *Bulletin of the School of Oriental and African Studies* 20, no. 1–3 (1957): pp. 409–16.

41. Lewis, "Muslim Discovery of Europe," p. 411.

42. Paolo Preto, *Venezia e i Turchi* (Florence: G. C. Sansoni Editore, 1975).

43. Andrew C. Hess, *The Forgotten Frontier: A History of the Sixteenth Century Ibero-African Frontier* (Chicago: University of Chicago Press, 1978); Andrew C. Hess, "The Moriscos: An Ottoman Fifth Column in the Sixteenth-Century Spain," *American Historical Review* 74 (October 1968): pp. 1–25; Andrew C. Hess, "The Battle of Lepanto and its Place in Mediterranean History," *Past and Present* 57 (1972): pp. 53–73; Andrew C. Hess, "The Ottoman Conquest of Egypt (1517) and the Beginning of the Sixteenth-Century World War," *International Journal of Middle Eastern Studies* 4, no. 1 (1973): pp. 55–76.

44. Robert C. Davis, *Christian Slaves, Muslim Masters: White Slavery in the Mediterranean, the Barbary Coast and Italy, 1500–1800* (New York: Palgrave Macmillan, 2003).

45. Samuel Huntington, *The Clash of Civilizations and the Remaking of World Order* (New York: Simon & Schuster, 1996).

46. E. Natalie Rothman, "Interpreting Dragomans: Boundaries and Crossings in the Early Modern Mediterranean," *Comparative Studies in Society and History* 51, no. 4 (October 2009): pp. 771–800.

47. Cf. Edward Said, "Clash of Ignorance," *The Nation*, October 22, 2001, http://www.thenation.com/article/clash-ignorance.

48. Fernand Braudel, *La Méditerranée et le monde Méditerranéen à l'époque de Philippe II*, 2nd ed. (Paris: Armand Colin, 1966).

49. Braudel, *La Méditerranée*, 1:155.

50. For an assessment of how Braudel used Ottoman sources, see Colin Heywood, "Fernand Braudel and the Ottomans: The Emergence of an Involvement (1928–50)," *Mediterranean Historical Review* 23, no. 2 (2008): pp. 165–84. See also Ruggiero Romano, *Braudel e noi: Riflessioni sulla cultura storica del nostro tempo* (Rome: Donzelli, 1995) and Maria Fusaro, Colin Heywood, and Mohamed-Sala Omri, eds., *Trade and Cultural Exchange in the Mediterranean: Braudel's Maritime Legacy* (London and New York: I.B. Tauris, 2010), especially Maria Fusaro's chapter, "After Braudel: A Reassessment of Mediterranean History between the Northern Invasion and the *Caravane Maritime*," pp. 1–22.

51. For example, for the reports by Beyazıt's spies on Selim's movements in the Balkans, see TSMA, Document 3703/1, 5994, 6306; Eroğlu, p. 27. For reports from the reign of Süleyman the Magnificent concerning the activities of Prince Beyazıt, see TSMA, Document 4265, 4575/2, 5997; Şerafettin Turan, *Kanuni Dönemi Taht Kavgaları*, 2nd ed. (Ankara: Bilgi Yayınevi, 1997), pp. 113, 123.

1

TWO EMPIRES, ONE SEA

The sixteenth century bore witness to an arduous struggle between two great powers aiming to become *the* global empire. This struggle lasted practically the whole century, and the other states in Europe had no alternative but to take sides. To help the reader gain a clearer understanding of numerous events and personalities that will feature in this book, I now offer a brief introduction to the actors in this bout and the phases of their rivalry.

One of these empires, the Ottoman Empire, first made its mark on history as a powerful state in the fifteenth century. The Ottoman principality had been established at the beginning of the fourteenth century, a small frontier state in the southeastern Marmara region of Anatolia, but in just a short time it managed to annex Byzantine territory and, from the second half of that century onward, the Ottomans extended their rule into the Balkans. Once they had fortified their position in the Balkans, under the reign of Sultan Bayezid I (r. 1389–1402), they set their sights on Anatolia and one by one dispensed with the other Turkish principalities in that peninsula.[1] This is how, by the beginning of the fifteenth century, "Turkish unity was ensured in Anatolia," as the cliché repeated in Turkish high school textbooks puts it. However, after the Turkish princes who had lost their territory appealed to Tamerlane to help them, this great Turco-Mongolian conqueror from the east occupied Anatolia and, in the Battle of Ankara in 1402, defeated the Ottoman armies, taking Bayezid captive. This is how the gains that the Ottomans had made were temporarily stalled. The Ottoman princes became engulfed in a no-holds-barred fight for the throne, sparking the eleven-year period that today's historians have dubbed the *Fetret Devri* (Interregnum Period). Thanks to the stability created by the bureaucratized system of military fiefdoms (*timar*), the Ottoman principality managed to emerge from the Interregnum Period in one piece and entered a phase of recovery under Mehmed (r. 1413–21), who can actually be regarded as a second founder of the Ottoman state. Although this consolidation continued in the reign of Murad II (r. 1421–44, 1446–51), in 1444 and 1448, the Ottomans faced two of the greatest crises in the Empire's history but were able to win two major battles, putting an end to the Christian powers' dream of ejecting them from the Balkans.[2]

It is often rightly claimed that the conquest of Istanbul by Sultan Mehmed the Conqueror (r. 1444–46, 1451–81) marked the Ottoman state's transformation from a mere principality into an empire in the full sense of the word. On the one hand, the Ottomans took up the legacy of the defeated Byzantines;[3] on the other hand, during the reign of Mehmed, a number of important steps were taken in the direction of centralization.[4] After Mehmed had achieved major victories in both the west and the east, his son Bayezid II (r. 1481–1512) was responsible for another period of consolidation. However, by the beginning of the sixteenth century, it had become clear that a more dynamic sultan was needed who was up to the multiple challenges that had emerged: the changes in trading routes following new geographical discoveries in the west; the Portuguese encroachment into the Indian Ocean; and the rise of a threatening Shi'ite power in the east, the Safavids.[5]

It was under these conditions that Selim I (r. 1512–20) would seize the throne by doing away with both his father and his brother, Prince Ahmed. He accomplished a great deal in just a short time and transformed the Ottomans into the sole power in the Eastern Mediterranean.[6] Having won a bruising struggle for the throne, Sultan Selim first tried to settle accounts with the Safavids. Ever since he had served as governor in Trabzon, Selim had been uneasy about the activities of Shah İsmail, who had suddenly gained considerable power in Iran. İsmail had instrumentalized Shi'ism as a means of propaganda and was constantly deploying it to incite the Turkmen elements in Anatolia against rule from Istanbul. These heterodox Turkmen, who practically deified their shahs, constituted a serious challenge to Ottoman domination in the region. Although Selim's victory over Shah İsmail at the Battle of Chaldiran (1514) did not mean that the danger was put to rest, for a while it was at least kept in check. Selim also had a good grasp of how to deal with the ongoing crisis weighing on the Mamluks, another major power in the region, who controlled Egypt and Syria. The Mamluks were losing in both power and prestige. They were plagued by factional infighting and were also faced with the threat to Mecca and Medina posed by the Portuguese, a rising force in the Indian Ocean. The Mamluks' defeat by the Ottomans at the Battle of Marj Dabiq in 1516 led to the demise of the Mamluk state, which had existed for 250 years. Instead of returning to Istanbul, Selim opted to strike a fatal blow to the Mamluks, now left without effective leadership, as their ruler had perished on the battlefield. Selim would achieve this objective at the Battle of Ridaniyah (1517) and annex Syria and Egypt into his empire.

Just as the Ottomans were achieving notable successes in the east, in the west the Habsburg dynasty was starting to consolidate its power. The rise of the Habsburgs, however, had been accomplished not through military victories but by means of diplomacy and marriages with the members of other dynasties. In reality, the Habsburgs were a rather insignificant family from present-day Switzerland, whose lands happened to lie within the boundaries of the Holy

Roman Empire. The head of state of this empire that was, as Voltaire put it wittily, neither holy nor Roman nor an empire (*ni saint, ni romain, ni empire*) was chosen by seven elector princes.[7] The first emperor from the Habsburg family to be elected (in 1273) was Rudolph, but he was chosen precisely because he was weak. In 1282, Rudolph managed to add the duchy of Austria to his family's domains, but after Rudolph and until the fifteenth century, no other member of the Habsburg family would be elected as emperor.

In the fifteenth century, through Albert Duke of Austria's marriage to the daughter of Emperor Sigismund, the Habsburgs were able to stake a claim to Bohemia and Hungary. Just a year after Albert was selected as emperor (1438), though, he lost his life fighting against the Ottomans. In 1452, Albert's son Frederick III was elected Holy Roman emperor, and by means of skillful diplomatic maneuvers, Frederick expanded the influence of the dynasty from its base in Central Europe to the continent. Frederick orchestrated the marriage of his son and successor, Maximilian, to Marie, daughter of Charles the Bold, the duke of Burgundy. When Charles was killed at the Battle of Nancy (1477), which pitched the duchy of Burgundy against the duchy of Lorraine and the Swiss Confederacy, control of both the region of Burgundy (in the east of France) and the Low Countries (today's Belgium and the Netherlands) fell to the Habsburg dynasty. Crowned emperor in 1486, Maximilian—together with Marie—continued the strategy of diplomacy by marriage, and the couple married off their son Philip to the Spanish princess Juana.

Juana's parents were the rulers of two of the five independent states on the Iberian Peninsula. The marriage of Queen Isabella of Castile to King Ferdinand of Aragon in 1469 had led to the unification of the two kingdoms. Through the annexation of Granada in 1492 and Navarre in 1512 by these so-called Catholic monarchs, the entire peninsula bar Portugal was united into a single state. The Aragon dynasty, moreover, possessed other territories in the Western Mediterranean: since 1282, the family had held control of Sicily, and from 1420 onward they held Sardinia. Due to the demise of the dynasty ruling the Kingdom of Naples, in 1504 Naples also fell under Ferdinand's control. It should also be pointed out that the glory of Castile was enhanced enormously by the discovery of the Americas in 1492 and especially by the conquest of vast territories in Peru and Mexico by conquistadors such as Cortés and Pizarro.

When Isabella died in 1504, though, Ferdinand ceased to be king of Castile, and he was also forbidden from interfering in the kingdom's internal affairs. Against this background, Ferdinand's marriage in 1505 to Germaine de Foix threatened to undermine the delicate union between the two kingdoms. However, the couple's only child would die when just a few days old, meaning that Juana retained the sole claim to both thrones.

On her mother's side, Juana was heir to the Castilian crown and on her father's side the successor to the Aragonese crown and on both sides could lay claim to all the territories of those kingdoms. Philip, for his part, was heir to the territory of Burgundy through his mother and to that of Austria through his father. In other words, the marriage of Juana and Philip meant that a single family could control numerous kingdoms, duchies, counties, and overseas colonies. As a consequence of Philip's early death in 1506 and Juana's descent into insanity, it was left to their son Charles to enjoy the fruits of their strategic diplomacy. Through the death of his father in 1506, this Ghent-born young prince inherited the territory linked to the Duchy of Burgundy. Following Philip's death, the royal assemblies (*Cortes*) of both Castile and Aragon endorsed Charles and his mother, Juana, as rulers of these kingdoms. Charles thus ended up controlling a vast range of territories. From his maternal grandmother he inherited Castile, Navarre, Granada, a number of citadels (*presidio*) in North Africa, and colonies in America, and these supplemented the territories of Aragon, Sicily, Naples, and Sardinia that he inherited from Ferdinand. With the death of his other grandfather, Maximilian, in 1519, Charles not only gained possession of the archduchy of Austria but also acquired the opportunity to stake a claim to the most important position in the Christian world.

The Holy Roman Empire was a complex structure made up of numerous principalities, duchies, counties, ecclesiastical fiefdoms, and free cities. The emperor at the top of this federative structure was chosen by a group of electors. Ever since 1356, the number of these electors had been set at seven. The electors were free to elect any Christian ruler; indeed, following the death of Maximilian, alongside Charles, King Francis of France and King Henry VIII of England had made overtures to try to be elected. However, using funds that they borrowed from the Augsburg banking families the Fuggers and the Welsers, the Habsburg dynasty offered irresistible bribes to the electors, as a result of which Charles was granted the title of emperor as Charles V in 1519. The de facto power he enjoyed was thus underpinned through the prestige carried by this title.

Charles V did not owe his massive empire purely to coincidences such as premature deaths and childless relatives; he benefited just as much from the shrewd diplomatic moves of his grandfathers. It was thanks to the marriages that had been arranged many years previously that a myriad of independent kingdoms, counties, and duchies came to be subordinated to the rule of a single figure. Put simply, whereas Süleyman's empire had been carved out by the sword, Charles V's was forged using rings. How right the Hungarian king Matthias Corvinus was when he purportedly penned the following lines about the marriage between Maximilian and Marie: "While everyone is fighting, may you marry, oh happy Austria! Whereas others are given [kingdoms] by Mars, it is Venus who grants them to you" (*Bella gerant alii, tu felix Austria, nube! Nam quae Mars aliis, dat tibi diva Venus*).

CHARLES V AND SÜLEYMAN THE MAGNIFICENT

Following the swift conquest of Egypt, Syria, and Hejaz, in an attempt to claim leadership of the Islamic world the Ottoman sultans placed special emphasis on the religious titles they carried, such as "*Hâdimü'l-Haremeyni'sh-Sherîfeyn*" (Servant of Two Holy Cities, Mecca and Medina). Similarly, Charles V took steps that involved him becoming the direct ruler of several merged territories and aspired to unify the Christian world (*Universitas Christiana*) under a single ruler. What no doubt inspired both rulers was the apocalyptic vision that prevailed in the sixteenth century; this led Süleyman and Charles to perceive themselves as the last ruler prior to the end of days. As the one thousandth year of the Hegira calendar approached, Ottoman intellectuals began to promote Sultan Süleyman as the "restorer" (*müceddid*) of the Islamic world. Particularly during the first 20 years of Süleyman's reign, the sultan was perceived as the individual who, in the run up to the Apocalypse, would help spread the True Faith and become the ruler of the whole world (*sâhibkırân-ı 'âlempenâh / sâhibkırân-ı rub'-ı meskûn*, "shelter for the universe, and victorious supreme leader of the inhabited world"). This, presumably, is the prism through which Süleyman viewed his rivalry with Charles V; destiny had ordained that the tenth sultan of the Ottoman dynasty would be the Mahdi, or Muslim messiah (*Mehdi-yi sâhib-zamân / Mehdi-yi* âhirü'z-zamân, "Mahdi, the owner of time / Mahdi, who will arrive in the last days") who, by defeating Charles, would bring about the ultimate victory of Islam.[8]

Charles's chancellor Gattinara conjured up a similar image of his superior as a "universal ruler" (*monarchia universalis*). According to this narrative, Charles V was the ruler who would precede the Messiah Jesus Christ and reconquer Jerusalem, paving the way for Jesus's millennial empire. Charles V's election as emperor in effect constituted *sacrum imperium*, that is, the realization of the Holy Empire.[9]

The rivalry between the two emperors manifested in their correspondence. Although one of the designations that Charles chose for himself was "the king of Jerusalem," Süleyman called him simply "the king of Spain" and refused to use the title "Emperor" to refer to him.[10] The competition between the two rulers was also played out on a symbolic level. In 1530, prior to his coronation ceremony in Bologna, Charles V entered the city by passing through several victory arches to the accompaniment of military music. Throughout the celebrations, the assembled crowd hailed him with cries of "Caesar, Caesar, emperor, emperor!" The Ottoman response to this ceremony, with its echoes of Roman military processions, came at the time of the 1532 military campaign, when Ottoman troops were stationed in Belgrade. At a military procession held in this city, which Süleyman had captured eleven years earlier, the Ottoman emperor deployed symbolism very similar to that used by Charles. A news bulletin from that time likened the victory arches (*li archi triomphal*) erected on the streets of Belgrade and the playing of military music (*suoni de instrumenti diversi*) to the military processions of ancient Rome (*secondo le antiquità de Romani*).[11] Sultan Süleyman was seated on a golden throne resting on four columns, and on his head he wore a Western-style crown with four different layers, which was decorated with incomparable jewels (fig. 2); Grand Vizier İbrahim Pasha had paid some Venetian jewelers the astronomical sum of 115,000 ducats to produce this remarkable work.[12] It is hardly difficult to understand why the chief treasurer, Mahmud, who had to arrange this payment, complained about it: at a time when a high-ranking governor-general would be earning a salary of 1 million *akçes*[13] and the Empire itself had an annual cash budget of 200 million *akçes*, the sum of 115,000 ducats was equivalent to 6 million *akçes*,[14] which was clearly a lot of money to spend on a crown! This ceremony was accompanied by immaculately rehearsed rituals and was performed in a semiotic language that was alien from both Islamic political culture and the imperial grammar of the Ottomans. The aim was evidently to lay down the gauntlet to the West in the West's own language. The Austrian envoys who attended the ceremony could not remain silent about what they had witnessed, and this remarkable event sent shock waves throughout Europe. In a nutshell, the Eastern empire's response to the Western empire certainly hit home!

From the 1520s onward, the Ottomans and the Habsburgs started in earnest to attempt to realize their dreams of founding a universal empire. In the last few years of his reign, even Selim had turned his gaze to the west, once he had seized Mamluk territory and staved off the threat that the Safavids posed to the Ottoman territories in Anatolia. Selim's premature death, however, put an end to a possible Ottoman campaign against Rhodes.

When Süleyman took the throne in 1520, he was soon confronted with a problem common to former princes when they returned to Istanbul from their respective provinces. When a new sultan assumed power, rivalry tended to emerge between the men whom the sultan brought with him from his province and his father's appointees at the center, who would try to cling on to the influence they held in the palace and the state. Sultans tended to overcome such crises—the gravest of which occurred during the enthronement of Selim II in 1566—by proving themselves through launching a successful military campaign; they would then use the prestige gained from success in war as a cover to install their own men. The rivalry that accompanied enthronements of new sultans goes a long way in explaining phenomena such as Mehmed II's execution of Çandarlı Halil Pasha (his father's grand vizier) following the conquest of Istanbul, the Siege of Eger (1596) under Mehmed III (r. 1595–1603), and the Battle of Khotyn (1621) involving Osman II (r. 1618–22).

To get rid of his father's entourage and to implement his own policies, Süleyman lost no time in seeking to conquer territory. To start with, he seized the fortress of Belgrade (1521), a city which could be regarded as the key to Central Europe. This was followed by an attack on Rhodes (1522), where the Knights of St. John were to be found, a monastic order consisting of Crusaders who were very much involved in piracy. After a siege, Rhodes fell. Sultan Süleyman made a lightning start to his reign by capturing two strategic locations that Mehmed the Conqueror had been unable to take, and he would use the prestige he gained from this to displace his father's associates. Ignoring all the precedents, in 1523 he appointed grand vizier İbrahim, who was merely the master of robes and hence lacking any administrative experience. This was something of a coup and reminded the pashas who had risen up from among the palace ranks (*Enderun*) that power now lay with the new sultan.

Feeling that he was entitled to be grand vizier, Second Vizier Ahmed Pasha requested to be assigned to the newly conquered province of Egypt. Even before the Ottomans had been able to enforce their sovereignty over Egypt, Ahmed Pasha raised the flag of rebellion in this prosperous governorship, which led Süleyman to delay his campaigns of conquest by a few years. However, with the fall of Belgrade, the gates to Central Europe had opened up. Ever since the reign of Murad II, the Ottomans had been unable to defeat the Kingdom of Hungary. Now, though, Hungary was unmistakably weak, lying in the hands of a young and inexperienced king and at the mercy of aristocratic factions. The powerful state once run by Matthias Corvinus, the son of the famous John Hunyadi, was a thing of the past. At the Battle of Mohács in 1526, the Ottoman army inflicted a stinging defeat on their Hungarian counterparts, and the young king of the Hungarians, Lajos, would himself die on the battlefield.[15]

This was actually the first occasion on which the Ottomans and the Habsburgs directly confronted each other. With the Habsburg Empire now consisting largely of territories in Western Europe, Charles V handed over control of the lands in Austria to his brother Ferdinand. The Habsburg family always had their eyes open for kingdoms that they could acquire with the help of Venus, so they had already jumped at the chance of arranging a marriage with the Jagiellonian dynasty that ruled Bohemia and Hungary. While Ferdinand had himself married the Hungarian princess Anna, his sister Maria had wedded Lajos.

Lajos's death at the Battle of Mohács actually created problems for the Ottomans; his demise meant that Ferdinand, as the husband of Lajos's sister, could now lay claim to the territory of Hungary. For two reasons, though, the Ottomans were prevented from expanding their territory at the expense of the Habsburgs. First, in 1505, Hungarian nobles decreed that no foreign prince would be able to become their king; second, an influential oppositional faction developed around the governor of Transylvania, John Zápolya. The Ottoman line of defense was along the River Danube. In order to administer the Hungarian territories directly from the Ottoman capital, this system was in need of fundamental change, and the Ottomans had to accept that they would be faced with logistical challenges. Rather than managing the area as if it were some kind of a province (*beylerbeylik*), the Ottomans preferred to monitor it in the manner of a buffer zone under their control. This is why Sultan Süleyman recognized Zápolya as king when he was elected by the Hungarian aristocrats in November 1526. Süleyman attempted to deploy the new king in his struggle with Ferdinand. However, when Ferdinand defeated Zápolya twice, in 1527 and 1528, and went on to seize Buda, the Ottomans resolved to launch a campaign, which got underway in 1529. In the course of this expedition, which would culminate in the Siege of Vienna, Süleyman the Magnificent took the initiative of personally crowning Zápolya with the holy crown of Saint Stephen in Buda.

The Habsburgs could not bring themselves to confront Süleyman's troops head on. They waited until winter was approaching, and as soon as the Ottomans started to head home, they resumed their pressure on Hungary.

When Ferdinand laid siege to Buda once more in 1530, the Ottomans had little choice but to respond by marching on Austria again, which they did in 1532. At the time of the Siege of Vienna (1529) and the so-called German Campaign (*Alaman Seferi*) of 1532, both Charles V and Ferdinand deliberately avoided a pitched battle with the Ottomans, and both campaigns did not turn out to be strategic successes for the Ottomans. Based on this experience, Istanbul, eager to launch a campaign toward the east, came to appreciate the merits of peace in the west. As a result of the agreement between Vienna and Istanbul in 1533, the Kingdom of Bohemia and some pieces of land in northwest Hungary remained the property of Ferdinand, while the Hungarian territory ruled by Zápolya became a tributary state of the Ottomans. In the south, the Ottomans were left with land sandwiched between the River Danube and the River Sava, which they would administer as the Province of Syrmia.

What undid the peace that had been restored was Zápolya's decision not to behave like an Ottoman tributary. Instead, he came to an agreement with Ferdinand and in his will stipulated that the lands he owned would be bequeathed to the Habsburgs. After the Hungarian king died in 1540, the Ottomans decided to initiate another campaign in the region, aimed at subordinating Hungary to the central Ottoman government by designating it the Province of Buda. Zápolya's infant son John and his mother, Izabela Jagiellonka, were sent away to the family's principal estate in Transylvania, which the young prince and his mother would run as an Ottoman tributary state.

This is how an Ottoman zone emerged in Hungary in the environs of Buda. While the Principality of Transylvania came under the rule of Istanbul, in the west things were heating up. Not since the time of Charlemagne had Europe witnessed such an immense empire controlled by a single ruler. As France was flanked on all sides by Habsburg territories and the pope fretted that he would lose his domination over the Christian faith, both were very concerned by the rise of the Habsburg Empire. Believing that something had to be done straight away, the French king Francis I did not hesitate to attack Charles V. Things, however, did not go according to plan, and in 1525 Francis would be taken captive by Charles V in the course of the Battle of Pavia. In search of a solution, Francis's mother, Louise of Savoy, decided to write to Süleyman the Magnificent to ask for his help. A letter held at the *Bibliothèque Nationale* reveals that the Sultan responded positively to this request.[16] In the Treaty of Madrid signed in 1526, Francis was forced to make concessions to the Habsburgs on a number of points, but he did not keep his promises and thought nothing of placing hurdles in Charles V's path. On top of that, he had no qualms about forging an alliance with the Ottomans, despite the fact that the Pope had granted him the title of *Rex Christianissimus*, that is, "The most Christian King"; most contemporaries concurred that being part of such an alliance hardly befitted a French king.[17]

The French needed to go to great lengths to hide the fact that they had formed this alliance with the Muslim Turks. This was not helped by the fact that, from 1535 onward, a permanent resident French ambassador was posted to Istanbul. The Ottomans were eager to prevent the Habsburgs from realizing their policy of uniting the Christian world, so they were pleased to have found in the French a second ally to join the Protestants.[18] To this end, in collaboration with the Protestant princes and the king of England, they lent Francis 100,000 gold coins, to encourage him to form an alliance against the Habsburg emperor.[19]

While the Ottomans were primarily interested in Hungary, the French wanted the alliance to concentrate on southern Italy. Several times, using as a pretext the claims that the dukes of Anjou had to the kingdoms of Naples and Sicily, the French crossed the Alps and "drove their armies beyond the Rubicon" (*Rubiconem duxit exercitum*). The last time the French had managed to expel the Habsburgs from Naples was in 1527. However, because Andrea Doria, the Genoese admiral employed by Francis I, abruptly changed sides and a wave of illness struck the French army, the French attack turned out to be a failure and their dreams came to nothing.

Following the plains of Hungary, the next area where the rivalry between the Ottomans and the Habsburgs would be played out was the Mediterranean (see map 1.1). In fact, the sudden emergence of the Mediterranean as a site of imperial conflict was a knock-on effect of the alliance that Muslim corsairs[20] in North Africa had established with Istanbul. It was clear that the Habsburg defense systems were insufficient for dealing with the threat posed by corsairs of Eastern Mediterranean origin, that is, with people like Oruc Reis, Hızır Reis, Sinan Reis, and Aydın Reis, all of whom had relocated to North Africa. In 1513,[21] Oruc and Hızır (known in the West as the Barbarossa brothers) first established a base on the island of Djerba and then entered into the service of the sultan of Tunis, settling in the harbor of La Goulette (Ott. Halkü'l-Vad). In 1516, Oruc and Hızır received an invitation from the leader of Algiers, Sâlim al-Tûmî, despite the fact that this city had been subject to the Habsburgs since 1510. The opportunist and cunning brothers not only accepted the invitation but also took advantage of the factionalism that was rife in the city and murdered Sâlim. From this point on, Oruc and Hızır were not run-of-the-mill sea-bandits but actually possessed their very own harbor.

However, as the powers in control of Algiers, they found themselves faced with the Habsburgs. With the fall of Granada in 1492, the focus of the war against Muslims shifted to North Africa. One by one, strategic cities like Melilla (1496), Mers El Kébir (1505), Peñón de Velez (1508), Oran (1509), Béjaïa (1510), and Tripoli (1510) fell to the Spanish. Algiers came to recognize Spanish sovereignty over it in 1510. Sâlim al-Tûmî's son Yahya appealed to the Habsburgs for assistance, and in 1516 the Habsburgs dispatched a fleet with the aim of occupying Algiers. The attempted siege, however, achieved nothing.

Now it was time for the Barbarossa brothers to go on the attack. Oruc Reis was able to seize Miliana and Tenes, but he was killed in 1518 while fighting against the Habsburgs, which left Hızır in a difficult position. Even though the Spanish navy suffered a debacle in the siege of Algiers (1519), this did not stop Hızır from withdrawing. In 1520, this experienced corsair evacuated Algiers

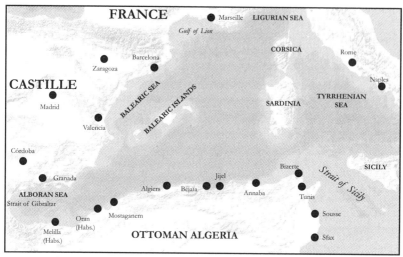

MAP 1.1. The Western Mediterranean

and retreated to Jijel. At the same time, he dispatched envoys to Istanbul in an attempt to preserve amicable relations with the Ottomans.

Struggling with problems in Italy and Germany, the Habsburgs rather neglected North Africa, and Hızır took advantage of this. Having seized El Kul in 1521 and Constantine and Annaba in 1522, he returned to Algiers in 1525 with a much stronger hand. After all, he now had his own corsair kingdom. Four years later, he would capture the Spanish fortress on the islet facing the harbor of Algiers (Peñón of Algiers / Ilot de la Marine), thereby wiping out the final residue of Spanish resistance. Hızır was therefore in total control of the town and the region.

Due to his success, other corsairs operating independently in the area, such as Sinan and Aydın Reis, recognized Hızır's leadership.[22] What also reinforced his status as a leader was İbrahim Pasha's decision to summon him to Istanbul in 1534 and appoint him as grand admiral. The ease with which the Habsburgs were able to seize some of the key harbors in the Peloponnese, namely Koroni, Patras, and Nakpaktos, underlined how inadequate the Ottoman navy was. Years later, Lütfi Pasha (grand vizier between 1539–41) would express very eloquently the disappointment that was felt in the Ottoman capital: "But because the person at the head of the navy (*baş ve buğ olan kimesne*) was a frequenter of taverns who drank wine (*harâbat ehli ve şâribül-hamr*), he did not see to the needs of the ships and, out of stupidity (*hamâkatından*), allowed the fleet to fall apart, returning to Istanbul on his own. Because of this, the infidels could take advantage of the situation and carried out these acts."[23]

Benefiting from the experience of Hızır (hence called Hayreddin)[24] Barbarossa and his corsairs, the Ottomans pursued a pragmatic policy and carried the war to the Western Mediterranean.[25] In 1534, the new Ottoman grand admiral conquered Tunis, an ally of the Habsburgs. A year later, though, when faced with a siege in which the Habsburg emperor himself was involved, he only just managed to save his navy and avoid being killed himself. Hayreddin waged a successful naval battle against the Venetian-Habsburg coalition that had emerged in response to the Ottomans' siege of Corfu in 1537. In 1538, by opting wisely for a strategy of wait-and-see at Preveza,[26] Hayreddin won a significant victory, thereby strengthening the Ottoman hold on the Eastern Mediterranean.

Having strengthened their naval forces by receiving assistance from North African corsairs, the Ottomans were motivated by their alliance with the French to set their sights on southern Italy. The siege of Corfu (a Venetian-controlled island across the Italian peninsula at the mouth of the Adriatic) in 1537 should be regarded as the first leg of this campaign; in the same year, Hayreddin would plunder Otranto, situated on the heel of Italy, across from Corfu. From then on, Hayreddin's naval activities in the seas off Christian countries would not be limited to the Adriatic alone. From the middle of the sixteenth century onward, the Ottomans started to undertake maneuvers in the Tyrrhenian and Ligurian seas, as well as in the Balearic Islands, that is, along coasts that were directly controlled by the Habsburgs. In 1543, having pillaged the coasts of Italy, in coordination with French forces Hayreddin besieged the city of Nice, which belonged to the Duke of Savoy, a Habsburg ally. Hayreddin would spend the winter in the city of Toulon. By the time their fleet returned to the same shores in 1550, 1552, 1553, 1555, and 1558, the Ottomans had developed links with fifth columns in Habsburg territories. In collaboration with oppositional nobles headed by the prince of Salerno, Ferdinando Sanseverino, the Ottoman intelligence service did its utmost to stir up an anti-Habsburg rebellion in the Kingdom of Naples. What is more, Istanbul received a visit from Sampieru Corso, the man who had initiated a revolt in Corsica against Genoa, the Habsburgs' chief ally.[27] With encouragement from the French, the Ottoman navy gave direct backing to the rebellion on the island.

The Barcelona-Genoa route was one of the key supply lines for the Habsburgs, and the actions of the Ottomans and their allies represented a serious danger to this line, leaving the Habsburgs in a vulnerable position. When it came to the Western Mediterranean, the Habsburgs staked everything on a campaign to seize Algiers, which got underway in 1541. The emperor participated in person in this attack, as he had done in the siege of Tunis six years before. However, due to the horrendous weather, a setback to be expected in late November, the siege of Algiers ended in failure, setting an example to Early Modern Age commanders of the harm that could be done by undertaking campaigns in the wrong season. From then on, Charles V acted much more cautiously, instructing his forces in North Africa to remain on the defensive. The corsairs' power in the region increased. Evidence of this is the success of Governor-General Salih Pasha's forces in occupying Fez and two years later installing Ali Abu Hassun as ruler and besieging Oran, the main Habsburg stronghold in the region.

Another corsair who made his mark on this period was Turgud Reis. Although in today's historiography he is depicted as the successor to Hayreddin Barbarossa, the reality was more complicated. During negotiations with Ferdinand and Charles V in 1545, the Ottomans let it be known that they were troubled by the raids that this ruthless corsair was carrying out from his base on the island of Djerba.[28] Still, when Andrea Doria captured Al-Mahdiyya, a port close to Tunis, in 1550, the Ottomans did not hesitate in assisting Turgud and breaking the ceasefire they had signed with the Habsburgs. In the following year, the Ottoman fleet would raid the island of Gozo, located close to Malta, before proceeding to seize Tripoli. Following the fall of Rhodes in 1522, Charles V handed over Malta and Tripoli to the Knights of St. John. However, it would be more accurate to see this transfer not so much as an award but as a liability; with only limited resources at its disposal, this order would always have its work cut out to hold on to this faraway harbor. Still, the fall of Tripoli in 1551 meant that now both Malta and Habsburg-owned Sicily were at risk. Although the Ottomans had placed Turgud Reis in charge of their fleet, if not on paper, at least in essence,[29] they resisted appointing him governor-general of Tripolitania until 1556 and they were quite open in expressing their distrust of this veteran corsair.

The Habsburg emperor was in a jam. He had not found what he had hoped for in North Africa; he had failed to pacify the Muslim corsairs who continued their plunder of coastal settlements; he seemed to be impotent with respect to the Ottoman navy right next door; and he had no end of worries in Europe. On top of the resistance from the French king Francis, he had to contend with opposition from the German Protestants, all of which left Charles V out on a limb. Using the soldiers and funds that he was able to extract from Habsburg territory, he tried to impose a more centralized structure on the Holy Roman Empire, but in 1552 this project was abandoned when Charles V had to abandon the Siege of Metz. The Peace of Augsburg signed in 1555 led to the adoption of the principle of *cuius regio, eius religio* (whose realm, his religion). According to this, the princes and cities of the empire could choose between Catholicism and Lutheranism and impose the selected denomination on their subjects.[30] In other words, in an era when the first steps were being taken to create centralized and more homogenized states, the Habsburg Empire found itself at the mercy of a force for decentralization.

In the aftermath of the debacle at Metz, the Habsburg dynasty had no choice but to divide its territory into two. It was inevitable that Charles V would be succeeded as emperor by his little brother Ferdinand, who in 1531 had been elected as "king of the Romans" (Lat. *Romanorum Rex* / Ger. *Römisch-deutscher König*). What had not been decided on was who would follow Ferdinand as king of the Romans and then as emperor. Although Charles insisted that his son Philip should be next in line after Ferdinand, Ferdinand did not want to pave his nephew Philip's way to the throne, Philip being the same age as his own son, Maximilian.[31] As a result, the assets of the dynasty ended up being divided into two. In 1556, Austria, Hungary, Bohemia, Styria, and the other territories of the Holy Roman Empire were assigned to the junior branch of the dynasty, for which Ferdinand and Maximilian were responsible; Spain, Italy, the Low Countries, and the empire's territories in America were given to Charles's son Philip II (r. 1556–98). From then on, in the Balkans the Ottomans would be dealing with Maximilian and his sons, whereas in the Mediterranean they would have to contend with Philip II. (In this book, the term "the Habsburgs" will be used to pertain to the Spanish [i.e., senior] branch of the Empire.)

DJERBA, MALTA, AND LEPANTO

Having proven its credentials in the 1550s through its actions in the Western Mediterranean, the Ottoman navy inflicted a heavy defeat on the Habsburg fleet commanded by the Duke of Medinaceli at Djerba in 1560. This defeat, in fact, came with much heavier losses than did the Battle of Preveza.[32] Interestingly, though, it has not received the attention it deserves, neither from contemporary chroniclers nor from modern historians. That said, from the work of Fernand Braudel we can get a sense of the panic and fear of an Ottoman attack that gripped Habsburg leaders in Italy between 1561 and 1564.[33]

However, the expected onslaught never materialized, and the conqueror of Djerba, Piyale Pasha, brought the navy to the Western Mediterranean only five years later, in 1565. When the Ottomans went to war with Ferdinand in 1564, the Mediterranean territories of Philip II were also expected to become a target once again, but instead the Ottoman fleet set its course for the island of Malta, the base of the Knights of St. John. After a grueling siege, in which Turgud Reis lost his life, the Ottoman navy was forced to retreat. The following year, the Ottomans seized the island of Chios in the Eastern Mediterranean, and in 1568 their navy pillaged the coast of Puglia. Other than that, though, the Ottoman fleet remained rather inactive.

Meanwhile, after reigning for 46 years, Süleyman the Magnificent died in 1566 and was succeeded by Selim II. When his father was still alive, Selim had emerged victorious over his younger brother in the fight for the throne. Although Selim signed an agreement with Vienna in 1568, it did not take long before he started eyeing up possibilities in the Mediterranean. Even before he took the throne, Selim had contemplated conquering Cyprus. Although the island was located deep inside Ottoman territorial waters, it was in Venetian hands. As shall become evident in later chapters, from the end of the 1560s onward, Ottoman agents started to gather intelligence about the island.

The background of the War of Cyprus was the rivalry between Grand Vizier Sokollu Mehmed Pasha on one side and a coalition of Lala Mustafa, Piyale Pasha, Pertev Pasha, and the Jewish powerbroker Joseph Nasi on the other. This cabal, which wished to increase its power over the grand vizier, was successful in persuading Selim, and in 1570 the invasion of Venetian Cyprus got underway. However, events took the course that Sokollu Mehmed Pasha had feared, and the attack on Cyprus actually ended up uniting the Christian world. Under Pope Pius V (r. 1566–72), a Holy Alliance had been established, and a Christian navy was assembled from galleys from Venice, the Habsburgs, Genoa, Malta, and Florence. Because the fleet took time to assemble and to set sail, it was unable to prevent the fall of Cyprus. In the second year of the war, though, this navy practically annihilated the Ottoman fleet at the Battle of Lepanto.[34]

The governor-general of Algeria, Uluc Ali, managed to survive the battle and to extricate his galleys from the war unscathed. This explains why the panicked Istanbul government appointed this corsair as grand admiral of the navy and embarked on a frenetic program of ship building. In 1572, Uluc Ali took the fleet out to sea, even though it was incomplete and the ships in it had been hastily constructed. All the same, he demonstrated his experience by undertaking tactical maneuvers and refusing to get embroiled in direct combat. With this strategy, he gained time, allowing disagreements to surface within the Christian alliance. Venice was eager to protect its overseas colonies and wanted to send ships to the heart of the Eastern Mediterranean to reconquer Cyprus. For their part, the Habsburgs were beleaguered by corsairs and were contemplating attacking North Africa.

In 1573, the Habsburg admirals Don Juan and Gianandrea Doria launched a concerted attack on the corsairs and recaptured Tunis, which had been conquered by Uluc Ali four years earlier. Meanwhile, Venice recognized that it would not be able to retake Cyprus but also that it would be impossible to live off the wheat that it imported from Sicily. Something had to be done, but the only solution for Venice was to betray its own allies and come to a secret agreement with Istanbul. Accepting the territorial losses, toward the end of 1573 Venice signed a peace agreement with Istanbul.

The Habsburgs were now all alone in their struggle with the Ottomans, while at the same time having to deal with a rebellion in the Low Countries. They were unable to prevent the Ottoman navy from conquering not just Tunis but also La Goulette, the port of Tunis (1574). With this victory, the Ottomans possessed a third province in North Africa. From then on, the corsairs based in the harbors close to Sicily would be a serious headache for the Habsburgs.

Western historians tend to emphasize that the Battle of Lepanto showed that the Ottomans could be defeated, and they claim that this battle marked the point at which Ottoman dominance of the Mediterranean was broken. Andrew Hess has maintained, however, that even after the battle took place in 1571, Istanbul continued to pursue a rigorous policy with respect to the Mediterranean. He also takes issue with the argument that the defeat at Lepanto set the Ottoman fleet on the path of decline. According to this American historian, imperial rivalry in the Mediterranean would not end until the Ottomans were clear victors in their conflict with the Habsburgs in North Africa.[35]

However, I would like to make it clear that I do not agree with Hess, who seems to think it would be easy to rebuild a navy that has lost a war. The galleys used by the Ottomans relied on a large number of oarsmen and were limited in terms of their cargo capacity and their operational quality. For that reason, the number of ships in the fleet was not in itself a reliable measure of the navy's competence. Moreover, it is not as significant as it may seem that the Ottomans rebuilt their fleet within just one year. Indeed, the fact that Uluc Ali went so far to avoid conflict with the enemy would suggest that he also acknowledged the fleet's poor quality. That said, contrary to what Hess maintains, incidents such as the expeditions of Tunis in 1574 and Fez in 1576 had very little to do with the strength of the navy. In the first case, the fleet remained on a defensive footing and was only used for transporting soldiers; the second case is concerned with a land offensive that departed from Algiers. In a recent study, Phillip Williams illustrated how crucial veteran oarsmen were to the performances of Mediterranean fleets, not least in that they had to be able to put up with tough living conditions.[36] In the Battle of Lepanto, the Ottomans lost many slave oarsmen. There was also another factor that reduced the manpower available to the Ottoman navy, thereby creating problems for the fleet: not only did sailors die in the course of duty, but the Pope insisted on executing any sailors captured by his forces.

At any rate, after 1574, the Ottomans did not pursue an active policy in the Mediterranean. Ramazan Pasha, the governor-general of Algeria, ensured that his own candidate, Abdulmelik, was enthroned in Fez. This, though, prompted an intervention by Sebastião, the king of Portugal, who saw his dreams of a new crusade shattered. The struggle for the throne of Morocco would culminate in the death of no less than three rulers (Sebastião, Abdulmelik, and Abu Abdullah Muhammed II) in the course of the Battle of Wadi al-Makhazin (Port. *Batalha de Alcácer Quivir*, 1578). The new man on the throne of Morocco, Ahmed al-Mansur, succeeded in maintaining a careful balance in his dealings with Madrid and Istanbul, and in so doing he saved Morocco from becoming a theater in the clash between empires. Throughout this period, the actions of the Ottoman navy in the Western Mediterranean were limited to sending a fleet to Algiers in 1581 under the command of Uluc Ali. However, this fleet did not engage in any kind of operations and returned to where it had come from.

There are several reasons for this policy of passivity. The first of these was Philip II's reluctance to invest in the Mediterranean. The money spent on wars had crippled Madrid, to the extent that by 1575 the central government was unable to repay its debts and was forced to declare bankruptcy. Meanwhile, the rebellion in the Low Countries was proving very difficult to suppress and was becoming an international issue. The Spanish were constantly having to transfer money in order to protect Habsburg interests in France and to fund the Catholic Alliance (*La Ligue catholique*) in its rivalry with the Protestant Huguenots.[37] In addition, there was no way of pacifying England, which was becoming increasingly influential in the north. In 1588, the Spanish Armada ended up a total fiasco, and under such circumstances, a war in the Mediterranean would be something of a luxury.

Secondly, since the Battle of Djerba, the Ottomans had refrained from pursuing an aggressive policy in the Mediterranean. They did not appear at all interested in reaping the benefits of the victory at Djerba, and after the failed siege of Malta in 1565 they waited another five years before engaging in a major campaign. The Ottoman-Safavid War that began in 1577 and lasted 13 years would impose a considerable financial burden on the Ottomans. When silver arrived in Europe from the Potosí mines of Peru, creating inflationary waves as it spread throughout the continent, it precipitated a serious economic crisis, resulting in devaluations in 1584. The Ottoman economy deteriorated, and disturbances were a regular occurrence in the capital. Under these conditions, Istanbul was not in a position to follow a dynamic policy with respect to Morocco, and neither could it prevent Philip in 1580 from acceding to the Portuguese throne.

As well as the aforementioned political and economic considerations, technological developments could also be said to have contributed to the Ottomans' passivity. As the American naval historian John Guilmartin has pointed out, from the middle of the sixteenth century galleys started to increase in size. This in turn increased the number of oarsmen required, while reducing the agility of such ships. In order to cater to the needs of these galleys, which brought with them ever-greater logistical challenges, galleys needed to berth more often so as to obtain fresh water and provisions. This impeded large fleets from carrying out operations in far-off seas.[38] This situation, which Guilmartin terms "strategic stasis," made it difficult for the Ottomans to send a navy to the West; this had been possible in the 1550s, but now it no longer was.

Against the background of these diverse factors, in 1578 Istanbul and Madrid embarked on peace talks, which bore fruit in an agreement in 1581. It was only natural that these negotiations bore the imprint of the struggle for superiority and diplomatic precedence that the two dynasties had been engaged in for the last 50 years. Both sides were war-wearied and longing for peace, but neither of them wanted to be the one that actually initiated negotiations. After all, pulling out of a war against "the infidel" constituted a loss of prestige, and the first party to sue for peace would be regarded as weak. Another reason why the Ottomans refrained from sending envoys to Europe was their worldview, which positioned sultans at the center of the universe. According to this perspective, all the world's rulers were free to send envoys to Istanbul, to the person that Güneş Işıksel had termed "a cosmocratic sultan,"[39] and there was no problem with them seeking his friendship.

This issue was solved thanks to a saboteur who would not hesitate to lie in order to save his life. Martin de Acuña, a Habsburg spy captured by the Ottomans, pretended that he had been sent by the Spanish king with the aim of initiating peace talks. With the help of fake documents prepared by Aurelio Santa Croce, the Habsburg station chief in Istanbul, and by Hürrem Bey, an interpreter at the Imperial Council, Acuña would manage to convince Sokollu Mehmed Pasha. The Ottomans returned de Acuña to his king, and Philip II's response was to send an informal ambassador. At the end of forty months of tough negotiations, in February 1581 a document was signed that was in no way an official peace treaty between two rulers. Rather, it was framed as a three-year ceasefire agreement signed on the one hand by a Spanish envoy who had no official status and on the other hand by the Ottoman grand vizier. This is how Philip was able to save face, while the Ottomans gained the opportunity of concentrating on their eastern border.⁴⁰

As a consequence of the Ottoman-Safavid peace agreement in 1590, things heated up in the Mediterranean once again, albeit temporarily. The ceasefire that Madrid and Istanbul had signed in 1581 was renewed in 1584, but when it came to the 1587 renewal, negotiations reached an impasse. Meanwhile, the new international conjuncture appeared to benefit the Ottomans by limiting the options available to the Habsburgs. In France, a seemingly never-ending civil war pitting the Protestants against the Catholic Church (supported by Madrid) had been underway since the 1560s. In 1589, the situation escalated due to the death of Henry III and the enthronement as king of France of Henri de Navarre, who was the leader of the Protestants. Although the latter was now the king of France, as Henry IV, he was unable to enter the capital, which was resisting a Protestant ruler. This is why he was open to any project that would allow him to play for time with Madrid. In Portugal, meanwhile, the death of the last member of the Aviz Dynasty in 1580 left the throne of that kingdom vacant. Although Philip II took the opportunity to seize the throne (his mother was a Portuguese princess), the illegitimate prince Dom António was eager to take back the land that had belonged to his grandfather. Another factor that weighed in favor of the Ottomans was the presence of an English ambassador in Istanbul since 1583. In 1588, although the Spanish Armada was repulsed, Elizabeth was not convinced that the Spanish would not try the same again.

An alliance between Elizabeth of England (r. 1559–1603), Henry IV of France, Dom António of Portugal, and the Ottomans would have put Madrid in a very difficult position. The key condition of this alliance was that the Ottoman navy would have the opportunity to make its presence felt in the Western Mediterranean. However, it would have been a challenge for Istanbul to find sufficient sailors, oarsmen, and funds to put such a plan into effect. There were numerous reasons for this. For one thing, there was the impact of the devaluation of the *akçe* in 1584, by which it lost almost 100% of its value. Also, since the navy had not embarked on a large-scale operation for quite some time, it had become sluggish and corsairs had gradually started striking out on their own. Grand Vizier Sinan Pasha's correspondence with Murad III captures the situation in all its nakedness: "There used to be corsair commanders and captains who served [us] very well; now that these have been forced out, the protection of the seas has become increasingly difficult." On top of this, experienced corsairs, such as Memi the Albanian and Murad Reis, rejected offers of governorships and did not hold back in their criticism of the passivity of the government: "We've been taught to fight with the enemy day and night and we are not coming there." The seasoned grand vizier was well aware of the severity of the problem and bemoaned the fact that, whereas in the 1570s there had been 350 captains, there were now just 70, most of whom were elderly and not much use (*kimi pîr ve kimi 'amel-mânde olmuşlardır*).⁴¹ An interesting solution was proposed by Koca Sinan,⁴² possibly one of the most accomplished commanders of the time, who had led Ottoman armies on three continents, from Tunisia to Yemen and from Iran to Hungary. According to this plan, which had actually been proposed previously, after the disaster of the Battle of Lepanto, viziers, governor-generals, governors, and treasurers of provinces would be expected to equip their galleys from their own pockets, albeit in line with their incomes. In exchange, they would be granted all the taxes that had not been collected since 1582 (which, frankly, were practically impossible to collect).[43] This practice amounted to the roundabout imposition of tax on the military class, who were supposedly exempt from tax. As one would expect, this plan, which aggravated a lot of people, also came to nothing. In any case, Sinan Pasha was dismissed in the summer of 1582.

In short, the Ottoman navy did not head west, and the anti-Habsburg alliance remained dormant. When, in 1593, the Ottomans could not escape becoming involved in a thirteen-year war with Austria, the Mediterranean once again became a lesser priority. Although the navy under the command of Cigalazade Yusuf Sinan Pasha plundered the coasts of southern Italy and Sicily, the Ottomans were unsuccessful in their attempt to spark an anti-Habsburg rebellion in Naples. It was Sinan's talents as a corsair that had led him to be appointed as grand admiral of the Ottoman fleet. By the time he died fighting against the Iranians in 1606, the Ottomans' Mediterranean policy had long been shelved.

NOTES

1. Feridun M. Emecen, İlk Osmanlılar ve Batı Anadolu Beylikler Dünyası (Istanbul: Timaş Yayınları, 2012), ch. 2.
2. Halil İnalcık, *Fatih Devri Üzerine Tetkik ve Vesikalar* (Ankara: Türk Tarih Kurumu, 1954).
3. Cf. Fuad Köprülü, *Bizans Müesseselerinin Osmanlı Müesseselerine Tesiri* (Istanbul: Evkaf Matbaası, 1931).
4. For detailed studies of Mehmed the Conqueror, see Franz Babinger, *Mehmet der Eroberer und seine Zeit: Weltenstürmer einer Zeitenwende* (Munich: F. Bruckmann, 1953); Halil İnalcık, "Mehmed II," *Türkiye Diyanet Vakfı İslam Ansiklopedisi*.
5. Feridun M. Emecen, *Yavuz Sultan Selim* (Istanbul: Kapı Yayınları, 2016).
6. Palmira Brummett, *Ottoman Seapower and Levantine Diplomacy in the Age of Discovery* (Albany: State University of New York Press, 1994).
7. Voltaire, *Essai sur les mœurs et l'esprit des nations et sur les principaux faits de l'histoire depuis Charlemagne jusqu'à Louis XIII* (1756), ch. 70.
8. Cornell Fleischer, "The Lawgiver as Messiah: The Making of the Imperial Image in the Reign of Süleymân," in *Soliman le magnifique et son temps*, ed. Gilles Veinstein (Paris: La Documentation Française, 1992), pp. 159–77; Feridun M. Emecen, *İmparatorluk Çağının Osmanlı Sultanları-I* (Istanbul: İSAM Yayınları, 2014), pp. 153–59.
9. John M. Headley, "The Habsburg World Empire and the Revival of Ghibellinism," *Medieval Renaissance Studies* 7 (1975): pp. 97–98; John M. Headley, "Germany, the Empire and *Monarchia* in the Thought and Policy of

Gattinara," in *Das römisch-deutsche Reich im politischen System Karls V*, ed. Heinrich Lutz and Elisabeth Müller Luckner (Munich: Oldenbourg, 1982), p. 22.

10. Jean-Louis Bacqué-Grammont, "Autour d'une correspondance entre Charles Quint et İbrahim Paşa," *Turcica* 15 (1983): p. 234.

11. Anonymous, *Copia de una lettera de la partita del Turcho. Particolare de giornata in giomata insino a Belgrado*, Belgrade, July 7, 1532. Cf. also Anonymous, *Copey unnd lautter Abschrifft ainsi warhafftigen Sendtbrieffs/ wieder Türckisch Kayser Solyman/disen sein yerzt gegen würtigen Anzug wider die Christenhait geordnet/von Constantinopel aussgezogen/und gen Kriechischen Weyssenburg ankommen ist/Wie volgt*, Belgrade, July 7, 1532; Gülru Necipoğlu, "Süleymân the Magnificent and the Representation of Power in the Context of Ottoman-Hapsburg-Papal Rivalry," in *Süleymân the Second and His Time*, ed. Halil İnalcık and Cemal Kafadar (Istanbul: The Isis Press, 1993), pp. 172–73, fn. 31.

12. Necipoğlu, p. 170. The ducat was the Venetian gold coin that served as the main currency in the sixteenth-century Mediterranean. One ducat was worth roughly 60 Ottoman *akçe*s in the middle of the century.

13. Metin Kunt, *The Sultan's Servants: The Transformation of Ottoman Provincial Administration, 1550–1650* (New York: Columbia University Press, 1983), p. 27. *Akçe* is the name of the Ottoman silver coin.

14. Ömer Lütfi Barkan, "Hicri 933–934 / Miladi 1526–1527 Yılına Ait Bir Bütçe Örneği," İktisat Fakültesi Mecmuası 15, no. 1–4 (1954): p. 255.

15. For an analysis of this important battle, which was a turning point in Hungarian history, see Feridun M. Emecen, *Osmanlı Klasik Çağında Savaş* (Istanbul: Timaş, 2011), pp. 159–216.

16. Annie Berthier, "Un Document Retrouve: La Premiere Lettre de Soliman au Francois Ier (1526)." *Turcica* 27 (1995): pp. 263–66.

17. Christine Isom-Verhaaren, *Allies with the Infidel: The Ottoman and French Alliance in the Sixteenth Century* (London: I.B. Tauris, 2011).

18. Stephen A. Fischer-Galati, *Ottoman Imperialism and German Protestantism, 1521–1555* (Cambridge, MA: Harvard University Press, 1959); Juan Sánchez Montes, *Franceses, Protestantes, Turcos. Los españoles ante la política internacional de Carlos V* (Granada: Universidad de Granada, 1995).

19. Feridun M. Emecen, *Osmanlı İmparatorluğu'nun Kuruluşu ve Yükselişi, 1300–1600* (Istanbul: Türkiye İş Bankası Kültür Yayınları, 2015), p. 249.

20. "Corsair" is the name given to privateers in the Mediterranean. I would like to emphasize the difference between pirates and corsairs/privateers. While the former are small-time thieves operating on their own accord, the latter function under the protection and support of a central government and thus have to observe certain rules.

21. Aziz Samih İlter, *Şimali Afrika'da Türkler* (Istanbul: Vakit Matbaası, 1936), 1:70–71; Svat Soucek, "The Rise of the Barbarossas in North Africa," *Turcica* 7 (1975): p. 246.

22. Rhoads Murphey, "Seyyid Murâdî's Prose Biography of Hızır ibn Yakub, Alias Hayrredin Barbarossa: Ottoman Folk Narrative as an Underexploited Source for Historical Reconstruction," *Acta Orientaliae Academiae Scientiarum Hungaricae* 54, no. 4 (2001): pp. 519–32.

23. Lütfi Paşa, *Tevârih-i Âl-i Osman*, ed. Kayhan Atik (Ankara: T.C. Kültür Bakanlığı Yayınları, 2001), vr. 343, p. 271.

24. Literally, "Goodness of the Faith," the sobriquet given to Hızır by the Sultan.

25. Gábor Ágoston, "Ideologie, Propaganda und Politischer Pragmatismus: Die Auseinandersetzung der osmanichen und habsburgischen Grossmächte und die mitteleuropäische Konfrontation," in *Kaiser Ferdinand I.—Ein mitteleuropäischer Herrscher*, ed. Maria Fuchs (Münster: Aschendorff, 2005), pp. 207–33.

26. For an evaluation of the strategy deployed in this battle, see John Francis Guilmartin Jr., *Gunpowder and Galleys: Changing Technology and Mediterranean Warfare at Sea in the Sixteenth Century* (London: Cambridge University Press, 1974), pp. 42–56.

27. Carlo Bornate, "La Missione di Sampiero Corso a Costantinopoli," *Archivio Storico di Corsica* 15 (1939): pp. 472–502.

28. ASV, *SAPC*, fil. 5, c. 161r (July 17, 1551).

29. The nominal admiral of the fleet was Sinan Pasha, the brother of Grand Vizier Rüstem Pasha.

30. The Calvinists would have to wait for the Thirty Years' War before they could be included in this agreement.

31. The most impressive depiction of the perennial debates within the family can be found in Karl Brandi's classic work *Kaiser Karl V: Der Kaiser und sein Weltreich* (Munich: König Verlag, 1973), pp. 488–95.

32. Guilmartin, pp. 123–34.

33. Braudel, *La Méditerranée*, 2:297–308.

34. Countless books and articles have been written on the Battle of Lepanto. The most impressive examination of the battle from a tactical perspective is John Francis Guilmartin's *Gunpowder and Galleys*, pp. 221–52. The most comprehensive document-based analysis of the War of Cyprus is the study by Alessandro Barbero, *Lepanto: La battaglia dei tre imperi* (Rome and Bari: Laterza, 2010). During the writing of this book, the French translation of Barbero's work was consulted: *La bataille des trois empires: Lépante, 1571*, trans. Patricia Farazzi and Michel Valensi (Paris: Flammarion, 2012).

35. Hess, "The Battle of Lepanto," p. 71.

36. Phillip Williams, *Empire and Holy War in the Mediterranean* (New York: I.B. Tauris, 2014), ch. 3.

37. "Huguenot" is the name given to French Protestants.

38. Guilmartin, pp. 221–29.

39. Güneş Işıksel, *La diplomatie ottomane sous le règne de Selîm II: paramètres et périmètres de l'Empire ottoman dans le troisime quart du XVIe siècle* (Paris: Peeters, 2016), p. 212.

40. For the details of these negotiations, see Braudel, *La Méditerranée*, 2:439–50; S. A. Skilliter, "The Hispano-Ottoman Armistice of 1581," in *Iran and Islam: In memory of the late Vladimir Minorsky*, ed. C. E. Bosworth (Edinburgh: Edinburgh University Press, 1971), pp. 491–515; M. J. Rodríguez-Salgado, *Felipe II, el "Paladín de la Cristiandad y la paz con el Turco"* (Valladolid: Universidad de Valladolid, 2004); Emrah Safa Gürkan, "Espionage in the 16th Century Mediterranean: Secret Diplomacy, Mediterranean Go-Betweens and the Ottoman-Habsburg Rivalry" (unpublished PhD diss., Georgetown University, 2012), pp. 291–312.

41. TSMK, Revan 1943, vr. 3b; Halil Sahillioğlu, ed., *Koca Sinan Paşa'nın Telhisleri* (Istanbul: IRCICA, 2004), p. 3.

42. This claim was first put forward by Feridun M. Emecen.

43. Pál Fodor, "Between Two Continental Wars: The Ottoman Naval Preparations in 1590–1592," *In Quest of the Golden Apple: Imperial Ideology, Politics, and Military Administration in the Ottoman Empire*, ed. Pál Fodor (Istanbul: Isis, 2000), pp. 171–90.

2

OTTOMAN SPIES AND
INTELLIGENCE OPERATIONS

Let us start our examination of Ottoman intelligence by focusing on the agents themselves and the dangerous operations that they carried out in enemy territory on the other side of the Mediterranean. What kinds of backgrounds did these spies have? What characteristics did they need to have in order to carry out their work effectively? When it came to operations such as intelligence gathering, assassinations, bribery, and agitation, what kinds of methods did they use, and how successful were they? These are the questions that I shall try to address in this chapter.

To start with, it is worth pointing out that the vast majority of Ottoman spies who operated around the Mediterranean and in Europe knew the region inside out. It was only natural that some of them were Christians or converts to Islam. As well as there being logistical reasons for this, it is also clear that, at a time when political factors limited the mobility of individuals, people who knew the region and its geography were in a better position to travel and forge contacts, which meant that it was much easier for them to gather information.

However, because the Ottomans made use of spies with a convert background, Christians who came from the "Well-Protected Lands" (i.e., Ottoman territory) started to be viewed with suspicion. For example, a report presented to Philip II in 1559 suggested that Greek sailors who arrived at harbors in the Kingdom of Naples should be checked to see if they were circumcised; in this way, one could identify whether they were Ottoman spies.[1] There were, moreover, cases of spies who had converted to Islam but who asserted that they wanted to return to "The True Religion" that they had previously abandoned. Such explanations were able to fool the authorities, and the spies in question continued to carry out their activities on enemy soil with little interference. Indeed, Istanbul sent agents of this kind to several locations across Europe.[2]

We know that the Christians and converts who served the Ottomans in the Western Mediterranean made effective use of their family networks when trying to gather information. In chapter 4, I shall explain in greater detail how Alvise Gritti sent his brothers to all four corners of Europe to function as spies.

We come across numerous comparable examples related to Ottoman grand admiral. The personal connections of Uluc Ali, for instance, a convert from Calabria, were important from the perspective of both Habsburg and Ottoman intelligence. This experienced sailor had previously been on a reconnaissance mission in the Adriatic together with Kara Hoca, the commander of the corsairs of Vlorë. In 1570, he would send Kara Hoca to Sicily to discover the location of the Allied Christian fleet.[3] Kara Hoca anchored in Messina under cover of darkness, got as close as he could to the fleet, and counted the number of galleys there. He then landed with his men in Calabria, where he received the news from a relative of Uluc Ali that the Christian fleet was about to put to sea.[4] However, Uluc Ali's acquaintances had caught the attention of Habsburg intelligence.

The Habsburgs made countless attempts to win back former subjects to their side. In one of these, Habsburg officials came up with the idea of dispatching a member of Uluc Ali's family in the hope of initiating negotiations aimed at winning him back. This plan, however, was bound to fail, since these relatives were either too young to know the grand admiral or too old to travel. Instead, the decision was taken to send Giovanni Battista Ganzuga, who happened to be both a childhood friend of Uluc Ali and his former slave. Ganzuga had come to specialize in raking in ransom money earned from getting captives released, while donning the uniform of the Mercédaire order of monks.[5] The offer that he made to his old master was that, if he returned to the Christian fold and handed over Algiers to the Habsburgs, he would be granted whichever title he desired—whether marquis or count—plus a bonus of 12,000 ducats.[6] As I have pointed out in another article,[7] Uluc Ali turned down several bribes and invitations to betray his side, remaining loyal to the Ottomans until the very end.

Another grand admiral with a background in piracy, Uluc Hasan Pasha, had no reservations about employing his own cousin, Livio Celeste, as a spy. Livio, however, turned out to be rather incompetent and ended up being caught no less than three times, in Marseilles, Malta, and Naples. He escaped with his life on all three occasions, but for this to happen Uluc Hasan Pasha had to speak up or even make open threats. For example, in 1590, when Livio was captured for the third time, Uluc Hasan Pasha is alleged to have warned that, if anything happened to Livio, he would roast alive every single Spaniard and Neapolitan that he could get his hands on. The viceroy of Naples, Juan de Zuñiga, appears to have taken this threat quite seriously; Livio was allowed to return to Algiers, and when he died, he was buried in the tomb of his savior, Uluc Hasan Pasha.[8]

A final example is that of the convert Cigalazade Yusuf Sinan Pasha from Genoa, né Scipione Cicala. In 1561, when he was just seventeen years old, Scipione was taken prisoner by corsairs, together with his father, the famous corsair Visconte Cicala. Turgud Reis, the governor-general of Tripolitania, subsequently sent Scipione to Istanbul as a present for Süleyman the Magnificent. In Istanbul, Scipione would be educated in the palace school and end up a favorite of the sultan. He rose up rapidly through the ranks. In recognition of his "skill in the science of the sea and his pedigree as the son of a corsair,"[9] that is, based on the experience he had gained thanks to his father's occupation as a corsair, Cigalazade Yusuf Sinan Pasha was placed in charge of the Ottoman navy. At that point, he took the step of inviting his younger brother Carlo Cicala to come and join him. At the time, Carlo was working for the Habsburgs in Sicily, where his Genoese family had settled at the beginning of the sixteenth century. He had to get permission from the Habsburg authorities to join his brother in the Ottoman Empire. For this, he offered the authorities his services as a spy, adding that he would persuade his brother to convert back to Christianity and to change sides, bringing with him the Ottoman navy under his command. Having been granted permission to leave, in 1593 Carlo moved to Istanbul, where he was reunited with his brother. From that point on, he traveled back and forth between Sicily and Istanbul on countless occasions.[10] As well as drawing attention to the complex and colorful history of the Cicala family, I would like to point out that, having gone to the Ottoman Empire with the objective of serving as a spy for the Habsburgs, a role he fulfilled by filing reports on a regular basis, eventually Carlo actually metamorphosed into an agent working for the Ottomans! According to a report prepared by the Venetian intelligence service, Carlo was joined on a visit to Corfu by a military engineer (*professor di cose militari*) by the name of Ambrosio Benedetti. Benedetti quickly drew up a plan of the Venetian fortress on this strategically important island in the Adriatic Sea, and he sent this plan to Istanbul.[11] A year later, Bernardino de Cárdenas, who was both viceroy of Sicily and duke of Maqueda, let it be known that he disapproved of Carlo's presence in Sicily, given that he was constantly on the move between Istanbul and Sicily. According to Cárdenas, the further away this lousy *vanissimo* was from the island, the less the Ottomans would find out about what was going on there.[12]

The Ottoman intelligence service did not hesitate to force Christians and converts to Islam to function as spies and sometimes even went so far as to put clergymen to use. A case in point is the man referred to in documents as the "Bishop of Heraclea" but who was probably the metropolitan bishop of Thessaloniki, Macharius Chiensis. Chiensis was an Orthodox clergyman, and he was planning to attend the Council of Trent (1545–63), at which a (re) appraisal of the Catholic faith was due to take place in response to the emergence of Protestantism. However, when it was demanded that he embrace Catholicism and obey the pope, he felt compelled to retract his request to attend the council. Meanwhile, the metropolitan contacted the Habsburgs and proposed a number of covert operations, which would actually have been difficult to carry out. Macharius believed that the Habsburgs should try to reach out to Prince Selim, the assumption being widespread that, in the struggle for the Ottoman throne, Selim would lose out to his brother Mustafa. Grand Admiral Sinan Pasha was uneasy about Mustafa becoming sultan, and there were other members of the Ottoman elite who would not hesitate to join a coalition backing Selim. By sowing discord among the Ottomans in this way, the Habsburgs would be able to conquer the Balkans. In addition, Macharius maintained that contact could be made with Grand Vizier Rüstem Pasha and his brother Sinan

Pasha and even that it might be possible to hold talks aimed at setting up an alliance also comprising Emperor Charles V and the Safavid Shah Tahmasp.[13] Behind all these fantastic plans lurked the reality that the metropolitan was an Ottoman spy, a fact that would only surface later. Without a doubt, Macharius's plan to attend the Council of Trent, like the other projects he proposed, was a well-thought-out pretext to travel with ease.[14]

Turning to another example, in 1574, a bishop from Ragusa (today's Dubrovnik, in Croatia) was arrested by the Habsburg authorities on the charge of being a spy and was sent to Rome. It was alleged that the bishop had been monitoring the coast and cities near Puglia, in southeast Italy, and had passed on whatever he learned to Istanbul.[15]

There were even cases of spies who had disguised themselves as clergymen in order to be able to move about freely. For instance, we know about a case where a five-oared frigate approached the Ottoman fleet, carrying two French spies in Neapolitan waters. They came aboard the Ottoman capitana and gave Grand Admiral Sinan Pasha a report of the latest developments. When they disembarked from Sinan Pasha's ship, though, they once more donned their sailors' uniforms. The duo had dressed as monks in the first place in order to provide a cover for their information-gathering activities. Two French sailors wandering around in Naples during a Franco-Spanish war was not something that the authorities would tolerate. The cape and robe of a monk could dispel all suspicions.[16]

Without a doubt, for people seeking the freedom to travel abroad, the best profession was to be a merchant. As I will explain in chapter 3, Ottoman merchants who returned from Christian territories were more than willing to share information about what they had seen with the authorities. The situation was no different for traders who were Habsburg subjects. Merchants had their ears open for gossip wherever they went, whether at the marketplace, in port, or in inns and taverns, where they would be likely to come across people from all walks of life. They might have the chance to observe military preparations, and by developing relationships with the people in the new towns they visited, they could get access to valuable information. That said, the capacity and ability of merchants to access confidential information depended on the precise type of business in which they were involved. Of all the merchants, those who were involved in slave-trading were the best suited to intelligence-related activities, a point that is worth dwelling on.

Slavery was, at this time, an integral element of Mediterranean naval life and of Mediterranean economies. Although the Mediterranean had nothing like the plantation slavery that would later become so widespread in the Americas, slaves were deployed as oarsmen on galleys as well as for a range of tasks in homes, shops, and workshops. Whenever captives were seized on a ship belonging to members of "the other religion," they would be sold at the marketplace as slaves and would only be freed if a ransom was paid for them or some kind of swap took place.[17] It was only natural that merchants, who were used to speaking and haggling with officials at every level on both sides of the Mediterranean frontier, became experts in ransom negotiations. With easy access to rich and powerful people, merchants were also the ideal candidates for the role of spy.[18]

In some cases, indeed, it is difficult to say whether a merchant was a spy or a slave ransomer. Generally, the reality was that the two occupations overlapped. A good example of this is Ali Moro. An excellent speaker of *lingua franca* (a hybrid language spoken almost everywhere in the Mediterranean), Moro had taken up the occupation of assisting in the freeing of slaves in Istanbul on behalf of Christian states (*scuotter et barattar schiavi*). Because of this he was able to gain access everywhere (*con il quale mezzo si fa intratura in ogni loco*). He held a letter of safe conduct, which had been granted to him by the viceroy of Naples, the grand duke of Tuscany and the grand master of the Order of St. John (Knights of Malta), a religious order which, as mentioned earlier, was mainly engaged in piracy. According to the *bailo* (the Venetian consul in Istanbul) Lorenzo Bernardo, Ali Moro was at the same time an Ottoman spy, being himself a Turk. In saying this, Bernardo was presumably referring to Moro's Muslim identity, since the surname Moro points to a Morisco (Moorish) origin, that is, a Muslim from the Iberian Peninsula. Moro wore clothing particular to Christians (*veste alla franca*), and thanks to the letter of safe conduct he carried with him, he was free to travel around Italy unhindered. He had told Bernardo that he would travel to Naples, followed by Malta, Florence, and Venice for "slave ransoming business" (*per negotio di riscattar schiavi*). The wily *bailo* figured out that Moro's involvement in slave ransoming was a pretext, which made it possible for Moro to travel to places that were of primary strategic importance to Ottoman intelligence. Bernardo was already suspicious of Moro because of the amount of time he spent conversing with Grand Admiral Uluc Ali. At the same time, though, Ali Moro was continuing with his official occupation, and because of this we cannot say that he was solely a spy or a slave ransomer. For example, at a meeting of the Ottoman state council held in the Ottoman Shipyard, to which Moro was invited by Uluc Ali, a discussion took place about exchanging a number of captive Ottoman captains in Malta for Christian slaves in Ottoman lands. Although Moro assured Bernardo that he would return the following March, Bernardo had his suspicions and took the step of passing on a description of Moro to the authorities in Venice. This olive-skinned, medium-height spy, with his short beard, was a lively and cagey (*accorto*) character.[19]

The field of activity of Ottoman spies was remarkably broad. As well as seeking out intelligence in cities closer to home, such as Rome, Naples, Messina, and Vienna, they could also be found further afield, such as in France, Spain, or the Low Countries. The competence and ingenuity of some agents are truly impressive; they seemed to have few difficulties in overcoming borders of culture, religion, and geography and accessing the most confidential information of that period. On occasion, a single document can provide insight into a broad network of agents. According to the testimony of two Habsburg agents in Istanbul, spies from Istanbul could be found in several Habsburg cities.

Among the numerous Ottoman agents in Naples was a Valencian Morisco working for Uluc Ali, who could easily gain access to both the palace and the fortress in the city.

Another notable agent managed to pass on to Istanbul all the news that Cardinal Antoine Perrenot de Granvelle, the viceroy of Naples, received from Spain. The news was as follows:

- During the siege of La Goulette in 1573, one Juan Çanoguera forged secret contacts with the Ottomans, something for which he should not escape punishment.
- One of the Neapolitan aristocrats that fell into Ottoman hands at the end of the siege, named Cesar Carafa, was indeed a spy in the employ of Joseph Nasi (see chapter 4), the favorite of Selim II. Carafa had been expelled from Naples for joining the anti-Habsburg rebellion led by the Prince of Salerno. After he was transported to Istanbul, far from being subjected to any kind of ill treatment, he was set free and moved on to Ragusa. All these details make it abundantly clear that he was a spy.
- Andrea Gasparo Corso was responsible for coordinating the secret negotiations between Algiers and Madrid concerning Uluc Ali's return to the Christian fold. At the same time, though, he was providing Istanbul with information.
- Another agent who worked for the Ottomans was a convert named Murad Agha, from the Pinatello family of Naples.
- Among the most serious allegations related to spying activities concerned Aurelio Santa Croce and his brother Giovanni Antonio. Since the 1560s, Santa Croce had been funneling Habsburg funds into their intelligence network in Istanbul, of which he was the station chief. It transpired, however, that both brothers were double agents and were also providing the Ottomans with intelligence.[20]

It is worth pointing out once more that all the aforementioned names emerged from a single document.

Luis de Portillo, a trickster from Ragusa, was infamous for his exaggeration and his fabricated reports. All the same, it would be wrong to skip over Portillo's claim that Ottoman ships transported no less than thirty spies to Sicily and Naples, the aim being for these agents to find out what preparations the Christian fleet was making and what aims they had in mind.[21] Given the circumstances of that era, this figure may seem exaggerated, but it is not impossible that it is accurate. After all, Aurelio Santa Croce would report that in 1569, 112 Habsburg agents were active in Istanbul,[22] and the Ottomans would see nothing untoward in dispatching four spies to Naples for a single mission, these spies consisting of a Florentine with a ruddy complexion, an old black-haired Neapolitan, and two Genoese, one of whom had a ginger beard.[23]

In order to see how agents working for Ottoman intelligence went about collecting information, let us turn to examine in detail some of the stories of spies that I have tracked down in European archives. The reasons why I have selected these particular stories out of the many available are not just that they are interesting and contain a lot of detail. They provide a snapshot of the personalities who made up the world of intelligence in the Early Modern Mediterranean, and they also offer good examples of the diverse formats and narrative styles that we encounter in documents in the archives. While some stories concentrate on intelligence gathering, others deal with covert operations such as assassinations, agitation, and bribery. Some narratives provide an overview of a spy's activities, but others follow the format of an interrogation when recounting the activities of an agent. As such, the latter kind of texts allows the reader to savor the flavor of the documents that the historian gets to examine.

MARXEBEN LENER

Marxeben Lener was a Transylvania-born agent working for Grand Vizier Sokullu Mehmed Pasha.[24] His story is short but well worth telling. Lener was born in Kronstadt,[25] or Brashov (Romania)[26] as it is called today, and at some point, he became a Muslim and adopted the name Mahmud or Ahmed before eventually getting married in Istanbul.[27]

We know nothing else about the past of this convert-agent, but we do know that he somehow succeeded in getting a meeting with Emperor Maximilian II and extorting a considerable amount of money from him. It is not certain what shadowy projects he used to entice Maximilian, but the kinds of stories you will read in this chapter should give you an idea.

Shortly after returning to Istanbul, Lener set off once again, this time to Naples. His aim was to infiltrate the entourage of the viceroy (*asentar en casa del Virey*) under the pretext of renouncing Islam. Once in Naples, he would keep the Ottomans briefed about what was happening there. From Naples, Lener planned to move on to Rome and Venice and after that to Spain.

According to a report from Istanbul, Lener was around forty years old, black-bearded, and rather partial to wine and gambling. While he could be talkative (*parlero*), at least he was a talented chatterbox. Apart from German, Lener understood Hungarian, Aromanian (*Valaco*), Venetian, and a sufficient amount of Turkish. Even this limited amount of information should suffice to show that Lener matched the typical profile of the spies of his era. He was used to conversing in taverns and inns with people of different nationalities, and he was constantly on the move. Given the ease with which he managed to fool Maximilian, one naturally arrives at the conclusion that he was a very persuasive con man! In 1575, this experienced and versatile agent was taken into custody in Naples by *alcalde* Ximenez Ortiz on suspicion of being a spy. What heightened Ortiz's suspicions was the large number of languages that Lener spoke, and Ortiz participated in the interrogation himself. When Lener's lies were exposed as such, he was arrested. After this, there are no more traces of Lener in the archive, so we unfortunately do not know what became of him.

A TRICKSTER FROM LANGUEDOC: BARON DE LA FAGE

Baron de la Fage was the name used by a fraudster who descended from one of the foremost families in the Languedoc region of southern France.[28] It is well worth examining the adventures he had when he traveled to Italy on behalf of the Ottomans in order to gather intelligence. A remarkably crafty convert, de la Fage was at the same time an agent for the English queen, Elizabeth! Having returned to Italy, purportedly to convert back to Christianity, he did much more than just gather information for Istanbul. In Florence, he established close relations with both the grand duke of Tuscany and the French ambassador, so much so that he received favors from them. Unfortunately, we can only guess what it was about de la Fage that made him so popular.

After Florence, the baron moved on to Rome, and in the capital of the Christian world he was able to obtain an audience with Pope Innocent IX and his cardinals. He informed them that several high-ranking Ottoman converts were yearning to return to The True Religion. The governor of Euboea, de la Fage alleged, could be convinced to change sides and to surrender the fortress under his command to the Habsburgs. De la Fage also told his interlocutors that it would be possible for Christian powers to get hold of a huge number of Ottoman galleys that were under the control of a significant number of Christian-born convert-captains. Of course, this would come at a price. It would appear that the baron succeeded in winning over the pope and his cardinals to implausible projects like this, of which there is copious evidence in the archives.

De la Fage's success inspired in him a sense of bravado. Having returned to Istanbul, he showed off the license (*patente*) and letter of safe conduct signed by Cardinal Lucio Sanseverino, which had been issued on the orders of the pope. In other words, he went so far as to publicly mock the highest authorities of the Catholic world. At this point, I would like to note that de la Fage might not have been the only Ottoman spy who appeared before the pope in this kind of covert operation. Notwithstanding the fact that the reports filed by Luis de Portillo cannot be entirely trusted, he likewise refers to a meeting that took place in 1573 between a Greek Ottoman agent, Pope Gregory XIII, and two cardinals. This convert agent boasted to Portillo that he had gone over to Naples and talked to Don Juan, the illegitimate brother of Philip II, no less than sixteen times.[29]

Having done what he needed to do in Rome, Baron de la Fage traveled to Venice. Here too, though, he was up to no good and tried to extract money from the Habsburg ambassador. Francisco de Vera generally had a soft spot for spies, but he recognized straightaway what kind of a person de la Fage was and sent him packing. Continuing with his mischief, our spy from Languedoc promised to take four young Christians—one a Spaniard, one a Frenchman from the high aristocracy, and two Italians—on a tour of Ottoman territory, and he persuaded them to return with him to the Eastern Mediterranean. At this point, though, the wily diplomat de Vera intervened and dissuaded the young men from taking part in the trip, warning them that de la Fage intended either to sell them as slaves or to force them to become Muslims. The Spanish ambassador remembered this incident ten years later, in 1602, after he had returned to Madrid and become one of the key figures in Habsburg intelligence. This testifies to the mark that colorful personalities could leave on others in the sixteenth century.

Upon his return, de la Fage concocted a number of schemes, including defrauding the captain of a ship he boarded to travel to the town of Kotor on the Adriatic coast. Telling him that he was going to Dalmatia to buy a horse, he persuaded the captain to give him 450 écus[30] as well as a quantity of goods that is not specified in the documents. The gullible captain never got his money back and, not surprisingly, was ruined. Another person whom the baron damaged economically, by ensuring that his assets were confiscated, was the Venetian merchant Marc'Antonio Stanga, one of the most active spies in 1590s' Istanbul. In order to recover his fortune, Stanga had no option but to say goodbye to two hundred ducats in the form of a bribe.

Throughout his many travels, Baron de la Fage would keep a sharp eye on everything around him, and his intelligence activities appear to have borne fruit. As soon as he returned, he blew the whistle on a number of spies and informants. Based on allegations made by de la Fage, a considerable number of people ended up being imprisoned by the Ottomans. These included David Passi (see chapter 4), a Marrano (clandestine Jew from Spain) spymaster, who was not averse to maintaining undercover links with the Habsburgs, as well as Passi's right-hand man, Guillermo de Saboya. Other victims of de la Fage's machinations were Juan Sequi from Majorca (a prominent member of the Habsburg intelligence network in Istanbul) and a convert-informer by the name of Captain Ramazan. Although Ramazan and Saboya were tortured, they denied all the charges against them. Not long after this, Saboya would die in jail, but the irony was that de la Fage's fate was not so different. Unfortunately, in the fall of 1592, one of the most colorful figures in Istanbul's intelligence scene succumbed to the plague, and just one and a half months after Saboya's death, de la Fage found himself on the other side, where he could avoid the cold of the coming winter.

FROM VLORË TO PIAZZA GIUDEA: JERONIMO AMIQUI AND FRIENDS

I mentioned previously that most of the spies sent to Europe were converts to Islam. If caught, though, such people risked being dragged before the Inquisition on the charge of apostasy, that is, abandoning The True Religion.[31] In their now-classic work, Bartolomé and Lucile Bennassar show us the lengths these "Christians of Allah" (*Les chrétiens d'Allah*) went to in order to hide their pasts; to be spared the horrors of the Inquisition, they would claim that they were born Muslim and had never been Christians.[32] In doing so, they aimed to position themselves beyond the scope of the Inquisition, which could judge heretics and converts but not infidels; in other words, Christians but not Muslims. On this point, though, it is important to offer some clarity regarding the fate that Spain's Muslims suffered because of the Inquisition. Although Moriscos remained Muslims in secret, they were forced to be baptized and become Christians, and the latter is what they technically were. When they became Muslims once more, they were classed as apostates, who would have to be judged by the Inquisition.

One of the Ottoman spies who attempted to avoid the Inquisition by concealing the conversion he had undergone was Jeronimo Amiqui, who was caught in 1552. During his interrogation, this Spanish spy from Zaragoza contended that he had set out for Italy but then had been taken captive by corsairs in Villefranche-sur-Mer, near Nice. The corsairs had shipped him off to Vlorë, the main port in Ottoman Albania. Having stayed there for more than a year, he was taken by the brother of his deceased former master to Thessaloniki, where he remained for four years. This part of the story appears quite reasonable. After all, during those years when the Ottoman fleet was heavily engaged in the Tyrrhenian and Balearic Seas, that is, in 1550, 1552, 1553, 1554, and 1558, Ottoman corsairs ran riot in the Western Mediterranean. Given that Vlorë was something of a headquarters for the corsairs operating in the Adriatic, it is not at all surprising that a captive should be brought to this port.

However, Amiqui's answer to the next question posed by his interrogators landed him in deep water. He was asked whether he was circumcised when he converted, and he answered yes. This made the interrogators even more suspicious of him. Like all the converts who found themselves in a similar situation, Amiqui tried to explain away his conversion by claiming that it had made it easier for him to escape. His interrogators, however, had had their fill of such excuses. Amiqui continued his narrative by recalling that he had fled Thessaloniki and found his way to the port of Lezhë on the Adriatic coast. A Christian grain merchant whom he met there, named Trifone, sneaked him onto the ship that he himself was traveling on and took him to Ulcinj, one of the Venetian ports on the Adriatic coast. Because there were a lot of Turks in Ulcinj, though, Amiqui was afraid of being recognized and carried on to Ragusa. From there, he was put on a ship by some priests and sailed on to Barletta, part of the Kingdom of Naples. A Spanish soldier who learned that Amiqui had escaped from captivity took a shine to him and accommodated Amiqui for three days. Amiqui traveled from Barleta to Naples, where he stayed for one day. Aiming to cross over to Santa Maria de lo Rito, he headed north but was arrested in the port of Gaeta once it was discovered that he was circumcised.

His captors believed he was lying, and they made the decision to apply torture during the interrogation. It is worth bearing in mind that, in the sixteenth century, the deployment of a moderate amount of torture was regarded as legally acceptable. It was frequently used with the proviso that any permanent damage should be avoided and certain rules should be followed. During the interrogation, in which the commander of Gaeta, the count of Altamira, participated in person, Amiqui was suspended upside down (*cuerda*, known today as the "Palestinian hanger"). Amiqui admitted being a Morisco who had gone to the Ottoman Empire of his own free will and embraced Islam. Nonetheless, Amiqui attempted to wrest victory from the jaws of defeat by claiming that Islam did not satisfy him and that this was why he had wanted to return to the Christian realm.

The interrogators, however, were good at their job. They lifted Amiqui onto the hanger once more and this time broke his resistance. "Untie me!" he pleaded, before admitting that he was an Ottoman spy who had been sent by Süleyman, the governor of Vlorë, to find out how many soldiers and cannons there were in the forts in the vicinity of Puglia, Naples, and Gaeta. Amiqui told his interrogators that the governor had promised him land in Vlorë and had given him just ten ducats toward his travel expenses. Apart from himself, Amiqui claimed, two other agents had set out on the same mission. Amiqui did not hesitate to provide the detailed descriptions that his interrogators needed to capture his associates; in the world of spies, it was every man for himself, and there was no room for loyalty. Amiqui revealed that one of his fellow spies was Francesco Aragones, whose Muslim name was Muhammad and who was slim, with a slight beard, and somewhat taller than himself. All he said about the other was that his name was Miguel Manchebo/Ali and that he too had a small beard.

The three spies had found a brigantin[33] to take them to Ragusa. From there, they had crossed over to Barletta on a merchant ship. There they separated, having agreed to meet again in Rome. For two days, Amiqui explored every inch of the fortress of Barletta, observing that it contained 150 soldiers under the command of Captain Portillo but a remarkably small number of cannons. From Barletta, Amiqui traveled to Naples, spending one day there, and was subsequently captured in Gaeta. Amiqui alleged that he did not know where the two other agents were. The three had arranged to meet again in the Piazza Giudea in Rome. From there, they would travel to Ancona, where a merchant ship owned by a Turk by the name of Muhammed would deliver them to Herceg Novi, where they could present their reports to Governor Süleyman.[34] It must have been difficult for Amiqui to accept that he would miss the grand reunion with his fellow agents. Let us hope that his colleagues did a better job than him!

CONSTANTINO OF HERAKLION / MUHAMMED AND AHMED THE JANISSARY

Another Ottoman agent who was a convert and who, like Jeronimo Amiqui, was caught red-handed in Southern Italy was Constantino.[35] A Greek by origin, he was born in the city of Heraklion on the Venetian-governed island of Crete. When he became a Muslim, he adopted the name Muhammad/Mehmed. The corsair harbors in North Africa were swarming with converts like him. As a matter of fact, while the literature presents Ottoman corsairs as holy warriors eager for action, a large proportion of them were opportunists who were born Christian but for one reason or other had become Muslims.[36] Constantino is likely to have been inspired by these kinds of people. It should also be noted that new converts to Islam often took on the name of the Prophet Mohammed or names found in Ahl al-Bayt, Mohammed's extended family.

In the winter of 1561 to 1562, the famous Ottoman corsair and governor-general of Tripolitania, Turgud Reis, sent Constantino and a Janissary by the name of Ahmed (*Ayamet*) to Sicily, where they were supposed to gather intelligence. Ahmed did not fit the mold of the classic Janissary; he was not a member of a Christian community in the Balkans who had been forced to convert to Islam and subsequently ended up serving in the rifle infantry, which was the elite unit of the central army. The Janissaries of North Africa consisted of Muslim volunteers of Western Anatolian origin, who constituted the local forces in their own towns.[37] In 1519, when Hayreddin Barbarossa agreed to be subordinated to Istanbul, he was not only sent a regiment from among the Janissaries in Istanbul but also got permission from Sultan Selim to recruit soldiers from among the Muslims of Anatolia, and he used this opportunity to form a unit who would remain loyal to him. This provides us considerable insight into the logic behind the systems that the Seljuks called *gulam*, Egyptians referred to as the Mamluk system, and the Ottomans called the method of *devşirme*: people who came from a different area would not have close ties with the local population, and this made them ideal candidates to be members of elite corps or military units, all of whom would remain loyal to the ruling class or dynasty to the very end.

Besides not being a convert, Ahmed had the advantage of being familiar with the area to which he was posted. He had previously been captured by Maltese corsairs, the Knights of St. John, and he'd had a chance to get to know Syracuse. Constantino was a veteran spy. According to the testimony he gave when he was captured, together with another Genoese, he had previously carried out an operation to another Sicilian city, namely Trapani. Turgud provided the two spies with a frigate.[38] In addition, he proposed to the spies that, should they manage to get into Syracuse and bring back information about the city's fortifications, cannons, and garrison, he would grant Constantino a substantial reward of five Christian slaves and 1,000 écus. In comparison to this, the 10 ducats that the governor of Vlorë paid his spy appear laughable. At the beginning of the sixteenth century, one écu was worth 50 *akçes*, and in the middle of the century its value was 55 *akçes*; thus, the money that Turgud was offering to Constantino was fifty times the average salary earned by Ottoman agents around the beginning of the century, which stood at 1,000 *akçes* (see chapter 4). In general, Habsburg spies earned no more than between 100 and 200 écus; even the Habsburg station chief in Istanbul in the 1570s, Aurelio Santa Croce, earned only 300 ducats, the equivalent of 340 écus.[39] Given that a seasoned corsair such as Turgud was unlikely to be so generous, the astronomical sum of 1,000 écus was probably an exaggeration by Constantino, an attempt to legitimize his own treachery.

Turgud ordered the two spies to meet up with a Greek in Syracuse named Juan, whom he had dispatched there two months earlier. Juan was a slave owned by a corsair called Memi Reis, but Memi Reis appears to have been quite willing to hand over Juan to his boss Turgud to use as a spy.

Three months prior to Constantino's interrogation, the two spies had set sail for Sicily (see map 2.1). Because of the bad weather, they were forced to take refuge several times in harbors along the coast of Tunisia, namely Djerba, Sfax, Monastir, and Kelibia. When they set out to cross the Strait of Sicily, their ship was accompanied by a brigantin that had been sent by Turgud for capturing Christian "tongues,"[40] who would be used as sources of information. However, no sooner than they had seized six Christians from a merchant ship sailing between Sicily and the island of Pantelleria, the brigantin turned around, leaving the two agents' frigate alone. At Cape Passero, located at the southeasternmost point of Sicily, they came across some Maltese corsairs. Taking four Turks with them, the two agents went onto land, and in order not to be spotted, they traveled overnight for 50 kilometers to arrive at Syracuse. When the group arrived in the city, it was decided that Constantino would enter the city ahead of the others. This was an unfortunate choice; when Constantino arrived at the city gate, he was recognized by a soldier who had previously been a slave in Tripoli. As a result, he was seized immediately.

At this point, I would like to make a short digression in order to explain why we should not actually be surprised to come across coincidences like this. In the sixteenth century, the "Mediterranean world" essentially meant its port

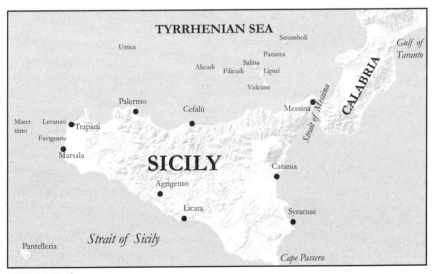

MAP 2.1. Sicily

cities. For this reason, spies, merchants, soldiers, corsairs, and slave ransomers would be likely to bump into one another from time to time in the busy ports, inns, and streets of these cities. For example, Martin de Acuña, who was sent to Istanbul by the Habsburgs in 1577 to sabotage the Ottoman Shipyard, would be denounced by a Greek named Esteban. Esteban had in fact once served as a spy for the Habsburgs, but he fled from Naples, converted to Islam, and entered the service of the Ottomans.[41]

The fact that Constantino had been captured meant that the hunter had now become prey. Turgud's spy was no longer a subject providing intelligence but rather an object from whom intelligence needed to be extracted. The Habsburgs began to fire questions at the failed spy in an attempt to find out what was going on in North Africa and what kind of mission the crafty corsair Turgud had assigned his agent. Who sent him? Were there other spies operating in the area? Was Süleyman the Magnificent planning to send the fleet to the Western Mediterranean? If he was, where was the navy going to attack? (Let us not forget that, just two years before, the Ottoman fleet had inflicted a serious blow to the Habsburg navy at the Battle of Djerba.) How many galleys were moored at Tripoli?

Constantino did not play hard to get and blurted out straightaway that he had been sent by Turgud Reis and that there were other Ottoman agents in the area. Juan and the aforementioned Genoese convert who had accompanied Constantino in the Trapani operation were just two of these agents. The Habsburg authorities must have been particularly interested in the operation that Constantino had undertaken together with the Genoese convert several years before, because Constantino went into considerable detail about it. Following a successful looting operation through which—to use an expression from that period—he had gained his fill of booty (*ganaimle doyum olmak*), a corsair named Ali Reis dropped off Constantino and the Genoese close to Trapani. Disguised in Christian garments, the duo arrived at a garden close to the city. The Genoese then left Constantino behind and entered the city on his own. Two hours later, he returned with a resident of Trapani, another Ottoman agent, who conversed with the Genoese for a while. When this conversation was over, the two agents left the man from Trapani behind and returned to Ali Reis's galley, where the Genoese gave an extensive report to his superior. According to Constantino's description, the agent from Trapani, who was heading toward Spain on a grain ship, was a red-bearded man aged between thirty-five and forty. His upper lip had been ripped off to the extent that it was possible to see his teeth. The investigation conducted by the Habsburg intelligence service confirmed that someone matching this description had boarded a ship. Indeed, this Ottoman agent had helped some men associated with Juan de la Cerda, the viceroy of Sicily and duke of Medinaceli, to load onto the ship some hawks that had been provided by the sultan of Tunis, hawks at that time being considered a symbol of subservience.

Now let us return once more to our spy Constantino, who was so generous with the information he provided in his confessions. According to his testimony, in the Fortress of Djerba there were eighty Turks as well as a galiot[42] that belonged to a Slav convert by the name of Kaid Mustafa.[43] There were a total of two thousand slaves in Tripoli, but when the corsairs sailed off to pillage, these slaves would mostly accompany them; otherwise, they could constitute a serious threat in such a small city temporarily bereft of her soldiers. Constantino continued: In the spring of 1562, a fleet totaling twenty to twenty-one galleys was supposed to set sail. It was going to consist of fourteen galleys directly owned by Turgud and six or seven galleys that belonged to his captains. Turgud, however, wanted to wait for the return of his steward, whom he had sent off to Istanbul five months earlier. The steward had delivered two important prisoners to the sultan: Visconte Cicala, one of the most notorious corsairs in the Mediterranean, and his son Scipione. The latter would enter the Ottoman palace school (Enderun) under the name Yusuf Sinan and go on in later years to serve as vizier, grand admiral of the Fleet, and even—albeit for just forty days—grand vizier. The name of this pasha, whom Ottoman sources refer to as Cigalazade, actually lives on in Cağaloğlu, the name of a famous district in Istanbul (see chapter 6).

Constantino told his interrogators that, in the following year, the Ottoman fleet planned to launch an attack on the port of La Goulette, located 12 kilometers east of Tunis (see map 2.2). Following the debacle at Djerba, Habsburgs were very much fearful of what the Ottoman navy could do. However, Constantino's warning proved to be inaccurate. The Ottomans did not attack this Habsburg *presidio*, or fortress, until 1574, and it was only in 1565 (with the Siege of Malta) that they once again sent their fleet westward. Constantino made a point of mentioning that the sultan of Tunis, Ahmed III, did try to persuade the Ottoman sultan to dispatch the navy.

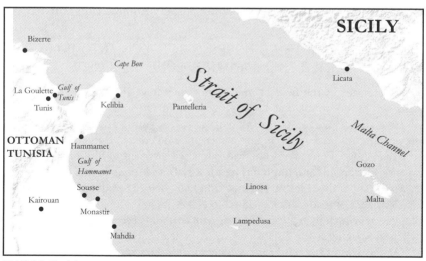

MAP 2.2. Tunisia

Unfortunately, we do not know what became of Constantino. At that time, it was customary, after converts had been captured and interrogated, to deploy them as oarsmen in galleys. When he fell into the hands of the enemy, even such a famous sailor as Turgud Reis was compelled to row a galley. Another possibility is that Constantino was handed over to the Inquisition; after all, he had deviated from The True Religion and was thus an apostate. The fact that he was Orthodox rather than Catholic would not have saved him; the Inquisition judged all Christians, regardless of their denomination. The only thing that might have come to the rescue of our Greek convert was that the Habsburg authorities constantly faced a shortage of oarsmen and were eager to place every Muslim they caught in a galley. Had he been handed over to the Inquisition, he would have been sent to Palermo, where he would have been expected to show remorse for his apostasy and would have served his sentence.

A wide range of sentences awaited victims of the Holy Inquisition. Some of them were able to get away with relatively mild punishments. One of these was to wear a penitential garment called a *sambenito* and wander around the streets to demonstrate to true believers that they regretted their sins and wanted to ask for absolution. Others underwent a catechism to reaffirm their faith; worse but quicker, some would receive a public flogging. But there were also more severe punishments, such as being forced to row in a galley, imprisonment, and even the death penalty. Those who insisted on their apostasy were burned, but we can be certain that this was not the fate suffered by Constantino. My reason for believing this is not that I am convinced that this cunning spy, who wasted no time in divulging what he knew, would have been unwilling to sacrifice his life for the sake of Islam. Rather, it is the fact that only five Muslims were burned to death in the Sicilian Inquisition. Four of them, moreover, were victims of the inquisitorial ritual of public penance (Por. *auto-da-fe*) that took place in the wake of the disaster of Lepanto, a ceremony that was held in the harbor of Messina in the presence of the Habsburg Admiral Don Juan himself.

A GOOD-FOR-NOTHING HOPPING BETWEEN ENTOURAGES: MEHMED THE SPANIARD / LOPE DE LLANOS

His capabilities in the field of intelligence may have been questionable, but there can be no doubt that Lope de Llanos, an Ottoman agent captured in Venice in 1580, had an interesting biography.[44] A young aristocrat, he started out working as a page (*paje*) in the service of Don Pedro Velazquez in Sicily, but for a reason we do not know, he was punished and had to find himself a new master. He worked for a limited time for Ruy Diaz Mendoza, the chamberlain (*mayordomo*) of the Habsburg Prince Don Juan, before deciding to seek his fortune abroad. Lope de Llanos escaped to Navarino and joined the entourage of Uluc Ali, serving him as a page (*paje de camara*) for three years. Later he would switch to working as the Calabrian Uluc Ali's head gatekeeper (*portero mayor*).

As this young Spaniard rose quickly in Uluc Ali's entourage, he caught the attention of Joseph Nasi, a Jew who was one of the most influential political figures in Istanbul at that time. In his capacity as the duke of Naxos, Nasi had taken over administration of the Dodecanese Islands from the Ottomans. He asked Uluc Ali to appoint Lope/Mehmed Bey as the governor of Lemnos. This district was subordinated to a province named Cezayir-i Bahr-ı Sefid, or "Islands of the Mediterranean," which lay under the control of the grand admiral of the fleet. By means of this appointment, Lope/Mehmed, now as coastal governor (*derya beyi*), would join together with Uluc Ali in times of war, providing a couple of galleys. When the fleet was not setting out on a mission, Lope/Mehmed would team up with the other captains in a fleet of between twelve and sixteen ships to ensure "coastal protection" (*derya muhafazası*).

The grand admiral was eager to keep on the right side of Nasi, who had considerable influence at the palace. This is why he agreed to dispatch Lope/Mehmed to Lemnos, sending with him another convert for good measure. The Spanish convert, however, bore a secret grudge against this companion, whom he had known since the days they both spent serving Uluc Ali as pages.

As soon as they arrived on the island, Lope/Mehmed stabbed this man, killing him and thereby getting into trouble once more. Outraged by this wholly unwarranted murder, the people of Lemnos seized Lope/Mehmed and sent word to Uluc Ali, who at the time happened to be on Chios, an island 180 kilometers south, together with his fleet. Uluc Ali was renowned for his temper, so much so that, when he wore black, indicating that he was in bad temper, his men were afraid of going anywhere near him. When he heard about Mehmed's butchery, he flew into a rage.

It looked like this was the end for the man from Zaragoza; Uluc was talking about breaking his servant into four parts (*hazer quartos*).[45] However, Joseph Nasi stepped in once more, saving the troublesome Spaniard from a messy fate and opening up opportunities in the Western Mediterranean. The sly admiral Uluc Ali certainly did not want to agitate the influential Jewish powerbroker and accepted that it would be wise to master his nerves and content himself with a moderate revenge on his protégé. Indeed, what made Uluc Ali a great seaman and distinguished him from the many reckless corsairs of his time was his patience and his strategic instinct. Nasi may have been successful in preventing Lope/Mehmed from being killed, but he could not save him from suffering a fate worse than death. Lope/Mehmed eventually found himself heading toward North Africa as an oarsman in the galleys of the governor-general of Algeria, Uluc Hasan Pasha.[46] When Uluc Hasan arrived in Algiers, he decided to send this troublemaker convert to the sultan of Fez. In so doing, he would ensure that Lope/Mehmed was finally beyond the reach of Nasi. We do not know whether Hasan made this decision himself or if it was passed down to him by his superior, Uluc Ali. At one time, Hasan had served in Uluc Ali's entourage, as his treasurer to be precise. It is possible that he felt sorry for Lope/Mehmed and that, by bringing him along to Fez, he had rescued him from the fury of the Calabrian. The fact that Lope/Mehmed arrived in Fez as a personal gift from the governor-general of Algiers leads one to assume that during his time in Fez he was not treated as just an ordinary slave. Later on, indeed, he would suddenly pop up in Venice, which points to his unusual status.

From this point on, the only sources we have regarding Lope/Mehmed's actions are rumors. Supposedly, he started by traveling to Spain and then on to France before eventually hanging up his hat in Venice. Just at this juncture, though, two Spaniards who had returned from a spell of imprisonment in Istanbul recognized Lope/Mehmed and reported him to the Venetian authorities, claiming that he was a spy. Lope/Mehmed landed in jail, his fate now sealed. Don García Hernandez, the secretary and head of the mission of the Habsburg embassy,[47] attempted to persuade the Venetians that Lope/Mehmed was a subject of Philip II and tried to get them to hand Lope/Mehmed over to the Spanish king. The Venetians, though, were not having anything of this and would later report that Lope/Mehmed died in prison. To the seasoned secretary, though, this seemed an out-and-out lie. He maintained that, like many of those who had been accused of espionage, Lope/Mehmed had been drowned in one of the numerous canals of Venice.

The story of Lope/Mehmed demonstrates once more that, contrary to the notion of a Mediterranean divided into two on the basis of religion, it was easy to move from one side to the other and even to change one's alignment. There is no doubt that, even though Lope/Mehmed lacked discipline, he must have been quite competent; if not, why would he have been offered so many chances? This young aristocrat had not been able to gain a foothold in any one entourage and sought the backing of various patrons. All the same, he was able to travel easily between Spain, Sicily, Istanbul, Morocco, France, and Venice. What he was unable to acquire in the entourage of a Christian master he sought in the company of a convert to Islam, just like himself. Uluc Ali's retinue was indeed a veritable paradise for converts. It contained corsairs and seamen from across the Western Mediterranean; however, it was also home to three thousand slaves, comprising people Uluc Ali was obliged to feed and whom he rented out to the state for use as oarsmen.[48]

TWO OTTOMAN ASSASSINS IN MESSINA

Spies certainly did more than just gather intelligence. They were prepared to do all kinds of dirty deeds for those spymasters who were willing to pay. In the sixteenth century, many people were the victims of assassinations, and not just rulers and nobles like Henry III of France, Jeanne d'Albret of Navarre, and William of Orange.[49] In a previous article, I have shown how much effort Habsburg intelligence invested in doing away with Uluc Ali.[50] In an age when quality personnel were few and far between, it made a lot of sense to have the competent commanders and administrators of one's enemy killed; the Ottomans were not averse to giving the go-ahead for assassination operations of this kind.

The story of two assassins working for the Ottomans who arrived in Messina in 1622 to carry out the murder of the viceroy of Sicily, Emmanuele

Filiberto, demonstrates how far the hand of Istanbul extended. It was only through a stroke of luck that the Habsburgs became aware of the danger posed by these assassins, one of whom was from Venice, the other a Trinitarian monk.[51] The cover of the two assassins was blown when they were recognized in Messina by a Franciscan monk (*fray [. . .]de la tercera orden de san francisco*) named Angelo Scarola, who had met them before.

Before he traveled to the Eastern Mediterranean, Scarola had been educated in Pavia. He had become good friends (*strectissima amicitia*) with a Venetian merchant named Giovanni Antonio Poleni, and it was Poleni who ensured that things went smoothly (*origine d'ogni mio comodo*) for Scarola, whether he was in Split (then controlled by the Venetians) or in the Ottoman cities of Sarajevo and Thessaloniki. Giovanni Antonio's brother Pietro, who lived in Split, was an agent working for both the Venetian and Ottoman intelligence services.

One day, while in Sarajevo, Scarola made the acquaintance of a Spanish convert, Mehmed Bey. Mehmed was a double agent, who offered his intelligence services both to Ottoman pashas and to the duke of Osuna, Pedro Téllez-Girón, who had been the viceroy of Sicily (1611–16) and Naples (1616–20). Like one of the assassins who had come to kill Emmanuele Filiberto, Mehmed was a onetime preacher affiliated with the Order of the Most Holy Trinity, or using a more familiar appellation, the Trinitarians (*spagnolo di Castiglia lavechia . . . religioso sacerd[o]te è pred[icato[re del ordine della St.^{ma} Trinità*). In order to obtain information from Scarola (who was on a pilgrimage to the Holy Land), he asked him a few questions about Sicily. In the course of this conversation, he revealed that plans had been made to assassinate Emmanuele Filiberto.

To cut a long story short, the preacher Mehmed whom the Franciscan monk encountered in Messina was an associate of the Venetian Pietro Poleni. When they first saw the monk, Mehmed and his fellow spy tried to slip away. Once Scarola had gone up to them and reminded them of the conversation they had had in Venice, however, they first turned pale and then offered him a bribe to keep mum, since this was the only solution they could think of. It should not come as too much of a surprise that they asked him a number of questions about Sicily. They went further and, with a recklessness born of arrogance, they even asked when Emmanuele Filiberto would be returning to Palermo, which to some extent confirmed Scarola's suspicions. The Franciscan monk refused to collaborate with them and asked them where they were staying. However, before he could get an answer to this question, the assassins vanished, and Scarola wasted no time in getting to the Habsburg authorities.

In his testimony, Scarola stated that these two spies were just the tip of the iceberg; the Ottomans, he claimed, possessed an extensive intelligence network on the island. The fact that he offered to travel to Venice and get the names of the other Ottoman agents on the island from Pietro Poleni leads us to suspect that a sense of duty might not have been the only factor that motivated him to make these allegations; he may have been exaggerating the threat in order to find himself some work and make a pretty penny. The viceroy must have applied a similar logic, as he turned down this offer and told Scarola to write to Poleni on another occasion, to inquire what was on his mind. Still, we have no way of knowing how much the Franciscan monk was exaggerating. All we do know is that the two assassins failed to meet their objective. When the viceroy died two years later, it was not the work of the Ottoman agents but rather the outcome of a plague that was ravishing the population.

LEARNING SPANISH ON THE STREETS OF ISTANBUL: THE UNUSUAL STORY OF A CAVALRYMAN FROM BURSA IN SALERNO

In the centuries prior to the foundation of modern intelligence services, no educational institutions provided the knowledge and skills needed for overseas espionage operations. Still, among the Ottoman spies there were spies of Turkish origin who had no prior connections whatsoever with the Western Mediterranean. One of these was a cavalryman from Bursa, who was apprehended in 1552 in Salerno. During his interrogation, he revealed that he had been a soldier for twelve years and had learned Spanish on the streets of Istanbul. What is more, he had developed his Spanish by conversing with Christian Spaniards, and not with Moriscos, the Muslims who had fled from Spain.[52]

According to his statement, six months earlier, when the Ottomans summoned provincial cavalrymen (*tımarlı sipahi* or timariots) to Istanbul in preparation for a new campaign, our man from Bursa went to the Ottoman capital together with a regiment commander (*capitan*) named Mehmed Bey (see map 2.3). There, he was assigned to serve on one of the galleys in the fleet

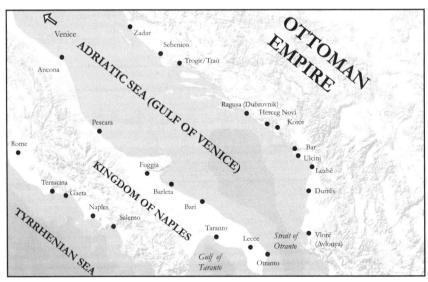

MAP 2.3. Adriatic Sea

at a rate of five *akçe*s per day. When the fleet, consisting of 130 galleys and great galleys,[53] arrived at Lepanto, Grand Admiral Sinan Pasha ordered Pirî Reis[54] to go on a reconnaissance mission in a galiot. The cavalryman from Bursa was instructed to do whatever Pirî Reis said. He also delivered two letters to him.

First of all, Pirî sailed to Otranto and then on to Salerno, without going ashore. The Ottomans planned to incite a revolt in the area, which would be headed by the prince of Salerno. Meanwhile, one of Pirî's Greek slaves informed him that his brother Nicolò lived in a village just 8 miles away from Salerno. At this point in the interrogation, our talkative cavalryman provided a description of Nicolò, referring to him as a Neapolitan Greek who was short and fat and had a black beard.

Pirî decided to send his slave ashore. He also commanded our cavalryman from Bursa to accompany him and gave him two letters that he had received from Sinan Pasha, which the cavalryman was supposed to hand over to a seaman in Salerno by the name of Juan Felipe. The plan was that the cavalryman would return to the same location a month later, bringing with him the replies to the letters, and he would meet up with Pirî. In return for his efforts, he would receive fifty écus plus a Christian slave. Since one écu was worth about fifty-five *akçe*s, the amount he was being offered corresponded to the pay he would have received for five hundred days' service in the navy!

The cavalryman also had another job to do: to gather intelligence. What were the people of Salerno saying about the Ottoman navy? Were people expecting the Habsburg navy to be dispatched? If the Habsburg navy was expected to come, where was it now? Were the people satisfied with their prince? In Naples, were preparations being made for an onslaught by the Ottoman fleet? Was there any news about Emperor Charles V? Was it true that Charles's brother Ferdinand had butchered twelve thousand Turks in Hungary? Other than the last two, these questions were quite logical. On the eve of a rebellion, it was understandable to want to gauge the mood of the population and to take precautions against a possible Habsburg intervention. On the other hand, it was quite odd to seek information in Salerno about far away events related to the Habsburg emperor, who already had his hands full with the Protestants and who was about to suffer a major defeat at Metz. Similarly, Salerno was hardly the ideal location for gathering news about a battle in Hungary between the Ottomans and the Austrians. To be sure, Pirî Reis's purpose in assigning this mission was not to gather news that could be shared with Istanbul or with Sinan Pasha; rather, he may have been trying to check the information he received from other sources. Perhaps he was curious about whether the population of Salerno had heard about an Ottoman defeat; in order to be able to instigate a pro-Ottoman revolt, it was more crucial than ever to propagate an image of "the invincible Ottomans."

During his interrogation, the cavalryman from Bursa claimed that he had not opened the letters that had been entrusted to him and that he did not know how to read anyway. This was why he had no idea about their contents. All he knew is that they had been written by a Sicilian in the presence of Sinan Pasha, and he presumed that they were in Italian. It is highly likely that the letters were written with the aim of inspiring Ottoman agents and collaborators in the area to take action. What we simply cannot know is whether the letters contained details concerning specific missions and, if they did, what these missions involved.

Exactly twenty-nine days before the interrogation, on a Sunday, the Greek slave and the cavalryman disembarked. After they had walked 2 miles, the Greek slave informed the man from Bursa that he was going to look for his brother and that they would meet up again in Citera in ten days' time. Having said that, he left the cavalryman. The latter started to hop from one harbor to the next. As he came to meet an ever-increasing number of people, his courage diminished and he started to fear being caught. He decided to seek some respite on a ship. He thought it would be wise to tell the people on board that he was a Christian and a Spaniard. The sailors took away his guns and the five écus in his pocket. They advised him that, if he did not want to be killed by the locals, he should not tell them that he was armed and came from Spain. Apparently, there was no love lost between the Neapolitans and their Spanish overlords, a fact that would have pleased the Ottomans seeking to stir up a rebellion in the region.

Finally, the man from Bursa arrived in Citera, and he was approached by more than fifty men. One of them asked him whether he was a Christian, and when he replied that he was, this man inquired further whether he could speak Turkish. The cavalryman responded that he could, whereupon his interlocutor started to speak Turkish; he was none other than Juan Felipe, the spy with whom the cavalryman was supposed to meet. The cavalryman wanted to give him the two letters straight away, but the more cautious Felipe waited until all the other men had gone. Then, Felipe introduced the cavalryman to the other Ottoman spy. Having spent one night in the home of someone called Juan Dominico, the cavalryman was taken up to the mountains by another agent, Micer Juanillo. This is how a team of four emerged: Juan Domenico, his brother Juan Sardo, Micer Juanillo, and our friend from Bursa.

The cavalryman's newly found collaborators answered his questions about the fleet and Charles V. It was true, they told him, that Ferdinand had massacred twelve thousand Ottoman soldiers. Emperor Charles, moreover, had on three occasions instructed Pedro de Toledo, viceroy of Naples, to take his fleet out to sea, but the latter was reluctant to do this. The cavalryman also learned that nine galleys had been sent from the Kingdom of Naples, to transport four thousand troops for an expedition against France. He heard too that, wherever one went, insurrection was in the air. The populace had had enough of Spanish rule and were waiting for their own princes to arrive, together with the Ottoman navy.

However, before the cavalryman was able to share this valuable information with Pirî Reis, he was captured by the Habsburgs. We saw earlier in the case of Constantino how the hunter had become prey, and the same turned out to apply to the cavalryman too. Although he had set out on his mission to gather intelligence, in the end he was made to answer questions about the

Ottoman fleet. And he turned out to be as forthcoming as the Greek from Heraklion, telling his interrogators everything he knew. He claimed that he did not know what had happened to the Ottoman navy after its departure from the port of Lepanto, but he was in a position to provide information about its current state. Besides the 130 galleys and great galleys that had arrived from Istanbul, the fleet contained 20 galiots and brigantins, carrying a total of ten thousand Janissaries and five thousand cavalrymen, one of whom was our friend from Bursa. Five hundred of these cavalrymen had brought their horses with them, whereas the others had left them behind; this suggests that they were expecting to fight from aboard the galleys, using their arrows. The naval personnel also included five hundred accomplished sailors. Our cavalryman explained that he did not know whether any other galleys would be joining the fleet, but everyone was well aware that the objective of the fleet was to install the prince of Salerno on the throne. The plan was this: An army made up of the prince's supporters was going to seize Naples, and with the help of a popular uprising, the kingdom would be wrested from Habsburg control. Apparently, things would not end here. The navy would either spend the winter in France, if the French king requested it, or it would return to Istanbul. According to the cavalryman's testimony, on the fifteenth day of the following month (unfortunately, the precise date of the document is uncertain) there would be a meeting between the Ottoman and French fleets.

The cavalryman was asked who represented the king of France in the Ottoman navy. He replied that, while he did not know the name of this person, the representative was a prominent (*principal*) Corsican who was well-liked by the sultan. Indeed, the same man was responsible for coordinating all the negotiations between Henry II and Sultan Süleyman. The person in question must have been Sampieru Corso of Bastelica, the leader of the Corsican rebellion against Genoa, an ally of the Habsburgs. Sampieru, who was backed by the French, had traveled all the way to Istanbul, where he had had an audience with the sultan at which he requested support from the Ottomans.[55] A year later, with the backing of the Ottoman navy, a rebellion was sparked in Corsica, inflicting numerous defeats on the Genoese. In the end, though, the plans of the Corsicans and Ottomans would come to nothing because the French would sign an armistice and then a peace agreement with Genoa.[56]

The cavalryman from Bursa also mentioned in his statement that the Ottoman fleet (which also included two French galleys) was headed by Rüstem Pasha, the son-in-law of the sultan. This was not true though. The commander of the fleet was not Grand Vizier Rüstem but his brother, Sinan. Furthermore, because Sinan Pasha lacked naval experience, he was supported by Turgud Reis, who probably called the shots when it came to naval strategy.

As a last point, let us ponder for a while the cavalryman's claim that he had learned Spanish by speaking with Christian Spaniards rather than with the Moriscos in Istanbul or with the Marrano Jews who had been expelled from Spain in 1492. This may have been the case. Istanbul was a key commercial and diplomatic center, a magnet for people of diverse nationalities and backgrounds from all over the Mediterranean region. It is an undeniable fact that, in such a Tower of Babel, every language would have been spoken and people of all religions and races would have socialized with one another.

Another possibility, though, is that our spy was actually a Morisco, in other words an apostate of Spanish origin and that, in order to evade the Inquisition, he preferred to present himself as a Turk from Bursa. The mirror image of this is known to have happened: when they were captured, Ottoman corsairs who had converted to Islam told their Christian interrogators that they were born-and-bred Muslims. In this way, they hoped to be spared the Inquisition; as was mentioned previously, only Christians could be judged by the Inquisition, and people who had not been baptized and were born Muslim were beyond its jurisdiction. There is an abundance of examples of steadfast converts who stuck to their stories even though their investigations lasted months. One of these was Francesco Guiccardo / *Gavur* (Infidel) Ali Reis, a convert-corsair from Ferrara who was caught in 1624. Contrary to the testimonies of nineteen witnesses, he insisted that he was a Turk from Sinop, a port in the Black Sea, giving the names of his mother, brother, uncle, and older sister. He even refused to eat anything unless it was prepared by a Muslim, and for eight months he resisted speaking Italian. Francesco's obstinacy is easier to understand when one considers that he had already escaped the Inquisition on two occasions by using the same method and paying a ransom.[57]

Let us return once again to our cavalryman from Bursa and his questionable testimony. Another sign that his testimony may have been fabricated is that some of the details were simply wrong. For one thing, contrary to what he claimed, Bursa is not 20 miles away from Istanbul but considerably more. In addition, throughout his interrogation, he referred to Rüstem Pasha rather than Sinan Pasha as the grand admiral of the Ottoman navy, which throws even more suspicion on him. He had purportedly spoken to this pasha in person, so how could he confuse his name? Was it possible for an Ottoman cavalryman not to know the name of someone who had led the Empire for eight years? Finally, could a cavalryman who was posted to the provinces have spent so much time wandering the streets of Istanbul that he was able to pick up Spanish there?

It is impossible to provide a definitive answer to these questions; the best we can do is to offer educated guesses. We may never know whether the Bursa cavalryman's testimony was true or fabricated, but at least we can conclude that his story appears to have convinced his interrogators, the Habsburg authorities.

JUAN PIMENTEL AND HIS OTTOMAN COLLABORATORS IN THE HABSBURG PORTS

According to correspondence in 1561 from Habsburg spies in Istanbul sent to Pedro Afán de Ribera, duke of Alcalá and viceroy of Naples, a number of soldiers and cannoneers in La Goulette, the port of Tunis, were hatching a conspiracy (*traychion*) together with the sultan of Tunisia and the governor-general of Tripolitania, Turgud Reis.[58] When the Ottoman fleet arrived with the aim of besieging the Habsburg-controlled port, the Ottomans' allies caused an explosion in the fortress's gunpowder mill and rendered the cannons useless by pouring mercury (*azogue*) into them, making the tin crystallize.[59] They also offered to poison the wells and keep the Ottomans updated concerning the fortress's weak points. Very soon after the duke of Alcalá had shared these details with the commander of the fortress, Alonso de la Cueva, he started to interrogate one of the cannoneers whom he suspected and, by applying torture, forced him to reveal what he knew.

The cannoneer alleged that the brains behind this plan was an Ottoman agent by the name of Juan Pimentel, who had left La Goulette a year and a half earlier and whose wife lived in Trapani, on the western tip of Sicily. While still at the fortress, Pimentel had come to an agreement with a soldier from Valladolid by the name of Cisneros, whom he had asked to find more volunteers for their planned actions. It was Pimentel who put Cisneros in touch with our cannoneer, who was now suspended from a Palestinian hanger. Having made this revelation, our cannoneer was found dead in his cell under mysterious circumstances; the plot thickens. When it was time for Cisneros to be interrogated, he confessed his crime. Pimentel, who invited Cisneros to participate in the plot, had written that he had been contacted by an Ottoman agent in Sicily and had been offered a generous sum of money.

It was clearly very important to the Habsburg authorities to capture Pimentel and ascertain the identity of this Ottoman agent in Sicily. According to news received from Trapani, however, Pimentel had set out for Spain with the aim of taking possession of some property that had been left to him by his brother-in-law. Quite possibly this excuse was made up; no one who goes somewhere to carry out espionage is going to admit that they are on a mission as a spy! What is more, in a letter that he sent to his mother-in-law from Naples, Pimentel stated outright that an Ottoman agent whom he met in Sicily had invited him to take part in a covert operation aimed at La Goulette. A search was carried out of the Ottoman spy's house, but this did not throw up any clues. Due to the atmosphere of mistrust that this conspiracy stirred up, seventy-nine Moriscos who came to Trapani by galleon were imprisoned in the fortress. Juan de la Cerda, viceroy of Sicily and duke of Medinaceli, whose strategic choices had already caused the destruction of the entire Habsburg navy one year earlier at the Battle of Djerba, was sure that Pimentel was a Morisco.

Several months later, in a letter he dispatched from Chios to Palermo, a Christian who had been freed from captivity shared the insights he had gained from a friend, an interpreter, who had participated in the Battle of Djerba. According to the letter, Turgud and the sultan of Tunisia had informed Sultan Süleyman of the covert operation they were undertaking in order to get control of La Goulette, and they persuaded the sultan to dispatch the imperial fleet. Some of the converts within the navy also mentioned the Ottoman collaborators to the interpreter friend of the Christian ex-captive from Chios. They told him that, during the siege, four Morisco cannoneers, who were unaware of one another's existence, would carry out numerous subversive acts. They would disable the cannons by pouring mercury or some kind of destructive mixture (*con ciertas mesturas de estripante o argento vivo*), ignite the gunpowder magazine, burn harquebuses, and—in an attempt at causing chaos—set fire to the houses inside the fortress. Within the garrison, aside from these infantrymen, there were twenty Morisco soldiers who were regularly supplying news to the sultan of Tunisia. Like the infantrymen, they too did not know that the others existed. Also like the cannoneers, they had been assigned to carry out a number of covert operations. Into the wells of the fortress, they were supposed to pour poison that the sultan had obtained from Jewish botanists (*botinarios*). These Morisco soldiers were also meant to initiate a mutiny in case Spanish troops did not receive their salaries, a likely event in the fortresses of North Africa, a place of exile where Spanish soldiers were paid late if at all.[60] Already in September 1559, that is, between eight and nine months prior to the Ottoman siege, there had been plans to launch a revolt of sorts. However, with the help of two galleys that arrived from Italy carrying fifty thousand ducats, these treacherous plans came to nothing. Finally, it should be noted that there were also plans to allow the Ottoman soldiers into the fortress by means of a bastion higher than the walls, which would be constructed from the sand transported with baskets manufactured from palm leaves and straw (*espuertas de palma y de esparto*).

The letter that winged its way from Chios to Palermo helped expose more than just one conspiracy. Subsequent pages will reveal the extent of the news-gathering network that the Ottoman intelligence service established across the Habsburg territories.

In the Sicilian city of Syracuse, a ring of spies had been established by Leone Strozzi. When this French admiral of Florentine origin passed away, responsibility for this ring passed to Turgud Reis. According to the plan, before besieging the city the Ottomans would send a frigate to inform agents of this spy ring and then deploy two ships (*barca*) to prepare a covert landing operation at the point where the ramparts had been eroded by the waves (*rotto por la mucha continuacion del conbatir de la mar*). In order to distract those guards stationed on the streets overlooking the crevice caused by the waves, these collaborators would then instigate a rebellion within the fortress. If this failed, though, the Ottomans would have no alternative but to set up camp and go ahead with a siege. Even in this case, the collaborators claimed, they would be able to take over the fortress within just a few days (*en breve dias*) because it would be easy to protect both of the locations from which help would come, one of them by digging trenches, the other by firing cannons from "the source of Salerno" (*desde la fuente de salerno*). Although the sultan did not hold out much hope for the rebellion, he was impressed by the fact that the plotters included residents of the city (*dentro de la ciudad*), and he gave the go-ahead for this operation.

Remarkably, the Ottomans' collaborators in Syracuse managed to conceal their identities. Members of one of the city's most prominent families, Antonio, Fortuno, and Valerio Bellomo, were imprisoned in the Matagrifone Castle, but even the viceroy himself had to admit that they lacked sufficient evidence to inflict torture on local notables of such stature.

Another plot was targeted at the Spanish island of Ibiza. The governor-general of Algeria, Hasan Pasha (the son of Hayreddin Barbarossa, r. 1544–51, 1557–61, 1562–67), maintained secret links with Morisco soldiers stationed there. They were prepared to hand over the fortress to the Ottomans if it meant that they could return to Islam. Hasan Pasha informed his father's old ally Turgud and requested a meeting at which the details of the attack could be discussed; to this end, a meeting point was designated for the Algerian and Tripolitanian fleets. Turgud's initial response to Hasan's request was positive. He acknowledged that he liked the plan, but he made the point that, should the attack be unsuccessful, he would be forced to explain this to the sultan. In order to avoid such a burdensome task, this operation had better be kept secret. This seemingly sincere request, though, was actually a sly pretense. The reason why the wily corsair advised Hasan to keep mum about this operation was that he disliked him and did not want to share with him the glory that such a victory would bring.

A VERY STRANGE INVESTIGATION: GIORGIO (ZORZI) CAVALÀ FROM HERAKLION (KANDIYE)

Zadar was a strategically important Venetian port in the Adriatic. When the Ottomans declared war on Venice and invaded Cyprus in 1570, the Adriatic borderlands became one of the war's most important conflict zones, and Zadar itself became one of the favorite destinations for Ottoman spies. One of these was the protagonist of this story, who was captured there in 1571.[61] He claimed that he was a Christian who had fled from the Ottomans. Because he was circumcised, all he needed to do to avoid being recognized was to dress up in Turkish style (*alla turchesca*), that is, donning Muslim clothes when he was going about his business. The experience of war had taught the governor-general of Dalmatia (*Provveditore Generale*) Giacomo Foscarini to be cautious, and he refused to swallow the captive's story and insisted that he be subjected to a body search. He was found in possession of two letters written by captives who were being held by the Ottomans. They were typical captives' letters: their writers complained to the relatives and friends about the conditions in which they were being kept. Noting that they would be transported to Istanbul, they asked their readers to send them money to cover their ransoms. These letters did not seem to have had much impact on the wily governor-general. He concluded that the prisoner was deliberately carrying them in order to have a more convincing defense if he was captured while traveling through Christian territory (*per far apparir la partita sua piu vera*). He seemed to be justified in his suspicions when two Ottoman documents (*polizze turchesche*) were discovered in a secret compartment in the shoes of our protagonist from Heraklion. A more thorough investigation was obviously called for. On March 28, 1571, the captive—named Giorgio Cavalà—was subjected to a tough interrogation. At first, he claimed that he was a Venetian soldier who had been on duty in Terraferma (*soldato della guardia della porta di Terraferma*)[62] and that while he was transporting letters from Novigrad to Zadar, he came across some Ottomans. To avoid imprisonment, he told the Ottomans that he was a Turk running away from the Christians and hid the official licenses (*patente*) he was carrying under a stone. Although the Ottomans imprisoned him for fifteen days on suspicion of espionage, he was later released.

This incident struck Giorgio's interrogators as suspicious, and they stepped up the pressure on him. How could the Ottomans have let him go? According to Giorgio, everything had actually been very straightforward. The Ottoman governor had first offered him a job paying five *akçe*s a day,[63] but when he insisted on returning to his hometown, Thessaloniki, he was allowed to leave. Furthermore, in order to make sure that he was not molested by local authorities, the governor provided Giorgio with a letter of safe conduct as well as a reference letter in which he requested a certain Mustafa Voyvoda to find work for him.

It did not take long before the Venetians asked the familiar question designed to test the loyalty and intention of captives in similar situations: Was Giorgio circumcised? Giorgio had no choice but to answer yes to this question, adding as a plausible explanation that he had been kidnapped by Muslim corsairs when he was a child. This was how the Ottoman governor had believed Giorgio was a Muslim who was on his way to Thessaloniki. In reality, though, he was still a Christian, and he actually had on his person two documents that showed that he had converted back from Islam.

One of them had been penned by Francesco Martines de Marcilla, a knight of Saint John from Aragon, who served as a castle bailiff in Malta. The knight affirmed that Giorgio had converted to Islam and joined Captain Durmuş's galiot as a free oarsman. However, on May 1, 1569, he took part in a mutiny alongside some Christian oarsmen, which resulted in the death of the captain and two Turks. Indeed, the other Muslims on board jumped into the sea, leaving the galiots in the hands of Giorgio and his fellow mutineers. Wrestling with storms, they made it to Malta in July.

The second letter was written by Ioan Seres de Aguilar, one of the clerks in the Holy Inquisition, the very institution where the likes of Giorgio who reneged on their faith had to appear to seek redemption. In this document, dated October 3, 1569, it was stated that Giorgio had been investigated just like all apostates and, having expressed his sincere regret, he had been admitted back into the Church.

Normally, these documents should have been more than enough to stop the Venetians from prying into the issue of Giorgio's Christianity. However, as Giorgio's story seemed to be falling apart, the Venetians did not relent and went on asking prickly questions. Given that Giorgio had been traveling across Ottoman territories and would frequently have had to show these documents to the authorities, why did he not keep his Ottoman documents in his pockets but instead choose to hide them in a secret compartment in his shoes? The answer Giorgio came up with was that he had meant to show these documents to the officials in Venice, but he calculated that, if they were found on his person in Zadar, this would have got him into trouble.

Around this time, word got out that a corporal from Novigrad, Gioan Battista d'Assiago, was currently in Zadar; it would therefore be possible to find out a bit more about Giorgio's army background. D'Assiago remembered Giorgio straightaway. According to his testimony, one day Giorgio had asked for permission from the castle bailiff to go and wash something (*far bugada*) together with the Sicilians in his regiment. Once this was granted, he had left the fortress and sailed away with some friends.

When Giorgio was asked why he did not present the letters that the castle bailiff in Novigrad had asked him to deliver to Zadar, he replied that he had thrown them away, fearing that the Ottomans might find them. But what about the other documents? Why hadn't he thrown them away too? Giorgio alleged that he had actually hidden all his letters, but when he returned twenty-six days later, all that he could find was a single, half-sodden document, and the letters penned by the castle bailiff were gone. When Giorgio's interrogators toughened up, warning him that, if he didn't tell the truth, they would deploy torture, our friend from Heraklion resorted to emotional blackmail and asserted that he had come back in order to be among Christians once more. If the interrogators did not believe him, he was in their hands, and they could take his life. At least he would die a Christian.

To save his skin, he tried another classic trick and began to provide the governor-general with information about Ottoman military and espionage plans. A cannoneer (*bombardiero*) named Michiel had supposedly offered to cast four cannons for the Ottoman governor. On learning that soldiers were gathering in Sebenico and that the Venetians had forced the Ottomans to retreat as far back as Scardona, the governor-general requested that five hundred cavalrymen be sent from Bosnia. He was planning to launch surprise attacks on Split, followed by Trau and Sebenico, and even on Zadar. The cannoneer Michiel recommended that, in the case of a siege of Zadar, the governor should fire his cannons from where the old city walls were located. He suggested that houses should be demolished and that a bastion made of earth (*spalto di terra*) be constructed behind this wall. On the Ottoman front, an animated debate was underway as to whether they should wait for the other governors before attacking. Meanwhile, the Ottoman governor had at his disposal a total of four cannons, one of which was large, the other three smaller. Giorgio had discovered from Michiel that the Ottomans had so few cavalrymen at their disposal that, if they wanted to attack somewhere, they would need to call soldiers from other fortresses in the area, even at the expense of leaving their borders defenseless.

Having been interrogated, Giorgio was thrown into a dungeon. The next day, a translator named Nicolò Cambio was brought in from Sebenico, and with his help it became clear that the documents in Ottoman did indeed bear the seal of the governor. The two letters—one addressed to Mustafa Voyvoda, the other to the local authorities—demanded that Giorgio be allowed to travel in Ottoman territory without being interrogated or harassed. In fact, these details do not contradict Giorgio's claim. However, as he came under increasing pressure during the interrogation, he came up with different arguments in his defense and revealed himself to be a liar when he said Mustafa Voyvoda would find a job for him.

Convinced that he was dealing with a spy, the Venetian governor-general decided to deploy the gruesome "Palestinian hanger" in order to get more information out of him. During the second interrogation, which occurred the day after the first one, the blunt accusation was fired at Giorgio: there was no doubt that he was an Ottoman agent, so he should stop lying that he had come to return to Christianity. What he needed to do was simply answer the questions directed at him. What was his purpose in coming to Zadar, and who had ordered him to come? Giorgio could not resist the temptation of making a fool of his interrogators one last time. He maintained that the governor had sent him, saying that if he was a Christian he should return to his homeland and, if he was a Muslim, he should go and do his duty and then come back. This, however, did not strike the interrogators as at all logical. In a time of war, what commander would allow someone to travel at will in a borderland zone, especially if that very person was a Christian who up until very recently had been accused of espionage? Moreover, there was another obvious contradiction: if the Ottomans had suspected Giorgio of being a Christian, there was no way they would have let him cross over the border and return during wartime. If Giorgio were a Muslim, he would not have been dispatched without having been assigned a specific mission.

Realizing that he was cornered, Giorgio tried to win some time by saying that he wanted to speak in his mother tongue, Greek. This appeal was to no avail though; there was no avoiding the Palestinian hanger. He resorted to a new strategy of painting a more innocent picture of the mission he had been given by the Ottomans: the governor had purportedly sent him to find out whether war or peace prevailed on the other side of the border, as well as to learn where the navies were located. If he were a true Muslim, he would certainly come back and inform the governor. Although these tasks fall within the remit of a spy, together they make up a mission that was much more straightforward than Giorgio's actual mission, which will be outlined next. Giorgio tried to get off lightly by presenting his acts of betrayal as actually being rather ordinary, but he was unable to convince the Venetians; the interrogators found his statement simply illogical. Giorgio's interrogators argued that no governor would provide him with travel documents without asking where he was going or giving him specific instructions. Giorgio must hang!

Compared with some other agents, Giorgio managed to hold his tongue for quite some time. However, when the pain became unbearable, his tongue loosened. The governor, he acknowledged, had asked him to observe everything around him. How many soldiers were stationed at Zadar and the other castles? What kind of preparations were being undertaken in Venice? Was any attempt being made to assemble a large fleet? Was Philip II helping Venice? When Giorgio was asked whether he had traveled beyond Zadar, he replied that he had planned to go as far as Venice because the governor had offered him a significant reward (*grandissimo premio*).

As the interrogation continued, the focus shifted to Giorgio's years in captivity. He repeated his story that, having been captured by corsairs, he became a Muslim in North Africa. Following that, he had taken control of Durmuş Reis's galiot and moved on to Malta and then to Sicily. We can assume that this story was true. After all, using a patently made-up tale, it would have been practically impossible to be granted documents by both the Knights of St. John and the Inquisition. On the journey from Sicily to Venice, Giorgio had met a Greek priest by the name of Father Todoro. This priest was part of a plot to recover for the Venetians the island of Euboea, which they had once held. In Venice, Giorgio stayed in the house of a clerk for a month, but when he announced that he did not want to participate in the conspiracy, he was thrown out onto the street. He then fell ill and slipped into poverty. To earn some money, he signed up for the military, a detail that coincided with the testimony of the corporal who had been interrogated the day before.

Giorgio was asked why he had not gone from Novigrad to Zadar, as he had promised the castle bailiff, and why instead he had returned to Ottoman territory. He had simply got lost, he claimed, and the road he took at night after leaving the fortress had led him to Nadin, an Ottoman fortress. He then thought it wise to ask for permission to enter Ottoman territory, and in order to dispel the suspicions of espionage, he was brought before the governor. Based on the testimony of Corporal d'Assiago the day before, Giorgio's interrogators knew that this part of the story was not true and that Giorgio had actually fled together with the Sicilians in his regiment. All the same, to turn the screws on their prisoner from Heraklion, they asked him what he had done with the letters that the castle bailiff had given him. Once again, he swore that he had lost them, a claim with an apparent flaw in its logic. If Giorgio really had lost these letters, how had he not lost the documents that were found on his person, namely the letters from captives and the two documents attesting to his conversion? All that Giorgio could say in response to this question was that he had hidden the letters in two different places and that later he was unable to find the documents in one of these. Hardly a convincing explanation!

Giorgio's interrogators had broken his resistance, but they still had not been able to get him to reveal everything. They continued to pile on the pressure. What Giorgio had said so far was very general—he should provide more details. Why had he gone to Zadar in the first place? What orders had he received from the governor? Had he spoken to anyone while he was on Venetian territory? Giorgio responded that the Ottomans had discovered that numerous new units had amassed at the border, leading them to fear that an attack was imminent. This was why he had been sent to ascertain the number of soldiers in the enemy's forces.

This answer seems to have satisfied Governor-General Foscarini; it is clear from the other questions he asked, though, that he harbored suspicions that Giorgio was not working alone. Where were the six Sicilians who had served in the same unit as Giorgio in Novigrad? Could he say more about Michiel from Verona, whom he had mentioned the previous day? Did the governor have any other secret connections (*intelligentia*) in Zadar or agents operating on Venetian territory? Giorgio claimed not to know the whereabouts of the Sicilians, just as he was unaware of whether the governor had other spies at his disposal. He could, though, say more about Michiel. Having been captured by the Turks, this cannoneer was brought before the governor, whom Michiel assured that he could help them conquer Zadar. Michiel asserted that, if the Ottomans constructed a bastion with olive tree branches and earth where the old town walls were located, they could fire cannonballs from there, and that would be enough to capture the town. A Christian who had escaped from Sebenico likewise advised the governor about which side the fortress in Zadar needed to be attacked from to make it easier to seize the castle. Finally, Giorgio divulged to his interrogators that the Ottomans were planning to build two fortresses in the pass on the way to Novigrad. Their purpose in doing this, he suggested, was to prevent the Venetians from sending aid, and he cautioned his interrogators to be wary of this new development.

In times of war, a spy apprehended at a border would most likely have received a harsh punishment, especially if the person in question was a former soldier who had abused the trust of his government. Foscarini appreciated that it was more or less impossible to save Giorgio's body, but he was willing to give him one last chance to save his soul. For this reason, he considered assigning a priest to Giorgio so that he could confess his sins and take his leave of this world as a Christian. The priest in question, however, was evidently as eager to get Giorgio to reveal more information—which would be for the benefit of Christianity—as to cleanse him of his sins. Indeed, what the Church needed was not so much his faith as the knowledge he possessed. It did not take long for the priest to persuade Giorgio; the latter put in a request to have an audience with Foscarini and tell him what he knew.

Giorgio said that, if his life were spared, he would be willing to share all the facts of which he was aware. Foscarini, however, did not offer him a cast-iron guarantee. All he said was that, if Giorgio told the truth, he would be treated justly, in a manner that the governor-general saw fit (*che la giustitia procedera per quelli termini che li parera*). Acknowledging that his situation was hopeless, Giorgio started once again to relate what he knew. He reported that, when he moved from Sicily to Rome, he got to know a young Albanian boy (*garzon*) who belonged to the entourage of the clerk Lascaris. Although everyone thought that Lascaris was Italian, he was actually of Greek origin.[64] He was a tall, old man who had been authorized by Gregory XIII to prepare certificates of indulgence (*absolution*) and papal edicts (*bolle*). Having arrived in Venice from Rome, Giorgio made the acquaintance of an Eastern Mediterranean Jew called Jacob, who was keeping the Ottomans up-to-date with current events.

When Giorgio was asked how he had met this man, he began to share even more interesting information. During his second interrogation, Giorgio had referred to a Greek priest who was involved in a plot related to Euboea. Now he admitted that sometimes he went to the house of a Greek noble (*zentilhomo*) to talk about this plot. He could not remember the name of this noble, who was medium height and middle-aged and had a brown beard. When he provided a detailed description of the house, though, this led to the conclusion that the location in question was the Square of St. Filippo and Giacomo.

In the same house, he also came across an associate (*compagno*) of Jacob, whom he would see once more when he left Venice and moved on to Cliuno. According to what this man said, while Jacob had sent himself off to Cliuno, he had dispatched another Jew to Istanbul. The latter claimed that the Jews were willing to pay to the sultan the taxes that they were currently paying to the Christians. He also pleaded for the Ottomans to keep up their fight against the Venetians. At this point, it is worth pointing out that the Ottomans' attack on Cyprus had inflamed anti-Jewish sentiment in Venice. It was widely believed that the war had been provoked by Joseph Nasi, the sultan's Jewish courtier. One of the claims linked to this belief was that the quality of Nasi's wine had enchanted the sultan to the extent that he was persuaded to seize Cyprus from the Venetians! Another prevalent myth was that a fire in September 1569, which almost destroyed the Venetian Arsenal, had been started by saboteurs acting on instructions from Nasi.[65] Throughout the duration of the war, these allegations would underpin the accusations that Jews in the territory of Venice were spying on behalf of Nasi; eventually these allegations would culminate in the expulsion of Jews from the city of Venice. It was only when the war ended and the Ottomans interceded that Jews were once again allowed to live in the city. When it came to the signing of the peace settlement, Sokollu Mehmed Pasha sent as the Ottoman ambassador one Salomon Ashkenazi, who had once been the doctor of the Venetian *bailo*. This Jewish notable would convince the Venetians to retract their anti-Jewish measure.[66]

Amidst this antisemitic climate in Venice, in which Jews were regarded with ever more suspicion, Giorgio's stories must have been all the more disturbing to the Venetians, who were already hypersensitive. However, Jacob's associate was not the only Ottoman agent whom our man from Heraklion encountered in Cliuno. Lascaris's young Albanian acquaintance would also pop up at different points along the border, and Lascaris sent him to Istanbul to debrief the Ottomans. As the second phase of his mission, he would return from Istanbul by ship and get involved in some kind of plot in an area under Christian control (*far qualche tradimento*).

Finally, Giorgio was made to answer questions related to the unnamed Ottoman governor. Did he have cannonballs at his disposal? If he did, how big were they and how many did he have? Our spy was aware that some cannonballs had been confiscated from a ship and sent to the governor from Herceg Novi. Since they had not arrived yet, he had not yet had a chance to see them. This was why he had no idea about their size and quantity.

Had the governor asked Giorgio anything about Novigrad? Yes, he asked whether Giorgio had been in Novigrad at the time of the Ottoman siege. When Giorgio replied that he had not, the governor wanted to know whether the city's ramparts were robust. Giorgio answered that the ramparts were in a good state, being protected by a recently constructed bastion as well as by cannons. It is difficult to know, though, whether Giorgio actually said this. In general, spies shape their responses according to what they think their interrogators want to hear, especially in cases like this where it is impossible for them to extricate themselves in some way. Giorgio might have felt the need to conceal the fact that he had provided the Ottomans with information that could actually place the Venetian fortresses in danger. The last thing our spy divulged was that the governor had told him that the only way in which the Ottomans could seize Zadar was by gaining control of the two castles in the pass on the road to the town. Cannons on their own would not suffice.

Having commented that he had nothing more to say, Giorgio was taken back to his cell. We do not know what happened to him from this point on. However, it would be reasonable to predict that things were unlikely to turn out well for a spy captured on borderlands during wartime, especially since he was a former soldier who had abused the trust of his government on countless occasions. However, if a more detailed investigation had been carried out into the story that Giorgio told toward the end of his interrogation process, he might have had a chance of staying alive somewhat longer. Even this is not certain; although Giorgio might have been kept alive for some time by Foscarini, who dispatched the interrogation records to Venice, the same Foscarini emphasized that the dungeons were not in a good condition and Venice should give its verdict as quickly as possible. Everyone who heard that Giorgio had been caught expected justice to be served. In addition, carrying out the death penalty on the man from Heraklion might have been an effective threat for any other Spaniards or Greeks who were thinking of registering as soldiers as a cover for functioning as spies.

The interrogation report concerning Giorgio is the longest of all those used to assemble the stories presented in this chapter. To provide a clearer picture of the questions that were targeted at captured spies and of the tactics that were employed during investigations, I have attempted to reproduce the original order of questions and answers, without skipping any details. One last point I would like to make is that the interrogation strategy applied in the case of Giorgio is not very different from that used in the Inquisition hearings, which have been characterized in great detail in the Bennassars' masterpiece. To start with, our spy was subjected to ordinary questioning, and the contradictions in his testimony convinced his interrogators that they were dealing with an agent. After this, two strategies were used to encourage him to share what he knew. On the one hand, he was tempted with the physical benefit of being spared torture, on the other hand he was advised that, in providing information, he would be a good Christian and ensure that his apostasy and treachery would be forgiven. Up until this point, practically all victims of interrogation would keep something hidden. As we have seen in the other interrogations that have been discussed so far, many suspects would really start to speak only when they were subjected to torture.

In contrast to the interrogations in the Inquisition, however, remaining silent at this point would not bring any benefits. There were two reasons why Inquisition courts regarded it as very important for defendants to confess their guilt and had no qualms about prolonging cases to make this possible. First, the Inquisitors considered it to be one of their responsibilities to get the people they were dealing with to confess their profanity, show repentance and, in so doing, save their souls. Furthermore, in Inquisition courts verdicts could not be declared solely on the basis of evidence, particularly in the case of crimes that were punishable with death; the guilty party had to acknowledge their guilt. This enabled several convert-corsairs to prolong their trials by years by claiming that they were Muslims and insisting that because of this they should not be tried. Among these was a French convert from Narbonne named Guillaume Bedos. Initially he accepted that he was a Christian, but later he changed his testimony and started to maintain that he was one Şaban from Chios and that both he and his parents were Muslims. Between 1619 and 1621, he maintained this position in no less than twenty-five hearings, and he managed to keep the Inquisitors busy until 1625.[67] A comparable example was the convert-corsair Francesco Giccardo/*Gavur* Ali Reis from Ferrara, who was mentioned earlier in this chapter. Contrary to the testimonies of nineteen witnesses, Ali asserted that he was the son of a Muslim and a Muslim himself. Although in 1626 he was sentenced to death, this sentence was rescinded by a higher court, who pointed out that, when Ali was forced to make a confession, he had not been subjected to torture.[68] This decision offers a particularly clear example of the fact that a defendant could actually get away with his life if he resisted the pressure to confess. Torture was used on Ali in 1627, three years after the beginning of his trial, but because of the state of his health he was able to get away with just a small dose. When Ali dug his heels in and still refused to accept that he was a Christian, his punishment was commuted to a term of life imprisonment. Given that he was still in prison fifteen years down the line in 1642, one can assume that his tactic of avoiding confessing acted in his favor.[69]

The same could not be said, though, for spies like Giorgio, who found themselves at the mercy of civil administrators. Even a mere suspicion could turn out to be their undoing. To be sure, the Venetians were not the only authorities who dispensed with the niceties of the judicial process if they had political motives for doing so. In chapter 5, we shall see plenty of examples of how the Ottomans did away with agents "politically" (Ott. *siyaseten*), that is, without any kind of legal decision.

To put it bluntly, there was no point in relying on legal impasses or in bearing up to torture and refusing to make any kind of confession. Aware of this, Giorgio opted to spare himself some pain by divulging at least a bit of what he knew; that said, because he thought he would be able to save himself, he did not go so far as revealing the whole truth. By means of his explanations, he was able to persuade Foscarini that he knew more. At this point, the crafty Venetian moved on to the third phase and sent a priest to Giorgio, with the aim of placing him under psychological pressure. The trick worked, and Giorgio's tongue loosened. Although we cannot know for sure whether Giorgio really felt pangs of conscience for abandoning his religion, his biography would suggest that it was the circumstances in which he lived that forced him to undergo this conversion. For Giorgio, Islam probably represented a door of opportunity. Like many other corsairs, spies, and mercenaries, he opted for conversion to Islam as a means of achieving a better life. Whatever the case, the priest proved to be effective, and the man from Heraklion was persuaded to reveal everything else that he knew. Apparently, what Giorgio said during the third interrogation satisfied Foscarini. Whereas at the outset of the investigation the governor-general had promised Giorgio that justice would be done in a manner that he saw fit, the very same man now called for the immediate liquidation of this Ottoman agent. This was how merciless the justice of the borderlands could be! Foscarini actually had doubts about the authenticity of the plots that Giorgio was talking about—perhaps he was making them up to save his skin (*per diferir la morte*). But the stories might also have been genuine. In order to find out for sure, we would need to draw on the services of the effective Greek priest we have met in Giorgio's story.

THE TWO AND A HALF YEARS OF GABRIEL DEFRENS

A Frenchman known as Gabriel Defrens, whose actual name was Gabriel de Bourgogne / *Frenk* (Frank) Mahmud bin Abdullah, was the first Ottoman spy whose story provided the material for an academic article: a short but groundbreaking study by Susan Skilliter based on a meticulous comparison of Ottoman and European documents.[70] According to Skilliter, Defrens was born in Blois in 1554 or 1555, the son of the French consul in the port of Alexandria, the heart of commerce in Egypt. He was raised in the entourage of the French princess Diane de France, the illegitimate child of King Henry II. When Defrens was young, he was captured by so-called Morlach bandits in Dalmatia, probably while he was on his way to his father in Alexandria. The Morlachs sold him to the Ottomans as a slave. He was subsequently somehow able to be freed from servitude, became a Muslim, and managed to establish close relations with circles connected with the palace.

On first sight, it might appear contradictory that the very same man was both an international trader responsible for procuring the luxury commodities required by the palace and an interpreter working for the French embassy. However, once we bear in mind that Defrens's main areas of activity were actually espionage and diplomacy, it becomes clear straightaway that he used his "trader's hat" as a guise to travel around with ease. His close relations with the Ottoman court won him the admiration of his French supervisor, Ambassador Germigny. The ambassador heaped praise on him in 1580 for setting up a meeting with Second Vizier Lala Mustafa Pasha, and in the following year

Germigny demonstrated his faith in Defrens through selecting him as a guide for the Ottoman ambassador who was sent to France.

Defrens was a typical example of a convert working in the Ottoman capital who maintained a successful balance between diplomacy and espionage. Besides speaking Ottoman Turkish and French, he was competent in Italian and Greek and knew just about enough Latin. He was a rather puny, medium-height man with a black beard. He had a wart on one cheek, and he would sometimes sniff while talking.

In February 1579, Defrens was sent to Spain. This was at the time of the talks that began (albeit accidentally) between the Ottoman and Spanish courts, aimed at formulating an agreement to put an end to the longest war of the sixteenth century. We have no information about what Defrens was expected to do in Spain, but what we do know is that he traveled on via France to England, where he presented a letter from the sultan to Queen Elizabeth I. It is worth pointing out that English merchants were eager to become directly involved in trade in the Eastern Mediterranean and that through the mediation of one William Harborne they had tried to get Sultan Murad III to grant them capitulations. Their efforts bore fruit in 1580,[71] and the letters that Defrens carried to London are likely to have been related to this issue.

In July 1580, Defrens returned to Istanbul. There, he set up the aforementioned meeting between Ambassador Germigny and Lala Mustafa Pasha, Germigny being eager to stymie the ceasefire negotiations between the Ottomans and the Spanish. There is evidence that in September of that year Defrens set off to Ragusa wearing his international trader's hat, purporting to procure clocks and similar mechanical devices for the palace. From there, he traveled to Venice, and it is presumed that he also went to Augsburg and Nuremberg in the Holy Roman Empire. His journey ended in England, where he was due to deliver the sultan's letters to the queen. By November, he had arrived in London. According to a report prepared by the Spanish ambassador Bernardino de Mendoza, in these letters Murad III indicated that English merchants would have the opportunity to conduct trade in Ottoman territory; he also appealed to Elizabeth to help Dom António, the claimant to the Portuguese throne, who was struggling against Philip II. As was explained in chapter 1, when the Portuguese king died on the battlefield in Morocco in 1578, Philip II became the successor to the Portuguese throne, since he was the son of a Portuguese princess. This came in addition to his titles as the king of Spain and king of Naples, Sicily, and Sardinia. There were in fact other claimants to the Portuguese throne, among whom was Dom António, who actually managed to occupy the position for a brief period. However, he was defeated in battle by the Spanish forces under the leadership of the famous commander the duke of Alba, Fernando Álvarez de Toledo. From this point on, Dom António pinned his hopes on an Ottoman-led coalition involving Elizabeth and Henry IV. These hopes turned out to be dashed, though, and the coalition never materialized. Dom António would die in Paris in 1595, a disappointed man, and until 1640 the Portuguese throne would remain in the hands of the Habsburg dynasty.

On December 11, 1580, Defrens left London for Holland. The Calvinist cities in that country, led by William of Orange, valued their autonomy and had had enough of the Habsburgs' oppressive policies with respect to religion. This drove them to revolt and form a confederation, which would later take on the name "the United Provinces" and constitute the foundation of today's Holland. It is not difficult to guess what Defrens talked about with William. He probably passed on letters from Murad III, and possibly also from Elizabeth I, as well as conveying the message that both rulers supported the rebellion. Indeed, the revolt was of crucial importance to the Ottomans' strategy. Because of the demanding geographical conditions in Holland,[72] for a long time the Habsburgs were unable to suppress the revolt and ended up spending a fortune on it. What is more, as the rebellion dragged on, the Habsburgs' defenses in the Mediterranean were weakened, and this in turn offered some respite to the Ottomans, who were engaged in a long and costly war in the East against the Safavids.

Defrens returned to Istanbul via Venice, but he did not spend very long in the Ottoman capital. At the request of Siyavuş Pasha, he accompanied the Ottoman ambassador Hasan Agha, who was sent to France to invite Henry III to the crown prince's circumcision in 1582, a lavish ceremony intended as a veritable show of imperial propaganda. Having traveled to Venice via Ragusa, Hasan Agha stayed in this Croatian city a while. Meanwhile, Defrens took the sultan's letter and presents to Paris. In September, he had an audience in Paris with the French king before returning to Venice, equipped with a letter from Henry III to the French ambassador. From Venice he would set out again, accompanied by Hasan Agha and an interpreter from the Imperial Council named Ali. The Ottoman diplomats followed a route to France that took them via Bergamo, Milan, Geneva, and Lyon, after which they headed north and arrived in the French capital on November 8, 1581, after passing through Orléans and Bourg-la-Reine. With them, the diplomatic delegation brought a renewed capitulation agreement. Having stayed in Paris for twenty days, they traveled back to the Ottoman Empire via Venice, eventually reaching Istanbul on March 29, 1582.

Unfortunately, there is no further trace of Defrens in the documents that Skilliter examined. All the same, we can learn a great deal even from the two-and-a-half-year fragment we have of what appears to have been a colorful career. Gabriel Defrens visited numerous locations in Europe, and while on the face of it his main occupations were interpreting and trade, it is not difficult to guess what else he got up to. The Austrian ambassador Joachim von Sinzendorff, an experienced diplomat, must have had good cause to send an urgent warning to Vienna to keep an eye on this spy. As we saw before, the fields of commerce and diplomacy were closely bound up with espionage. Diplomats and merchants took advantage of their occupations to travel around with ease, to do business with members of political elites, and to earn money; this applied particularly to people like Defrens who were engaged in international commerce involving luxury goods. If diplomats were the employers in the world of espionage, merchants were the employees. Once a merchant knew that he would be able to earn well, he would not hesitate to sell intelligence to whoever was willing to pay the most, in much the same way that wheat, fabric, or jewels were sold to the highest bidder.

Defrens's story allows us to expand on another point. The interconnectedness between the activities of espionage, commerce, and diplomacy demonstrates how blurred the line was between the official and the unofficial in the Ottoman capital. But it does more than just this. It is quite unclear who this Frenchman actually worked for; as such, his career illustrates the fact that political and diplomatic powerbrokers like Defrens were individual agents who were independent of central governments. How else can one explain the career of Defrens? Here we have a French-born merchant who became a Muslim, was freed from slavery, and ended up conducting international trade on behalf of the Ottoman palace but who also worked as an interpreter in the French embassy, receiving his salary from Henry III. On the one hand, he was working for the French ambassador, while on the other hand he functioned as an envoy, delivering Murad III's letters to London and Queen Elizabeth's letters to William of Orange. When a French ambassador wanted to meet with an Ottoman vizier, why did he feel the need to request the assistance of an interpreter who was actually his subordinate?

An answer to these questions can be found in the nature of governments in the Early Modern Age, which did not yet make such a fuss about demanding the absolute loyalty of their employees. At the time, the structures of centralized bureaucracies were in their infancy and cannot be compared to the governments of today, with their basis in rational bureaucracies. A state reliant on grandee households cannot be expected to resemble the modern state. Even if one can claim that there was such a thing as "the interest of the state" that existed in both eras, the interest of the state was in fact the combined interest of all the groups that made up the state, or rather the lowest common denominator of these groups.

This explains why it was quite possible for people of various occupations to work for a multitude of employers, whether these people were spies, merchants, interpreters, soldiers, or even diplomats. A shining example of this can be found in the history of the ceasefire talks between Istanbul and Madrid. These negotiations actually began by mistake. The Habsburgs had dispatched one of their agents, Martin de Acuña, to carry out sabotage, but when he was captured, he came up with the excuse that he was a spy who had been sent to participate in ceasefire talks. The documents that were needed to back up this defense were prepared by the head of the Habsburg intelligence network in Istanbul, Aurelio Santa Croce, in collaboration with Hürrem Bey, an interpreter in the Imperial Council.

De Acuña was replaced by Giovanni Margliani, and he spent no less than forty months in lengthy negotiations with the Ottomans. What is unsure, though, is who his interlocutors were actually working for, these being Hürrem Bey and Salomon Ashkenazi, whose names we have seen before.

Hürrem was an official interpreter at the Imperial Council. As for Ashkenazi, while he was working as doctor to the *balio*, Marc'Antonio Barbaro, he also began to serve Sokollu Mehmed Pasha. As we shall see further on, the Ottomans imprisoned him twice for his involvement in enabling Barbaro's correspondence to be smuggled over to Crete. Thanks to the intervention of Sokollu, this Jewish man was released from prison and was later assigned as the Ottoman ambassador to Venice, where he was responsible for overseeing the signing of the Ottoman-Venetian treaty of 1573, which he had done so much to bring to fruition.

During the Ottoman-Habsburg peace talks, Ashkenazi and Hürrem assisted both Margliani and Sokollu. Besides functioning as mediators between the two sides, they made sure that they themselves got something out of the negotiations. It barely needs stating that Madrid rewarded them generously, but it was not just the Habsburgs who were willing to splash out. The grand duke of Tuscany, Ferdinando de' Medici, had long been trying in vain to establish lasting diplomatic and commercial links with Istanbul, and he decided to ask Hürrem and Ashkenazi for help.[73] Once more, Hürrem was more than happy to provide interpretation for both the *balio*[74] and the Austrian ambassador,[75] and neither did he hold back from leaking information in return for a fee.[76] These political and diplomatic powerbrokers worked in legitimate professions (as doctors and interpreters) and lent their services to the Ottomans as well as to the other European states, but the ways in which they exploited the relationships that emerged from their work were hardly innocent. To put it in a nutshell: the failure of central states to guarantee the loyalty of their employees resulted in a serious security deficit, and powerbrokers jumped in to take advantage of this and make themselves a pretty fortune by dealing in intelligence.

CONCLUSION

There can be no doubt that for every spy who was captured and whose story has been documented, there were many more whose adventures have been forgotten because they managed to get away with it. It has been no mean feat to extricate the small number of stories I have presented from among the often-chaotic archive holdings. Archive documents written with poor syntax and in antiquated language and poor-quality ink understandably make the job of the historian more difficult still. Notwithstanding this, in this chapter I have tried for the first time to provide readers with a compact portrait of the Ottoman spies in the field and of the operations in which they were engaged. I hope that one day this chapter will be supplemented by studies concerned with other centuries and other areas.

As was stated in the introduction, contrary to the myth that has been reproduced in numerous works from the sixteenth century and from the present day, the borders between the Muslim and Christian worlds were by no means impermeable. The ten stories that have been examined here in some detail show us that travelers, soldiers, adventurers, seamen, corsairs, and spies were able to cross from one realm to the other and, in so doing, supplied the manpower on which intelligence networks could draw.

Even though these people did not receive any training, they were competent at what they did. After all, due to their normal occupations, they were used to roaming, eavesdropping, and doing things on the sly. What made them so brazen in their opportunism was the generosity of the rulers commissioning them, who were keen to invest money in intelligence. As long as empires continued to come to blows, central governments continued to invest money in agents, who worked out much cheaper than cannons, guns, galleys, and sails.[77] This meant that they went on filling the pockets of some very colorful characters.

NOTES

1. AGS, *E* 1049, fol. 145.
2. ASV, *SDelC*, reg. 7, c. 161r (May 26, 1589); Tobias Graf, "'I am Still Yours': Christian-European 'Renegades' in the Ottoman Elite during the Late Sixteenth and Seventeenth Centuries" (unpublished PhD dissertation, Heidelberg University, 2013), p. 212.
3. The Allied Christian fleet consisted of Habsburgs, Venetians, and a few Papal, Maltese, and Savoyard ships. Christian fleet is used here as a shorthand.
4. Gustavo Valente, *Vita di Occhiali* (Milan: Casa Editrice Ceschina, 1960), pp. 121–25; Emrah Safa Gürkan, "The Centre and the Frontier: Ottoman Cooperation with the North African Corsairs in the Sixteenth Century," *Turkish Historical Review* 1, no. 2 (2010): p. 136.
5. The official name of the order was the *Ordo Beatae Mariae de Mercede Redemptionis Captivorum*.
6. AGS, *E* 487, documents dated December 15, 1568, and March 18, 1569; Emrah Safa Gürkan, "My Money or Your Life: The Habsburg Hunt for Uluc Ali," *Studia Historica: Historia Moderna* 36 (2014): pp. 139–40.
7. Gürkan, "My Money or Your Life."
8. Antonio Fabris, "Hasan 'il Veneziano' tra Algeria e Costantinopoli," *Quaderni di Studi Arabi* 5 (1997): pp. 59–61.
9. Selânikî Mustafa Efendi, *Tarih-i Selânikî*, ed. Mehmet İpşirli (Ankara: Türk Tarih Kurumu, 1999), 1:246.
10. AGS, *E* K 1675, fol. 44 (April 30, 1591); Gino Benzoni, "Cicala, Scipione (Čigala-Zade Yûsuf Sinân)," *Dizionario Biografico degli Italiani* 25 (1981).
11. ASV, *IS*, b. 460, document dated July 25, 1600.
12. AGS, *E* 1159, fol. 243 (July 23, 1601).
13. Masiá, pp. 39–41, 118–24.
14. BNE, *Correspondencia del Cardenal Granvela*, ms. 7905/189 8r; Masiá, p. 168.
15. ASV, *AMP*, fil. 3082, fol. 76 (June 5, 1574), 96 (July 17, 1574).
16. AGS, *E* 1044, fol. 86 (July 16, 1552).
17. There is extensive literature on the slave trade and ransom practices in the Mediterranean. For an introduction to these subjects, see Ellen G. Friedman,

Spanish Captives in North Africa in the Early Modern Age (Wisconsin: The University of Wisconsin Press, 1983); Daniel J. Vitkus, ed., *Piracy, Slavery, and Redemption: Barbary Captivity Narratives from Early Modern England* (New York: Columbia University Press, 2001); Davis, *Christian Slaves*; María Antonia Garcés, *Cervantes in Algiers: A Captive's Tale* (Nashville: Vanderbilt University Press, 2002); Wolfgang Kaiser, ed., *Le Commerce des Captifs: Les intermédiaires dans l'échange et le rachat des prisonniers en Méditerranée, XV–XVIII siècle* (Rome: École française de Rome, 2008); Giovanna Fiume, *Schiavitù mediterranee: corsari, rinnegati e santi di età moderna* (Milano: Bruno Mondadori, 2009); Gillian Weiss, *Captives and Corsairs: France and Slavery in the Early Modern Mediterranean* (Stanford: Stanford University Press, 2011); Daniel Hershenzon, "The Political Economy of Ransom in the Early Modern Mediterranean," *Past and Present* 231 (May 2016): pp. 61–95. On Muslim slaves in Europe, see Salvatore Bono, *Schiavi musulmani nell'Italia moderna: galeotti vu' cumprà, domestici* (Naples: Edizioni Scientifiche Italiane, 1999). On slavery in the Ottoman Empire in the Early Modern Period, see Yvonne J. Seng, "Fugitives and Factotums: Slaves in Early Sixteenth-Century Istanbul," *Journal of the Economic and Social History of the Orient* 39, no. 2 (1996): pp. 136–69; Géza Dávid and Pál Fodor (eds.), *Ransom Slavery along the Ottoman Borders (Early Fifteenth–Early Eighteenth Centuries* (Leiden and Boston: Brill, 2007); Joshua Michael White, "Catch and Release: Piracy, Slavery, and Law in the Early Modern Ottoman Mediterranean" (unpublished PhD diss., University of Michigan, 2012); Nur Sobers-Khan, "Slaves without Shackles: Forced Labour and Manumission in the Galata Court Registers, 1560–1572" (unpublished PhD diss., Pembroke College, 2012); Will Smiley, "'When Peace Comes, You Will Again be Free': Islamic and Treaty Law, Black Sea Conflict, and the Emergence of 'Prisoners of War' in the Ottoman Empire, 1739–1830" (unpublished PhD diss., University of Cambridge, 2012), p. 19. On Ottoman slavery in the period under examination here, see the works of Ehud Toledano.

18. Gürkan, "Espionage in the 16th Century Mediterranean," pp. 102–3.
19. ASV, *SDC*, fil. 22, cc. 279v–280r (December 8, 1585).
20. AGS, *E* 1072, fol. 232; *E* 1144, fol. 212, 335 (December 30, 1575).
21. AGS, *E* 1332, fol. 198 (July 16, 1573).
22. AGS, *E* 487, document dated April 16, 1569.
23. AGS, *E* 1330, fol. 135 (January 5, 1572); Hernán, "The Price of Spying," p. 235.
24. AGS, *E* 1072, fol. 232.
25. In the document, the city is referred to as *Corsotat*. The Ottomans tended to use the Hungarian name, Brasso.
26. The name *Bresoya* is used in the document.
27. The name *Amut* is used in the document.
28. AGS, *E* K 1675, fol. 142, 167b (August 15, 1592), 172 (September 5, 1592), 83 (October 24, 1592); K 1677, fol. 5 (February 2, 1602).
29. AGS, *E* 1332, fol. 180 (May 6, 1573).
30. *Écu:* A gold coin minted by the French.
31. AGS, *E* 1072, fol. 232.
32. Bartolomé Bennassar and Lucile Bennassar, *Les chrétiens d'Allah: l'histoire extraordinaire des renégats, XVIe et XVIIe siècles* (Paris: Perrin, 1989), stories in the First Section.

33. This was a small, oared gallery with a single lateen sail, containing between eight and sixteen seats, each of which had room for a single oarsman. For more on Mediterranean oared vessels, see Emrah Safa Gürkan, *Sultanın Korsanları: Osmanlı Akdenizi'nde Gazâ, Yağma ve Esaret, 1500–1700* (Istanbul: Kronik, 2018), ch. 3.

34. AGS, *E* 1043, fol. 26.

35. AGS *E* 1127, fol. 103–4.

36. For a critique of the simplistic view of corsairs as adventurers eager to fight in the name of religion, see Emrah Safa Gürkan, "Batı Akdeniz'de Osmanlı korsanlığı ve gaza meselesi," *Kebikeç: İnsan Bilimleri İçin Kaynak Araştırmaları Dergisi* 33 (2012): pp. 173–204; Gürkan, *Sultanın Korsanları*, ch. 2.

37. Gürkan, *Sultanın Korsanları*, pp. 202–4.

38. *Fregata* or *fusta:* An oared type of ship with a single lateen sail attached to a single mast. In the ship there would be six to twelve pairs of oars, each of which would be controlled by one rower.

39. AGS, *E* 1071, fol. 189.

40. "Tongue" is a literal translation of the Ottoman term *dil*, used to denote captured enemy soldiers and subjects who were interrogated to elicit information.

41. AGS, *E* 1071, fol. 191 (March 5, 1577).

42. *Galiota* (galiot): A compact and nifty oared galley, with a board that was lower than that of a normal galley. It contained between sixteen and twenty seats from which pairs of oarsmen would row. Galiots had a single lateen sail suspended from a single mast. The versions used by North African corsairs did not include fore- or aftcastles.

43. *Kaid:* The title used for governors and castle commanders in North Africa.

44. AGS, *E* 1337, fol. 32 (March 18, 1580); *E* 1337, fol. 51 (April 29, 1580); *E* 1547, fol. 272.

45. Quartering: Literally meaning dividing into four parts, quartering refers to a very painful, yet common, method of execution. The victim was generally tied to four horses, or probably in this case four ships, and then pulled in opposite directions until he was disemboweled and split into four parts.

46. Uluc Hasan Pasha should not be confused with Grand Admiral Uluc Ali Pasha, his former master and protector. Uluc, meaning renegade, was a common sobriquet among the convert sailors of the time.

47. In 1558, a diplomatic crisis over precedence resulted in the withdrawal of the Habsburg ambassador from Venice. When Philip II inherited the throne from his father, Emperor Charles V, he expected his ambassador to be given precedence over that of his uncle Ferdinand. However, as the latter was the emperor, Venetians argued otherwise. This infuriated Philip II and Spain was represented by the ambassadorial secretary until 1571. Miguel Ángel Ochoa Brun, *Historia de la Diplomacia Española, VI: La Diplomacia de Felipe II* (Madrid: Ministerio de Asuntos Exteriores, 2000, 2nd ed., 2003), pp. 225–26.

48. ASV, *SDC*, fil. 9, c. 353r (January 9, 1576, m.v.).

49. AGS, *E* 1894, fol. 94–96 (October 20–21, 1622).

50. Gürkan, "My Money or Your Life," pp. 121–45.

51. Trinitarian monk: Member of the Order of the Holy Trinity (*Ordo Sanctissimae Trinitatis*).

52. AGS, *E* 1043, fol. 71.

53. *Galea grossa*: A large galley, used as a flagship, which contained between 27 and 31 benches and three lanterns.
54. One of the associates of Turgud Reis, this Pirî Reis should not be confused with his elder namesake, the renowned seaman and cartographer famous for his book, the *Kitab-ı Bahriye* (Book of Navigation) and his world map which, as early as 1513, included America.
55. Kemal Beydilli, "Korsika," *Türkiye Diyanet Vakfı İslam Ansiklopedisi.*
56. France's plans concerning Corsica would only be realized in 1767 when Genoa, tired of fighting with the rebels, sold the island to the French. It was thanks to this acquisition that Napoleon Bonaparte could enter the famous École Militaire and go on to change the map of Europe instead of remaining an insignificant Corsican nobleman.
57. Bennassar and Bennassar, pp. 78–106.
58. AGS, *E* 1126, fol. 41, 47, 48, 94, 107, 141, 152, 168, 169, 176; *E* 1127, fol. 78–79; Canosa and Colonnello, *Spionaggio a Palermo*, pp. 75–77.
59. Per Hadsund, "The Tin-Mercury Mirror: Its Manufacturing Technique and Deterioration Processes," *Studies in Conservation* 38, no. 1 (February 1993): p. 12. I would like to thank Kahraman Şakul for sharing this reference with me.
60. Braudel, *La Méditerranée*, 2:185–87; Beatriz Alonso Acero, *Orán Mazalquivir, 1589–1639: Una sociedad española en la frontera de Berbería* (Madrid: Consejo Superior de Investigaciones Científicas, 2000), pp. 133–35.
61. ASV, *CCX-LettRett*, b. 302, document dated March 30, 1571.
62. The name given to the territories in Northern Italy controlled by Venice. It included the areas of Friuli, Padova, Brescia, Treviso, Verona, Vicenza, and Bergamo.
63. The interrogation report that I have been able to access does not contain the name of the governor in question and does not even specify which district he was in charge of. All the same, it may help to know that the districts in the vicinity of Zara were Bosnia, Herzegovina, and Izvornik.
64. The Lascaris were an aristocratic Byzantine family.
65. Bartolomeo Sereno, *Commentari della guerra di Cipro e della lega dei principi cristiani contro il Turco* (Monte Cassino: Tipi di Monte Cassino, 1845), pp. 16–17.
66. Benjamin Arbel, *Trading Nations: Jews and Venetians in the Early Modern Eastern Mediterranean* (Leiden: E. J. Brill, 1995), ch. 5.
67. Bennassar and Bennassar, pp. 57–75.
68. The logic of this was that the court was supposed to have done everything needed to force him into confession. It did not, however, do this and instead chose to convict Ali without a confession. Unlike in modern accusatorial systems, in inquisitorial systems of justice, courts could not sentence someone to death if they had not made a confession.
69. Bennassar and Bennassar, pp. 78–106.
70. Skilliter, "Gabriel Defrens."
71. S. A. Skilliter, *William Harborne and the Trade with Turkey, 1578–1582: A Documentary Study of the First Anglo-Ottoman Relations* (Oxford: Oxford University Press, 1977).
72. In this region, referred to as "The Low Countries," the land is below sea level. It is only possible to conduct agriculture in those parts of the region that have been protected using dams and dykes.

73. Sola Castaño, *Uchalí*, p. 214; ASV, *SDelC*, reg. 8, c. 100r (June 23, 1591).
74. ASV, *SDC*, fil. 25, cc. 195r, 197r (April 21, 1587); fil. 32, cc. 52v–53r (September 4, 1590).
75. Graf, "I am Still Yours," p. 223.
76. The Venetians paid him thirty ducats in 1585, four hundred in 1587, and two hundred in 1592. ASV, *SDelC*, reg. 7, cc. 19v (September 7, 1585), 71r (June 13–15, 1587), 80v (January 9, 1587, m.v.); reg. 8, c. 89v (September 23, 1592).
77. Emrah Safa Gürkan, "Fitilin ucunda Tersane-yi Amire," in *Osmanlı İstanbulu: I. Uluslararası Osmanlı İstanbulu Sempozyumu Bildirileri, 29 May–1 June 2013, Istanbul 29 Mayıs Üniversitesi*, ed. Feridun M. Emecen and Emrah Safa Gürkan (Istanbul: İstanbul 29 Mayıs Üniversitesi Yayınları, 2014), pp. 67–69.

3

SOURCES OF OTTOMAN INTELLIGENCE

Without a doubt, agents gathering intelligence in the field are not the only means by which a state can obtain information. Even in earlier times, when diplomatic relations and methods of observation had not reached the level of sophistication they possess today, central governments found indirect ways of accumulating intelligence. In this chapter, we shall focus on the civilian, military, and diplomatic sources of Ottoman intelligence.

MERCHANTS AND CAPTIVES

There is a widespread belief that Ottoman Muslims left dealing with trade to Christians; even in the case of Europe, though, this view is mistaken. Although Muslims were not as intensely involved in commercial activities in Europe as were their Christian counterparts in the Islamic world, Muslim traders could be found in important European cities such as Venice, Ancona, and Marseilles. When we also consider the large number of non-Muslim merchants within the Ottoman population, it becomes clear that merchants were an important source of news for the Ottomans. There were even cases of merchants transporting spies on their ships. You may remember, for example, that in chapter 2 we saw the story of an Ottoman spy, Jeronimo Amiqui, who visited the shores of southern Italy and then met up in Ancona with a Turk by the name of Muhammed, who carried him in his ship to Vlorë.[1]

An even more efficient source of news than merchants were Muslim ex-captives who had spent many years in Christian territories but then returned home, having fled or having been ransomed. In 1570, Sokollu Mehmed Pasha interrogated a Turk who had previously been a slave in Malta about the fortifications, supplies, and ammunition on that island. The grand vizier had been opposed to a campaign against Cyprus from the very beginning, and perhaps he was contemplating sending the navy to Malta again, as he had done five years previously. If that was the case, what he heard must have disappointed him, as the slave informed him that the fortress on the island was large, the soldiers were in good condition, and the knights had ample supplies and munitions.[2]

The records in the Registers of Important Affairs (*Mühimme Defteri*) for the critical year 979 in the Hegira calendar (Greg. 1571–72) make it abundantly clear that captives and slaves who had been freed from the enemy provided up-to-date information about the plans and preparations of the Holy League's fleet. When one of Grand Admiral Uluc Ali's men, Yusuf, was freed from captivity and made it to Tripoli, he immediately reported to the governor-general there what he had found out about the Holy League's fleet from his master, a captain. The governor-general then passed on this information to Istanbul.[3] Other freed captives who proved to be useful sources of information included six former sailors and a ship captain named Memi Shah. They provided up-to-date information about the Venetian fleet in Corfu to Vizier Hüseyin Pasha, who was then serving as the commander in chief (*serdar*) in the Balkans.[4] In the days after the debacle at Lepanto, when panic reigned along the coasts of the Ottoman Empire, which had been left defenseless, another ex-captive reported to the governor of Morea that the enemy fleet was planning an attack on that area.[5]

Another piece of intelligence provided by freed captives was that the Christian notables (*ayan*) of Ioannina, Narda, and Ayamavra had gone to Corfu and come to an agreement with the Venetians. To use the language of the Ottoman document, these notables had sided with the heathens (*küffârla yek-dil*). At a time when Ottoman dominance in the western Balkans was being severely threatened, the notables encouraged the Venetians to attack the Ionian island of Ayamavra (today's Lefkada). They gave the assurance that, if the Venetians managed to retake this island, which the Venetians had handed over to the Ottomans in 1503, Christian notables could easily seize the castles of Ioannina, Narda, and Preveza.[6] Finally, three prisoners who had escaped from Corfu in 1573 informed the governor of Morea about the "condition of the ships belonging to Venice."[7]

Ex-captives of this kind did not just bring with them news about large fleets; they also reported on more unexpected activities, which would have been more difficult to find out about. For example, in 1585 two prisoners who had escaped from Malta and come to Rhodes revealed that ships belonging to Florence (*Düka Françe*)[8] and Malta were acting in concert and intending to sail into the Strait of Rhodes. Alarmed by this, Istanbul sent orders to its coastal governors (*derya beyleri*), commanding them to protect the seas (*derya muhafazası*), that is, to organize the defense of the Ottoman coast.[9] In another case, five months after former prisoners from Rhodes let on that eleven galleys and one galleon had headed off toward Alexandria, the same governors were sent another command.[10]

Muslim captives did not just help the Ottoman government. In fact, they gave considerably more assistance to corsairs than they did to the imperial fleets. One of the most renowned of these corsairs was Turgud Reis, who was always eager to take advantage of the element of surprise and was thus constantly on the lookout for up-to-date news. Nicola Maria Caracciolo offers insight into the way in which Turgud Reis received news from Muslim captives in Naples and Sicily. Caracciolo was himself a slave, and as soon as he was liberated by Turgud, he recorded his experiences in a book. According to Caracciolo, whenever an attack was underway, Muslim captives in Italy would use signs from the mainland in an attempt to direct the corsairs.[11] We have already seen in the story of Constantino/Mehmed how the slaves who were being deployed by the corsair passed on to Turgud the news that they had received from their relatives in Sicily. In exchange, he set some of them free and sent them back to their homeland, where they were supposed to function as spies.

OTTOMAN INTELLIGENCE AND FIFTH COLUMN ACTIVITIES

One of the main sources of information that the Ottomans deployed in areas controlled by the Habsburgs was ethnic or religious groups opposed to the Habsburg government. To employ a twentieth-century term for such groups that Andrew Hess has borrowed from General Emilio Mola in the Spanish Civil War, I refer in this section to "fifth columns."[12]

Foremost among these were the Muslims living in Spain, that is, Moriscos. Following the fall of Granada in 1492 and the demise of the last Muslim state on the Iberian peninsula, Muslims were initially granted the freedom to practice their religion. However, this climate of tolerance was short-lived, and an attempt was made to force Muslims to convert to Christianity. These policies were destined to backfire and transformed Muslims into potential rebels. Eventually, all the Moriscos would be expelled from the peninsula between 1609 and 1613, but until then, many maintained strong contacts with North Africa and Istanbul and collaborated with both. Although the Ottomans were not a key player in the Moriscos' Alpujarras Rebellion of 1569, it would appear that Istanbul had been tipped off about it beforehand.[13] The Ottomans did not supply military units to back up the rebellion, but they sent weapons, ammunition,[14] and envoys and expressed a willingness to help.[15]

How intelligence figured within this collaboration is evident from the Spanish documents. In 1565, a Morisco was tortured into revealing the names of a number of Ottoman spies. According to this man, there was a spy operating in Lyon who passed on to Istanbul the news that he had obtained from Spanish Moriscos. Information was also being sent on a regular basis from the shores of Granada to the governor-general of Algeria, which would have made things much easier for the corsairs, who were very eager to attack the Spanish coast.[16] Because the Ottomans were preoccupied with the War of Cyprus, Istanbul was unable to lend a hand in the Alpujarras Rebellion, but they requested the rebels to press on patiently with the war and to go on providing news.[17] Even after the revolt had been suppressed and the rebels had been exiled to various areas of Spain, the Moriscos would retain their links with Istanbul.[18]

While some Moriscos chose to stay in Spain, others opted of their own free will—*buena voluntad*,[19] as the Spanish document phrases it—to migrate to the Ottoman Empire. They proved more than willing to serve the Ottoman government in its struggle with the Habsburgs; it was the latter who had forced them to leave in the first place. It was only natural that the Ottomans deployed several of them as soldiers and spies. After all, they were familiar with the language, culture, and geography of the area.[20] In 1552, Süleyman, the governor of Vlorë, sent a Morisco to Puglia with the mission of surveying the fortifications there.[21] In 1610, a Morisco marshal (çavuş) passed through Venice on his way to France.[22] Finally, it is worth noting that there were actually Spanish Muslims within the Habsburg army who provided the Ottomans with intelligence.[23]

Even after their expulsion from Spain, the Moriscos continued to fulfill an important role for Ottoman intelligence. Indeed, Spain had very little idea of where the Moriscos it had expelled had gone,[24] and this constituted a major security risk. That said, the Habsburgs recognized how important the Moriscos were for the Ottomans, and they went as far as trying to assassinate one by the name of Mehmed / Mahmud Çelebi / Manuel Enriquez, who had dedicated himself to transporting Moriscos to Istanbul. According to Habsburg intelligence, Mehmed/Mahmud, a merchant who had been living in Venice for many years, gave himself the mission of persuading Moriscos to enroll in the Ottoman army. Furthermore, he collected bills of exchange in lieu of the properties that expelled Spanish Muslims had left behind and encouraged the Ottomans to send ships to North Africa for the purpose of bringing back the eighty thousand Moriscos waiting there.[25] In 1613, in the Sicilian port of Trapani, the Habsburg authorities took eleven Moriscos aboard a French ship to Palermo for interrogation. The Moriscos maintained that they were planning to settle in the French port of Marseille, but these claims were deemed suspicious because they had left their families behind in Tunis. The viceroy of Sicily realized the danger in allowing Moriscos to move freely between the Habsburg ports. This would make the kingdom vulnerable against Ottoman spies; whenever the latter wanted to gather information about Habsburg ports and coasts, they could send similar spies in French, English, or Dutch ships. However, his hands were tied. The Moriscos were traveling in a French ship, which meant that he could not arrest them. He simply did not know what to do. The solution he found was to consult the capital.[26]

Another fifth column consisted of the rebels in Naples, who are referred to in foreign sources as *fuorusciti*. Ottoman intelligence wanted to exploit the anti-Habsburg sentiment that prevailed in the Kingdom of Naples and did not hold back from agitating among the Neapolitans, who were eager to be rid of the Spanish viceroys ruling them and the infantry troops (*tercio*) stationed in the kingdom. Presumably as a result of these efforts, a number of regions requested to become Ottoman subjects: these were Taranto in 1496 and Brindisi and Otranto in 1509.[27] In 1532, the son of the recently deceased commander of the fortress at Brindisi openly proposed offering Brindisi to the Ottomans.[28] Indeed, influential local nobles who had participated in uprisings aimed at overturning Habsburg rule were part of the Ottoman fleet during the campaigns of 1537[29] and 1553.[30] These nobles placed their local connections at the disposal of the Ottoman intelligence network. For example, one of the prince of Salerno's men offered to seize Naples in collaboration with the local population, who were ready to open the gates to the castle. He also summoned two engineers who were experts on the castle's fortifications.[31] These secret negotiations came to nothing, though. Since the Ottomans always regarded Southern Italy as a front of secondary importance, they did not carry out any serious military operations there.

An even more interesting example is a conspiracy involving a group of Dominican monks that the Habsburgs uncovered in 1599. This group was headed by the famous philosopher Tommaso Campanella. The monks, who wanted to replace Habsburg rule with a republic, were able to secure the support of the Ottomans and forged contacts with the Grand Admiral of the Ottoman Fleet, Cigalazade Yusuf Sinan Pasha.

In the previous year, Cigalazade and a sizable fleet had sailed up to the coasts of Sicily and carried out devastating attacks on a number of settlements. Before returning to Istanbul, Cigalazade cast anchor 7 kilometers away from Messina and managed to get permission from the viceroy to meet his mother, Lucrezia, and his brothers, who lived in the city. In Ottoman sources, this strange rendezvous is glossed over in just a couple of sentences.[32] What is striking, though, is that while the Ottoman fleet lay anchored, one of the Dominican plotters, a man named Maurizio, sailed up to Murad Reis's galley and requested that the fleet come back the following year. On his return, Maurizio showed the conspiracy leader, Campanella, a document he had been given by the Ottomans. Judging from what the Venetian consul in Naples reported, the reunion between Cigalazade and the rebels was scheduled for September 7 of the following year. The Ottoman navy did indeed show up in the sea off southern Italy a year later, dispatched ships to the shores of Calabria, and on September 13 tried to establish contact with the coast by means of signals. However, because the conspirators had been caught, Cigalazade was forced to return to Istanbul empty-handed.

The close links between Istanbul and Calabria were also demonstrated by the case of Dionisio Poncio de Nicastro, one of the conspirators who managed to evade the Habsburgs by escaping to Istanbul. The fact that a Dominican monk who was wanted everywhere could travel to the realm of Islam with such ease is further proof that the political boundaries separating the two religions were not as insurmountable as some historians have suggested. Poncio's escape to Istanbul testifies to the fact that the Ottoman capital had become a migration destination for people who wanted to escape the Spaniards or the difficult conditions of their region. Istanbul was now home to a considerable number of Calabrians, with Uluc Ali being the most eminent. Remarkably, another Dominican monk who fled to Istanbul and converted to Islam had actually killed Poncio's uncle ten years earlier.[33]

It is impossible to know whether the Dominican monks devised the conspiracy on their own or whether it was dictated to them by the Ottoman intelligence service. However, another of the conspirators, Giulio Contestabile, complained that the Turks and the French had not come to the aid of the plotters, implying that people who were fed up with Spain saw the Ottoman sultan himself as a beacon of hope. Indeed, Contestabile himself had an image of the sultan suspended over his breast, and he took this out and showed it to Campanella, as well as recommending that he travel to Istanbul and ask for help.

Another community eager to cooperate with Ottoman intelligence was the Jews. In contrast to the mistreatment that they had endured in Europe, after settling on Ottoman soil Jews had enjoyed a comparatively high level of freedom when it came to religion and culture. They ended up taking on a number of political and economic responsibilities for the good of the Istanbul regime. In chapter 4, we deal in greater detail with the favored Marrano political brokers who had an important role in steering the policies followed by Istanbul. For the moment, though, suffice it to say that it was thanks to these powerbrokers that the Ottomans were able to maintain close contacts with Jews in a large number of major cities in Europe and the Mediterranean, from whom the Ottomans received a regular flow of information.

Jews living in Europe were frequently accused of espionage. It is quite challenging to determine whether there was some basis for such claims or whether they were simply the fruit of antisemitic paranoia. At the time of the War of Cyprus (1570–73), for instance, several Jews were arrested on the charge of being Ottoman spies. In July 1570, the Venetian *bailo* complained that the authorities in Ragusa had allowed one of Nasi's spies to pass through.[34] As a matter of fact, in April of that year Nasi had sent not one but two men from Lucca—Carlo Saminati and Benedetto Simoni—to serve as spies in Venice.[35] Simoni was captured in Naples, but although he was subjected to all manner of torture and psychological pressure (the Habsburgs even summoned a priest to try to intimidate him) he refused to speak.[36] In July, another of Nasi's men, Salamò Zizie, was captured while disguised as a Christian merchant, and the letters that he was supposed to be taking to Venice, Bologna, and other cities were confiscated.[37] In August, the *bailo* would refer to another agent in Thine.[38]

To be fair, the Ottomans maintained good relations with the Jews of Venice in peacetime as well. In 1585, a Jewish informant named Cain Saruch revealed to the state inquisitors that five Ottoman spies were active in Venice. In order to nurture the commercial links that they had established with Istanbul, these agents, who were also successful businessmen (*di gran negotio*) sent news to the Ottomans on a regular basis.[39] According to what the *bailo* wrote in 1577, Nasi's lieutenant on Naxos, Francesco Coronella, was in charge of a number of spies on Crete.[40] A month later, another of Nasi's agents was spotted in Corfu.[41]

The Jewish community in the Kingdom of Naples also maintained close relations with the Ottoman intelligence network. The confessions of two spies captured in Naples point to the existence in the city of a complex network, which was overseen by Hayreddin Barbarossa, grand admiral of the Navy. The official in charge of following up on the claims made by these captured spies proceeded to arrest several Marranos in the city of Malfredonia on the

Adriatic coast, located directly across from Ottoman territory. The captives later admitted to sending information to the Ottomans via their siblings and sons in Thessaloniki. Aware that it was inconceivable to tolerate an active fifth column like this so close to the Well-Protected Lands, Viceroy Pedro de Toledo of Naples wasted little time in expelling the Jewish community from the city. According to Toledo, the spies in Malfredonia had done more than just keep Istanbul briefed on military preparations; when French armies occupied the kingdom in 1528, Jewish agents had also carried out espionage on behalf of France and the Ottoman Empire.[42] Three years later, a Jewish miracle maker named Astrume Elia was arrested, and the confessions he eventually made were extraordinarily interesting. Elia claimed that he was born in Naples but had traveled to many places around the Mediterranean and could speak Spanish, French, Arabic, Turkish, Italian, and Greek. He also admitted spying on behalf of the Ottoman grand vizier, İbrahim Pasha. When (according to Elia) İbrahim Pasha died in the war against the Safavids—in fact, this is simply not true, as İbrahim was strangled in Istanbul on the orders of the sultan—Elia returned to Naples with letters of reference in his pocket and was given a warm welcome by the Jewish community. Later on, he joined a ring of spies who were working for the Ottomans, many of whose members were Jews.[43]

We do not know the extent to which Elia's claims reflect reality, whether they manifest the delirium of a lunatic or are actually examples of deliberate disinformation on the part of an agent trying to conceal his mission. Whatever the case, the details are worth sharing. Furthermore, even if they were made up, they needed to be convincing to have the desired effect. Above all, the information that Elia allegedly provided is worth considering because it tells us something about how the Neapolitans judged the effectiveness of Ottoman intelligence. After subjecting Elia to torture and numerous interrogations, Toledo set this mysterious Jewish character free. His aim in doing this was to try to find out more about Elia's secrets and connections by having him followed. This plan, however, proved a failure, as in 1537 Elia was found dead in the sea, taking everything he knew with him to the grave.

OTTOMAN DIPLOMACY AND INTELLIGENCE

As well as having diplomatic duties to fulfill, ambassadors also functioned as station chiefs, that is, local coordinators of intelligence networks. In a book he wrote in 1716, François de Callières dubbed such men "honourable spies" (*espion honorable*).[44] Particularly from the second half of the sixteenth century onward, at a time when envoys were writing their correspondence in an ever more orderly manner, a large share of the letters they sent to their governments was made up of the confidential information they obtained from informants and spies. According to the calculations of Alain Hugon, 61.6 percent of the content of what Paris-based Habsburg envoys wrote between 1598 and 1635 consisted of information about France; just 7.1 percent of the people who provided this content were embassy employees specialized in Habsburg-Bourbon relations.[45] The active role that spies played in generating and reporting intelligence was indeed acknowledged by governments, who frequently treated ambassadors as if they were spies. In fact, ambassadors lived up to the expectations of governments and got embroiled in all manner of conspiracies, resulting in a fair number of diplomatic crises. For example, in 1584, Bernardino de Mendoza, the Habsburg ambassador to England, was involved in a plot to dethrone Queen Elizabeth I, and when news of this emerged, he was forced to leave London.[46] As a consequence of a similar affair, in 1542 the French ambassador Guillaume Pellicier was expelled from Venice when it was revealed that he had bribed clerks on the Council of Ten and intercepted instructions that had been sent related to the peace talks between the Venetians and the Ottomans.[47] The Ottomans also tended to regard ambassadors with suspicion; in 1492, the *bailo* Girolamo Marcello, who was accused of sending intelligence to his government, was expelled from Istanbul.[48]

The politics and diplomacy of the Ottoman Empire were shaped in the image of what Güneş Işıksel has termed a "cosmocratic" emperor,[49] who saw himself as the center of the universe. Because of this, the Empire was reluctant to send ambassadors to Europe and only did so at the end of the eighteenth century, when the balance of power had changed. In accordance with the sultan and Empire's views of themselves, it was expected that other monarchs would send ambassadors to Istanbul, and this included rulers who were subordinate to the Empire. The door of the sultan was supposedly open to all, friends and enemies alike, a sentiment that was expressed in countless variations within the Ottoman diplomatic sphere, one variation being this: "This Threshold of Felicity (i.e., Istanbul) is not closed [to anyone], and by the grace of almighty Allah it has always been open; nothing should deter anyone from visiting here, wherever they come from and whether they are friend or foe."[50]

The Ottomans were disadvantaged in not having permanent ambassadors in Europe, but it is difficult to believe that envoys sent on specific missions to Europe did not carry out intelligence activities. No wonder Venice did everything it could to keep an eye on what Ottoman ambassadors were up to and to ensure that ambassadors' contacts were limited;[51] the residence of an ambassador was deliberately chosen to prevent him from speaking with informants and spying out the land. For instance, in an attempt to cut his ties with the outside world, an Ottoman official who came to take part in the peace negotiations in 1500 was accommodated in Ca' Dandolo, situated near the Doge's Palace, the "Palazzo Ducale."[52] Similarly, in 1522, to prevent another unspecified envoy from grasping the size of the city and its distance from Venice's hinterland territories (Terraferma), this envoy was housed in Ca' Ghisi, in the city center.[53]

It should also be noted that the Venetians were eager to be rid of such envoys as soon as possible, since they cost them a lot of money. As a matter of fact, the famous historian Sanudo captures the discontent caused by those Ottoman envoys who kicked up a fuss about leaving.[54]

The extent to which Ottoman envoys in Venice could move around freely depended on the current state of the relationship between the two states.

Whereas some of them, such as Ali Bey, had to put up with de facto house arrest,[55] others were able to dine together with Venetian officials, examples being Yunus Bey and another envoy who arrived in 1522 but whose name is unknown. At one of these dinners, an aristocrat went rather too far with his hospitality and gifted an Ottoman envoy a map of Istria and Dalmatia, an action that was not well-received by his government.[56] Limiting the mobility of an envoy was not always enough on its own. The Habsburg ambassador, Rodrigo Niño, was unable to conceal his admiration for an Ottoman envoy who, though being held permanently captive on the island of Giudecca, still managed to receive news. Niño made the interesting observation that the Ottoman ambassador was aware of everything that was going on and that anyone who wanted to pass on information to him could do so via his men who roamed around Venice at leisure.[57]

Ottoman envoys tried hard to ensure that all their efforts bore fruit. In 1504, suspicions arose that an envoy by the name of Mustafa had been involved in the escape of three youths from a monastery, but later these rumors dried up.[58] In 1517, Ali Bey wanted to climb up to the top of the bell tower in San Marco and tried to sound people out about the territory and defenses of Venice. He posed a number of awkward questions, such as how far the cities of Terraferma were from Venice, on which side Friuli was located, and what type of precautions were being taken against an Ottoman attack. The following year, Yunus Bey would arrive again on another espionage mission. In 1520, a man by the name of Adamo was expelled from Venice on the grounds of having engaged in suspicious relations with an Ottoman palace official (*müteferrika*) called Ahmed.[59] Four years before the Cyprus campaign, in 1566, the Imperial Council interpreter İbrahim came to Venice. In his home, he had maps of Venice and Corsica, which had been given to him by a Morisco from Granada.[60] İbrahim was not only interested in what was happening in Venice but also used his position and contacts to elicit information about the world at large. He took great care to maintain a regular correspondence with Emperor Maximilian II,[61] but he also bombarded the Venetians with questions about power relations between the Kingdom of France and the other states, at the same time as he tried to get a sense of how Nasi was perceived in Venice. A year later, Kubad Çavuş quizzed the Venetian interpreter Michele Membre about Cyprus' income and about the Venetian land and naval forces stationed on Cyprus.[62] In 1600, a Habsburg envoy suspected that an Ottoman marshal who had come to Venice purportedly to take delivery of the goods of a Turk who had died in Venice[63] had actually come to serve as a spy.[64]

The fact that Ottoman envoys were so interested in gathering information leads one to ask whether they had been sent for the purpose of diplomacy or espionage. This was a question often on the lips of European rulers in the sixteenth century, which was when the phenomenon of the resident ambassador started to become something of the norm. It is well known that the diplomatic duties of ambassadors were intertwined with their duties as intelligence operatives. In any case, the responsibilities of Ottoman envoys included attending events that did not involve important negotiations and doing things that did not require any knowledge of diplomacy. Examples of these were presenting victory missives (*fetihname*) and inviting the doge of Venice to the celebrations for the circumcision of the sultan's sons.[65]

Ottoman intelligence may not have used diplomats as effectively as their European competitors, but they certainly benefited from diplomacy to a considerable degree. Thanks to the diplomatic weight that the Empire enjoyed because of its political and military might, Ottoman intelligence was in a position to pressure its vassal states and close allies into sharing their intelligence information. The intelligence that these allies and vassal governments bordering the empire provided appears to have partly compensated for the lack of resident ambassadors, which had inhibited the regular flow of information. At the same time, since these intelligence networks possessed different characteristics and had different areas of operation, by collaborating with them the Ottomans significantly enriched the intelligence at their disposal.

The Ottomans were constantly requesting their vassal states to supply them with intelligence.[66] This explains why Transylvania,[67] Moldavia,[68] Crimea,[69] and Ragusa[70] sent spies into enemy territories and shared the information they acquired about developments on the other side of the border not just with Istanbul but also with governor-generals of neighboring areas.[71] The Ottomans expected to be able to rely on similar assistance from their ally France, as well as from Venice. Venice was not a vassal of the Ottomans, of course, but due to its role in Eastern Mediterranean trade, it was eager to maintain close relations with the Ottoman Empire.

Ragusa was the vassal state that was most forthcoming in providing the Ottomans with intelligence concerning developments in Europe and the Western Mediterranean. A Catholic city-state in the Orthodox Balkans, Ragusa enjoyed good relations with Europe; at the same time, though, as a tributary state of the Ottomans, it possessed commercial privileges in the Well-Protected Lands. Put simply, Ragusa was stringing along the Habsburgs and the Ottomans at the same time,[72] and all parties were well aware of this.[73] Even though, from time to time, the Ottomans issued harsh warnings on this matter (see chapter 5), they mostly turned a blind eye to the Ragusans' double game, factoring in the value of the information that Ragusa was providing them. The Ragusans had consuls in numerous cities in Europe,[74] and they made a point of sharing with Istanbul the news that these consuls were able to gather; according to Istanbul, the Ragusans were obliged to do so since they were subordinate to the sultan and their servitude required them to act in this way (*ubudiyyetleri muktezasınca*).[75] It was the Ragusans who informed the Ottomans about some key events, such as Charles V's capture of Mahdia;[76] Ippolito Aldobrandini's election as pope (under the name Clemens VIII);[77] the so-called *cose di Francia* (i.e., recent events in a France shaken by civil war), the Habsburg fleet's setting out from Naples on its way to the Portuguese Campaign;[78] the Duke of Alba's defeat of Dom António, heir to the Portuguese throne;[79] and the formation of the Habsburgs' "Invincible Armada" to be sent against England in 1588 (*Grande y Felicísima Armada*).[80] Given the quantity and significance of the news that Ragusa supplied to the Ottoman Empire, the latter must have been quite satisfied with the service it was receiving.

Ragusa also occasionally dispatched spies to Europe on behalf of the Ottomans.[81] At the time of the Great Siege of Malta, when Istanbul lost all contact with its fleet, a Habsburg agent indicated how important the intelligence provided by Ragusa was: "Every ten days, news reaches here (Ragusa) from Messina, especially concerning the deeds of His Majesty's general, Señor Don Garcia (de Toledo). . . . Whenever he washes his face, we hear about it in Ragusa, and straight away a Turk sets out to take this news to Istanbul."[82]

There were also Ottoman agents operating in Dubrovnik itself. For example, in 1580, rumors abounded that the Ragusa government had secretly ordered the murder of a Jewish spy working for the Ottomans.[83] Around the same time, Archbishop Filippo Trivulzio of Ragusa (of. 1521–43) established a network of spies who provided intelligence not just for the French but also for the Ottomans, the latter taking place on the orders of Francis I.[84]

As far as the Ottomans were concerned, the sharing of information was one of the conditions for an alliance. It was what "friendship" demanded, "friendship" (*dostluk*) being a concept constantly referred to in treaties between two states. On numerous occasions, Istanbul asked Venice for information,[85] and when its requests fell on deaf ears, Istanbul was not averse to demonstrating an aggressive stance.[86] Venice was dependent on Ottoman exports for the grain it consumed, and after the Ottoman-Venetian War over Cyprus, it became even more inclined to follow a policy of cooperation. The eagerness of the Venetians to establish good relations with the Ottomans did not escape the attention of the Habsburgs, and Madrid accused its slippery ally of being the Ottomans' concubine (*amancebada*).[87] Furthermore, suspecting that Venice was leaking intelligence to the Ottomans, the Habsburgs concealed important information from the former. In 1530, for instance, the Habsburgs hid the fact that the fleet they were preparing in Genoa was aimed at Vlorë.[88] Such cautiousness was quite understandable. After all, between 1533 and 1535, when the Habsburgs and the Ottomans had been at each other's throats, the Council of Ten provided the *bailo* with up-to-date information about the Habsburg fleet to share with the Ottoman pashas.[89] Two years before, when requesting the Venetian envoy Pietro Zen to provide information about the Venetian fleet, the Ottomans had quipped that the Venetians even knew what the fish at the bottom of the sea were up to; they had good grounds for doing so.[90] This information exchange continued even in the following century. In 1611, when Venice suspected that Austria was going to launch an attack on Serbia and Albania, the Venetians dispatched two nobles to Herceg Novi, who subsequently informed the Ottomans.[91] As this example demonstrates, the flow of information occurred not just between the two capitals; a degree of local information exchange also took place at different points along the border, and actors in Ottoman provincial organizations made requests for intelligence.[92] Finally, it should be noted that at those times when the Ottomans lost contact with their own fleets, they tried to get news about them from the Venetians.[93]

For ambassadors in the capital, sharing intelligence was an easy way of gaining prestige in the eyes of Ottoman grandees. The rivalry between these envoys could sometimes metamorphose into competition. As the Ottomans saw it, an ambassador who did not receive news from his king on a regular basis was not doing his job. When, in 1547, the French ambassador D'Aramon failed to provide any news about the Lutherans in Germany, Grand Vizier Rüstem Pasha poked fun at him, asking what he was actually doing in Istanbul if he could not even receive a letter from France.[94] It was precisely this kind of pressure that had pushed ambassadors from allied countries such as France and England into being more forthcoming about sharing intelligence. To avoid being repetitive and overburdening the reader, I will not be dealing with these issues here.

Before ending this section, it is necessary to point out one of the drawbacks of the exchange of intelligence between states. The Ottoman Empire was a powerful state whose foreign policy had a direct effect on the countries with which it dealt; given this, it would be naïve not to expect that these countries manipulated the information that they supplied to the Ottomans.[95] While they happily passed on information that accorded with their political goals, "inconvenient intelligence" was liable to be swept under the rug. To be sure, the Ottomans' interlocutors were not the only ones who resorted to such methods. As I shall explain in chapter 4 in relation to Uluc Ali and his Mediterranean faction, the Ottoman pashas also undertook manipulations of this kind. There was no such thing as "objective intelligence." What is more, since they gathered information from a variety of sources, the Ottomans also had the opportunity to compare reports.

While the Ottomans displayed a reluctance to send diplomats to Europe, it should be remembered that one of the reasons for this was that Istanbul was a leading diplomatic center anyway.[96] There had been a Venetian *bailo* in the city since 1453, and he was joined in 1535, 1547, 1580, and 1612 by representatives of the French, Austrian, English, and Dutch states respectively. While these envoys were themselves very enthusiastic about espionage, the Ottomans regarded every one of them as a legitimate source of news and tended to fire question after question at them.[97] In 1522, a new ambassador arrived from Venice, and the questions that were directed at Marco Minio typify the kinds of dialogues that ensued between ambassadors and Ottoman pashas. Let us examine an example:

> When they started by asking me how powerful the Pope was and how he could find money, I exaggerated his power, although I did this in a measured way (*convenientemente*), in order that they would believe me; I told them that he would manage to accumulate a considerable sum of money. Later they asked me how many soldiers (as both infantry and cavalry) the Emperor would be able to deploy on

the battlefield; once again, I inflated the figures and, to back up what I had said, I listed all the kingdoms that were under the control of the Emperor [i.e., Charles V], including Germany, which had recently been added to the list because he was elected the Emperor. . . . They also asked me questions about the Most Christian King [i.e., Francis I], to which I again gave overblown answers. When they asked how relations were between your Sublime Highness (*Vostra Sublimita*) and the French and Habsburg rulers, I replied that you maintained peaceful relations with both of them. They responded that "You are more tied (*congiunti*) to France than you are to the Emperor." My reply was that your Sublime Highness did indeed maintain a special relationship (*particolar intelligenza*) with France, but this was precisely why you were able to enjoy peaceful relations with the Emperor. They also requested information about Rome (*particolarità di Roma*). How long did it take to get from Istanbul to Rome? Which was the most convenient route to take to get there? The kinds of questions they asked lead one to a single conclusion: that they were planning a campaign against Christendom. They asked me whether I thought the Pope would assist the King of Hungary, and I replied that I did. They also asked me what kind of relationship there was between His Serene Highness (*Serenissimo*) the Emperor and the King of Hungary, and I answered that they were related by blood.[98]

As can be seen from this quotation, the Ottomans had the opportunity to compare the information the ambassador was giving them with the information they already possessed. This is evidenced by the fact that the Ottomans were not convinced by Minio's claim that Venice enjoyed good relations with the Habsburg emperor. Sure enough, a short time later France and Venice would find themselves at war with the Habsburgs. In reality, there are reasons to believe that the pashas were following a strategy of disinformation and manipulation; this is suggested by the simplicity of some of the questions they asked Minio and the fact that the Ottomans were able to verify what they heard from him by consulting alternative sources. It is likely that these questions were intended to scare Minio and to spread rumors of a possible Ottoman attack. At the same time, as I shall explore further in chapter 5, deploying simple questions in order to coax the other party into speaking was a frequently used technique.

Having said this, the example cited here also demonstrates the risks associated with this method of questioning ambassadors. All the information that Minio provided was distorted with the aims of serving Venice's interests and keeping the Ottomans away from Europe. A similar example is the dialogue between Grand Vizier Rüstem Pasha and the *bailo* at that time, Domenico Trevisan. Having heard that the Ottomans' ally France had signed a peace agreement with the Habsburgs, Rüstem summoned Trevisan and asked him what kind of news he was receiving from his government. The *bailo* told Rüstem Pasha that the pope had served as an intermediary between Charles

V and Francis and that soon the English monarch would likewise come to an agreement with the Habsburg emperor. This baseless news was enough to make Rüstem's blood boil (*escandalizado*). Seeing that the *bailo* was trying to undermine their relations with the Ottomans, the French were quick to respond. The French ambassador in Istanbul assured the Ottomans that Henry III would certainly not be party to such an agreement and lodged a complaint with the Venetian government about the envoy in Venice and the *bailo*.[99]

It is likely that the reason why the Council of Ten was so eager to share news with the Ottomans is that this exchange presented them with the opportunity to carry out disinformation and manipulation. Three years after the end of the War of Cyprus, the Council sent the then *bailo*, Giovanni Correr, a batch of news to pass on to Sokollu Mehmed Pasha: a rebellion in Genoa had been suppressed through the combined intervention of Pope Gregory XIII, the Spanish king Philip II, and Emperor Maximilian II; a peace treaty had been signed between the French king, Henry III, and the Protestant Huguenots (the Edict of Beaulieu, or the Peace of Monsieur); following the death of Philip's commander Don Luis de Requesens, there had been no more news of further insurrections (*moto*) in Flanders; the Habsburg fleet was scattered across different regions, and Don Juan was due to travel to Vigevano, in the vicinity of Milan.[100] Essentially, the Council was sending the message that peace reigned across Europe and that the Habsburgs were not involved in any preparations for a military attack on the Ottomans. Based on this news, which certainly played into Venice's hands, the Ottomans would neither perceive any threat nor sense an opportunity; as a consequence, they would not see any need to invest in their navy.

To forestall manipulations of this kind, the Ottomans sometimes attempted to recruit informants and agents from among the staff of foreign embassies. It was particularly easy to put pressure on those embassy dragomans (interpreters, translators, and guides) who were Ottoman subjects.[101] In addition, embassy staff could be seduced by using money, and this applied especially to officials working in chanceries. Chancery employees were particularly handy: they were in a position to pass on the latest news from Venice, warts and all, and because they knew everything that was going on in the chancery, they would be helpful when it came to decryption. For example, the Ottomans were only able to decipher the letters of the *bailo* Vettore Bragadin because they were assisted by a certain Colombina, who was one of the "language boys" (*giovani di lingua* [It.] / *dil oğlanları* [Tur.]) employed at the embassy, that is, an apprentice interpreter. Having been sent to Istanbul to learn the local language, Colombina became a Muslim at the insistence of Sokollu Mehmed Pasha[102] and spent many years working in the Ottoman chancery. The Ottomans rubbed salt into the Venetians' wound when, in 1578, they expressed the desire to appoint this traitor as their ambassador to Venice, a move which met with a stern response from the Venetians.[103]

Besides opportunists like Colombina, another group of people who were easy targets for Ottoman intelligence were those employees who were disgruntled with the way an ambassador was treating them. A case in point was Ladislaus Mörth, the housekeeper of the Austrian ambassador, Frederick von Kregwitz. When he was caught performing an act of homosexuality and punished by the ambassador, Mörth decided that the best way to escape would be to seek asylum in the Ottoman Empire and become a Muslim. He took revenge on his former master by exposing the letters that the ambassador had kept hidden. Not only did Mörth do this right before the outbreak of a new Ottoman-Austrian war but he also took the outrageous step of planting himself in front of the embassy gate, accompanied by marshals. When it emerged from the letters that Safiye Sultan (the wife of Murad III) was having secret dealings with the ambassador, the cautious Grand Vizier Koca Sinan Pasha immediately set about trying to cover this up.[104]

The Ottomans discovered that the *bailo* Hieronimo Lippomano was actually being held in house arrest by an envoy sent from Venice named Lorenzo Bernardo, after it was revealed that Lippomano had been leaking intelligence to Madrid. They were certainly not going to let this matter drop! The grand vizier was eager to get to the root of the scandal. In accordance with diplomatic custom, Sinan Pasha requested to meet with Lippomano before he left Istanbul so that they could give the permission that Lippomano needed to depart from the Ottoman capital. Might Lippomano also have shared information with the Ottomans? It is impossible to know for sure. What we do know, though, is that Lorenzo Bernardo did not leave anything to chance and prevented the traitorous Lippomano from having an audience with the grand vizier. Explaining that this custom did not apply to ambassadors who had been dismissed, he politely turned down Sinan Pasha's request.[105]

In a similar case of betrayal, in 1582, a certain Maksud Bey, who had once served as the Safavid ambassador to Istanbul, went over to the Ottoman side together with his son and his entourage. In the time he spent as the ambassador to the Ottoman capital, Maksud Bey had recognized the need to form good relations with the Ottoman pashas. To that end, he passed on the latest news from Iran and informed the Ottomans that certain high-ranking figures back home were keen to settle matters with the Ottomans. He also gave some advice regarding a possible conquest of Tabriz. Istanbul took Maksud's advice at face value and ordered the governor-general of Van to send spies to Iran, the aim being to steer the thinking of the local rulers in Iran.[106] These spies appear to have done a good job, because three months later a subsequent order was conveyed to the governor-general of Yerevan province to award a district (*sancak*) to Timur Khan, who had gone over to the Ottomans; Ustaclu Hasan, meanwhile, was to be rewarded with a suitable fiefdom.[107]

MILITARY INTELLIGENCE

An intelligence organization has to do more than just ascertain the enemy's strategy and keep up-to-date with important developments in the area. There have been many cases in which agents changed outcomes on the battlefield by obtaining information about unforeseeable factors that determined who came out on top. While it is clear that the strength of the Ottomans' armies cast fear into their neighbors, how did the Ottomans manage to gather information about their enemies' military plans, their preparations for war, and their fortifications?

To answer this question, let us turn first to the cornerstones of all military planning, namely maps and plans. At the time when the first preparations were being made for a war, the Ottomans would have had access to a lot of data about the enemy's fortifications and military resources. This is clear from the military maps and plans held at the Topkapı Palace and from the testimonies accessible in archival documents.

For example, according to the report of Giacomo Contarini, dated March 1507, Ottoman Grand Admiral Davud Pasha frequently held secret meetings with a caulker (*calafado*) known as Andrea R. At these meetings, Davud Pasha made sure that a navigation map (*una carta da navichare*) was provided, and he posed questions about the Adriatic coast, with a particular focus on Puglia. Davud Pasha was especially interested in military details such as the harbor of the Venetian-controlled Zara, the length of its walls, and the current stock of weapons and ammunition within the fortress.[108] In another example, sixty-three years later, on the very eve of the War of Cyprus, Lala Mustafa Pasha pored over a map of the island while listening to a detailed report presented by an engineer from Tripoli, Josefi Attanto. Because of some crimes he had committed, Josefi had been sentenced by the governor of Famagusta to row in galleys. After five years of hard labor, though, he managed to escape to Istanbul. There, he did what many a fugitive and exile did and decided to try his hand at espionage. Shortly before his briefing with Lala Mustafa Pasha, Attanto had returned from Acre, where he had gone to look for attractive columns that could be used in the building of the Selimiye Mosque in Edirne. He reported that there were no harbors in Cyprus big enough to accommodate a large fleet; the harbor at Famagusta could take no more than ten galleys. Since the water was very shallow on Anatolia's Cyprus-facing coast, the navy could not anchor there either. Receiving this news, Lala immediately ordered the creation of detailed plans of the island and its fortresses, as well as wooden siege engines (*alcune machine di legname*).[109] It is worth mentioning that at this point, two years before his discussions with Lala Pasha, the very same Josefi Attanto had been stationed in Nicosia, as part of the Ottoman fleet commanded by Müezzinzade Ali Pasha. Then too he had traveled up and down Cyprus, again under the pretext of looking for columns! Because he was carrying a letter of recommendation from the Venetian *bailo*, he was not faced with any obstacles. This is how this former galley-convict was free to wander around the island carrying out surveillance, without anyone saying a word. It should come as little surprise that again Attanto failed to find the four elegant columns that he was looking for![110]

Sometimes, opportunists in pursuit of money would approach the Ottomans themselves, offering plans of enemy fortifications. In 1568, a man named Giulio di Scudi, who had converted to Islam and adopted the name Mustafa, handed over the plans of the fortress of Famagusta.[111] By means of this generous present, di Scudi was no doubt attempting to kick-start a new career in the Ottoman capital. According to a letter written in 1594 by Carlo Cicala, a Ragusan ship captain named Marino Stagnese supplied Grand Admiral Cigalazade Yusuf Sinan Pasha with plans of Malfredonia and Taranto, both located in southeastern Italy, opposite the Ottoman Adriatic coast.[112] Later, in 1612, a French pirate named Saint-Pierre, who was working for Florence, presented Grand Admiral Halil Pasha with plans of the Venetian fortresses.[113]

Notwithstanding such cases, the Ottomans also took the step of sending their own military experts into enemy territory. In 1576, at the request of Uluc Ali, the military engineer of the fortress at Navarino (*ingeniero che ha carico della fortezza di Navarino*) drew up plans of the island of Corfu and its fortress.[114] A year later, another engineer (*matematico*) working for the Ottomans—this time a Portuguese man by the name of Juan Sebastian—was captured by the Venetians.[115] These detailed plans provided the basis for models that were created as part of military preparations.[116]

It was customary to send numerous spies to selected military targets. There were even occasions when the grand admiral himself would go to observe such places, coming up with some kind of excuse for doing so. For example, although the Ottomans were able to seize Chios without any military intervention, when Piyale Pasha first arrived on this Aegean island, he concealed his intention to seize it. Instead, accompanied by governors and an engineer, he toured all the island's strategic locations.[117] Two years later, Müezzinzade Ali Pasha and the Ottoman fleet sailed into the Cypriot harbor of Nicosia in search of a guide with knowledge of the Gulf of Alexandretta (İskenderun). While they were in Cyprus, they saw nothing amiss in exploiting the Venetians' hospitality, however superficial it may have been. The pasha donned a disguise and went ashore, mingling with the other people who were purportedly there to get water. While on land, he used the opportunity to scrutinize the island's shipyard. The fact that Müezzinzade did not actually make it to Alexandretta but returned to Istanbul after capturing a few Venetian soldiers from Nicosia en route leads one to believe that he had ulterior motives for sailing around in this part of the Mediterranean: his actual objective was to keep tabs on Cyprus. Once he returned to Istanbul, the grand admiral relayed to the sultan everything he had seen.[118] Rumors abounded in 1593 among the seamen of Istanbul that Cigalazade Yusuf Sinan Pasha had sailed as far as the sea off Corfu and had been able to have a good look at the castle.[119] Although this was probably not the case, what is significant is that Ottoman seamen found it credible that one of their commanders embarked in person on an intelligence-gathering mission.

Military intelligence was not targeted at fortifications alone. Successful commanders know that the outcome of battles can be determined if they are immediately alerted to the movements of enemy troops. For an example, we can look at the career of a sultan who proved himself countless times on the battlefield. In August 1516, Selim I received news from a spy that the Egyptian army had retreated from Aleppo, being "stuck in steel" (*fûlâda müstağrak*). After marching for two stations (*menzil*), the army ended up settling next to a stream (*ab-ı revân*) situated in the plain of Marj Dabiq, believed to be the location of the tomb of the prophet David. Selim immediately ordered his army to get moving, and they set off for a battle that would eventually demolish the Mamluk sultanate.[120]

To be sure, one does not have to be a master spy to observe that a massive army has moved from A to B and then file a report on this. The same could not be said, though, for infiltrating enemy units. Some Ottoman agents did succeed in fulfilling this difficult task, and considerable value was attached to the regular reports they sent regarding the morale of troops and the state of the army's supplies. For example, in 1565, when the Ottoman army under the command of Pertev Pasha arrived at the border with Timişoara, Ottoman spies within the enemy ranks[121] reported that the Hungarian commander and five thousand soldiers had locked themselves away in the castle at Gyula and were busy trying to strengthen the castle's fortifications.[122] One year on, during the challenging days that followed the fall of Szigetvár and the death of Süleyman the Magnificent, "experienced renegades and payrolled spies"[123] referred in their reports to the animosity that existed within the Habsburg imperial army between soldiers of different ethnic origin. In response to this, the Imperial Council interpreter İbrahim Bey, Sokollu's privy secretary Feridun Ahmed Bey, and Lala Mustafa Pasha's chamberlain Mustafa Kethüda drafted inflammatory letters in Hungarian, Croatian, German, and Latin: "Letters were written in the respective languages of each of the tribes and peoples, letters that aimed to set these against one another; these letters were delivered by spies to the battalions and companies."[124] In the words of the Ottoman chronicler Selaniki, these letters stirred up strife between the soldiers and caused hostility and discord.[125]

Sokollu's deployment of the Hungarian and Austrian spies against their own emperor can only be described as a stroke of genius; these were the very same spies who had been regularly informing the Habsburg forces about the state of the Ottoman army. The crafty grand vizier had letters in Hungarian written for the Hungarian spies and letters in German prepared for the Austrians, in all of which he promised to spare the spies' lives. By doing this, he succeeded in setting different units against one another. According to the bogus letter targeted at the Hungarian spies, an Austrian nobleman had turned up at the Ottoman camp, bringing with him a treaty from the other noblemen. This treaty stated that the Austrian chieftains bore no ill will toward the sultan and always valued peace. The drafters of this letter continued by blaming "Hungarian thieves" for the war and promising that, if the Ottoman sultan guaranteed not to attack their territory, the Austrians would turn their backs on the Hungarians and withdraw from the war.

The letter dispatched to Austria was equally misleading. According to this letter, Hungarian noblemen had written to the Ottomans, complaining that everything bad that had happened to their land was because of "the filthy house of Austria" (*Nemçe murdarı*). Purportedly, they asked the sultan for a guarantee that, if they pulled out of the army, he would not attack their land. The two letters had the desired agitating effect, and the troops of the Habsburg army fell apart and started to retreat toward the north.[126] Around this time, Sultan Süleyman died, but news of this was kept hidden from the army until Prince Selim arrived at the Ottoman camp. At this point in time, the retreat of the Habsburg forces came just at the right moment!

The Ottoman intelligence apparatus also took an active role during sieges and made sure that there were a number of spies within the besieged castle. During the siege of Famagusta, Muslim captives managed to escape from the castle and made their way to the Ottoman camp.[127] Besides them, several soldiers[128] and aristocrats[129] joined the Ottoman side and converted to Islam. These ex-captives, soldiers, and aristocrats, who "performed the service and displayed the camaraderie required of them" at this time, were granted fiefdoms, the value of which depended on the skills and experiences of the recipients. This is how these "new Muslims" were incorporated into the Ottoman army. Some were even granted tax exemptions. A certain Mehmed, one of the residents of the castle at Kyrenia, was informed that he did not have to pay the taxes known as *tekalif-i* örfiye and *avarız-ı divaniyye* because he had ensured that the Ottomans captured the castle without a fight (*bilâ-harb*). Given that Mehmed was one of the residents of the castle at the time of the siege, he must have been of Christian origin. Following the fall of Nicosia, our Mehmed not only convinced the people of Kyrenia and the Venetian commanders of the castle to surrender but also turned out to be the very person who actually handed over the castle keys to the Ottomans.[130]

From the perspective of Ottoman intelligence, the navy was as important an object of attention as were castles. In naval battles that took place between oared vessels, logistical factors were paramount, so it was very important to get information about the preparations that the enemy was making. Furthermore, in cases where between 144 and 216 oarsmen were crammed into a war galley with a very limited capacity, the operational quality of the navy in question was severely restricted. It would have been impossible, for example, for such a ship to stay out at sea for a long time without its seamen needing to go ashore to get water. This is why keeping track of such fleets was easier than it might seem.

By carrying out reconnaissance missions using small and agile subtypes of galleys, such as galiots, brigantines, and frigates, the Ottomans managed to ascertain the whereabouts and size of enemy navies. For example, Piyale Pasha sailed with a large fleet from Istanbul to Rhodes in order to boost the naval forces at Cyprus. On August 20, 1570, one month on from the beginning of the siege of Nicosia, Piyale Pasha sent five galiots into the waters off Crete, with the aim of gathering information about the Christian navy. By interrogating five "tongues" whom they captured on the island, the Ottoman seamen on these reconnaissance ships learned that the Habsburg fleets had not yet joined up with the Venetian navy. What is more, because of widespread sickness, the Venetian fleet itself was in poor shape and remained all on its own in Crete. Realizing that his path would not be blocked by a fleet, Piyale set sail straight away for Cyprus. A month later, a small part of the Ottoman navy in Cyprus, consisting of six galiots and headed by Kaya Çelebi, was dispatched to Heraklion to bring back some tongues. From the inhabitants of a sailing ship[131] seized on September 15, they discovered that the Venetian and Habsburg fleets had merged and moved on from Heraklion to Sitia. This information reached Cyprus on September 23.[132]

In the following year, Ottoman galiots continued to stay in close pursuit of the Christian navy. Several months before the debacle at Lepanto, Karaca Ali had a frigate painted black so that it would not be spotted, and with this he surreptitiously entered the harbor of Messina one night, counted the naval ships anchored there, and even took a few more captives. Once the Christian navy had departed from Messina, the experienced seaman Karaca Ali followed the fleet as far as the Gulf of Taranto. In the course of a number of landings that he undertook, he managed to capture not just several tongues but also a frigate.[133] Around the same time, another corsair, Captain Kara Hoca, who was also the head of the corsairs located in Vlorë (*Avlonya Azapları Ağası ve Gönüllü Levend Reisleri Kapudanı*), sailed circles around the Christian navy but was still incapable of arriving at a full count of the galleys. While the navy was traveling through the strait between Corfu and Igoumenitsa, a count was carried out, the outcome of which was 150 to 160 ships. This result was erroneous, though.[134] Finally, it should also be noted that in 1573 Ottoman galleys were assigned the task of depositing thirty spies on the coasts of Naples and Sicily.[135]

These corsairs also started to explore the shores and islands of the enemy's territory. In this regard, the confessions of an Ottoman spy captured in Calabria in 1543 are remarkably illuminating. The spy had traveled to Messina four years earlier. When the Ottoman navy under the command of Hayreddin Barbarossa pushed on into the Western Mediterranean, the spy was dispatched to the coast of Faro in the northeast of Sicily, where he was supposed to look for an appropriate place for the Ottomans to stage a landing. After completing this mission, the spy was supposed to cross over to the island of St. Giovanni and be reunited with the Ottoman fleet. He figured that, if the fleet was not going to return to Istanbul—in the end, the fleet did not return but spent the winter in the French port of Toulon—he would travel across land, continuing with his reconnaissance activities before joining up with Barbarossa again at La Spezia.[136] To give an example from the Ottoman-Venetian War, in July 1570 three Ottoman frigates turned up in the open sea off Paphos, from which men went ashore. Pretending to be Christians from the Western Mediterranean, these seamen tried to entice a Greek monk to divulge information, but their efforts came to nothing. Before departing from Cyprus, they went to the trouble of taking two fishermen captive.[137]

NOTES

1. AGS, *E* 1043, fol. 26.
2. ASV, *SDC*, fil. 4, c. 268r (January 21, 1569, m.v.).
3. BOA, *MD*, X, hk. 5 (H. Muharrem 14, 979 / Greg. June 8, 1571); XIV, hk. 1532.
4. BOA, *MD*, X, hk. 171 (H. Şaban 21, 979 / Greg. January 8, 1572).
5. BOA, *MD*, X, hk. 292 (H. Zilkade 26, 979 / Greg. April 10, 1572).
6. BOA, *MD*, XVI, hk. 312 (H. Zilhicce 23, 979 / Greg. May 7, 1572); Peter Bartl, *Der Westbalkan zwischen spanischer Monarchie und osmanischem Reich: zur Türkenkriegsproblematik an der Wende vom 16. zum 17. Jahrhundert* (Wiesbaden: Harrassowitz, 1974).
7. BOA, *MD*, XXI, hk. 709 (H. Muharrem 11, 981 / Greg. May 13, 1573).
8. For a similar case, see BOA, *MD*, LII, hk. 816.
9. BOA, *MD*, LV, hk. 315 (H. Safer 8, 993 / Greg. February 9, 1585), hk. 348.
10. BOA, *MD*, LVIII, hk. 60, 78, 79 (all three dated H. Recep 19, 993 / Greg. July 17, 1585).
11. Bono, *Schiavi musulmani*, p. 220.
12. Hess, "An Ottoman Fifth Column."
13. AGS, *E* 1324, fol. 84 (February 2, 1561); *E* 1056, fol. 197 (August 31, 1568).
14. BOA, *MD*, IX, hk. 204, 231.
15. AGS, *E* 1327, fol. 7 (January 28, 1570); *E* 1499, fol. 189 (February 22, 1570).
16. M. L'Abbé Douais, ed., *Dépèches de M. de Fourquevaux ambassadeur du Roi Charles IX en Espagne, 1565–1572* (Paris: Ernest Leroux, 1896), vol. 1, no. 5.
17. BOA, *MD* XIV, hk. 283 (H. Safer 3, 979 / Greg. June 27, 1571).
18. AGS, *E* 1073, fol. 52 (March 24, 1577).
19. AGS, *E* 1043, fol. 26 (1552).
20. AGS, *E* 1324, fol. 84 (February 2, 1561).
21. AGS, *E* 1043, fol. 26 (1552).
22. AGS, *E* 1887, fol. 5 (April 10, 1610).
23. AGS, *E* 1126, fol. 152 (April 30, 1561), 47 (May 11, 1561), 48 (May 8, 1561), 107 (October 4, 1561), 141, 168, 169, 176 (July 26, 1561); *E* 1132, fol. 28 (December 4, 1567); *E* 1893, fol. 144 (February 1, 1621). See also Canosa and Colonnello, *Spionaggio a Palermo*, p. 73.
24. AGS, *E* 1928, fol. 334 (December 14, 1609).
25. AGS, *E* 1929, fol. 12 (April 9, 1610), 41 (February 4, 1611), 52 (March 13, 1611).
26. AGS, *E* 1166, fol. 18 (March 27, 1613).
27. Marino Sanuto, *I Diarii*, vol. 53, ed. Rinaldo Fulin et al. (Venice: Federico Visentini Editore, 1899), col. 288, 417, 436–37, 448; Jean Aubin, "Une frontière face au péril ottoman: la Terre d'Otrante (1529–1532)," in *Soliman le Magnifique et son temps: Actes du colloque de Paris Galeries Nationales du Grand Palais, 7–10 March 1990*, ed. Gilles Veinstein (Paris: La Documentation Française, 1992), 469, fn. 36.
28. Sanuto, vol. 55, col. 424.
29. José María del Moral, *El Virrey de Nápoles Don Pedro de Toledo y la Guerra contra el Turco* (Madrid: Consejo Superior de Investigaciónes Cientificas, 1966), p. 87.

30. Camillo Manfroni, *Storia della marina italiana* (Rome: Forzani E C. Tipografi Del Senato, 1917), 3:386.

31. AGS, *E* 1121, fol. 105–6, 111–12. (March 25, 1552).

32. Selânikî, 2:776.

33. Emilio Sola Castaño, *La conjura de Campanella* (Madrid: Turpin Editores, 2007), pp. 37, 56, and pt. 2, ch. 5, Campanella's testimony, and ch. 7.

34. Preto, *Servizi Segreti*, p. 102.

35. AGS, *E* 1058, fol. 40 (April 5, 1570).

36. AGS, *E* 1058, fol. 42, 214.

37. ASV, *CX, Parti Criminali*, reg. 11, c. 78r–78v (July 3, 1570); Preto, *Servizi Segreti*, p. 102.

38. ASV, *CX-ParSec*, reg. 9, c. 87r (August 19, 1570).

39. ASV, *IS*, b. 416, document dated January 13, 1585.

40. ASV, *CX-ParSec*, reg. 11, c. 118r–18v (January 16, 1576, m.v.).

41. ASV, *CX-ParSec*, reg. 11, c. 119v–20r (February 15, 1576, m.v.), 130v (May 17, 1577).

42. AGS, *E* 1017, fol. 39 (March 28, 1533); Moral, p. 75.

43. AGS, *E* 1026, fol. 36 vd.; Moral, pp. 80–82.

44. François de Callières, *De la manière de négocier avec les souverains* (Amsterdam: La Compagnie, 1716), p. 30.

45. Hugon, *Au service du Roi Catholique*, illustrations 2 and 3 on pp. 122–23.

46. Ochoa Brun, 6:178.

47. Preto, *Servizi Segreti*, p. 75.

48. Francesco Longo, ed., *Annali veneti dall'anno 1457 al 1500 del Senatore Domenico Malipiero* (Florence: Gio. Pietro Viesseux, Direttore-Editore, 1843), 1:141–42.

49. Işıksel, p. 212.

50. "Âsitâne-i sa'âdet-ünvânımız mesdûd olmayup inâyet-i Hakk celle ve alâ ile dâimen mekşûf olup etrâf u cevânibde eğer dostluğa ve düşmanlığa kimesne gelüp gitmesine men' ü redd yokdur."

51. Walter Zele, "Aspetti delle legazioni ottomane nei *Diarii* di Marino Sanudo," *Studi Veneziani* 18 (1989): p. 275.

52. Maria Pia Pedani, *In Nome del Gran Signore: Inviati ottomani a Venezia dalla caduta di Costantinopoli alla guerra di Candia* (Venice: Deputazione Editrice, 1994), 14:115.

53. Sanuto, vol. 33, col. 447–50; Zele, p. 267.

54. Zele, p. 267.

55. Sanuto, vol. 5, col. 25. See also Arturo Segre and Roberto Cessi, eds., *I Diarii di Girolamo Priuli (AA. 1494–1512)* (Città di Castello: Casa Editrice S. Lapi, 1912), 1:286–87.

56. Sanuto, vol. 19, col. 339; vol. 34, col. 100, 115–16; vol. 39, col. 118; vol. 53, col. 250; Zele, p. 266.

57. AGS, *E* 1310, fol. 42 (September 24, 1532).

58. Segre and Cessi, eds., *I Diarii di Girolamo Priuli*, 2:338; Sanuto, vol. 5, col. 98.

59. Preto, *Servizi Segreti*, pp. 98–99.

60. Pedani, *In Nome del Gran Signore*, p. 193.

61. HHStA, *Turcica* 21, konv. 4.

62. Pedani, *In Nome del Gran Signore,* pp. 161, 193.

63. Cemal Kafadar, "A Death in Venice (1575): Anatolian Muslim Merchants Trading in the Serenissima," *Journal of Turkish Studies* 10 (1986): pp. 191–218.
64. AGS, *E* K 1677, fol. 46 (July 3, 1600).
65. Pedani, *In Nome del Gran Signore,* App. I. In the sixteenth century, of the eighty-four envoys that the Ottomans sent to Venice, seventeen had the mission of delivering a victory missive. Another three had been assigned to carry out a different diplomatic duty but still took a victory missive with them.
66. For orders issued to Transylvania to send spies into enemy territory, see BOA, *MD*, III, several provisions; LX, hk. 536 (H. Rebiülahir 27, 994 / Greg. April 17, 1586); LXX, hk. 247 (H. Rebiülevvel 15, 1001 / Greg. December 19, 1592). For similar orders issued to Moldavia, see BOA, *MD*, III, hk. 93, 350 (H. Zilhicce 22, 967 / Greg. September 13, 1560). For orders to Ragusa, see *MD*, X, hk. 383 (*ubudiyyetiniz muktezasınca* [as required by your servitude]); XII, hk. 266 (H. Zilkade 21, 978 / Greg. April 16, 1571). See also Ágoston, "Information, Ideology, and Limits," p. 89.
67. BOA, *MD*, V, hk. 953, 1548 (H. Şevval 16, 973 / Greg. May 6, 1566), 1925; VI, hk. 1134 (H. Şevval 13, 972 / Greg. May 14, 1565); VII, hk. 2540, 2743; XXIII, hk. 19; LXX, hk. 296 (H. Safer 28, 1001 / Greg. December 3, 1592). See also *MD*, VII, hk. 1008; XXIII, hk. 19; Géza Dávid, "The Mühimme Defters as a Source in Ottoman-Habsburg Rivalry in the 16th Century," *Archivum Ottomanicum* 20 (2002): p. 199.
68. BOA, *MD*, V, hk. 747 (H. Cemaziyelahir 9, 983 / Greg. October 1, 1566); XIV, hk. 507, 508 (H. Rebiülevvel 12, 978 / Greg. August 14, 1570).
69. BOA, *MD*, XXX, hk. 610, 611 (H. Rebiülevvel 28, 985 / Greg. June 15, 1577).
70. BOA, *MD*, VII, hk. 503, 704, 705, 1261, 2767; XII, hk. 266 (H. Zilkade 21, 978 / Greg. April 16, 1571), 529 (H. Muharrem 22, 979 / Greg. June 15, 1571), 856 (H. Rebiülevvel 29, 979 / Greg. August 20, 1571); XIV, hk. 97 (H. Muharrem 16, 979 / Greg. June 9, 1571), 307 (H. Safer 14, 978 / Greg. June 18, 1570), 758 (H. Cemaziyelahir 28, 978 / Greg. November 27, 1570), 854 (Cemaziyelahir 6, 978 / Greg. November 5, 1570), 1644 (H. Şevval 21, 978 / Greg. March 18, 1571); XIX, hk. 128 (H. Gurre-yi Şaban 980 / Greg. December 7, 1572), 254, 656, 710, 711; XXII, hk. 208; XXIII, hk. 175 (H. Receb 6, 981 / Greg. November 1, 1573); XXXIX, hk. 679 (H. Rebiüelevvel 10, 988 / Greg. April 24, 1580); LIII, hk. 357 (H. Receb 27, 992 / Greg. August 4, 1584); DAD, *Acta Turcorum*, A8 9a, A8 10, K 68, K 113, A7 29a, K 82; Biegman, "Ragusan Spying," pp. 237–55.
71. See BOA, *MD*, VI, hk. 1134 (H. Şevval 13, 972 / Greg. May 14, 1565). According to this document, first Transylvania would send news to the province of Timişoara, and then Timişoara would inform Istanbul about the matter at hand.
72. On relations between Ragusa and the Ottoman Empire in the sixteenth century, see Nicolaas H. Biegman, *The Turco-Ragusan Relationship according to the Firmāns of Murād III (1575– 1595) Extant in the State Archives of Dubrovnik* (The Hague: Mouton, 1968); Metin Ziya Köse, *Doğu Akdeniz'de Casuslar ve Tacirler: Osmanlı Devleti ve Ragusa İlişkileri, 1500–1600* (Istanbul: Giza Yayınları, 2009).
73. BOA, *MD*, XVI, hk. 633 (H. Rebiülevvel 9, 979 / Greg. July 31, 1571); AGS, *E* 1331, fol. 35 (April 10, 1572), 99 (September 2, 1572).

74. Steven Dedijer, "Ragusa Intelligence and Security (1301–1806): A Model for the Twenty-First Century," *International Journal of Intelligence and CounterIntelligence* 15, no. 1 (2002): see the map on p. 108.

75. BOA, *MD*, X, hk. 383.

76. Sola Castaño, *Los que van y vienen*, p. 82.

77. DAD, *Lettere di Levante*, document dated February 11, 1592.

78. DAD, *Lettere di Levante*, documents dated November 24, 1579, and January 20, 1580.

79. AGS, *E* 1338, fol. 64 (October 28, 1580).

80. Biegman, *Turco-Ragusan Relationship*, pp. 129–30; Biegman, "Ragusan Spying."

81. AGS, *E* 1047, fol. 8 (March 22, 1554); *E* 1331, fol. 99 (September 2, 1572) contain references to spies in Rome, Naples, and Messina. As far as Portillo was concerned, frigates from Ragusa arriving at Naples on the pretext of delivering news should be turned away in an appropriate manner. This would help to prevent espionage. *E* 1332, fol.185 (May 30, 1572).

82. AGS, *E* 1054, fol. 173 (August 5, 1565).

83. AGS, *E* 1541, fol. 199 (November 25, 1599).

84. J. Tadić, *Španija I Dubrovnik* (Belgrade: Sirpska Kraljevska Akademija, 1932), pp. 60–62, as cited in Robin Harris, *Dubrovnik. A History* (London: Saqi Books, 2003), p. 111; AGS, *E* 1028, fol. 23 (April 20, 1538); *E* 1311, fol. 83–85 (March 19, 1534).

85. ASV, *DocTR*, b. 3, no. 315, 336; b. 4, no. 467; b. 5, no. 655.

86. ASV, *DocTR*, b. 3, no. 338, 340, 343.

87. Preto, *Servizi Segreti*, p. 117.

88. AGS, *E* 1308, fol. 31 (April 11, 1530).

89. ASV, *CX-ParSec*, reg. 4, cc. 11v (June 11, 1533), 36r (October 26, 1534), 51r–51v (August 14, 1535).

90. Pierre Sardella, *Nouvelles et spéculations à Venise: Au début du XVIe siècle* (Paris: Librarie Armand Colin, 1948), p. 15.

91. AGS, *E* 1335, fol. 220 (September 22, 1611).

92. ASV, *DocTR*, b. 5, no. 705.

93. ASV, *DocTR*, b. 4, no. 507 (July 14–23, 1543); BOA, *MD*, VI, hk. 1424 (H. Evasıt-ı Zilhicce 972 / Greg. June 9–18, 1565).

94. Jean Chesneau, *Le voyage de Monsieur d'Aramon, ambassadeur pour le Roy en Levant, escript par noble homme Jean Chesneau*, ed. Charles Schefer (Paris: Ernest Leroux, 1887), p. 187.

95. Ágoston, "Információszerzés és kémkedés," p. 151.

96. Emrah Safa Gürkan, "Bir Diplomasi Merkezi Olarak Yeni Çağ İstanbul'u," in *Antik Çağdan 21. Yüzyıla Büyük İstanbul Tarihi: Siyaset ve Yönetim I*, ed. Feridun M. Emecen and Coşkun Yılmaz (Istanbul: İ.B.B. Kültür A.Ş., 2015), pp. 372–99.

97. Ágoston, "Information, Ideology, and Limits," p. 84; Ágoston, "Birodalom és információ," pp. 45–48.

98. Eugenio Albèri, ed., *Le relazioni degli ambasciatori veneti al Senato durante il secolo decimosesto* (Florence: Società Editrice Fiorentina, 1855), 9:75–77.

99. AGS, *E* 1321, fol. 101.

100. ASV, *CX-ParSec*, reg. 11, cc. 99r–99v (June 6, 1576).

101. Ágoston, "Information, Ideology, and Limits," p. 86.

FIGURE 1. A period depiction of the expanse of the Ottoman Empire from the *Orbis Terrarum* atlas by Abraham Ortelius, published in Antwerp in 1570. *Science History Images/Alamy*

FIGURE 2. Sultan Süleyman I, "the Magnificent," wearing the crown produced by Venetian jewelers under orders from Grand Vizier İbrahim Pasha to be worn by during the military procession that İbrahim Pasha orchestrated on the streets of Belgrade in 1532. The crown resembled the three-layered crown worn by the pope, and the ceremony İbrahim organized was intended as a riposte to the pope's crowning of Emperor Charles V in Bologna in 1530. With these symbolic gestures, which were not part of the vocabulary of the Islamic political tradition, Süleyman was letting it be known what he thought about Charles's claim to be an emperor. *Wikimedia Commons, Metropolitan Museum of Art, Harris Brisbane Dick Fund*

FIGURE 3. A woodcut portrait of Charles V Habsburg (1500–58) by Giovanni Britto, after Titian, made c. 1535–45. He was the Holy Roman Emperor, archduke of Austria, king of Spain, and duke of Burgundy. *Metropolitan Museum of Art*

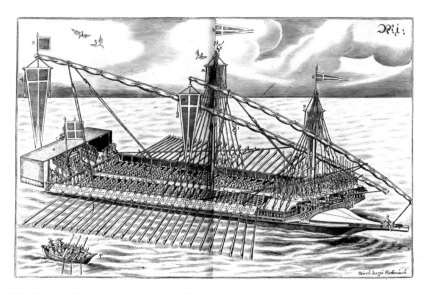

FIGURE 4. A 28-seater Maltese admiral's galley. From *Josephum Furttenbach, Architectura Navalis: Das ist von dem Schiffgebäw, auff dem Meer und Seekusten zu gebrauchen (Ulm: Jonam Saurn, 1629), no. 1*

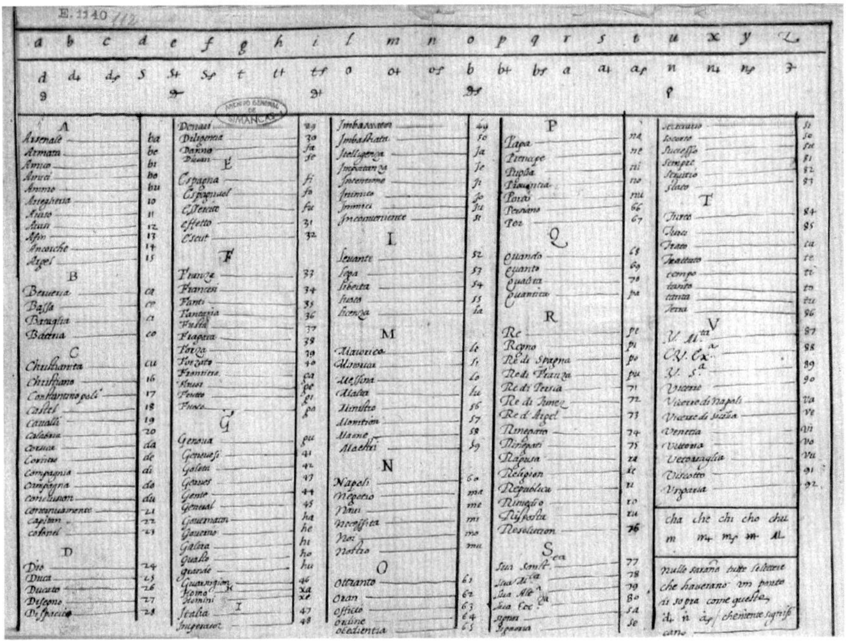

FIGURE 5. An encryption key for the code that Habsburg spies, ambassadors, and commanders used in their secret correspondence. Encryption keys of this kind, which were renewed at regular intervals, were vital for secure communication. As can be seen in the picture, frequently used words, such as galley, France, king, war, and ducat, were encoded using different combinations of numbers and letters. *Archivo General de Simancas, Valladolid, E 1140, fol. 112*

FIGURE 6. Letters written in code were subsequently decoded by clerks with the help of an encryption key. Around the margins of this document, you can see a transcription of the encrypted passages. *Archivo General de Simancas, Valladolid, E 1127, fol. 13 (April 20, 1537)*

FIGURE 7. A 1586 portrait of Philip II Habsburg (1527–98) by Jeronimus Wierix. As king of Spain, king of Naples and Sicily, and duke of Milan, he was the Ottomans' principal antagonist in the Mediterranean in the second half of the sixteenth century. *Library of Congress*

FIGURE 8. An encoded *dispaccio*. The important parts of the letters that the Venetian *bailo* regularly sent were encoded. In contrast to the documents in the Spanish archives, the transcriptions of encoded messages in letters from the *bailo* were done on a separate page, rather than in the margins. *Archivio di Stato di Venezia, Venice, SDC, fil. 3-C, c. 35r (April 9, 1561)*

FIGURE 9. Letter written to the Genoese nobleman Ottavio Sauli by the Genoese Gregorio Bregante, one of the key members of the Habsburg intelligence network in Istanbul, who was part of the Ottoman fleet at the time of the Siege of Malta. The letter, which was written at the height of the siege, gives a day-by-day account of the navy's movements up until reaching Malta and of the various stages of the siege itself. As well as presenting interesting stories, such as the fate of the two knights who wanted to surrender Malta to the Ottomans but who were captured and decapitated, it mentions the type of illegible, encrypted letter referred to in chapter 5. *Archivio di Stato di Genoa, Genoa, Archivio Segreto, Lettere Ministri Costantinopoli, fil. 2169, fol. 1r (July 13, 1565)*

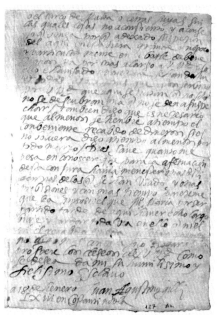

FIGURE 10. *Sacar al fuego.* This is a spy's letter that was written using lemon juice or another solution. The contents of the front page of the letter was intended not to arouse suspicion; often, pages like this gave the impression that the letter was written to the family of a captive or a merchant. However, Habsburg governors, viceroys, and ambassadors understood from the "honorando" (literally meaning "honoring") affixed to the name of the recipient that this was in fact a letter from a spy. Then, by "torturing" the letter by holding a flame to it, they made the invisible ink turn red. It should be noted that documents of this kind are particularly difficult to read. *Archivo General de Simancas, Valladolid, E 1392, fol. 63 (February 18, 1563)*

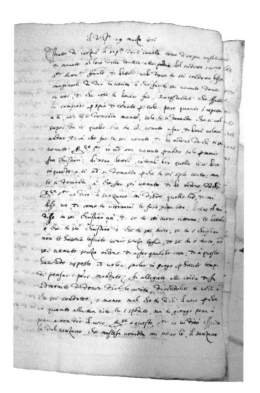

FIGURE 11. The record of the Venetians' interrogation of the Ottoman spy Giorgio (Zorzi) Cavalà from Heraklion (Kandiye), whose story was told in chapter 2. The report is in the form of a question-and-answer dialogue. *Archivio di Stato di Venezia, Venice, LettRett, b. 302 (March 29, 1571)*

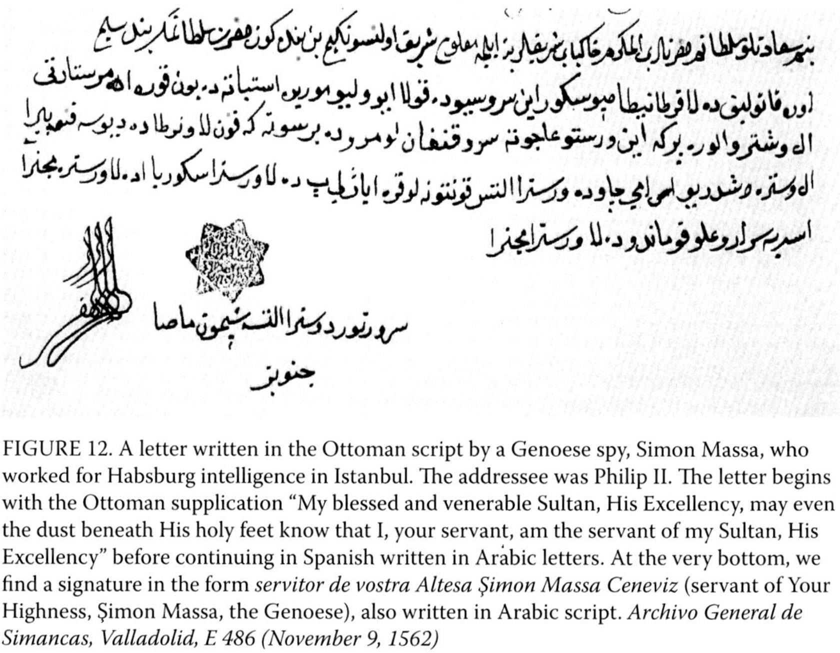

FIGURE 12. A letter written in the Ottoman script by a Genoese spy, Simon Massa, who worked for Habsburg intelligence in Istanbul. The addressee was Philip II. The letter begins with the Ottoman supplication "My blessed and venerable Sultan, His Excellency, may even the dust beneath His holy feet know that I, your servant, am the servant of my Sultan, His Excellency" before continuing in Spanish written in Arabic letters. At the very bottom, we find a signature in the form *servitor de vostra Altesa Şimon Massa Ceneviz* (servant of Your Highness, Şimon Massa, the Genoese), also written in Arabic script. *Archivo General de Simancas, Valladolid, E 486 (November 9, 1562)*

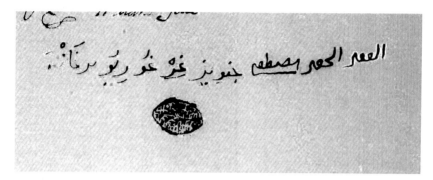

FIGURE 13. The signature of Gregorio Bregante, a Habsburg spy operating in Istanbul. Written in Arabic letters, it reads "Your humble servant, Mustafa Ceneviz (the Genoese), Girgor Bregante." *Archivo General de Simancas, Valladolid, E 486 (October 29, 1562)*

FIGURE 14. A depiction of a spy. From Cesare Ripa's *Iconologia di Cesare Ripa Perugino* (Venice: Christoforo Tomasini, 1645), p. 592, a book about occupations in the sixteenth century.

FIGURE 15. A stylized depiction of "Mahmut the Turkish Spy, Aged 72," from *Letters Writ by a Turkish Spy Who Lived Five and Forty Years, Undiscover'd, at Paris*, 5th ed., vol. 7 (London: H. Rodes, 1702), cover page. Written by the Genoese Giovanni Antonio Marana and published simultaneously in Italy, France, and England, this eight-volume work offers a critique of political, social, religious, and cultural issues, based on the letters of a fictitious Turkish spy named Mahmut (Mahmud), who purportedly served in the court of Louis XIV. This popular work underwent numerous reprints and had an important role in shaping the image of the Turkish spy in Europe.

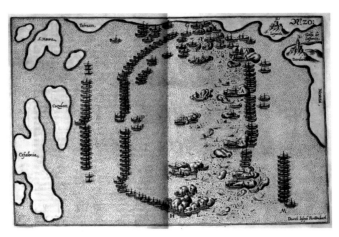

FIGURE 16. Formation of the navies at the time of the Battle of Lepanto, 1571. The Ottoman fleet is the line of ships located closer to the coast. The only part of it to emerge from the battle unscathed was the left flank, which was where the Muslim corsairs under Uluc Ali's command were positioned. The outcome of the battle was in fact determined by six Venetian galleasses with a high broadside, indicated on the map with an "A." *From Josephum Furttenbach*, Architectura Navalis: Das ist von dem Schiffgebäw, auff dem Meer und Seekusten zu gebrauchen *(Ulm: Jonam Saurn, 1629), no. 20*

102. ASV, *CCX-LettAmb*, b. 3, fol. 55; Christiane Villain-Gandossi, "Les Dépêches Chiffrées de Vettore Bragadin, Baile de Constantinople (12 Juillet 1564–15 Juin 1566)," *Turcica* 10 (1978): p. 77; Pedani, *In Nome del Gran Signore*, p. 42.

103. ASV, *CX-ParSec*, reg. 11, cc. 154v (March 24, 1578), fil. 20, document dated March 24, 1578.

104. A. H. Wratislaw, *Adventures of Baron Wenceslas Wratislaw of Mitrowitz* (London: Bell and Daldy, 1862), pp. 109–17. For the rest of the story, see Tobias P. Graf, "Of Half-Lives and Double-Lives: 'Renegades' in the Ottoman Empire and Their Pre-Conversion Ties, ca. 1580–1610," in *Well-Connected Domains: Towards an Entangled Ottoman History*, ed. Pascal W. Firges et al. (Leiden: Brill, 2014), p. 136.

105. P. Augusto Tormene, "Il bailaggio a Costantinopoli di Girolamo Lippomano e la sua tragica fine," *Nuovo archivio veneto*, n.s. 4, t. 7 (1904): pp. 83–84.

106. BOA, *MD*, XLVIII, hk. 311, 313 (both dated H. Ramazan 15, 990 / Greg. October 3, 1582).

107. BOA, *MD*, XLVIII, hk. 635 (H. Zilhicce 9, 990 / Greg. January 4, 1583).

108. Sanuto, vol. 7, col. 19.

109. Barbero, *La bataille des trois empires*, pp. 278–79.

110. Kenneth M. Setton, *The Papacy and the Levant (1204–1571)* (Philadelphia: American Historical Society, 1984), 4:394–95.

111. ASV, *CCX-LettAmb*, b. 3, fol. 146–47 (May 11, 1568).

112. AGS, *E* 1158, fol. 26 (November 3, 1594).

113. A. H. de Groot, *The Ottoman Empire and the Dutch Republic: A History of the Earliest Diplomatic Relations, 1610–1630* (Leiden and Istanbul: Nederlands Historisch-Archaeologisch Instituut, 1978), p. 59; ASV, *SDelC*, reg. 11, fol. 44 (October 17, 1612).

114. AGS, *E* 1335, fol. 77 (September 10, 1576).

115. AGS, *E* 1336, fol. 132 (March 18, 1577).

116. COSP, *Venice* 8, no. 1030 (March 16, 1591).

117. Philip P. Argenti, *Chius Vincta or the Occupation of Chios by the Turks (1566) and their Administration of the Island (1566–1912)* (Cambridge: Cambridge University Press, 1941), p. xcviii.

118. Setton, *Papacy and the Levant*, 4:394–95.

119. ASV, *SDelC*, reg. 8 c. 101v (February 6, 1592, m.v.).

120. Selâhattin Tansel, "Silahşör'un Feth-nâme-i Diyâr-ı Arab Adlı Eseri," *Tarih Vesikaları* 17 (1958), vr. 18a–18b, p. 307. My thanks to Feridun M. Emecen for drawing my attention to this source. Also, see Emecen, *Yavuz Sultan Selim*, p. 224.

121. "yarar ve içlerinde tedbîr ü tedârükde bile çalışub hidmetde olan berü cânib- den ulûfelü câsûslar."

122. Selânikî, 1:12–13.

123. "yarar mürtedler ve ulûfelü câsûslar."

124. "her bir kavm ve kabîlenün hilâfına dillerince kağıdlar yazılub taburda lonca- larında câsûslar eliyle bırağılub."

125. Selânikî, 1:32.

126. Feridun Ahmed Beg, *Nüzhet-i Esrâr-ü'l-Ahyâr der Ahbâr-ı Sefer-i Sigetvar*, ed. H. Ahmet Arslantürk and Günhan Börekçi (Istanbul: Zeytinburnu Belediyesi Kültür Yayınları, 2012), vr. 66a–69a.

127. BOA, *MD*, XIII, hk. 110 (H. Zilkade 4, 978 / Greg. March 30, 1571).

128. BOA, *MD*, XIII, hk. 134 (H. Zilkade 7, 978 / Greg. April 2, 1571), 498 (H. Zilhicce 978 / Greg. May 11, 1571), 1211 (H. Muharrem 20, 979 / Greg. June 14, 1571), 1340 (H. Muharrem 25, 979 / Greg. June 19, 1571), 1072 (H. Muharrem 14, 979 / Greg. June 8, 1571).

129. BOA, *MD*, XIII, hk. 290 (H. Gurre-yi Zilhicce 978 / Greg. April 26, 1571), 713 (H. Zilhicce 28, 978 / Greg. May 23, 1571); XLII, hk. 1925 (H. Rebiülevvel 18, 984 / Greg. June 15, 1576).

130. BOA, *MD*, XIII, hk. 684 (H. Zilhicce 26, 978 / Greg. May 21, 1571).

131. The term *nave* is used in the document. *Nave/nao/nef*: A merchant sailing ship with a high broadside, also used for smaller carracks. The term "carrack" is used for smaller and more agile versions, but Ottomans called both types of ships "*barça*" (barge).

132. Tommaso Contarini, *Historia delle successe dal principio della guerra mossa da Selim Ottomano a Venetiani, fino al dì della gran giornata vittoriosa contra Turchi* (Venice: Francesco Rampazzetto, 1572), fol. 12r, 13v, 16r, 19r.

133. Barbero, *La bataille des trois empires*, p. 656.

134. Barbero, *La bataille des trois empires*, p. 684.

135. AGS, *E* 1332, fol. 198 (July 16, 1573).

136. ASF, *AMP*, fil. 4148, "Avvisi di Napoli e Messina," fil. 370; Angelo Raffa, "L'ultima impresa di Hayreddin (Barbarossa). La guerra marittima turco-franco-spagnola del 1543–4," *Aspetti ed attualità del potere marittimo in Mediterraneo nei secoli XII–XVI*, ed. P. Alberini (Rome: Ufficio storico della marina militare, 1999), p. 408.

137. Barbero, *La bataille des trois empires*, p. 277.

4

THE INSTITUTIONAL STRUCTURE OF OTTOMAN INTELLIGENCE IN THE SIXTEENTH CENTURY

In the introduction, I noted the lack of systematic analyses of Ottoman intelligence. This chapter aims to remedy this lack by exploring the institutional structure of the Ottoman secret service during a century in which centralized bureaucracies were just beginning to emerge. My thesis is that Ottoman intelligence in the sixteenth century differed from its European counterparts in two distinct ways. Firstly, the Ottoman secret service did not have an institutional structure and functioned primarily on the basis of personal networks, in keeping with the patrimonial structure of the Empire. Secondly, this lack of institutionalization prevented the capital from directly organizing and managing operations in the provinces. As you will see, governors in the provinces were broadly left to their own devices to establish their own intelligence networks. Aware of its incapacity to intervene directly, Istanbul set greater store by the results it achieved than the means it used to get them.

A PATRIMONIAL EMPIRE

Premodern states were entities that, unlike contemporary sovereign states, had not yet completely institutionalized, so they depended more on clusters of personal connections. In the sixteenth century, centralized bureaucracies began to emerge across the Mediterranean and the first steps were taken toward a method of corporate government that was not based solely on the individual ruler. This process of centralization and bureaucratization was not uniform, however, and differed according to both geographical setting and function.

What distinguished the Venetian and Habsburg secret services from their Ottoman counterpart was their dissimilar levels of centralization and institutionalization. Venice and the Habsburgs strove to create institutions that would oversee intelligence efforts from one central point. As a republic, Venice was governed by elected members of the nobility (Ven. *patrisi*) who served for a predetermined period on one of the many governing councils (Ven. *magistrato*); the council responsible for intelligence work was the Council of Ten (*Consiglio di*

Dieci). This council not only oversaw the activities of spies but also censored the reports about such activities before they were presented to the Venetian Senate. In line with the view that documents of this kind containing such sensitive information should be viewed by as few people as possible, 1539 saw the first election of three members of the Council of Ten to serve as state inquisitors (*Inquisitori di Stato*). These completely secular officials, who were entrusted with the task of guarding state secrets and overseeing intelligence efforts, should not be confused with Holy Inquisitors in the Spanish sense.[1]

As for the Habsburgs, intelligence was the purview of state clerks who would both oversee the chancery and regulate the functions of the councils, which constituted the state's main decision-making apparatus. Philip II, known as the "Paper King" (*Rey Papelero*) due to his fondness for red tape, was especially interested in the secret service. A further step was eventually taken to institutionalize the central management of intelligence, and a department was created that started functioning in the final years of Philip II's reign but was fully institutionalized only in 1613. Officially called the "Secret Intelligence Superintendent" (*Superintendente de las inteligencias secretas*), the holder of this post was generally referred to as "the Great Spy" (*Espia Mayor*).[2] Although the post was scrapped shortly after its establishment for reasons unknown, its creation is important insomuch as it reflects the general tendency toward centralizing and standardization.

In the Ottoman Empire, there were no comparable attempts at institutionalization or regulation of intelligence. This was not due to the Empire's shortcomings in establishing a centralized bureaucracy; rather, increasing revenue requirements in the sixteenth century had heightened the need for the creation of a centralized state run by professional bureaucrats.[3] This period witnessed the emergence of a class of bureaucrats (*kalemiyye*) independent of the class of scholars (*ilmiyye*); from then on, those tasked with the administrative duties of the state would follow a distinct career trajectory.[4] Slowly but surely, a distinction emerged between the Chancery and the Ministry of Finance.[5]

Another noticeable tendency of the era was the domination of administrative positions in the provinces by palace circles and by members of the households of grandees.[6] As governor-generals of provinces were increasingly appointed from among palace-trained personnel, local military commanders and administrators were inhibited from rising through the ranks. As a result, grandee households, which lay outside of the newly emerging centralized bureaucracy, gained an immense amount of importance and became, in the words of Metin Kunt, "the building blocks of the Ottoman political edifice."[7] The Ottoman Empire's patrimonial structure was made up of a large number of intertwined households (called *kapu*, literally meaning "gate"), and at the heart of this system was the sultan himself and his family.[8] This method of government, which was not institutionalized but relied on personal connections, blurred the line between the state and the dynasty and between the public and the individual. While the sultan's private income could be used for state expenditure,[9] celebrations such as weddings and circumcisions could go beyond being family matters and become ceremonies attended by the state's highest-ranking bureaucrats.

All Ottoman administrators, from the lowest- to the highest-ranking, had to finance a retinue of individuals, as they relied on the clerks, spies, translators, and soldiers who worked for their office to perform their administrative and military duties. Many of these employees received a salary from the treasury; most, however, were paid out of the pashas' own pockets. The pashas themselves had incomes much greater than their official salaries, thanks to the bribes, gifts, and commissions that they received.[10] Rather than seeing the latter kinds of financial resources as a salary, they were regarded as a budget that allowed Ottoman governors to fulfill their administrative and military duties and to provide for their entourages.[11] For this reason, when a pasha died or was dismissed, it was traditional to seize his possessions; nothing could be more natural than to reclaim the budget of a pasha who no longer had any function for the state and to transform it into a financial resource that the state could redistribute as it wished.

INTELLIGENCE OPERATIONS AND THE HOUSEHOLDS OF OTTOMAN GRANDEES

In this system, the households of grandees were also tasked with establishing intelligence networks and gathering information. In short, there was no central institution, which meant that, often, numerous intelligence networks were operating simultaneously and independently, sometimes in competition with one another. This plurality did not go unnoticed by contemporary commentators. The Spanish ambassador to Venice, Lope de Soria, did not know whether the Ottoman spy he captured in 1534 worked for Süleyman the Magnificent, Grand Vizier İbrahim Pasha, or Alvise Gritti, the Venetian power broker and a favorite of the sultan.[12] Furthermore, in his compendium of midseventeenth century Ottoman legal codes, Hezarfen Hüseyin Efendi records that sultans asked their grand viziers to employ a network of spies who were *müstakil ve mahfi*, that is, self-reliant and secret.[13]

The lack of an institutional structure does, of course, make the historian's job difficult. The Ottoman archives in Istanbul consist primarily of documents from the sultan's own council, that is, the Imperial Council. Since they contain no information about the grandee households, in order to explore Ottoman spy activity in detail, one needs to consult European archives.

As the highest-ranking official in the Ottoman administration, the grand vizier was the foremost patron of spies. Numerous documents exist related to the intelligence activities of two of the three most important grand viziers of the century. İbrahim Pasha (of. 1523–36),[14] who had a keen interest in European affairs, sent many spies to the West, one of whom was the jeweler Marco de Nicolò, whom he tasked with gathering intelligence on Venice, Spain, and France.[15] Another of his spies was a Jewish man by the name of Astrume Elia, who admitted he was one of numerous Jews working for the Ottomans in

Naples (see chapter 3).[16] To facilitate intelligence-gathering on Habsburg territory, another quartet of spies working for the pasha came up with a proposal targeted at the Habsburg authorities, namely to carry out a number of covert counteroperations.[17]

Sokollu Mehmed Pasha valued his spies highly, as evidenced by the lengths he went to save one of his spies from the Venetians. Once the Ottoman-Venetian War of 1570–73 was over, an exchange of prisoners was arranged between the two sides, but the Venetians did not release Mahmud of Castelnuovo (present-day Herceg Novi), who was considered a dangerous spy. When Sokollu persisted in demanding the return of his agent, the Venetians told him that Mahmud had not been captured during the war but during peacetime, and they dragged their feet until 1579. Mahmud's fate was sealed after his patron was killed by the dagger of a traitorous assassin as part of a palace plot to eliminate him. The Venetians did not waste time in ridding themselves of Mahmud and poisoned him immediately, although they told the Ottoman authorities that he had died in prison following a long illness.[18] One might be inclined to interpret the Venetians' persistence in not releasing the Ottoman spies they had captured, even at the risk of drawing the ire of a powerful grand vizier like Sokollu, as an indication of their capabilities as spies; Sokollu's concern for the plight of Mahmud over the years can be seen as reflecting the robust and close relationship that Ottoman spies had with their patrons.

Mahmud was not the only spy working for Sokollu who was captured in Europe. According to the Venetian *bailo*, Sokollu Pasha used his spies to encourage the Moriscos in Spain to rebel.[19] In a secret meeting with the pasha, one of Don Juan de Cardona's captives assured Sokollu Mehmed Pasha that, if he dispatched the navy to Spain, one hundred thousand Moriscos would take up the weapons they had buried underground and start an uprising.[20]

In February 1570, months before the Ottomans landed in Cyprus, one of Sokollu's spies arrived in Istanbul from Venice and reported that the Venetians were preparing seven galleys that they intended to use to protect the island from attack.[21] In September 1572, another spy left Ragusa to travel to Rome, disguised as a slave ransomer. The same man had traveled to many other cities in the past, Naples in particular, and was a famous spy[22] who had even been spotted aboard the Maltese capitana.[23] In January 1574, Kasım Çelebi, working for the Ottoman governor of Delvine, leaked to the Habsburgs that two converts bringing letters from Sokollu had arrived in Delvine. Previously, one of these converts had traveled to the Venetian-ruled island of Corfu and scouted the fortifications there. Now the duo was tasked with traveling first to Corfu, disguised as slave ransomers, and then on to Puglia in southern Italy, on the other side of the Adriatic.[24] Within the same year, the *bailo* issued a warning to Venice regarding another convert dispatched by Sokollu: this spy was from Rome and in his midforties and of average height, with pale skin and a black goatee.[25]

In the mid-1570s, we come across two Transylvanian spies working for the same legendary grand vizier. Marxeben Lener, whose Turkish name was

Mahmud or Ahmed, first defrauded Emperor Maximilian II through certain projects. Although the details of these projects are lost to us, we know that Lener made the emperor lose a significant amount of money. The year after that, he was planning to secure the patronage of the viceroy of Naples by pretending to reconvert to Christianity, which would also give him an opportunity to gather intelligence. Prior to arriving in Naples, he intended to visit Rome and Venice and then travel to Spain (see chapter 2). Another spy from Transylvania was Markus Benkner / Ahmed, who was arrested in Naples. Also pretending to be a convert to Islam who was escaping from the Ottomans, he arrived in Spain and declared his desire to reconvert to Christianity; meanwhile, he was sending Sokollu letters written in code. When he was unmasked by the Austrian ambassador, however, Benkner's mission was rescinded and his plans came to nothing.[26]

One cannot fail to be impressed by the geographically far-reaching intelligence network that Sokollu created. In 1567, he sent a great many Moriscos to "Sicily, Spain, Italy, and Germany,"[27] and in the same year the Habsburgs realized that the pasha was receiving regular news from La Goulette, the strategic outpost in North Africa, via a Morisco[28] who owned a shop in Galata.[29] In 1578, in order to receive the latest updates regarding the Dutch Revolt, the pasha assigned a Dutchman to his city of birth, Antwerp.[30]

Another important official who shaped Ottoman strategy in the Mediterranean was the grand admiral of the Navy. Whichever pasha held this post was duty bound to follow the latest developments in Europe closely. The Ottoman grand admiral who left behind him the largest trail of documents was Uluc Ali Pasha, born Giovanni Dionigi Galeni in Calabria, who converted to Islam after being captured by corsairs and who became a formidable corsair himself (of. 1572–87).

Naturally, this experienced corsair, who knew the Mediterranean like the back of his hand, had ears everywhere. In September 1570, when a Maltese slave who arrived in Florence after leaving Uluc Ali's fleet disappeared, everyone reached the conclusion that he was an Ottoman spy and began to look for him.[31] Another spy working for the Calabrian convert found himself in the town of Messina in Sicily in September 1572, from where he reported to his patron that the Christian navy would be sailing out soon. For this reason, Uluc Ali Pasha, who had assumed command of the Ottoman navy after the disaster at Lepanto, should not return to Istanbul but instead remain at sea.[32] A year later, Uluc Ali Pasha sent an entire retinue of spies to Naples, their mission being to ascertain how the Habsburgs had taken the news that the Venetians had dumped their allies and instead were engaging in peace talks with Istanbul.[33] According to a 1575 account by a Habsburg prisoner in Istanbul, a Majorcan monk named Diego, among the pasha's spies in Naples was a Morisco from Valencia, who was evidently able to go in and out of the castle and the viceroy's palace at will.[34] In 1576, Uluc posted to Corfu the military engineer of the fortress at Navarino, and he proceeded to draw up plans of the island and the fortress.[35] Two of the four spies who arrived in Venice in 1584 were Calabrian converts who had got hold of plans of the castle at Heraklion; the other two had just returned from an intelligence-gathering mission in Naples.[36] Another spy of the pasha, a Sicilian convert who was captured on the island of Tabarka in August of the same year, confessed that every year he traveled along the Spanish coast on a reconnaissance mission, giving particular importance to Valencia. And he was not alone, as many other spies were performing similar tasks; the Sicilian spy even gave the names of two such individuals.[37] Sure enough, a few months later three spies working for Uluc set out from Bizerte in Tunisia for Naples and Valencia.[38]

In 1585, it seemed as if Uluc Ali had set his sights on Heraklion, that is, Crete, because the reports being filed by the *bailo* Lorenzo Bernardo were a cause for concern. In a letter dated June 22, the *bailo* recorded how a Greek metropolitan bishop visited Uluc Ali at his home, entering through a secret door. He also pointed out that this visit was subsequently repeated two more times. The *bailo*'s sources told him that the metropolitan bishop, who never visited the pasha's house during the day, was actually the metropolitan bishop of Monemvasia. According to the *bailo*'s report, though, the only thing that was overheard during the long talks between the admiral and the metropolitan bishop was the word "Cythera," an island to the south of the Peloponnese peninsula. Even that much was enough to ring alarm bells in Bernardo's head, and the *bailo* immediately sent news to Heraklion. In the same letter, Bernardo mentioned a Greek man from Heraklion, Nicolò Andriopulo, who had visited Uluc Ali's home with the aim of converting to Islam. When his request was refused and he was told that this was not a good time, he went instead to Mehmed Pasha's palace.[39] Three weeks later, the *bailo* learned from Uluc's Venice-born chamberlain Rıdvan Agha that an Italian soldier had visited the admiral and had a private discussion with him on Heraklion and Corfu. Later, the *bailo*'s interpreter Pasquale encountered the soldier-spy in the admiral's residence and found out that he was from Bergamo. As he was about to leave the palace, the spy approached the interpreter and insisted that he was not actually from Bergamo. The *bailo* was reluctant to arrest the spy, partly because of his close links to Uluc Ali, partly because Bergamo lay under the control of a different ruler. For this reason, he went no further than writing to the authorities to warn them, also informing them that the soldier would return to Heraklion to rejoin his troop. In a letter posted a fortnight later, he corrected this information and stated that the soldier was still in Istanbul.[40] Around the same time, another interpreter working for the *bailo*, Giannettino, reported that, just as he was exiting the dungeon where Uluc Ali kept his slaves, he saw four Greeks carrying a model castle. According to the admiral's slaves, the model was of the Heraklion fortress, and the admiral used it to calculate distances and to shape his plans.[41] A month later, a one-handed man from Heraklion whom Uluc Ali had assigned as a spy returned to Istanbul, having gathered intelligence in his hometown and in Naples.[42]

Another group, whom I shall term "powerbrokers," employed informants at various locations in the Mediterranean to gather information on behalf of the Ottomans. While these powerbrokers did not occupy any official governmental posts, they used their international commercial, financial, and diplomatic connections to carry out important duties for the Ottoman state. Their close relationship with the imperial palace allowed them to wield considerable political influence.

Alvise Gritti, a close collaborator of İbrahim Pasha, exemplified this group.[43] He was the illegitimate son of Andrea Gritti, doge of Venice.[44] Alvise was a favorite of the palace and maintained an intelligence network that was surprisingly powerful and effective. His contemporaries attributed a myriad of intentions and actions to him, claiming that he wished to seize the Hungarian throne, that he incited the Ottomans to send their navy to attack Italy, that he encouraged the French king to attack Milan, that he wished to become the king of Naples, that he organized a Protestant uprising, and that he wished to conquer Vienna on behalf of the Ottomans and to destroy Venice.[45] Some of these claims are true. Subsequent events would show that he did have his eye on the Hungarian throne, and Gritti was not one to shy away from clandestine operations. We know, for instance, that he sent one of his men to speak to the Genoese admiral Andrea Doria, who had betrayed the French king and aligned with the Habsburgs; the envoy was supposed to persuade Doria to side with the Ottomans.[46] Some of the claims I have listed, though, were unsubstantiated rumors; nonetheless, even those are important as examples of how Gritti's diplomatic influence and operational capabilities were perceived.

When two of Gritti's sources were captured by the Habsburgs in November 1533, they produced some very interesting statements. They revealed that, acting on behalf of the Ottomans, the doge of Venice's son was engaged in talks with the kings of France and England, as well as with some German princes. The aim of these talks was to establish an alliance against Emperor Charles V. According to this plan, while an Ottoman navy (whose expenses would be fronted by France) would attack the coastal areas of the Habsburg Empire, Gritti himself would target Croatia and Hungary. In the meantime, the dukes of Bavaria and Würtemberg and the count of Hesse would pressure the emperor from within.[47] Gritti knew very well how to use his exceptional family connections to his advantage. From his father, he received a constant stream of intelligence regarding political and military developments, which he then passed on to Grand Vizier İbrahim Pasha.[48] He was no stranger either to involving his brothers and having them act as his personal spies. In 1531, the Habsburgs received a report that Alvise's brother Giorgio had begun to gather intelligence for the Ottomans as soon as he arrived in Ragusa.[49] Giorgio traveled to Venice from Ragusa in February, and then from Venice to Paris in May, his task ostensibly being to demand back the ten thousand ducats that a Frenchman in the palace of the Voivode of Transylvania, John Zápolya, owed Alvise. On his way back, he was arrested by the Habsburg authorities at a tavern in the Savoy region, and he was released only a week later, on the order of Emperor Charles V. Since he was the son of the doge of Venice, he was not subject to the routine treatment given to other suspects, and neither was he tortured to extract a confession.[50] Escaping by the skin of his teeth, Giorgio continued his intelligence activities; in 1535, when Habsburg spies captured Serafin de Gozo of Ragusa, a go-between between Istanbul and Paris, they found letters from Giorgio in his bag.[51] Another Gritti brother, Lorenzo, was also part of this intelligence network. In 1534, when Lorenzo brought a number of jewelers from Venice to Istanbul, among them was none other than the Marco de Nicolò mentioned previously.[52]

Another influential group within the Ottoman imperial palace were Jews who had fled from the Iberian Peninsula, in other words, Marranos. Marranos traveled to all corners of Europe, particularly Italy and the Low Countries, and from there some moved on to Ottoman territory. They did not hesitate to deploy the intelligence networks they possessed to increase their influence within the Ottoman capital.[53] A document from the Spanish archives testifies to the geographical reach of the Marrano spy network: Joseph Nasi had sources in many different cities, including Bologna, Ferrara, Prague, Candia, Livov, Lublin, Krakow, and Kutina.[54] This mysterious individual, who was perhaps one of the most famous Jews of the sixteenth century, was considered by his contemporaries to be hugely powerful. It is even believed that Nasi had something to do with the fire that broke out in the Venetian arsenal shortly before the Cyprus campaign, a campaign which Nasi himself had convinced the sultan to launch.[55] During the Ottoman-Venetian War, which lasted three years, many Jews in Eastern Mediterranean territories controlled by the Venetians were arrested and accused of acting as spies for Nasi (see chapter 3).[56]

Other Marranos, such as Alvaro Mendes and David Passi, were influential spy patrons. It was Mendes who told the Ottomans in 1588 that the Spanish Armada had been wrecked in the English Channel[57] and who provided Grand Vizier Siyavuş Pasha with information about Portuguese military fortifications near the Indian Ocean.[58] Mendes and Passi are also known to have had informants in Venice. While Mendes received regular updates from his brother and nephew living in the lagoon,[59] the correspondence between Passi and his sources in Europe did not escape the attention of the Venetians, who operated the only regular postal service between Istanbul and Europe. Venetian state inquisitors wrote to the *bailo* in Istanbul to alert him to the fact that Passi's spies were writing letters to him from all around Europe. The *bailo* was tasked with opening the letters sent to Passi and reporting their contents back to Venice.[60] In his reply, the *bailo* wrote that Passi had informants in every palace in Christendom and that in four days' time "an uncircumcised Portuguese Marrano" called Bentonunus would be traveling to Venice, and then to Flanders, to gather intelligence.[61]

The existence of numerous intelligence networks acting in the service of different political actors meant that spies and the decision-making processes they nourished came to occupy a central position in the factional politics of the Ottoman capital. Competition between different interest groups turned intelligence into a political football, and it was not too long before a struggle over intelligence broke out among the Ottoman grandees. They did not hesitate to give undue importance to certain information while doing away with other details or concealing information from the Palace and the Imperial Council if it did not suit their ends. In this way, they directed Ottoman foreign affairs in line with their own political ambitions. Some took it as far as fabricating news. A good example of this is the interest group I like to call the "Mediterranean faction," a team of captains and corsairs led by Grand Admiral Uluc Ali, who went to great lengths to convince Murad III and Grand Vizier Mesih Pasha to start a war in the Mediterranean. As I have stated in an earlier article, this group not only pressured Ottoman pashas by overstating the Habsburgs' military preparations via exaggerated reports but also tried to deceive the sultan himself by means of a piece of theatre, the details of which will be presented next.[62]

One day, when Uluc Ali was inspecting the shipyard, accompanied by the chief treasurer and a number of shipyard clerks, a Greek priest appeared out of nowhere. With tears in his eyes, he told the group how his ship, sailing from Rhodes to Istanbul, had been attacked by Maltese corsairs and how he, together with all the Muslims on board, had been taken captive and forced to work as oarsmen. "With God's help," the priest had managed to flee to Istanbul. Presumably to enhance the effect of his tale, he added the detail that the Maltese corsairs had asked him where Uluc Ali was. When they found out he was far away in the Black Sea with his fleet, they breathed a sigh of relief. In the months prior to this event, Uluc had been trying to convince Mesih Pasha and Sultan Murad III to send a powerful fleet into the Mediterranean, but the response he always received was that this would be impossible due to the ongoing challenge of the Ottoman-Persian war, which had been dragging on for some time. The conclusion that could be derived from the Maltese corsairs' alleged relief suited Uluc. According to this line of thought, as long as the grand admiral and his fleet did not chase the Maltese away, they would be able to continue attacking Ottoman ships at will.

The Calabrian listened to the priest and told him there was nothing he could do; if he were to tell the story to the grand vizier, the latter would assume he had made it up. In front of everyone, he scolded the priest and sent him away, but he also advised him to visit Mesih Pasha and tell him the exact story he had told him, not neglecting to mention how Uluc Ali had dismissed him. The priest visited Mesih Pasha and told him his story. However, the pasha was a cunning man, and after listening to the story, he told his men to give the priest a good feet-whipping. After fifty strokes of the whip, the crafty priest's tongue loosened. He confessed that the entire story was a fabrication and that he had not seen any corsairs anywhere. He also confessed that he had received money from Uluc Ali's men. In fact, the admiral himself had been spreading rumors for some time: a Maltese fleet of thirteen galleys and a galleon had allegedly been raising hell in the Aegean Sea. The aim of the legend surrounding the priest was—in the words of the Venetian *bailo*—to add some "color" (*colorire*) to such fabricated stories.

What is even more interesting is Uluc Ali's response when his plan was foiled. Having dismissed the priest, Mesih Pasha summoned Uluc Ali and told him that, even though what he did was wrong, he would not report him to the sultan. Despite being caught red-handed, the Calabrian corsair showed no signs of being repentant. He simultaneously denied the accusations levelled at him and his men and, taking the priest's made-up story as truth, criticized Mesih Pasha for not doing anything to combat the Maltese corsairs and shirking from spending any money on the navy. Mesih Pasha's reluctance to tell the sultan about the incident and Uluc's haughty attitude when faced with the grand vizier lead us to conclude that such pieces of theatre and attempts at misinformation were normal features of political life in the capital, which often saw factions pitted against one another.[63]

The biggest advantage to emerge from outsourcing intelligence-gathering to third parties was that it enabled Ottoman intelligence to draw on information from a wider geographical domain and from a bigger pool of informants. The entourages in question included people from different ethnicities all across the Mediterranean and Europe. To use Uluc Ali as an example once more, the Calabrian corsair's entourage did not consist solely of people from the same city as him but rather of corsairs and sailors who had strong familial connections with all corners of the Mediterranean. Another example is Koca Sinan Pasha, who found out about European developments through his relatives in Albania.[64] Cigalazade Yusuf Sinan Pasha, who served briefly as grand vizier and was made grand admiral twice, also benefitted from his family connections. His brother Carlo, whom he summoned to Istanbul, shuttled back and forth between Sicily and the Ottoman Empire gathering information. In order to obtain permission from the Habsburgs, Carlo offered to spy for them and promised that he would make his older brother return to the Christian fold.[65] This did not, though, prevent him from also gathering intelligence on behalf of the Ottomans.

The situation was no different for the political powerbrokers themselves. Alvise Gritti received regular news from his father, the doge. The family used their name to their benefit even when spying; what saved Giorgio from being interrogated and tortured was nothing other than Charles V's reluctance to anger his father. Finally, Marrano spymasters who employed spies to work for the Ottomans retained their close relationships within the Jewish community across the world, from the Mediterranean to the Indian Ocean, and from the Low Countries to Poland.

In the sixteenth century, resident embassies, which had emerged at the tail end of the previous century, became the norm in Europe;[66] however, the Ottomans refrained from establishing permanent embassies until the late eighteenth century. Bearing in mind that resident ambassadors performed the function of competent intelligence station chiefs (see chapter 3), this delay was a disadvantage for the Ottomans. However, the Ottomans were able to compensate for this deficiency with the help of their broad vision: Ottoman grandees and their entourages, all of whom came from diverse backgrounds, kept close track of global military, political, financial, and even artistic developments. Gazanfer Agha, for instance, a eunuch of Venetian origin who was a major political figure for three decades at the end of the sixteenth century,[67] scolded the *bailo* when he claimed that the grand clocks (*horoglio grande*) that the sultan requested could not be bought in Venice. Gazanfer Agha pointed out that such clocks could be found in St Mark's Square and other parts of the city (*piazza et in altri lochi*). [68] Furthermore, transimperial relationships of this kind allowed Ottoman pashas who were converts from Christianity to foster close relationships with those from their own homeland, both in the Ottoman capital and across Europe.[69] To give a striking example, the Venetian *bailo* Lorenzo Bernardo was a childhood friend of Grand Admiral Uluc Hasan Pasha.[70] During his tenure in Istanbul, Hasan also befriended other *bailo*s and exchanged information with them.[71]

That said, although this system was flexible, specialized, and influential, it also made double-crossing and betrayal possible; these were its primary faults. The transimperial relationships of non-Muslim powerbrokers in particular could be as harmful as they were beneficial, since such figures had no qualms about sleeping with the enemy, as it were. In 1531, for example, Alvise Gritti, who provided Venice with a regular stream of intelligence,[72] revealed to Venice, Rome, and Vienna that the Ottomans would attack Austria and Italy.[73] In the end, the Ottoman campaign against Austria did not happen until a year later, but this does not change the fact that Gritti had double-crossed the Ottomans. He was clearly not doing this out of the goodness of his heart, and he was shrewd enough to offer to mediate for Pope Clement VII, a cunning Medici, in Istanbul.[74] For his part, Joseph Nasi was not beyond bargaining with Philip II, despite the fact that Spanish king had previously commissioned an assassin to kill him! Nasi offered to return to Christianity and asked for a letter of safe conduct for himself and his family. He claimed that, if he were provided with the right opportunity, he could hand over the fortress at Herceg Novi to the Spanish.[75] Nasi also maintained clandestine connections with another sworn enemy, Venice. It was this master strategist who prewarned the Venetians about the Ottoman expedition to Cyprus, which would take place upon his insistence three years later.[76]

Another Marrano in cahoots with the Habsburgs was David Passi. Like Nasi, he was a double agent. On the one hand, he toyed with Madrid; on the other, he played the role of a middleman in an anti-Habsburg alliance consisting of the following monarchs: Dom Antonio, the heir to the Portuguese throne (Portugal now lay under Spanish control); the king of France, Henry IV, who was fighting a civil war against the Catholic alliance supported by Philip II; the queen of England, Elizabeth I; and Sultan Murad III. Passi also acted as an intermediary in the case of Spanish aristocrats taken prisoner during wars or corsair attacks and brought to Istanbul,[77] the release of whom required the payment of ransoms. By 1585, he had started talking about returning to Christianity.[78] In 1590, Guillermo de Saboya, Passi's right hand man and a Marrano like him, traveled to Naples and proposed a series of interesting clandestine operations to the viceroy. According to de Saboya, Passi was capable of a lot more than just sending news from Istanbul. De Saboya touched on a series of audacious projects, including enabling the Habsburgs to capture Ottoman galleys, drawing Grand Admiral Uluc Hasan Pasha and his fleet into a trap, identifying Ottoman spies working in Europe, and preventing the Ottoman navy from sailing into the Western Mediterranean.[79] These plans, many of them nearly impossible, were obviously fabricated to extort money from the Habsburgs; however, the fact that Passi was able to keep the Habsburgs engaged in discussions for many years testifies to the extent to which Ottoman spies were able to engage in double-dealing.

A DECENTRALIZED SYSTEM

The lack of an administrative structure to manage intelligence operations created a decentralized system. While the Habsburgs and the Venetians established state institutions to oversee every financial and operational aspect of intelligence activities, in the Ottoman Empire such details were entrusted to provincial authorities. The rulers of the Empire were eager to ensure that provincial military and administrative affairs were managed from the center, but when it came to intelligence, they took a laxer approach and, particularly with respect to border areas, tended not to interfere. In any case, it would have been impossible for Istanbul to take the lead in responding to a sudden military threat or opportunity.[80]

On paper, border authorities had to get Istanbul's approval on a variety of matters, including the appointment of administrators, repairs, and the allocation of *timar* fiefdoms.[81] Due to logistical obstacles, however, the sultan's influence over border areas was limited. How restricted it was depended on various political and diplomatic factors, the most important of which were whether it was war or peacetime, the political stability of the Empire, the personal characteristics of the province's governor-general, and the reputation he had in Istanbul.

There was no reason for the capital to concern itself with how intelligence was gathered, provided that it was fed a steady stream of information by its commanders in the provinces. The most important evidence proving that the Ottomans cared little about the personal qualities or experiences of the spies they sent abroad is no doubt the type of language used in archival documents. Orders sent to provincial commanders to encourage the creation of intelligence networks specified no qualities to look for in prospective agents aside from their being "competent" (*yarar*).[82] The process of determining the preferred characteristics and personality traits of recruited spies was left entirely to the provincial administration tasked with creating, dispatching, and managing intelligence networks.

There were various reasons why provincial administrations were left to their own devices on this matter. First, when military and political crises unfolded on the other side of the border, it would only have been possible to send spies to the right place and at the right time if Istanbul did not interfere but instead settled for playing a regulatory role. Second, in terms of logistical constraints, it would have been difficult for Istanbul to make any prompt military or political response to the intelligence it received, as this information would have been weeks out of date by the time it reached the capital. For these reasons, it was up to the province's governor-general to decide whether to take immediate action on the basis of the information obtained or to deploy a special messenger to consult Istanbul about the required course of action. It was vital to react immediately to military intelligence, especially during times of war. For this reason, when the majority of governor-generals and governors in the Balkans left their provinces to sail with the navy during the Ottoman-Venetian War, Vizier Hüseyin Pasha was appointed as commander-in-chief (*serdar*) and given the responsibility of coordinating the region's defense.[83] Because the pasha bore sole responsibility for this, he needed to have all the latest information at his fingertips so that he could make suitable preparations and act quickly in case of an attack. For this reason, Istanbul issued a decree to all the governors who remained in their posts, telling them to send Hüseyin Pasha, and not Istanbul, any intelligence they had obtained.[84]

A third factor worth mentioning is the high cost of sending news via special messenger. It was for this pecuniary reason that King Philip II of Spain asked his men to use regular messengers, to cut back on expenses.[85] In the same vein, governors were requested to take greater care when using the central postal organization (the so-called *menzil* system) and not to use messengers for their own private business or for unimportant news.[86] A "decree on messengers" (*ulak hükmü*) issued regarding this subject curtailed governors' authority to call for messengers and bestowed this privilege on governor-generals alone.[87]

The fourth reason why the central administration kept a lax hold on provincial outposts was the lack of resident Ottoman ambassadors abroad until the late eighteenth century. I have already observed that diplomacy and spying were intertwined; such ambassadors gathered intelligence in foreign capitals through their spies and informants and conveyed this information to the central authority. The Ottomans, however, lacked a diplomatic network to fulfill this duty, and the task of bridging this gap fell to borderland administrators and commanders.

The fifth and most important aspect of this decentralized system was that it enabled speculative and superfluous information to be filtered and, where deemed appropriate, discarded. In the sixteenth century, centralized bureaucracies were just starting to be established, which meant there were not many clerks working for the chancery. Since the state lacked the staff to cope with an avalanche of information, it could well have been overwhelmed by a flood of information—as Parker claims happened to Philip II[88]—and paralyzed as a result. This is where provincial administrators stepped in and used their experience and local connections to verify the information passed on to them, analyzing it in political and military terms, and prioritizing it as required. In short, by sifting accurate information from false information and spreading the responsibility for intelligence-gathering across the imperial administration, the Ottomans gained the capability to react swiftly and disburdened a centralized bureaucracy that was still in its infancy.

That said, we should pause here and acknowledge that Istanbul did not completely withdraw from all administrative matters. There were many instances of civil servants in the provinces being asked to send Istanbul the prisoners of war they had captured, in order that they could be interrogated.[89] Members of the Imperial Council, the highest decision-making mechanism in the Ottoman Empire, attended these interrogations in person.[90] What determined whether such a bigwig would attend was the nature of the information sought from the captive. For example, in 1572 Istanbul commanded the governor of Scutari to send the spies he had captured to Serdar Hüseyin Pasha rather than to the capital,[91] the reason being the nature of the information such captives would be able to provide. The information to be obtained from these prisoners concerned the location, condition, and strength of the Allied Christian fleet commanded by Habsburg Prince Don Juan. It would take weeks for this intelligence to be sent to Istanbul, and by the time the orders from the Council had arrived back on the Adriatic coast, the information would no longer be current anyway. Another order sent to all governors, judges, and castle wardens along the Ottoman coast up to Ioannina made a distinction between intelligence regarding corsairs and intelligence on enemy fleets; in the first case, intelligence should be conveyed to a marshal sent by Istanbul, while information in the second category, which was more important, needed to be communicated to the capital immediately (*ber-vech-i isti'cal*) via private messenger.[92] Another decree noted that, of the five infidels captured by one Şaban Reis, none had any information to share, so he should send their statements to Istanbul instead of delivering them in person.[93]

It appears that the central administration generally settled for the role of coordinator and auditor. Many of the records in the Registers of Important Affairs use expressions such as "the information you provided has been received"[94] or "I have understood the information,"[95] pointing to intelligence received from the provinces while encouraging provincial governors to continue gathering intelligence and making the necessary military preparations based on the intelligence received.[96] Besides sharing intelligence received via other means with the provincial authorities,[97] the central administration also took it upon itself to compare intelligence obtained from less trustworthy sources (e.g., other countries) with that received from its own provincial governors.[98] Sometimes, authorities in the provinces would be instructed to perform a specific intelligence task or told to use a particular spy.[99] It was not unheard of for the capital to dispatch an official to a province to gather information. On the very eve of the Maltese campaign and the Ottoman-Austrian war, a decree was sent to all governors, judges, and castle wardens, informing them that an official would be dispatched to ascertain whether enemy fleets were active near Ottoman shores.[100] News concerning corsair ships should be sent to Istanbul using the same official.[101]

In conclusion, it is clear that Istanbul wanted provincial administrators to take the initiative when collecting intelligence. When provincial governors were derelict in this duty, the tone of the decrees sent from the capital became sterner.[102] These orders contained scathing remarks, accusing officials of negligence (*sû'-yı tedbîr ve ihmâl ü müsâhele*) and lax behavior (*gaflet*) and threatening them with dismissal (*'azl*) and heavy punishment (*eşedd-i ikâb*), even politely insinuating execution.[103]

In the provinces, it was not just high-ranking officials such as governor-generals, governors, and judges who were ascribed duties related to intelligence;[104] many local authorities such as castle wardens[105] and regiment commanders (*alaybeyi*),[106] as well as the commander of corsairs and naval troops in Vlorë (*Avlonya Azap Ağası ve Gönüllü Levend Reisleri Kapudanı*),[107] were expected to gather intelligence through spies and to inform the capital about the "conduct and current state of the enemy."

Spying was also one of the duties of Christian *voynuk*s[108] and *martolos*,[109] who served in army units stationed in border regions during the centuries of Ottoman expansion in the Balkans. By the sixteenth century, *voynuk*s and *martolos* were no longer serving on the frontlines, but military units stationed in border areas were still expected to gather intelligence. These troops would raid enemy territory on reconnaissance missions and return with captives who are referred to in documents of the period as *dil*s, that is, "tongues." In 1572, the governor of Ohri sent two men called İbrahim and Pervane into enemy territory; they were supposed to return with "*dil*s and captives."[110] A year later, Şahin Agha, a cavalry agha from Székesfehérvár, and Sefer, a *mutasarrıf* with *timar* land worth eight thousand *akçe*s, killed enemy soldiers they came across while returning from capturing *dil*s: "We set out to capture *dil*s, and running into infidel soldiers, we destroyed their weaponry and cut off their heads."[111] It is worth noting here that the expression *dil almak*, referring to taking captives, was also synonymous with receiving news, as captive prisoners were the source of the latest news. Phrases with a similar double meaning also exist in other languages: *tomar lengua* (Spanish), *prendere/tuor/pigliare lingua* (Italian/Venetian), *prendre langue* (French), and *zeban averden* (Persian).

As we have seen, large numbers were not needed to undertake reconnaissance missions. When a unit under the command of a cavalryman Süleyman, the lieutenant of the Akkerman governor, captured eight enemy soldiers, the unit killed five and spared the lives of the other three for interrogation purposes.[112] The killing of five prisoners, despite their potential material value, tells us that Süleyman's reconnaissance expedition felt itself to be under threat. The year before, the Ottoman administration ordered the governors of Kilis and Herzegovina, who were preparing to launch a joint attack on Venetian territory in collaboration with Crimean Tatars, to send competent spies to those lands to see whether the enemy were aware that they were going to be attacked and learn whether they had enough weapons and cavalryman.[113]

The *akıncı* (raider) troops, who were constantly launching attacks on enemy regions in the Balkans and Central Europe, were required to possess extensive knowledge regarding the state of the enemy before they undertook such attacks. They shared the information they obtained from their spies with governor-generals and Istanbul.[114] Although the majority of *akıncı*s were of Turkish origin, they had a good command of local customs and languages because they came from families who were long established in border areas. For example, famous Ottoman traveler Evliya Çelebi describes how the veterans in the fortress of Nova "all spoke Bosnian and Serbian and Latin, and many were fluent in Albanian."[115]

It goes without saying that reconnaissance operations conducted by border troops with the aim of gathering intelligence were perfect opportunities for those seeking promotion; the Ottomans were known for consistently rewarding successful military operations. A soldier by the name of Mustafa, who was a subordinate of the Şahin Agha mentioned previously and who had a wage of eight *akçe*, was rewarded with a fiefdom for his usefulness.[116] Mehmed had previously had his fiefdom in Smederevo province taken away from him yet had in his possession a decree promising him land in Timişoara. However, on the recommendation of Mustafa Bey, governor of Vidin, he was rewarded with an even more valuable *timar* than that allocated to him in the decree, since he had slain enemy soldiers and captured *dil*s.[117] Our final example is another Mehmed, who was bereft of *timar* land in the province of Silistra but who was given a bonus for capturing a *dil* who was an armored enemy soldier.[118]

Border troops around the Mediterranean were similarly relied upon for their intelligence-gathering capabilities. The empires of the era had limited regular navies, so central authorities did not shy away from employing adventure-seeking irregular divisions, including corsairs and pirates. Ottoman corsairs such as Hayreddin Barbarossa, Uluc Ali, and Turgud were vitally important when it came to the Empire's policies with regard to the Mediterranean. They assumed many different military and political duties throughout the sixteenth century, both because they knew the sea and coastlines very well and because they had good connections in the Western Mediterranean.[119]

What Istanbul expected more than anything else from these corsairs was gathering intelligence. Their actions were sometimes perceived as banditry, which caused diplomatic problems,[120] but the fact that these corsairs were engaged in such activities on behalf of a state lent them legitimacy. This is precisely why, when their ships were sunk by the Venetians, they told Sokollu Mehmed Pasha that they were on a voyage for intelligence-gathering purposes, not for piracy—they wanted the state to look after them because they were spying on its behalf. The Venetian *bailo* also seemed to recognize the distinction between illegitimate piracy and legitimate spying. Instead of accusing the intelligence-gathering Ottoman corsairs of being bandits, he chose to deny that Venice sunk their ships in the first place.[121]

In 1562, Süleyman the Magnificent is said to have sent Uluc Ali with a fleet of three galiots to the Western Mediterranean to ascertain whether the Habsburgs were preparing an armada.[122] In 1589, a shipmaster by the name of Yusuf was rewarded with a five *akçe* increase for sailing in his galiot from Navarino to infidel regions and then returning to Tripolitania with the useful *dil*s he had captured.[123]

These examples are from the Western Mediterranean, but such corsairs were also active along the Adriatic coast.[124] In 1566, when a Venetian frigate transporting letters was captured by corsairs, the Venetians once again realized the true extent of the danger corsairs posed.[125] In 1572, the governor of Elbasan sent captains Memi and Şaban to "sail out to sea with two galiots and return with captured *dil*s."[126] A galiot captured by a volunteer captain called Cafer was on its way to join the Christian fleet with two Ottoman *dil*s on board; Cafer rescued the *dil*s and killed the enemy sailors.[127] Fast and agile corsair ships could sometimes pass right under the enemy's nose; in 1576, for example, corsairs aboard a galleon and a galiot had the temerity to gather intelligence in the waters off the Calabrian shore.[128] Finally, as I have stated in a previous article,[129] Kara Hoca, the head of the Ottoman corsairs in the Adriatic, undertook many successful intelligence operations during the Ottoman-Venetian War.[130]

Doing business with corsairs undoubtedly caused certain problems. Archival documents clearly reveal the extent of issues that emerged between Istanbul and corsairs who were constantly overstepping boundaries.[131] A good example of how intertwined piracy, marauding, and spying were can be found in the arrest of three men working for Hayreddin Barbarossa—Şaban, Yusuf, and Köse—by the governor of Lepanto. Istanbul commanded the governor to immediately release these captains, who were returning with valuable *dil*s on board.[132] It is not surprising that reconnaissance missions by corsairs were more important still in the Western Mediterranean, which was outside the capital's sphere of influence.[133] A good portion of these corsairs were Christian converts,[134] and they knew the Italian, Spanish, and French coastlines like the back of their hands; their topographical knowledge was so impressive that they won the praise of famous admirals, including Gianandrea Doria.[135]

The Ottomans were dependent on collaboration with local powers on the "forgotten frontier"[136] of the Western Mediterranean, just as they required assistance in the Indian Ocean. The region lay outside of their sphere of influence; without French or North African ports, they could not send their navy further than Sicily. As a result of these logistical limitations, the governor-generals of the three North African provinces of Algeria, Tripolitania, and Tunisia were able to take the initiative without Istanbul breathing down their necks.[137] The harbors of these three provinces, which lived off piracy, were home to corsairs, slaves, merchants, ransomers, and all manner of adventure seekers, who brought with them the latest information from every corner of the Mediterranean. As well as serving as intermediaries in the relationship between Istanbul, Morocco, France, and the Moriscos, these North African provinces also established their own intelligence network. In keeping with the flexibility and pragmatism to which Gábor Ágoston refers,[138] the capital was aware of its limitations, so in the orders it sent,[139] it settled for simply asking governor-generals to gather intelligence; however, it also knew how to chastise them when they could not fulfill this duty.[140]

These governor-generals knew well how to take advantage of North Africa's geographical proximity to Europe and of its commercial connections to Christian ports. For this reason, they were not prepared to settle for news that found its way to them indirectly. They went as far as dispatching spies to

Habsburg territories,[141] sending corsair ships on reconnaissance missions,[142] holding secret meetings with Habsburg soldiers,[143] and interrogating captured slaves.[144] In this way, they managed to send regular updates to Istanbul about the latest developments in the Mediterranean,[145] the Habsburgs' military preparations, and the location of their fleets.[146] A decree sent to Hasan Pasha, governor-general of Algeria, indicates how seriously Istanbul took the information arriving from North Africa. According to the document, the reason why the Ottoman navy was being sent to the Western Mediterranean—it would besiege Malta in 1565—was Hasan Pasha's reports on the Habsburgs' military preparations.[147]

SPIES ON THE PAYROLL

In this decentralized and household-based system, the central administration played an important role in two additional areas besides regulation: payment and the postal system.

Although we do not know anything about how much these spies were paid by local authorities and by the Ottoman grandees to whose entourage they belonged, we do have some information about the payments made by the central government. It was an Ottoman tradition to give *timar* fiefdoms as a reward to those who proved useful in military expeditions. The criteria for competence also included spying. Many individuals who brought news from the enemy were rewarded with new *timar*s,[148] and sometimes even *zeamet* (a more lucrative type of *timar*, with an annual income of between twenty thousand and one hundred thousand *akçes*).[149] Those who previously possessed *timar*s but who were later divested of them could be reinstated to their duties if they provided the authorities with important information.[150] Additionally, the Registers of Important Affairs contain many records showing that soldiers who captured enemy spies or who brought intelligence were rewarded with raises.[151] Such raises included upgrading *timar* land to *zeamet*.[152]

Timar rewards were usually given to people who gathered intelligence in the field of battle, that is, through reconnaissance and *dil*-capturing missions. Clearly, this method of remittance would not have been suitable for spies working in the Mediterranean and undertaking long journeys abroad.

As is manifest in the phrase "payrolled spies" (*ulufeli casuslar*)[153] that we find in the Ottoman sources, in addition to indirect methods of payment such as *timar*, cash wages, called *ulûfe*, were also given. Palace officials who were already being paid wages might also be asked to conduct spying activities. Other spies were rewarded for their intelligence-gathering directly from the coffers of the palace.

From a payment logbook detailing expenditure by the palace between 1503 and 1527, it is clear that spies were being paid in cash.[154] According to this early record kept in Persian, payments were made to 266 individuals during the nine years between H. 909 and 917, as found in table 4.1.

The patrons of many of the spies are not actually stated, but the patrons who are named are shown in table 4.2.

The princes at the top of this chart were the same grandees who sent the greatest number of men to capture *dil*s (*zebân âverden*). Nine out of the forty-three men were working for Ahmed, three for Selim, and two for Korkud; Osman Çelebi, son of the late Prince Alem Şah, also had ten men who captured *dil*s on his behalf. Karagöz Pasha, the governor-general of Anatolia, who often sent spies abroad, employed only one person to capture *dil*s; this number increases, however, when we factor in the men working for the governors

TABLE 4.1. Ottoman spies listed in a payment logbook

H. 909 / M. 1503–1504	23 spies
H. 910 / M. 1504–1505	26 spies
H. 911 / M. 1505–1506	27 spies
H. 912 / M. 1506–1507	29 spies
H. 913 / M. 1507–1508	79 spies
H. 914 / M. 1508–1509	43 spies
H. 915 / M. 1509–1510	20 spies
H. 916 / M. 1510–1511	13 spies
H. 917 / M. 1511–1512	6 spies
Total	266 spies

TABLE 4.2. Ottoman spy controllers

Prince Ahmed	27 spies
Governor-general of Anatolia, Karagöz Pasha	17 spies
Governor of Kayseri	13 spies
Prince Selim	5 spies
Prince Şehinşah	5 spies
Governor of Sivas	1 spy
Governor of Niğde	1 spy
Governor of Elbasan	1 spy
Governor of Vidin	1 spy
Şahruh b. Alaüddevle	1 spy
Sinan Bey, *Zaim* (Commander)* of Karahisar	1 spy
Süleyman Bey, *Zaim* (Commander) of Toro	1 spy

*Here, *zaim* denotes the commander of a region who was awarded a zeamet in exchange for his services.

of Manisa, Karahisar, and Sultanönü, all of whom were subordinate to the governor-general of Anatolia.

Sometimes, the location where the spies gathered intelligence was also stated in the payment record. According to this, eight spies brought information from Hungary, four from Iran, three from Aleppo, and two from the province of Rum (in and around Sivas, near the border with the Safavids). However, out of a sample of 266 spies, this information is not sufficient for any meaningful analysis.

When we consider that Prince Ahmed served as the governor of Amasya and Trabzon, and Prince Şehinşah was the governor of Konya, and taking into account the spies working for the Anatolian governor-general, the governors under him, and the *zaim*s, it is clear that between 1503 and 1512, Ottoman intelligence was more concerned with the eastern frontier—that is, the increasing threat from the Safavids—than with the western frontier. The total number of spies working for the governors of Vidin and Elbasan, plus the additional eight men who brought intelligence from Hungary, is lower than the number of spies working in the east of the Empire. The majority of intelligence operations in the West involved capturing *dil*s. Out of the forty-three people who returned with captives from enemy lands, fourteen were working in the Balkans, namely for the governors of Bosnia (four), Euboea (three), Semendire (three), Vidin (one), and Vlorë (one), and the *zaim* of Zvornik (two).

In the case of many of the spies mentioned in the records, job descriptions are not given; these must have been intelligence operatives who provided information in exchange for payment and who had no other duties within the Ottoman military and administrative system. Of those with stated job titles, eighteen were cavalrymen in the central army (*gureba*), fifteen were *timar*-owning cavalrymen, five were palace marshals, one was a cavalryman with a *zeamet* (*sipah zaim*), one was the keeper of the imperial standard (*mir-i alem*), and one was a castle guard (*an merdân-ı kal'a*).[155] There were also two sheikhs and a Christian captain called Gioan, who transported spies on his ship (*Cuvân Efrencî, re'îs-i gebr ki câsûsi âverd*).[156] Only eight of the spies were non-Muslims: four brought information from Hungary, and one was working on behalf of the governor of Vidin.

Spies' salaries appear to have been quite standardized. The payment was often 1,000 *akçe*s, although forty-three people were paid half that amount. The highest wage was paid to a sheikh working for Prince Ahmed in the İsfendiyar region, who earned 3,000 *akçe*s.[157] This was followed by four people paid 2,000 *akçe*s each, one of them being a member of the *ebnâ-i sipâhiyân*, the most important of the six cavalry divisions of the central army (*Altı Bölük Halkı*).[158] Another, a man working for Sultan Ahmed, was tasked with both spying and capturing *dil*s (*be-câsûsî firistâde ve zebân âverd*),[159] and the other was a keeper of the imperial standard. One spy received 1,500 *akçe*s, while the smallest amounts paid per person were 300 *akçe*s for two individuals and 200 *akçe*s for four. Considering that, in 1490, the average daily wage for a skilled worker was 7.7 *akçe*s and the average daily wage for an unskilled worker was 4.7 *akçe*s,[160] 1,000 *akçe*s was not an insignificant amount of money.

Those given the job of capturing *dil*s were paid smaller amounts of money. Twenty-seven out of forty-three were paid 500 *akçe*s, eight 1,000 *akçe*s, and just two 2,000 *akçe*s, one of the latter being the man working for Sultan Ahmed mentioned previously, who functioned as a spy as well as capturing *dil*s. Two people were renumerated with a relatively low fee of 200 *akçe*s; in contrast, one person was paid a record-breaking 5,000 *akçe*s. However, the reason for this generosity was probably not the nature of the intelligence provided but rather the fact that the spy was a member of the Komnenos family, a Greek aristocratic dynasty who had once ruled the Byzantine Empire between 1081 and 1185 and the Empire of Trebizond between 1204 and 1461. A note next to the name of Hüseyin Bey, who was one of the comrades (*nöker*s) of the Ottoman governor of Trebizond and served as a cavalryman in the prestigious regiment of *ser-ebnâ-i sipâhiyân*, refers to him as "the elder son of the former Emperor of Trebizond (*ser-veled-i Tekfur-ı köhne-i Trabzon*)."[161] In fact, Byzantine aristocrats of comparable status received similarly high payments, without providing any services at all. For example, a person appearing in the records as "Manol b. Tekfur-ı Mora,"[162] who was most likely the son of Demetrios Palaiologos II, the last coprince of Morea who defected to the Ottoman side, received regular payments from the palace (*der-cemâ'at-i müşâhere-horân*); he was paid a sum of 5,000 *akçe*s on three separate occasions.[163] After Manol's death in 1507, his children were gifted with *hilat*s (an expensive ceremonial kaftan) as a condolence offering,[164] and his son Yanol was paid 3,000 *akçe*s on three occasions.[165]

In addition to receiving a cash payment, each spy was rewarded with a certain amount of cloth. This was usually an embroidered cloth known as *câme-i münakkaş-ı Bursa* (Bursa-made embroidered fabric); sometimes, however, fabrics of other types and colors were given instead, including *câme-i mîrâhûrî-i kemhâ-i kırmızı, câme-i benek-i Bursa, câme-i pûrî, câme-i rişte-i Bursa, câme an kadîfe-i rişte-i Bursa*, and *câmehâ-i mîrâhûrî an kadîfe-i alaca-i Bursa*. One person was paid an additional 200 *akçe*s so he could purchase a beast of burden (*be-cihet-i bahâ-i bârgîr*),[166] while another was paid the same "as was the custom with treasurers and marshals" (*âdet-i hazînedârî ve çavuşî*).[167]

Those who captured dils were rewarded in the same manner, receiving gifts of cloth, particularly the fabric known as *câme-i münakkaş*, as well as other types, including *câme-i çatma-i Bursa* and Peshwari fabric. One person was paid 200 *akçe*s in travel expenses (*be-cihet-i harc-ı râh hem-râh-ı mezkûr*).[168]

While these figures are important in showing that the imperial palace had a budget set aside for spying activities, the fact that such payments appear under different headings points to the lack of a central, coordinating institution. For example, one spy was paid alongside apprentice treasury clerks, under the heading "Şakirdân-ı Kâtibân-ı Hızâne-i 'Âmire."[169]

These records are not the only proof we have of cash payments. It would obviously have been impossible to entice spies and informants in Europe and the Western Mediterranean using indirect methods of payment, such as the allocation of rent-generating land. One of the conspirators in the Cisneros trial, which was covered at length in chapter 2, claimed that an Ottoman spy in Sicily offered him a vast sum of money.[170] The *dhimmi*[171] who convinced the people of Crimea to surrender without a fight was awarded a salary of 30 *akçes* per day from the revenue of the island of Cyprus.[172] The magnitude of this payment becomes clear when we compare it with the daily wages of builders in Istanbul in 1573 (unskilled: 5.8 *akçes* per day, 1,800 *akçes* per annum; skilled: 9.4 *akçes* per day, on average 2,900 *akçes* per annum);[173] it should help to point out that an income of 10,950 *akçes* per year was equivalent to the average yearly income of a cavalryman with *timar* land.

Just as those gathering intelligence on the Persian border were rewarded with *timar* land, those doing the same in the Mediterranean could be recompensed with salaried jobs in the shipyard and the navy. For example, İlyas Reis (nicknamed "the Hungarian captain"), who brought *dil*s in 1570, was given the job of captain with a salary of 10 *akçes* per day.[174] Four years later, Hasan, who was both the commander of corsairs and naval troops in Vlorë (with a daily wage of 100 *akçes*), used his galiot three times during the siege of La Goulette to capture *dil*s from amongst the infidels. As a reward, he asked to be made an imperial (*hassa*) captain, and his request was accepted.[175] In 1581, Musa, who brought news from Spain, was rewarded with the post of caulker at the Imperial Shipyard.[176] Captains who brought intelligence from the Western Mediterranean were also rewarded with salary increases.[177] Corsairs were sometimes rewarded with *timar* land in exchange for performing intelligence-related activities.[178] In such cases, too, a raise could mean switching from one method of payment to another. For instance, in 1573, a lieutenant (*mutasarrıf*) called Mustafa, who worked for a wage of 8 *akçes* as a cavalryman at Székesfehérvár castle, was awarded with a *timar*.[179] Finally, we should add that in the so-called *salyaneli* provinces, where the *timar* system was not practiced and the Ottoman administration collected a certain amount of tax from the regional treasury instead, such salaried positions were ready and waiting for successful spies. Our Mustafa, for instance, who captured useful *dil*s during the Ottoman-Venetian War, was rewarded with a position in the 124th division of the Egyptian riflemen, at a salary of nine *akçes* per day, which was paid from tax revenues.[180]

Those who brought critically important news were sometimes honored with crucial administrative positions. For example, Koca Sinan Pasha's steward, who brought the news of the fall of La Goulette, was granted the post of the governor of Lesbos.[181] Around the same time, Kaid Mehmed, who conveyed news from Algiers, was bestowed with the district of Cherchell, which boasted an annual income of 200,000 *akçes*.[182] Such postings had nothing to do with the nature of the news delivered; bad news was equally well recompensed. Having converted to Islam, a Granadian who delivered the news that the siege of Malta had failed was given the post of imperial captain, with a daily wage of 15 *akçes*.[183]

As part of the Ottoman Empire's policy of *istimalet* (reconciliation), individuals who aided the Ottomans during times of siege were exempt from paying certain taxes. For example, a convert by the name of Mehmed, who convinced the people of Kyrenia to hand over the fortress to the Ottomans "without battle" and delivered the keys to the castle to the Ottomans himself, was exempt from the taxes known as *tekalif-i örfiyye* and *avarız-ı divaniyye*.[184]

THE MENZIL SYSTEM

The *menzil* (stopping-points) system was one of the things that in the sixteenth century the Istanbul regime regarded as vitally important. *Menzilhane*s (stopping-point facilities), which were intended to feed the army as well as make communications easier, were administered directly by the central government.[185] In the race toward centralization, Istanbul seems to have gone further than Madrid with this tactic, as the latter was forced to rely on private enterprise to meet this need. There are two main reasons for the empires' different choices. First, unlike the Ottoman Empire, which was a unified whole, Habsburg-owned lands were scattered across Europe. When delivering letters from one Habsburg region to the next, one had to pass through land belonging to other countries, starting with France, which meant that Habsburg messengers could not be imperial officials. Second, it is impossible for a country that has resident ambassadors abroad to rely solely on its own postal system to deliver letters; for example, to communicate with Europe, the Ottomans used the Venetian postal system.

Until the sixteenth century, the Ottoman Empire did not have an organized postal system. Messengers, known as *ulak*s, would carry a special document called an *ulak hükmü* (messenger license) and could seize the horse of anyone they liked. Their food and accommodation were also the responsibilities of the local population. A report in the Topkapı Palace Archives clearly shows how people in possession of a messenger license took advantage of people by having the public provide them and their horse with food at every opportunity and claiming horses without the owner's permission.[186] According to Lütfi Pasha, who was the greatest opponent of this system, even people in infidel lands did not exploit others in this way; Sultan Selim I had more complaints about it than anyone. He is even reputed to have said, "Thanks to this *ulak* cruelty, there will be no rest for us, neither in this world nor the next. In the eyes of God we are very guilty in this regard."[187] The fact that everyone, from governors to pashas, was issuing needless *ulak* licenses for anyone in their entourage made the system ripe for misuse. *Ulak* license-holders would confiscate the horse of anyone they happened to come across and beat the owner up if he did not surrender his horse. What's more, they often left the horse to die after they were done with riding it and moved on to the next victim, which exasperated the local populace. The grand vizier, the man at the very apex of the governmental hierarchy,

lashed out at those members of the Ottoman administration who were allowing such abuses to happen. He remarked, "It seems that when it comes to the
cruelty of *ulak*s, the Ottomans are copying the Mongolians."[188] He even went
so far as to say, "The laments of the victimized owners of horses taken by *ulak*s
manifested themselves to the sultan through his son Cihangir,"[189] referring to
the death of Süleyman the Magnificent's favorite son, Cihangir, which he associated with the abuse of the *ulak* system.[190]

Lütfi Pasha, who would articulate his criticisms in years to come, had
designed a network of *menzil*s. These stopover locations were set up at intervals of three to eighteen hours, the distance between them depending on
topographical conditions.[191] The system aimed at faster delivery of letters, as
horses would be waiting for messengers at the stopover points. The money
required for these facilities would be provided by the local community, dubbed
the *menzilkeş*, who would undertake hard labor in lieu of paying *avarız* and
bedel-i nüzul taxes; messengers would pay the *menzil*-keepers for the horses
they used. In this way, some of the burden on the locals would be alleviated.
The system remained functional for a long time, attesting to its success at some
level; all the same, we do come across records attesting to abuses.[192]

Civil servants such as the *menzil* custodian (*menzil emini*), *menzil* ser-
geant (*menzil kethüdası*), and barn lieutenant (*ahur kethüdası*) worked at these
stopover locations, and it was the local judge's responsibility to make sure they
were doing their jobs properly. Unlike its Habsburg counterpart, this postal
system could not be used by the public. The horses kept at *menzil*s were to be
deployed only for government purposes, and it was strictly forbidden for local
notables to use the *menzil* system for their private business.[193]

Letters which needed to be delivered as soon as possible because they concerned important governmental issues (*mühim ve müsta'cel husus*)[194] could not
be entrusted to messengers traveling between two *menzil*s; these were delivered from Istanbul right up to the door of the recipient by especially assigned
messengers "summoned on private orders."[195] Although it was forbidden for
messengers without written orders to pick up horses from *menzil*s, messengers
coming from frontier locations were exempt from this ban.[196]

The *menzil* system helped the Ottomans solve their internal communication problem, but it was of no use when it came to correspondence with
Europe. So, how did Istanbul communicate with European rulers or with intelligence officers working outside of the boundaries of the Empire?

Diplomatic correspondence was generally conducted via the foreign
ambassadors in Istanbul, and palace staff of various ranks,[197] such as marshal
(*çavuş*), *müteferrika*,[198] *silahdar* (sword bearer), and *kapıcıbaşı* (head of imperial gatekeepers), as well as interpreters, treasurers, *çeşnigir* (imperial food
tasters), *bölükbaşı* (commander of central army regiments), Janissaries, and
cavalrymen, would be sent as envoys to foreign capitals when important matters needed to be discussed. As Nicolas Vatin states, the letters carried by such
envoys acted as a type of passport and attested to the authority of the bearer.[199]

They did not contain any details of the matter at hand; this would be discussed verbally between the envoy and the foreign ruler.

When it was impossible to send anyone to Europe, the Ottomans were at the mercy of the *bailo*, as the Venetians ran the only regular postal service between Istanbul and Europe. Merchant, prisoner, diplomat,[200] and pasha alike had to entrust their letters to the *bailo*.[201] The Venetians, who were extremely keen on discovering others' secrets, would open the letters they were transporting, give them a good read, and then reseal them before delivering them to their recipients.[202]

Ottoman spies were expected to write intelligence reports for their masters on a regular basis, but we know very little about how these reports reached their addressees. Even those who left Istanbul on a specific mission and returned immediately afterward had to share the information they obtained with Istanbul as soon as they obtained it. The findings of Venetian counterespionage operations revealed that the Ottomans relied upon the Venetian postal system. Ludovico Veggia,[203] who wrote to Cigalazade from Rome, and the Marranos who wrote to David Passi from all corners of Europe (as we explored in detail previously) always used fake names and, trying to dupe the Venetians, endeavored to pass off their writings as nothing but innocent letters.

Another realm not covered by the *menzil* system was the sea. Communication between Istanbul and its overseas provinces in the Maghreb, or with its own navy, was managed through oared galleys.[204] For example, during the siege of Oran (1556) by the governor-general of Algeria, Salih Pasha, Uluc Ali was tasked with delivering the sultan's orders from Istanbul. The pasha had to return to the Eastern Mediterranean at once along with forty galleys.[205] There was no issue when the navy was close by; a lieutenant such as Süleyman in 1573 could deliver the required communiqués.[206] Another method, when communication on sea was not an option, was to send an *ulak* to the nearest port.[207] Sometimes, two messengers were sent, one over the sea and one over land, to ensure that the navy received the necessary instructions.[208]

However, this system was prone to disruptions when the fleet was stationed in the Western Mediterranean, as it was not possible to send messengers beyond the borders of the Ottoman Empire. Communication via galleys was also dangerous if there was an enemy fleet waiting nearby. The siege of Malta is a good example of this. Communication was rendered impossible between Istanbul and the pashas Mustafa and Piyale, who were undertaking a difficult siege in the middle of the Mediterranean; the reason was most likely the Habsburg navy commanded by Don Garcia de Toledo, which was lying in wait in Sicily.[209] As Istanbul became increasingly nervous, Venice once again rushed to the rescue. This old friend, who five years later would find the Ottoman navy breathing down its neck, not only delivered letters from the capital to Piyale and Mustafa but also regularly updated Istanbul about how the siege was proceeding.[210]

OTTOMAN INTELLIGENCE: HOW DID IT PERFORM?

Let us now turn to assess how this patrimonial and decentralized system performed. How successful were the Ottomans compared with their adversaries when it came to keeping on top of political and military developments in Europe?

The prevailing view in studies of intelligence in recent years has been that directly comparing intelligence organizations is methodologically problematic and does not yield the desired results. While this claim was initially proposed with respect to modern intelligence networks, it holds even truer for their sixteenth-century counterparts. Institutionalization was rare in this era, and the historical evidence we have is fragmented. However, it is possible to put forward some claims about the intelligence performance of an Early Modern state.

In his famous article on the Ottomans' grand strategy, Gábor Ágoston demonstrates that the Ottomans did possess the intelligence channels required for a meaningful strategy and a functional foreign policy.[211] The Hungarian historian, though, simply lists these channels and does not proceed to assess the performance of Ottoman intelligence. The aim of this last section is to remedy the gaps in the literature on the subject and to analyze the Ottomans' success at receiving news from the outside world, particularly regarding Europe.

The Ottoman-Venetian War over Cyprus can serve as a case study for such a performance assessment. Faced with a large Christian coalition, headed by the Venetians and the Habsburgs, the Ottoman Empire seems to have come out on top from the perspective of intelligence. For example, seventeen days before the fall of Nicosia, on August 23, 1570, they were able to predict that the enemy fleet stationed on Crete would not advance to Cyprus but retreat when they heard the news of the fall of the castle.[212] A short time before the disaster at Lepanto, in the autumn of 1571, Istanbul had extensive knowledge of the types of ships that the enemy fleet possessed.[213] Two years later, they were able to foresee that the Christian armada would attack Tunis and forewarned the governor-generals of Tunisia and Algeria two months before the attack, on August 12, 1573.[214] Again, during the same war, a Venetian nobleman informed the Ottomans that the Venetians would attack Herceg Novi. Four months later, when the event he had foretold came to pass, the Ottomans were more than prepared: the fortress was packed with ammunition, and five governors were tasked with repelling a possible siege.[215] In short, this timely delivered information meant that the Venetians' "surprise" attack was a fiasco.[216]

At this point, it should be reemphasized that Istanbul had an exceptional status, not just as the capital of a vast empire but also as a center for international diplomacy and commerce.[217] It was also home to many local and foreign communities of different religious and ethnic backgrounds. In short, it was a center of information,[218] receiving regular updates and intelligence from as far afield as the Indian Ocean and China.[219] No European or Mediterranean city had a comparable status, except perhaps Venice. This exceptional status must, to some extent, have made up for the lack of resident ambassadors. The Ottomans might have lacked the ambassadors in Europe whom they needed to manage intelligence operations and send regular news; however, they had at their disposal a vast community of European diplomats, merchants, ransomers, adventurers, and turncoats, all of whom were following the latest developments in Europe.

Another point which must be kept in mind when measuring performance is that gathering *correct* information is not the sole criteria. As is evident from the example of Herceg Novi given previously, the timeliness of information provision was also vital; otherwise, it would not have been possible to give the appropriate political or military response. The Ottomans were also successful in this aspect. As table 4.3 shows, news of important events in Europe, such as war, conquest, deaths, and coronations, did not take too long to reach Istanbul.

When we measure the Ottoman performance in intelligence against the contemporary average, it is clear that the Ottomans were successful. First of all, Ottoman decision-makers received news of many European events before the foreign ambassadors resident in Istanbul did.[220] We do indeed possess the figures needed to carry out a systematic comparison. According to French historian Pierre Sardella's calculations, based on senator Marin Sanudo's *I Diarii*, which sums up in a fifty-eight-volume journal all the correspondence that arrived in Venice between 1496 and 1533, the time required for news from Istanbul to reach Venice was between fifteen and eighty-one days. This wide time window will not mean much to us, so it would be more accurate to use the weighted average instead: thirty-seven days.[221] Extraordinary timeframes such as fifteen days are no doubt impressive, but the Ottomans received news from locations much further afield than Venice in fewer than thirty-seven days. Examples include the information they were sent regarding the Battle of Pavia and the election of Pope Sixtus V, as well as the devastation of the Spanish armada in 1588, which took place quite far north. We should add that, according to Sardella's numbers, communication between Venice and Paris took an average of twelve days, while that between Venice and Valladolid took an average of twenty-nine days. These figures tell us that the Ottoman averages (less than two months for France and less than three months for Spain) were no worse than those of its contemporaries.

We can see that the Ottomans diversified their news sources, particularly during times of war, thereby gaining the possibility of making comparisons. Once again, the best example to use would be the Ottoman-Venetian War, about which thousands of documents can be found in European and Ottoman archives. Even though Istanbul lost the majority of its navy and saw its reign in the Balkans threatened by rebelling Christian subjects encouraged by foreign intelligence services, it still managed to receive news from various sources:[222] General Vizier Hüseyin Pasha; the governor-generals of Rumelia and Buda; and the governors of Elbasan, Delvine, Mora, Ohri, Zaçasna, and Herzegovina, as well as the castle wardens in these areas, immediately relayed to Istanbul the information that had been brought to them by spies, *akıncı* troops, and

TABLE 4.3. The speed of European news arriving at the Ottoman Empire

Event	Date	Location	Date news arrived in Istanbul	Source	Time it took for news to reach Istanbul
Battle of Pavia	February 25, 1525	Pavia, Northern Italy	March 26/29, 1525[265]	Venetian *bailo*	Twenty-nine or thirty-two days
Death of Don Carlos, Philip II's son	July 24, 1568	Madrid	Already known by October 19, 1568	Unknown	Less than three months
Death of Isabelle de Valois, Queen of Spain	October 3, 1568	Madrid	Known days before January 7, 1569[266]	Unknown	Three months
Battle of Jarnac	March 13, 1569	Jarnac, France	May 11, 1569[267]	Venetian *bailo*, who learned it from a letter dated April 2	Less than two months
Battle of La Roche-l'Abeille	June 25, 1569	La Roche-l'Abeille, France	A few days before August 22, 1569[268]	Rumor: "un bruyt partout"	Less than two months
Battle of Lepanto	October 7, 1571	Patras Bay, Ionian Sea	October 24, 1571[269]	Letter from Uluc Ali Pasha	Seventeen days
Battle of Alacantara	August 25, 1580	Lisbon	October 17/20, 1580[270]	October 17: French ambassador October 20: Messenger from Ragusa	Less than two months
Sixtus V's Election as Pope	April 24, 1585	Rome	Known by May 31, 1585[271]	Private messengers from Ragusa, "corrieri espressi"	About a month
The Defeat of the Spanish Armada	August 8, 1588	Off the coast of Gravelines, Flanders	Before September 9, 1588[272]	Three different channels: Alvaro Mendes, ambassador of Ragusa, British ambassador	About a month
Murder of Duke of Guise, Henry, leader of the Catholic League	December 23, 1588	Paris	Before March 10, 1589[273]	As the veracity of the information could not be ascertained, the grand admiral asked the *bailo* to verify	More than three months
Assassination of the French King Henry III	August 1, 1589	Saint Cloud, Paris	Before September 18, 1589[274]	An ulak who reached Istanbul in 17 days from Ragusa	Seven weeks
Battle of Ivry	March 14, 1590	Ivry, France	The week before May 12, 1590[275]	A private messenger bringing a letter dated April 12, 1590 from Ragusa (messo espedito in diligenza)	Approximately two months

corsairs working on the frontiers. While the Ottoman navy gathered its own intelligence, the North African provinces reported on the military preparations of the Christian fleet on the Italian coast. King Charles IX of France sent letters to Istanbul detailing military and political developments, while his ambassador François de Noailles generously shared the information at his disposal with the Ottomans.[223] Ragusa was also constantly passing on to Istanbul news that its spies in Europe were bringing;[224] according to a Habsburg spy, a private messenger came to Istanbul weekly to bring information regarding the advance of the Christian fleet.[225] Additionally, the Ottomans were able to get information from captured *dil*s, Ottoman merchants trading in Europe, and Muslim prisoners released from captivity. Finally, we should note that a large number of spies belonging to the entourages of various grandees were constantly active.[226] They not only delivered news but also came up with suggestions for undercover operations. Fed by such a wellspring of information, the government settled for assiduously comparing the information brought to it and warning its civil servants regarding any discrepancies, that is, playing the part of inspector.[227]

Meetings between Ottoman pashas and European envoys clearly show how up-to-date the Ottomans were with the latest political and military developments. This leads to the conclusion that spy patrons such as Rüstem,[228] Sokollu Mehmed,[229] Sivayuş,[230] Koca Sinan,[231] and Uluc Ali[232] did not settle for just demanding and collecting information. They meticulously analyzed the information brought to them by European envoys,[233] placed it within a framework,[234] corrected it if necessary,[235] and even falsified it;[236] they were also not averse to asking for additional information regarding specific events.[237] They evidently followed political and military developments closely, including the Schmalkalden War,[238] the fate of the Polish throne,[239] the French Wars of Religion,[240] the Dutch Revolt,[241] the competition between the Habsburgs and the Valois,[242] interdynastic marriages in Europe,[243] and diplomatic relations.[244] Furthermore, they had extensive knowledge about military preparations and the state of fortifications in the Western Mediterranean.[245] Finally, we should add that Ottoman decision-makers and spymasters were able to filter out many incorrect pieces of information that arrived in Istanbul and successfully distinguished between rumor and reliable knowledge. It could not have been for nothing that an expert like the Venetian *bailo* described them as "skilled people" (*persone prattiche*) and praised their intelligence capabilities.[246]

These pashas sometimes asked the ambassadors surprisingly simple questions: "Where is Rome?"[247] "Are Florence and Ferrera on the coast?"[248] "Does Granada have a port?"[249] "Where is Cadiz, and to which ruler does it belong?"[250] "Does the Pope own any land near Puglia?"[251] "What is the German (i.e., imperial) diet?"[252] "How much is a doubloon[253] worth?"[254] "When did the Venetians and the Habsburgs sign a peace agreement?"[255] Some of these questions might have been asked with the genuine intention of eliciting information. Moses Benveniste, who inquired of Giovanni Margliani about the value of the doubloon—which was more commonly used in Spain and South America—also asked the ambassador to give him ten doubloons, as the sultan wanted to see them with his own eyes and weigh them. It is also understandable that Rüstem Pasha might not have remembered the exact date of a peace agreement signed twenty-two years earlier. However, it is difficult to imagine grand viziers such as Sokollu Mehmed Pasha and Köprülü Fazıl Ahmed Pasha lacking the simplest of geographical knowledge; after all, for many years they had administered a vast empire stretching from North Africa to Crimea, and from Buda to Yemen. Furthermore, even if they did lack this knowledge, there was no reason for them to ask such questions in the presence of foreign envoys, toward whom they might end up feeling both indebted and embarrassed. Istanbul was filled with Christians, Jews, and converts who knew those regions like the back of their hands and who hailed from all corners of the Mediterranean. The only reason for the pashas to ask such simple questions must have been to broach the subject and to ask more specific questions further on or, to be more precise, to play the idiot in order to extract information from the ambassadors.

No contemporary accounts accuse the Ottoman intelligence network of being a failure; on the contrary, there are many admiring references to it. For example, in 1565 a Spanish spy stated that people in Ragusa received information every ten days about what the Habsburg admiral Don Garcia was doing in Messina; they even knew when this admiral washed his face, and here we are talking about a man who commanded the fleet that would force the Ottomans to withdraw from the siege of Malta a few months later! Whatever news they received, they shared straightaway with Istanbul.[256] In 1581, the Austrian ambassador Joachim von Sinzendoff stated that the Ottomans had exact knowledge (*exactissimam cognitionem*) of the secret meetings the emperor held with his closest advisors.[257] Similarly, in 1570, Archduke Carl II lauded the efficiency of Ottoman spies on the Ottoman-Austrian border.[258] The unofficial envoy Margliani, who conducted the Ottoman-Habsburg peace talks in 1581, did not shy away from commenting on how successful Ottoman intelligence was and said in a letter written to Philip II from Lisbon in 1582, "All His Majesty's thoughts are known here just as they are known in Venice" (*si sano a quella porta i pensieri di S. M.ta come si sano anche in Ven.a*). It should not come as a surprise that the Ottomans found out about the duke of Alençon's entrance into Hesingas through the French ambassador.[259] Finally, when the Grand Admiral Cigalazade Yusuf Sinan Pasha anchored off the coast of Messina following his fleet's plunder of the Italian coast, he requested the viceroy of Sicily's permission to see his mother and siblings who resided in the city and said in his letter, "Don't think that I'm sending you him [a Christian slave freed by Yusuf Sinan who was carrying the letter] with the purpose of gathering information, as both you and I know full well that we have a sufficient amount of reliable information brought to us from all around the world."[260]

In short, by devising their own methods, the Ottomans passed the test when it came to espionage and managed to collect reliable and timely intelligence using a variety of sources. This success helped them to draw up comprehensive strategies, to make effective decisions, and to make better use of their limited resources. How, then, can we account for the effectiveness of the

Ottoman intelligence network, given its lack of an institutionalized structure? How were they able to make sensible military and political decisions in the absence of a centralized intelligence agency?

The answer to these questions can be found in the fact that institutions were not the be-all and end-all in a period in which rational bureaucracy had not yet been established and modern states were still in their infancy. In the sixteenth century, the impact of these initial attempts at centralization and institutionalization remained exceedingly limited. In a previous article on Ottoman diplomacy, I argued that an understanding of history that holds the European experience as the sole measure of success should no longer be given credence.[261] In parallel to this view, I add that following exactly the same processes as its European counterparts would not have meant success for Ottoman intelligence, not to mention that even the examples of Venice and the Habsburg Empire were anything but standardized, and improvisation and exceptions to the rule were the norm. It would also serve us well to remember that some experiments ended in disappointment, and important institutions disappeared without leaving a long-lasting tradition behind. For example, the French postal service created during the reign of King Louis XI was not used after his death;[262] similarly, for reasons unknown to us, the position of great spy of the Habsburgs we mentioned earlier lost its importance after the 1620s and became a ceremonial post.[263] As Alain Hugon has stated, such sequences of trial and error (*une suite de avancées et reculs*) do not sit easy with the tele-ological view that history is a constant forward march (*marche en avant vers le progrès*); they stop us from making the mistake of deducing causes from their supposed effect, namely the linear emergence of the modern state.[264]

NOTES

1. Preto, *Servizi Segreti*, ch. 2, 3; Ioanna Iordanou, "What News on the Rialto? The Trade of Information and Early Modern Venice's Centralized Intelligence Organization," *Intelligence and National Security* 31, no. 3 (2015): pp. 1–22.

2. Carnicer and Marcos, *Espías de Felipe II*; Gürkan, "Espionage in the 16th Century Mediterranean," ch. 4; Arndt Brendecke, *Imperium und Empirie: Funktionen des Wissens in der spanischen Kolonialherrschaft* (Köln: Böhlau, 2009).

3. Cornell Fleischer, *Bureaucrat and Intellectual in the Ottoman Empire: The Historian Mustafa Âli (1541–1600)* (Princeton: Princeton University Press, 1986), p. 212.

4. Cornell Fleischer, "Gelibolulu Mustafa Âli Efendi, 1541–1600: A Study in Ottoman Historical Consciousness" (unpublished PhD diss., Princeton University, 1982), 310–40; Fleischer, *Bureaucrat and Intellectual*, pp. 35, 215–17.

5. Fleischer, *Bureaucrat and Intellectual*, p. 218.

6. The word "grandee" is used here rather than "pasha"—the latter implying a Muslim state official—because Jewish and Christian powerbrokers with

no official ties to the state were also among the sponsors of spies, as will be seen later.

7. Metin Kunt, "Royal and Other Households," in *The Ottoman World*, ed. Christine Woodhead (London and New York: Routledge, 2012), p. 103.

8. Kunt, *Sultan's Servants*, pp. 62–67; Metin Kunt, "A Prince Goes Forth (Perchance to Return)," in *Identity and Identity Formation in the Ottoman World: A Volume of Essays in Honour of Norman Itzkowitz*, ed. Baki Tezcan and Karl K. Barbir (Wisconsin: Wisconsin University Press, 2007), pp. 63–71.

9. According to Metin Kunt, although in theory the government of the Ottoman Empire was the responsibility of all those for whom the state provided an income, in practice it consisted of the sultan and his household. Similarly, despite the sultan's private treasury and the state treasury being theoretically separate, Ottoman state budgets were shaped by the income and expenses of palace dwellers, and the sultan's private income was used to fund military and administrative spending. Metin Kunt, "Sultan, Dynasty and State in the Ottoman Empire: Political Institutions in the 16th century," *The Medieval History Journal / Special Issue on Tributary Empires* 6, no. 2 (November 2003): p. 228. Another historian who refers to the blurry line between the Ottoman dynasty and the Ottoman government is Rhoads Murphey, *Exploring Ottoman Sovereignty: Tradition, Image and Practice in the Ottoman Imperial Household, 1400–1800* (London: Continuum, 2008), pp. 149–50.

10. The best example of an Ottoman official who accrued formidable wealth through his political powers is Grand Vizier Rüstem Pasha. At the time of his death, he had amassed a fortune of 155,600,000 *akçe*s (approximately 2.5 million ducats), which outstripped the annual cash income of the Ottoman state (128,608,946 *akçe*s). Semiz Ali Pasha, who held the office of the grand vizier for just four years, had a more modest fortune of 15 million *akçe*s. Baki Tezcan, "Searching for Osman: A Reassessment of the Deposition of Sultan Osman II (r. 1618–1622)" (unpublished PhD diss., Princeton University, 2001), pp. 147–48. One did not necessarily need to be a pasha to get rich; on the fortune accumulated by Ali Efendi, judge of Mecca, see Tezcan, p. 111–12.

11. Kunt, *Sultan's Servants*, p. 51; Metin Kunt, *Sancaktan Eyalete: 1550–1650 Arasında Osmanlı Ümerası ve İl İdaresi* (Istanbul: Boğaziçi Üniversitesi Yayınları, 1978), p. 99.

12. AGS, *E* 1310, fol. 155 (August 7, 1534).

13. Even though the spies mentioned here were concerned with internal intelligence, it is clear that the sultan was referring to the establishment of a parallel network of spies to audit the information provided to him by his grand viziers. Hezarfen Hüseyin Efendi, *Telhîsü'l-Beyân fi Kavânîn-i Âl-i Osmân*, ed. Sevim İlgürel (Ankara: Türk Tarih Kurumu, 1998), p. 179.

14. Ebru Turan, "The Sultan's Favorite: Ibrahim Pasha and the Making of the Ottoman Universal Sovereignty in the Reign of Sultan Suleyman (1516–1526)" (unpublished PhD diss., University of Chicago, 2007); Necipoğlu, "Representation of Power." On İbrahim Pasha, see Hester Donaldson Jenkins, *Ibrahim Pasha, the Grand Vizir of Suleyman the Magnificent* (New York: Columbia University Press, 1911); Feridun M. Emecen, "İbrâhim Paşa, Makbul," *Türkiye Diyanet Vakfı İslam Ansiklopedisi*.

15. AGS, *E* 1311, fol. 40–42 (August 9, 1535), 45–47 (July 15, 1535), 48–51 (July 6, 1535), 60–61 (June 24, 1535), 149. ASV, *CX-ParSec*, reg. 4, cc. 38r–37v (October 7, 1534), 50r (June 23, 1535), 50v (July 12, 1535), 51r (August 8, 1535). De Nicolò was among the jewelers Lorenzo Gritti brought to Istanbul in 1534. AGS, *E* 1311, fol. 23 (May 21, 1534). As will be seen in chapter 5, when they realized that the Venetian jeweler was a double agent, the Ottomans beheaded him. *E* 1312, fol. 12 (March 27, 1536).

16. Moral, *Pedro de Toledo*, pp. 80–82.

17. AGS, *E* 1310, fol. 55 (August 7, 1535), 166 (October 30, 1534), 189 (August 17, 1534), 191 (August 11, 1534); *E* 1311, fol. 67 (April 7, 1535), 80 (March 13, 1535), 103 (January 11, 1534), 124 (November 28, 1534).

18. ASV, *CX-ParSec*, reg. 11, cc. 83v–83r, 84v–85r, 85v–86r, 86r–86v (all dated February 1575); reg. 12, cc. number missing (May 21, 1579); reg. 13, cc. 6r (June 23, 1583), 30v (January 20, 1585, m.v.), 34v (July 9, 1586); fil. 20, documents dated October 16 and 26, 1577; *CCX-LettAmb*, b. 6, fol. 56–57 (December 22, 1582).

19. ASV, *SDC*, fil. 4, c. 269r (January 21, 1569, m.v.).

20. COSP, *Venice*, VIII, no. 519.

21. ASV, *SDC*, fil. 4, c. 295r (February 6, 1569, m.v.).

22. AGS, *E* 1331, fol. 232 (September 10, 1572).

23. Capitana: A huge galley with thirty-five seats and powered by seven rowers, generally used as a flagship.

24. AGS, *E* 1064, fol. 100.

25. ASV, *CCX-LettAmb*, b. 4, no. 156, in Noel Malcolm, *Agents of Empire: Knights, Corsairs, Jesuits, and Spies in the Sixteenth-Century Mediterranean World* (London: Allen Lane, 2015), p. 229.

26. Malcolm, p. 229.

27. Sola Castaño, *Uchalí*, p. 141.

28. The document actually employs a different term, *Mudéjar*. Whereas *Moriscos* were Muslims who left Spain or who stayed there after 1492 on the condition of converting to Christianity, *Mudéjar* refers to Muslims who had been living under Spanish rule during the earlier medieval period. It is odd that such a term was being used centuries later, especially given that the same document mentions the city from which the *Mudéjar* in question came, namely Malaga. The misnomer presumably stems from the fact that the report was penned by the Maltese chancellery. Not exactly experts on Spanish bureaucratic terminology, the Maltese must have simply confused the two terms.

29. AGS, *E* 1132, fol. 28 (December 4, 1567).

30. ASF, *AMP*, fil. 4277, fol. 222.

31. ASF, *AMP*, fil. 3080, fol. 826 (September 30, 1570).

32. AGS, *E* 1331, fol. 232 (September 10, 1572).

33. AGS, *E* 1332, fol. 179 (May 6, 1573).

34. AGS, *E* 1144, fol. 212 (probably 1575).

35. AGS, *E* 1335, fol. 77 (September 10, 1576).

36. AGS, *E* 1517, cuaderno XIII, fol. 21 (January 21, 1584).

37. AGS, *E* 1417, fol. 172 (August 7, 1584).

38. AGS, *E* 1417, fol. 181 (October 28, 1584).

39. ASV, *SDC*, fil. 21, cc. 383r–383v (July 22, 1585).

40. ASV, *SDC*, fil. 21, cc. 449r–49v (July 12, 1585), 482r (July 28, 1585).

41. ASV, *SDC*, fil. 21, c. 397v (July 22, 1585).
42. ASV, *SDC*, fil. 21, c. 523v (August 5, 1585).
43. For the life story of this highly interesting figure, see Francesco della Valle, *Vita di Alvise Gritti*, BNM, mss. It VI 122 (6211); published manuscript: Francesco della Valle, "Una breve narrazione della grandezza, virtù, valore et della infelice morte dell'Illustrissimo Signor Conte Alouise Gritti, del Serenissimo Signor Andrea Gritti, Principe di Venezia, Conte del gran Contado di Marmarus in Ongaria et General Capitano dell'esercito Regno, appresso Sulimano Imperator de Turchi, et alla Maesta del Re Giovanni Re d'Ongaria," *Magyar Történelmi Tár* 3 (1857): pp. 9–60. Heinrich Kretschmayr, *Ludovico Gritti: Eine Monographie* (Vienna: Gerold, 1896); Carla Coco, "Alvise Gritti fra Veneti, Turchi e Ungheresi," *Studi Miscellanei Uralici e Altaici* 20, ed. Andrea Csillaghy (Venice: Libreria Editrice Cafoscarina, 1984): pp. 379–96; Aurel Decei, "Aloisio Gritti au service de Soliman le Magnifique d'aprés des documents turcs inédits (1533–1534)," *Anatolia Moderna-Yeni Anadolu* 3 (1992): pp. 10–60; Ferenc Szakály, *Lodovico Gritti in Hungary: 1529–1534: A Historical Insight into the Beginnings of Turco-Habsburgian Rivalry* (Budapest: Akadémiai Kiadó, 1995); Gizella Nemeth and Adriano Papo, *Ludovico Gritti: Un principe-mercante del Rinascimento tra Venezia i Turchi e la corona d'Ungheria*, (Friuli: Edizioni della Laguna, 2002); Gábor Barta, "Gritti Ludovicus'un Macar Valiliği (1531–1534)," *Belleten* 263 (2008): pp. 251–93; Elvin Otman, "The Role of Alvise Gritti within the Ottoman Politics in the Context of the 'Hungarian Question' (1526–1534)" (unpublished master's thesis, Bilkent University, 2009).
44. The name of the famous European-style district of Istanbul, *Beyoğlu*, comes from this interesting historical personality. As the Ottomans referred to the doges of Venice simply as *bey*s, Alvise, as the son of Andrea Gritti, was simply the son (*oğlu*) of the *bey*, that is, *beyoğlu*.
45. Robert Finlay, "Al Servizio del Sultano: Venezia, i Turchi e il mondo Cristiano, 1523–1538," in *Renovatio Urbis: Venezia nell'età di Andrea Giritti*, ed. Manfredo Tafuri (Rome: Oficina Edizioni, 1984), p. 100.
46. AGS, *E* 1367, fol. 60.
47. COSP, *Spain* 4/2, no. 1152 (November 19, 1533).
48. ASV, *Ducali et Atti Diplomatici*, b. 22; Coco, p. 383.
49. AGS, *E* 1308, fol. 186.
50. Finlay, p. 94.
51. AGS, *E* 1311, fol. 140–43 (October 5, 1535), 144 (October 8, 1535), 194–96 (October 11, 1535).
52. AGS, *E* 1311, fol. 23 (May 21, 1534).
53. Emrah Safa Gürkan, "Touting for Patrons, Brokering Power and Trading Information: Trans-Imperial Jews in Sixteenth-Century Constantinople," in *Detrás de las apariencias. Información y espionaje (siglos XVI–XVII)*, ed. Emilio Sola Castaño and Gennaro Varriale (Alcalá de Henares: Universidad de Alcalá, 2015), pp. 127–51.
54. AGS, *E* 656, fol. 2; *E* 664, fol. 91.
55. Sereno, pp. 16–17.
56. Preto, *Servizi Segreti*, p. 102; AGS, *E* 1058, fol. 40 (April 5, 1570), 42, 214. ASV, *CX, Parti Criminali*, reg. 11, cc. 78r–78v (July 3, 1570); *CX-ParSec*, reg. 9, c. 87r (August 19, 1570).

57. COSP, *Venice*, VIII, no. 753 (October 9, 1588); Salo Wittmayer Baron, *A Social and Religious History of the Jews, vol. 18, The Ottoman Empire, Persia, Ethiopia, India and China* (New York: Columbia University Press, Second Pressing, 1982), p. 144; Avram Galanti, *Türkler ve Yahudiler* (Istanbul: Gözlem Gazetecilik Basın ve Yayın, 1995), p. 138; Ágoston, "Information, Ideology, and Limits," p. 83.

58. AGS, *E* 1090, fol. 9 (September 20, 1588).

59. ASV, *IS*, b. 416, document dated October 15, 1586.

60. ASV, *IS*, b. 148, fol. 1 (September 25, 1585). Also see b. 416, January 8, 1585, m.v., documents dated March 25, 1586, and August 2, 1590.

61. ASV, *IS*, b. 433, document dated October 30, 1585; *SDC*, fil. 22, c. 193r (October 30, 1585).

62. Emrah Safa Gürkan, "Fooling the Sultan: Information, Decision-Making and the 'Mediterranean Faction' (1585–1587)," *Journal of Ottoman Studies* 45 (2015): pp. 57–96.

63. ASV, *SDC*, fil. 21, cc. 240r–42r (May 14, 1585).

64. Malcolm, ch. 14.

65. AGS, *E* 1157, fol. 151 (February 26, 1593); *E* 1158, fol. 26 (November 4, 1594), 53 (June 15, 1595), 54 (March 29, 1595), 67 (April 21, 1595), 187; *E* 1160, fol. 139 (September 25, 1602); *E* 1344 K 1675, fol. 4 (September 13, 1590), 8 (December 8, 1590), 44 (April 30, 1591), 70 (July 3, 1591), 125 (February 16, 1592), 150 (December 12, 1592); *E* 1885, fol. 6 (June 1592); *E* 1157, fol. 151 (February 26, 1593), 152.

66. Garrett Mattingly, *Renaissance Diplomacy* (New York: Dover Publications, 1988, first edition 1958), pp. 87–93, 123–39. For a revisionist perspective, see Isabella Lazzarini, *Communication and Conflict: Italian Diplomacy in the Early Renaissance, 1350–1520* (Oxford: Oxford University Press, 2015).

67. Levent Kaya Ocakaçan, "Geç 16. ve Erken 17. Yüzyılda Osmanlı Devleti'ndeki Patronaj İlişkilerinin Gazanfer Ağa Örneği Üzerinden Venedik Belgelerine Göre İncelenmesi" (unpublished PhD diss., Marmara University, 2016).

68. ASV, *SDC*, fil. 29, cc. 80r–82r (April 1, 1589).

69. E. Natalie Rothman, *Brokering Empire: Trans-Imperial Subjects between Venice and Istanbul* (Ithaca: Cornell University Press, 2012).

70. ASV, *SDC*, fil. 30, c. 379v (January 20, 1589, m.v.); Fabris, "Hasan 'il Veneziano,'" p. 52. Known as *Hasan Veneziano* in the West since he was a convert from Venice, this corsair was also immortalized in the work of his erstwhile captive Cervantes.

71. ASV, *SDC*, fil. 28, cc. 58r–60v (September 24, 1588), 265r (December 17, 1588), 434r (January 27, 1588, m.v.), 497r–98r (February 25, 1588, m.v.); fil. 29, cc. 26v–26r (March 10, 1589), 87r–87v (April 4, 1589), 133v–35v (April 27, 1589), 207r–7v (May 13, 1589), 402v (July 21, 1589); fil. 30, cc. 236v (December 23, 1589), 249v (December 9, 1589), 317v (June 22, 1589), 335v (January 20, 1589, m.v.). For an article examining an Ottoman convert's teetering between his past and his future, as played out in the thorny relationship between Uluc Hasan Pasha and the Venetian *bailo*s, see Emrah Safa Gürkan, "His Bailo's *Kapudan*: Conversion, Tangled Loyalties and Hasan *Veneziano* between Istanbul and Venice (1588–1591)," *Journal of Ottoman Studies* 48 (2016): pp. 277–319.

72. See Sanuto, vol. 51, col. 312, 379, 434, 517–18.

73. Aubin, p. 476.
74. Finlay, p. 95.
75. AGS, *E* 1132, fol. 155 (July 26, 1569), 164 (September 15, 1569), 193 (October 23, 1569), 194 (November 12, 1569), 196, 205, 207; *E* 1137, fol. 53 (March 17, 1572), 65 (April 21, 1572), 66, 130 (August 17, 1572), 223 (February 20, 1572); *E* 1141, fol. 11 (February 15, 1574). Also see José M. Floristán Imízcoz, "Felipe II ya la empresa de Grecia tras Lepanto (1571–1578)," *Erytheia* 15 (1994): pp. 155–90.
76. ASV, *SDC*, fil. 2, fol. 137 (July 10, 1567).
77. AGS, *E* 1531, fol. 107, 111, 134, 136, 137, 144–49, 163, 183; *E* 1532, fol. 149–51, 154, 169, 172, 174, 175, 178–80, 183 (all dated 1584); *E* 1533, fol. 202, 222, 257–62, 296–98; *E* 1534, fol. 130–6, 165–66; *E* 1535, fol. 121–22; *E* 1537, fol. 203–5, 317, 330, 342, 417; *E* 1538, fol. 109, 180–84, 276, 293, 367; *E* 1539, fol. 234–39, 360–62, 493–98.
78. AGS, *E* 1535, fol. 183 (July 9, 1585).
79. AGS, *E* 1090, fol. 116 (September 2, 1589); *E* 1092, fol. 72 (April 3, 1590).
80. For an example, see Casale; Gürkan, "Centre and the Frontier," pp. 156–63.
81. Local governors were only allowed to hand out *timar* plots of lesser value.
82. Selânikî, 1:25, 116; TSMA, *Evrak* 12321, hk. 215; Halil Sahillioğlu (ed.), *Topkapı Sarayı Arşivi, Mühimme Defteri E-12321* (Istanbul: IRCICA, 2002); BOA, *MD*, XVI, hk. 410 (H. Zilhicce 27, 979 / Greg. May 10, 1572); XIX, hk. 8 (H. Muharrem 5, 980 / Greg. May 17, 1572), 194 (H. Muharrem 29, 980 / Greg. June 10, 1572); *MZD*, V, hk. 27 (H. Şevval 24, 999 / Greg. August 14, 1591); XXVIII, hk. 520 (H. Receb 25, 984 / Greg. October 18, 1576), 801 (H. Şevval 8, 984 / Greg. October 30, 1576); XLII, hk. 953 (H. Zilkade 12, 988 / Greg. December 19, 1580); XLIX, hk. 65 (H. 991 / Greg. 1583); LXIII, hk. 48 (H. Rebiülahir 15, 996 / Greg. March 13, 1588), 56 (H. Rebiülahir 19, 996 / Greg. March 17, 1588). Only two orders are exceptional in their use of additional adjectives. *MD* XXVII, hk. 486 (H. Şevval 19, 983 / Greg. October 21, 1576) states that "a capable captain" (*muktedir levent re'isi*) should be sent to take "tongues," while *MD* VI, hk. 1134 (H. Şevval 13, 972 / Greg. May 14, 1565) refers to a "trustworthy spy" (*mu'temed câsûs*).
83. BOA, *MD*, XIX, hk. 547.
84. BOA, *MD*, XIX, hk. 521 (H. Rebiülahir 2, 980 / Greg. August 11, 1572), 527 (H. Ramazan 26, 980 / Greg. January 30, 1573).
85. AGS, *E* 1344 K 1675, fol. 66, 74 (July 13, 1591), 89 (August 16, 1591).
86. BOA, *MD*, XIX, hk. 487 (H. Ramazan 24, 980 / Greg. January 28, 1573), 488 (H. Ramazan 22, 980 / Greg. January 26, 1573), 521 (H. Rebiülevvel 2, 980 / Greg. July 12, 1572); XLIV, hk. 233; XLIX, hk. 499; LI, hk. 63.
87. BOA, *MD*, XLIV, hk. 233.
88. Geoffrey Parker, *The Grand Strategy of Philip II* (New Haven and London: Yale University Press, 1998), pp. 21–31, 65–71, conclusion.
89. BOA, *MD*, XII, hk. 787; XVIII, hk. 21; XIX, hk. 136, 490 (H. Ramazan 24, 980 / Greg. January 28, 1573), 521 (H. Rebiülevvel 2, 980 / Greg. August 11, 1572); LVIII, hk. 294 (H. Cemaziyelevvel 17, 993 / Greg. May 17, 1585); LXVII, hk. 188 (H. Selh-i Rebiülevvel 999 / Greg. March 26, 1591).
90. ASV, *SAPC*, fil. 5, c. 385r (May 13, 1552); *SDC*, fil. 5, fol. 19 (June 11, 1569).
91. BOA, *MD*, XIX, hk. 521 (H. Rebiülahir 2, 980 / Greg. August 11, 1572).

92. "Ol taraflarda küffâr-ı bed-girdârun donanma-yı hezîmet-eserlerinden
    harâmî ve korsan gemilerinden zuhûr itmiş gemi var mıdur, nicedür; vâkıf
    u muttali' olduğunuz sahîh haberi çavuşumla arzeyleyüp min-ba'd dahi a'dâ
    gemilerine müte'allik vâkıf olduğunuz haberi ber-vech-i isti'câl ihbâr itmek-
    den hâlî olmayasız."
93. ". . . içleründe çendan haber bilür kâfir bulunmamağın gönderülmediğin
    ve mektubların gönderdüğin." BOA, MD, XII, hk. 403 (H. Zilkade 16, 978 /
    Greg. April 11, 1571).
94. "Her ne demiş isen ma'lûm oldu."
95. "Ma'lûm-ı şerîfim olmuşdur."
96. BOA, *MD*, III, hk. 518, 878 (H. Cemaziyelevvel 27, 967 / Greg. February
    24, 1560), 1208 (H. Ramazan 11, 967 / Greg. June 6, 1560); XII, hk. 938 (H.
    Rebiülevvel 7, 979 / Greg. July 29, 1571); XIV, hk. 356 (H. Rebiülevvel 14, 978
    / Greg. August 16, 1570), 786 (H. Rebiülahir 978 / Greg. September 1570);
    XVI, hk. 410 (H. Zilhicce 27, 979 / Greg. May 10, 1572); XVIII, hk. 109 (H.
    Ramazan 22, 979 / Greg. February 7, 1572); XIX, hk. 8 (H. Muharrem 5, 980
    / Greg. May 17, 1572); XXVII, hk. 486 (H. Şevval 19, 983 / Greg. January 21,
    1576); XXVIII, hk. 245 (H. Receb 25, 984 / Greg. October 18, 1576), 801
    (H. Şaban 8, 984 / Greg. October 30, 1576), 520 (H. Receb 25, 984 / Greg.
    October 18, 1576); XXX, hk. 513 (H. Rebiülevvel 13, 985 / Greg. May 31,
    1577), 610 (H. Rebiülevvel 28, 985 / Greg. June 15, 1577), 611; XXXI, hk. 76
    (H. Rebiülahir 28, 985 / Greg. July 15, 1577); LXI, hk. 953 (H. Zilkade 12,
    988 / Greg. December 19, 1580); LXIX, hk. 65 (H. 991 / Greg. 1583), LXI, hk.
    46 (H. Receb 9, 994 / Greg. October 2, 1576).
97. BOA, *MD*, III, hk. 1265 (H. Ramazan 23, 967 / Greg. June 18, 1560);
    VII, hk. 202 (H. 975–76 / Greg. 1567–69); X, hk. 166 (H. Şaban 21, 978
    / Greg. March 18, 1571), 198; XII, hk. 1194 (H. Zilkade 24, 979 / Greg.
    April 8, 1572); XIV, hk. 343 (H. Safer 20, 978 / Greg. July 24, 1570), 463 (H.
    Rebiülevvel 12, 978 / Greg. August 14, 1570); XVI, hk. 109 (H. Receb 7,
    979 / Greg. November 25, 1571), 649 (H. Receb 9, 979 / Greg. November 27,
    1571); XIX, hk. 268 (H. Safer 3, 980 / Greg. June 14, 1572), 300; XLIX, hk.
    96; LVIII, hk. 518 (H. Şaban 8, 993 / Greg. August 4, 1585); LX, hk. 650 (H.
    Cemaziyelevvel 5, 994 / Greg. May 24, 1586).
98. BOA, *MD*, III, hk. 1256 (H. Ramazan 23, 967 / Greg. June 18, 1560); XIX, hk.
    710, 711 (both H. 980 / Greg. 1572).
99. TSMA, *Evrak* 12321, hk. 434; Sahillioğlu, *E* 12321; BOA, *MD*, VI, hk. 1134
    (H. Şevval 13, 972 / Greg. May 14, 1565); VII, hk. 630 (H. 975–76 / Greg.
    1567–69); XII, hk. 851 (H. Rebiülahir 2, 979 / Greg. August 23, 1571);
    XVI, hk. 192 (H. Zilkade 10, 979 / Greg. March 25, 1572), 411 (H. Zilhicce
    27, 989 / Greg. January 22, 1582), 636 (H. Cemaziyelevvel 21, 979 / Greg.
    November 9, 1571); XIX, hk. 268 (H. Safer 3, 980 / Greg. June 14, 1572), 300;
    XLVII, hk. 165, 166 (both H. Rebiülevvel 24, 990 / Greg. April 18, 1582); LX,
    hk. 273 (H. Zilhicce 17, 993 / Greg. December 9, 1585), 570, 571 (both H.
    Cemaziyelevvel 8, 994 / Greg. April 27, 1586); *MZD*, V, hk. 27 (H. Şevval 24,
    999 / Greg. August 14, 1591).
100. ". . . hâliyâ deryâda küffâr-ı hâksârun donanması olduğı istimâ' olunup ol
     taraflara karib hareket itmiş gemileri var mıdur, sahîh haber almağiçün."
101. BOA, *MD*, VI, hk. 1287 (H. Zilkade 20, 972 / Greg. June 19, 1565).
102. BOA, *MD*, VI, 1288 (H. Zilkade 20, 972 / Greg. June 19, 1565); IX, hk.
     246 (H. 977–78 / Greg. 1569–70); X, hk. 209 (H. Ramazan 27, 978 / Greg.

February 16, 1571), 274; XII, hk. 1021 (H. Şevval 29, 979 / Greg. March 14, 1572); XIV, hk. 781 (H. Rebiülahir 978 / Greg. September 1570), 816 (H. Selh-i Cemaziyelevvel 978 / Greg. October 30, 1570); LI, hk. 246 (H. 983 / Greg. 1585).

103. "... gaflet üzere olmak nice muhâfazadır, livâ-i mezbûrda seni vali nasb eyle- mekden murâd-ı hümâyûnum ol cevânibe onat vechile hıfz u hırâset eyleyüb a'da tarafından bir mahale zarar u güzend erişdirmemekdir, sebeb nedir ki ol vechile gaflet üzre olasın?" BOA, *MD*, X, hk. 274. "sû'-yı tedbîr ve ihmâl ü müsâhele sebebiyle Memâlik-i Mahrûse'mden bir mahalle zarar ü gezend irişmek ihtimâl olursa aslâ beyan idecek özrün makbûl olmayub mansıb alınmağla konulmayub envâ'-ı itâb u ikâba müstehak olman mukarrerdür," BOA, *MD*, LI, hk. 246 (H. 983 / Greg. 1585). "... azlile konılmayup eşedd-i ıkâbla mu'âkab olman mukarrerdür," BOA, *MD*, VI, 1288 (H. Zilkade 20, 972 / Greg. June 19, 1565).

104. BOA, *MD*, VI, hk. 1287, 1288 (both H. Zilkade 20, 972 / Greg. June 19, 1565).

105. BOA, *MD*, VI, hk. 1287, 1288 (both H. Zilkade 20, 972 / Greg. June 19, 1565).

106. BOA, *MD*, VI, hk. 1288 (H. Zilkade 20, 972 / Greg. June 19, 1565).

107. BOA, *MD*, XII, hk. 403 (H. Zilkade 16, 978 / Greg. April 13, 1571), 532 (H. Gurre-yi Safer 979 / Greg. June 24, 1571), 787.

108. Yavuz Ercan, *Osmanlı İmparatorluğu'nda Bulgarlar ve Voynuklar* (Ankara: Türk Tarih Kurumu, 1986), p. 75.

109. Robert Anhegger, "Martoloslar Hakkında," *Türkiyat Mecmuası* 7–8 (1942): p. 286; Abdülkadir Özcan, "Martolos," *Türkiye Diyanet Vakfı İslam Ansiklopedisi* 28 (2003).

110. BOA, *MD*, XIX, hk. 119 (H. Muharrem 21, 980 / Greg. June 2, 1572).

111. BOA, *MD*, XXV, hk. 16 (H. Şaban 13, 981 / Greg. December 8, 1573).

112. BOA, *MD*, XXV, hk. 315 (H. Ramazan 17, 981 / Greg. January 11, 1574).

113. "... vilâyet-i mezbûreye yarar ve mu'temedun-aleyh câsûslar gönderüb vilâyet-i mezbûre keferesinin ahvâl ü etvârın tetebbu' idüb garet olacaklarını haber almışlar mıdır yohsa gaflet üzre midür yat u yarağı ve atlı askeri var mıdur nicedür tamam mertebe vukûf tahsil. . ." BOA, *MD*, XIX, hk.194 (H. Muharrem 29, 980 / Greg. June 10, 1572), 201.

114. Ayşe Karapınar and Emine Erdoğan Özünlü, eds., *Mihaloğulları'na Ait 1586 Tarihli Akıncı Defteri* (Ankara: Türk Tarih Kurumu, 2015), p. 3.

115. Evliyâ Çelebi b. Derşiv Mehemmed Zıllî, *Evliyâ Çelebi Seyahatnâmesi, VI. Kitap*, ed. Seyit Ali Kahraman and Yücel Dağlı (Istanbul: Yapı Kredi Yayınları, 2002), p. 254.

116. BOA, *MD*, XXV, hk. 17 (H. Şaban 3, 981 / Greg. November 28, 1574).

117. BOA, *MD*, XXV, hk. 1846 (H. Rebiülevvel 9, 982 / Greg. June 28, 1574).

118. "... düşman taburundan cebeli ve cevşenli bir dil tutub. . ." BOA, *MD*, XXV, hk. 2193 (H. Rebiülahir 20, 982 / Greg. August 8, 1574).

119. Gürkan, "Centre and the Frontier," pp. 145–47.

120. Gürkan, "Centre and the Frontier," pp. 151–55.

121. ASV, *SDC*, fil. 2, fol. 24 (May 28, 1567).

122. AGS, *E* 1052, fol. 27.

123. BOA, *MD*, LXV, hk. 96 (H. Şevval 24, 997 / Greg. September 5, 1589).

124. İdris Bostan, *Adriyatik'te Korsanlık: Osmanlılar, Uskoklar, Venedikliler, 1575–1620* (Istanbul: Timaş Yayınları, 2009), pp. 36–56.

125. ASV, *SDelC*, reg. 3, c. 51v (August 29, 1566).

126. "iki kalyete ile deryaya salunub dil alub getirme"; BOA, *MD*, hk. XIX, hk. 87 (H. Safer 28, 980 / Greg. July 9, 1572).

127. BOA, *MD*, XXV, hk. 2686 (H. Cemaziyelevvel 26, 982 / Greg. October 12, 1574).

128. AGS, *E* 1070, fol. 77.

129. Gürkan, "Centre and the Frontier," p. 136.

130. BOA, *MD*, XII, hk. 403 (H. Zilkade 16, 978 / Greg. April 13, 1571), 532 (H. Gurreyi Safer 979 / Greg. June 24, 1571), 787; XIV, hk. 469 (H. Rebiülevvel 12, 978 / Greg. August 14, 1571); ASV, *SDC*, fil. 5, fol. 19 (June 11, 1569).

131. Gürkan, "Centre and the Frontier," pp. 151–55.

132. TSMA, *Evrak* 12321, hk. 380; Sahillioğlu, *E* 12321.

133. BOA, *MD*, III, hk. 139; XIV, hk. 539 (H. Rebiülahir 27, 978 / Greg. September 28, 1570); XVI, hk. 640 (H. Cemaziyelevvel 23, 979 / Greg. October 13, 1571); XIX, hk. 629 (H. Rebiülahir 18, 980 / Greg. September 8, 1571), 631 (H. Rebiülahir 9, 980 / Greg. August 30, 1571), 668.

134. According to a list drawn up by the Portuguese priest Antonio Sosa, who was enslaved in Algiers at the time, out of the thirty-five captains in Algiers in 1581, only thirteen were Muslims, and three out of those thirteen had convert fathers (such first-generation Muslims were called *kuloğlu* in the region). There was also a Jewish captain. The twenty-one non-Muslim captains were as follows: six Genovese, three Greek, two Venetian, two Spanish, one French, one Albanian, one Hungarian, one Corsican, one Calabrian, one Sicilian (Trapani), and one Neapolitan. One was of unknown ethnicity. Diego de Haedo, *Topographia e Historia General de Argel, repartida en cinco tratados, do se veran casos estraños, muertes espantosas, y tormentos exquisitos, que conuiene se entiendan en la Christiandad: con mucha doctrina, y elegancia curiosa* (Valladolid: Diego Fernandez de Cordoua y Ouiedo, 1612), ch. 22, p. 18.

135. AGS, *E* 1541, fol. 159 (November 20, 1591).

136. Hess, *The Forgotten Frontier.*

137. Emrah Safa Gürkan, "Osmanlı-Habsburg Rekabeti Çerçevesinde Osmanlılar'ın XVI. Yüzyıl'daki Akdeniz Siyaseti," in *Osmanlı Dönemi Akdeniz Dünyası*, ed. Haydar Çoruh et al. (Istanbul: Yeditepe Yayınevi, 2011), pp. 11–50.

138. Gábor Ágoston, "A Flexible Empire: Authority and Its Limits on the Ottoman Frontiers," *International Journal of Turkish Studies* 9, no. 1–2 (2003): pp. 15–31; Gábor Ágoston, "The Ottomans: From Frontier Principality to Empire," in *The Practice of Strategy: From Alexander the Great to the Present*, ed. John Andreas Olsen and Colin S. Gray (Oxford and New York: Oxford University Press, 2011), pp. 105–31.

139. For orders sent to Algerian governor-generals, see BOA, *MD*, VI, hk. 561 (H. Cemaziyelevvel 29, 972 / Greg. January 2, 1565), 904 (H. Şaban 22, 972 / Greg. March 25, 1565); XLIV, hk. 287 (H. *c.* Muharrem 23, 991 / Greg. February 16, 1583). For orders sent to Uluc Ali Pasha, governor-general of Tripolitania, see *MD* VII, hk. 653 (H. Receb 6, 975 / Greg. June 6, 1568), 1060 (H. *c.* Ramazan 14–16, 975 / Greg. March 13–15, 1568), 1472 (H. Zilhicce 25, 975 / Greg. May 22, 1568).

140. For an example of a stern order sent to the governor-general of Algeria, see BOA, *MD*, XLIV, hk. 297 (H. *c.* Muharrem 28, 991 / Greg. February 21, 1583).

141. Emrah Safa Gürkan, "An Ottoman Spy in Syracuse (1562): Constantino/ Mehmed from Candia," Archivo de la Frontera. Also see AGS, *E* 1070, fol. 77. AGS, *E* 1119, fol. 95–20 (December 14, 1547), which states that, when the Habsburgs captured Turgud's nephew in Messina, he had been travelling across Sicily undeterred. Most likely, Turgud's spies on the island were providing him with a steady stream of information.

142. Seyyid Murâdi Re'îs, *Gazavât-ı Hayreddin Paşa*, ed. Mustafa Yıldız (Aachen: Verlag Shaker, 1993), vr. 280b–81a, 296b. In 1558, Uluc Ali undertook a similar expedition. AGS, *E* 1124, fol. 135 (August 25, 1558). We should remember that there were two corsairs by the name of Uluc Ali in the 1550s, and it is impossible to discern which of them any given document is referring to.

143. Canosa and Colonnello, p. 73.

144. According to the *Gazavât-ı Hayreddin Paşa*, Barbarosa would interrogate slaves as soon as they were brought to Algiers: "If there were any infidels who spoke the language, he would have them brought before him and ask them all about recent events in the lands of the infidel." *Gazavât*, vr. 233b–35a, also see vr. 238b.

145. For news of a sea battle between the Spanish, English, and Calvinists, which reached Istanbul via Algiers thanks to the *dil*s whom Murad Reis captured off the coast of Sicily, see BOA, *MD*, XXIII, hk. 645 (H. Zilhicce 22, 980 / Greg. August 25, 1573). One of the duties of the governor-general of Algeria was to report to Istanbul about events in Fez and Marakkesh. *MD*, XXX, hk. 348, 424.

146. BOA, *MD*, VII, hk. 653 (H. Receb 6, 975 / Greg. January 6, 1568), 1060, 1472; XIX, hk. 255 (H. Rebiülevvel 3, 980 / Greg. July 13, 1572); XXVII, hk. 555 (H. Zilkade 2, 983 / Greg. February 2, 1576); LV, hk. 283 (H. Safer 22, 993 / Greg. February 22, 1585).

147. ". . . küffâr-ı hâksârun ol taraflarda donanma-yı hezîmet-esere azîm tedârükleri olub deryâ yüzünden vâkı' olan def'-ı mazarrat u fesâdı içün Donanma-yı Hümâyûnum irsâl olunmak lâzim idüğin i'lâm eyledüğün ecilden. . ." BOA, *MD*, VI, hk. 904 (H. Safer 22, 972 / Greg. September 28, 1564).

148. BOA, *MD*, I, hk. 132; II, hk. 47, 576; VIII, hk. 132, 151, 849, 943; LIII, hk. 7; LVI, hk. 70.

149. BOA, *MD*, XLII, hk. 1791.

150. BOA, *MD*, VIII, hk. 1040.

151. BOA, *MD*, I, hk. 13, 15, 18, 19, 20, 22, 42, 54, 123, 135, 166, 246, 247, 378, 610, 639, 996, 1056, 1593; II, hk. 576, 1039; XLII, hk. 1792.

152. BOA, *MD*, I, hk. 46, 140.

153. Selânikî, 1:13, 32.

154. AK, *Muallim Cevdet Yazmaları*, O.071. The Latinized version of this logbook exists in the form of a doctoral thesis. İlhan Gök, "Atatürk Kitaplığı Mc.O.071 Numaralı 909–933/1503–1527 Tarihli İn'âmât Defteri (Transkripsiyon-Değerlendirme)" (unpublished PhD diss., Marmara University, 2014). A portion of the notebook was published earlier by Ömer Lütfi Barkan. Ömer Lütfi Barkan, "İstanbul Saraylarına Ait Muhasebe Defterleri," *Belgeler: Türk Tarih Belgeleri Dergisi* 13 (1979): pp. 1–380.

155. AK, *Muallim Cevdet Yazmaları*, O.071, 69; Gök, p. 139.

156. AK, *Muallim Cevdet Yazmaları*, O.071, 227. Gök, p. 527. İlhan Gök reads the name here as "Han," which is incorrect. I would like to thank Professor

Feridun M. Emecen on this point, who shared the original notebook with me to compare it with.

157. AK, *Muallim Cevdet Yazmaları*, O.071, 326; Gök, p. 830.
158. AK, *Muallim Cevdet Yazmaları*, O.071, 226; Gök, p. 526.
159. AK, *Muallim Cevdet Yazmaları*, O.071, 223; Gök, p. 512.
160. Şevket Pamuk, *İstanbul ve Diğer Kentlerde 500 Yıllık Fiyat ve Ücretler, 1469–1998* (Ankara: T.C. Başbakanlık Devlet İstatistik Enstitüsü, 2000), p. 69.
161. AK, *Muallim Cevdet Yazmaları*, O.071, 195; Gök, p. 414; Emecen, *Yavuz Sultan Selim*, p. 33.
162. AK, *Muallim Cevdet Yazmaları*, O.071, 33; Gök, p. 67.
163. AK, *Muallim Cevdet Yazmaları*, O.071, 33, 71, 112; Gök, pp. 67, 143, 244.
164. AK, *Muallim Cevdet Yazmaları*, O.071, 212; Gök, p. 485.
165. AK, *Muallim Cevdet Yazmaları*, O.071, 279, 332, 387; Gök, pp. 677, 847, 1008.
166. AK, *Muallim Cevdet Yazmaları*, O.071, 226; Gök, p. 525.
167. AK, *Muallim Cevdet Yazmaları*, O.071, 267; Gök, p. 659.
168. AK, *Muallim Cevdet Yazmaları*, O.071, 196; Gök, p. 417.
169. AK, *Muallim Cevdet Yazmaları*, O.071, 11; Barkan, "Muhasebe Defterleri," p. 308; Gök, p. 18.
170. AGS, *E* 1126, fol. 41, 152 (April 30, 1561).
171. *Dhimmi*s were members of other revealed religions—that is, Christians and Jews—who were permitted to continue living within their autonomous communities and worshipping according to their customs in exchange for a special tax, called *cizye*.
172. BOA, *MD*, VIII, hk. 356 (H. Cemaziyelevvel 14, 978 / Greg. October 14, 1570).
173. Pamuk, *Fiyat ve Ücretler*, p. 69.
174. BOA, *MD*, VIII, hk. 18 (H. 978 / Greg. June 1570–June 1571).
175. BOA, *MD*, XXV, hk. 2804 (H. Receb 10, 982 / Greg. October 26, 1574).
176. BOA, *MD*, XLV, hk. 2529 (H. Şaban 27, 989 / Greg. September 26, 1581).
177. BOA, *MD*, VIII, hk. 15; LXV, hk. 96.
178. BOA, *MD*, XXV, 2686.
179. BOA, *MD*, XXV, hk. 17 (H. Şaban 3, 981 / Greg. November 28, 1573).
180. BOA, *MD*, VIII, hk. 951 (H. Safer 19, 978 / Greg. July 23, 1570).
181. AGS, *E* 1068, fol. 31 (January 9, 1575).
182. BOA, *MD*, XXV, hk. 1163 (H. Zilhicce 13, 981 / Greg. December 13, 1574).
183. AGS, *E* 1054, fol. 215 (October 19, 1565).
184. BOA, *MD*, XIII, hk. 684 (H. Zilhicce 26, 978 / Greg. May 21, 1571).
185. See Colin Heywood, "Some Turkish Archival Sources for the History of the Menzilhane Network in Rumeli during the Eighteenth Century," *Boğaziçi Üniversitesi Dergisi, Beşeri Bilimler. Humanities* 4–5 (1976–1977): pp. 39–54; Colin Heywood, "The Ottoman Menzilhane and Ulak System in Rumeli in the Eighteenth Century," *Türkiye'nin Sosyal ve Ekonomik Tarihi (1071–1920)*, ed. Osman Okyar and Halil İnalcık (Ankara: Meteksan, 1980), pp. 179–86; Colin Heywood, "The Via Egnatia in the Ottoman Period: The Menzilhanes of the Sol Kol in the Late 17th/Early 18th Century," *Via Egnatia under Ottoman Rule (1380–1699)*, ed. Elizabeth Zachariadou (Resmo: Crete University Press, 1996), pp. 129–44. All three articles can be found in Colin Heywood, *Writing Ottoman History: Documents and Interpretations* (Aldershot, Hampshire: Ashgate, 2002). Also see Yusuf

Halaçoğlu, *Osmanlılarda Ulaşım ve Haberleşme: Menziller* (Ankara: PTT Genel Müdürlüğü, 2002); Ali Yücel Yürük, "Lütfi Paşa'nın (ö. 970/1563) Osmanlı Haberleşme ve Ulaşım Sistemine Ulak Zulmü Bağlamında Getirdiği Yenilikler," in *Kitaplara vakfedilen bir ömre tuhfe: İsmail E. Erünsal'a Armağan* (Istanbul: Ülke Armağan, 2013), 1:597–626.

186. TSMA, *Evrak* 3192.

187. "Bu ulak zulmi bize ne dünyâda ve ne âhiretde rahatlık virir, Hak Te'âlâ katında bu husûsda gâyet şermsârız deyu ah."

188. ". . . ve 'Osmânlu dahi ulak zulmünden Cengizîleri taklîd gibi itmişlerdi."

189. ". . . ol zulümle ulak alub bindikleri atları sâhibleri mazlûmlarının ahı pâdişâh-ı rû-yı zemîn tarafına tesir idüp oğlı Cihângir'de zuhûr buldu."

190. Lütfi Paşa, vr. 373–84, pp. 284–92.

191. BOA, KK, no. 2555, (H. 1003 / Greg. September 1594–September 1595); Yusuf Halacoğlu, "Klasik Dönemde Osmanlılarda Haberleşme ve Yol Sistemi," in *Çağını Yakalayan Osmanlı! Osmanlı Devleti'nde Modern Haberleşme ve Ulaştırma Teknikleri*, ed. Ekmeleddin İhsanoğlu et al. (Istanbul: IRCICA, 1995), pp.14–15.

192. BOA, *MD*, XLIV, hk. 233; XLIX, hk. 499.

193. BOA, *MD*, XXX, hk. 62 (H. Muharrem 25, 985 / Greg. April 14, 1577); XLIV, hk. 233; LI, hk. 63.

194. BOA, *MD*, XIX, hk. 488 (H. Ramazan 22, 980 / Greg. January 26, 1573), 521 (H. Rebiülahir 2, 980 / Greg. August 11, 1571).

195. "Hususî emirle gelen ulak." Halaçoğlu, *Menziller*, p. 4. Additionally, we must add that specially assigned messengers were sometimes referred to simply as *ulak*s. BOA, *MD*, XIV, hk. 442 (H. Safer 23, 978 / Greg. July 27, 1570); XIX, hk. 487 (H. Ramazan 24, 980 / Greg. February 19, 1571); XLIV, hk. 233.

196. Halaçoğlu, "Osmanlılarda Haberleşme ve Yol Sistemi," p. 20.

197. Pedani, *In Nome del Gran Signore*, vol. 14, appendix I.

198. *Müteferrika*s were palace officials who, like marshals, were entrusted with a variety of tasks. Unlike other palace officials, they generally came from an elite background, with their ranks including the sons of vassal princes, high-ranking Ottoman officials, and Ottoman princesses.

199. Nicolas Vatin, "Remarques sur l'oral et l'écrit dans l'administration ottomane au XVIe siècle," *Revue du monde musulman et de la Méditerranée* 75–76 (1995): p. 147.

200. ASV, *CX-ParSec*, reg. 8, cc. 82v–83v (April 9, 1567).

201. ASV, *DocTR*, b. 6, no. 805; b. 8, hk. 1014.

202. Emrah Safa Gürkan, "Laying Hands on *Arcana Imperii*: Venetian Baili as Spymasters in Sixteenth-Century Istanbul," in *Spy Chiefs*, eds. Paul Maddrell et al. (Washington, DC: Georgetown University Press, 2018), 2:67–96.

203. ASV, *CX-ParSec*, reg. 14, cc. 128v (November 22, 1601).

204. İdris Bostan, *Osmanlılar ve Deniz: Deniz Politikası, Teşkilat, Gemiler* (Istanbul: Küre Yayınları, 2007), p. 126.

205. İlter, *Şimali Afrika'da Türkler*, 1:133. Also see BOA, *MD*, III, hk. 580, 581, 582, 583, 624, 629.

206. BOA, *MD*, XIX, hk. 508 (H. Ramazan 21, 980 / Greg. January 21, 1573).

207. BOA, *MD*, LXXIII, hk. 987 (H. Şevval 11, 1003 / Greg. July 10, 1593).

208. BOA, *MD*, XIV, hk. 442 (H. Safer 23, 978 / Greg. July 27, 1570).

209. Guilmartin, pp. 176–93; Bruce Ware Allen, *The Great Siege of Malta: The Epic Battle between the Ottoman Empire and the Knights of St. John* (Lebanon, NH: University Press of New England, 2015).

210. ASV, *CX-ParSec*, reg. 8, cc. 79r–80r (February 18, 1566, m.v.); BOA, *MD*, VI, hk. 1424 (H. Evasıt ı Zilhicce 972 / Greg. July 9–18, 1565).
211. Ágoston, "Information, Ideology, and Limits," p. 78.
212. BOA, *MD*, XIV, hk. 520 (H. Rebiülevvel 21, 978 / Greg. August 23, 1570).
213. BOA, XVI, hk. 34 (H. Cemaziyelevvel 20, 979 / Greg. October 10, 1571).
214. BOA, *MD*, XXII, hk. 416 (H. Rebiülahir 14, 981 / Greg. August 12, 1573), 419.
215. AGS, *E* 1331, fol. 221 (May 20, 1572).
216. Malcolm, p. 183.
217. For a study of Early Modern Istanbul as a center of diplomacy, see Gürkan, "Bir Diplomasi Merkezi Olarak Yeni Çağ İstanbul'u."
218. ASV, *SDC*, fil. 2, cc. 236v–37r (September 23, 1567).
219. See Ágoston, "Birodalom és információ."
220. ASV, SDC, fil. 3, c. 359r (January 7, 1568, m.v.); Ernest Charrière, ed., *Négociations de la France dans le Levant, ou, correspondances, mémoires et actes diplomatiques des ambassadeurs de France à Constantinople et des ambassadeurs, envoyés ou résidents à divers titres à Venise, Raguse, Rome, Malte et Jérusalem, en Turquie, Perse, Géorgie, Crimée, Syrie, Egypte, etc., et dans les états de Tunis, d'Alger et de Maroc* (Paris: Impr. Nationale, 1853), 3:69; Mario Infelise, "From Merchants' Letters to Handwritten Political Avvisi: Notes on the Origins of Public Information," in *Cultural Exchange in Early Modern Europe, vol. 3, Correspondence and Cultural Exchange in Europe, 1400–1700*, ed. Francisco Bethencourt and Florike Egmond (Cambridge: Cambridge University Press, 2007), p. 38; Infelise, *Prima dei giornali*, p. 7.
221. Sardella, pp. 56–57.
222. See BOA, *MD*, XIX, numerous points.
223. BOA, *MD*, XIX, hk. 247 (H. Safer 4, 980 / Greg. June 15, 1572), unnumbered, after hk. 667; XXII, hk. 108.
224. DAD, *Acta Turcorum*, A7 29a (H. Evahir-i Zilkade 978 / Greg. April 16–25, 1571), K 82 (H. Evail-i Rebiülahir 979 / Greg. August 23–September 1, 1571), K 113 (H. Evasıt-ı Safer 978 / Greg. July 15–24, 1570). For the texts, see Biegman, "Ragusan Spying," pp. 245–49.
225. ASV, *CCX-LettRett*, b. 292, cc. 175r–77q; for the text, see Michel Lesure, "Notes et documents sur les relations vénéto-ottomanes, 1570–1573, I," *Turcica* 4 (1972): pp. 158–64.
226. Preto, *Servizi Segreti*, p. 102. AGS, *E* 1058, fol. 40 (April 5, 1570), 42, 214. ASV, *Parti Criminali*, reg. 11, cc. 78r–78v (July 3, 1570); *CX-ParSec*, reg. 9, c. 87r (August 19, 1570). ASF, *AMP*, fil. 2979, cc. 336 (April 8, 1570), 374 (May 27, 1570); fil. 3080, c. 826 (September 30, 1570).
227. BOA, *MD*, IX, hk. 237, 239.
228. ASV, *SAPC*, fil. 5, cc. 3v–5r (August 6, 1550), 104v–5v (May 28, 1551), 159v–60r (July 7, 1551), 305r–5v (February 6, 1551, m.v.), 398r–98v (June 18, 1552).
229. ASV, *SDC*, fil. 2, cc. 43r–43v (April 10, 1567), 372v–73v (January 12, 1567, m.v.), fil. 3, cc. 163r (July 27, 1568); Charrière, 3:72 (August 30, 1569).
230. ASV, *SDC*, fil. 25, cc. 48r–48v (March 2, 1587).
231. Sola Castaño, *Uchalí*, p. 359.
232. ASV, *SDC*, fil. 21, cc. 283r–84r (June 12, 1585).
233. ASV, *SAPC*, fil. 5, cc. 3v–5r (August 6, 1550), 398r–98v (June 18, 1552).
234. ASV, *SAPC*, fil. 5 cc. 159v–60r (July 7, 1551); *SDC*, fil. 25 cc. 48r–48v (March 2, 1587).

235. ASV, *SDC*, fil. 2, cc. 43r–43v (April 10, 1567).
236. ASV, *SAPC*, fil. 5, cc. 104v–5v (May 28, 1551); *SDC*, fil. 2, cc. 372v–73v (January 12, 1567, m.v.), fil. 3, c. 163r (July 27, 1568), fil. 21, cc. 283r–84r (June 12, 1585), fil. 31, cc. 470r–70v (August 18, 1590).
237. ASV, *SAPC*, fil. 5, cc. 3v–5r (August 6, 1550), 159v–60r (July 17, 1551), 305r–5v (February 6, 1551, m.v.), 371v (May 18, 1552); *SDC*, fil. 2. cc. 43r–43v (April 10, 1567), 373v (January 12, 1567, m.v.), 384r–84v (January 19, 1567, m.v.), fil. 3, cc. 162r–62v (July 27, 1568), fil. 21, c. 405r (June 30, 1585), fil. 25, cc. 48r–48v (March 2, 1587); Charrière, *Négociations de la France dans le Levant*, 3:72 (August 30, 1569).
238. ASV, *SAPC*, fil. 5, cc. 371v (April 24, 1552), 386v (May 12, 1552).
239. Charrière, 3:73, dn. 1 (August 30, 1569).
240. ASV, *SDC*, fil. 21, c. 405r (June 30, 1585); Charrière, 3:69 (August 30, 1569).
241. ASV, *SDC*, fil. 21, c. 405r (June 30, 1585).
242. ASV, *SAPC*, fil. 5, cc. 305r–5v (February 6, 1551, m.v.).
243. ASV, *SAPC*, fil. 5, cc. 159v–60r (July 7, 1551); *SDC*, fil. 25, cc. 48r–48v (March 2, 1587); Charrière, 3:72 (August 30, 1569).
244. ASV, *SAPC*, fil. 5, cc. 305r–5v (February 6, 1551, m.v.).
245. ASV, *SDC*, fil. 21, cc. 283r–84r (June 12, 1585).
246. For an example, see ASV, *SDC*, fil. 3, cc. 383v–84r (January 28, 1568, m.v.).
247. ASV, *SAPC*, fil. 5, c. 19v (December 18, 1550).
248. ASV, *SDC*, fil. 4, c. 273r (January 21, 1569, m.v.).
249. Alain Servantie, "Charles Quint aux yeux des Ottomans," in *Carlos V: Los moriscos y el Islam*, ed. María Jesús Rubiera Mata (Madrid: Sociedad Estatal para la Conmemoración de los centanarios de Felipe II y Carlos V, 2001), p. 305.
250. Ghobrial, p. 77.
251. Michel Lesure, "Notes et documents sur les relations vénéto-ottomanes, 1570–1573, II," *Turcica* 8 (1976): pp. 144–45, fn. 47.
252. ASV, *SDC*, fil. 1, c. 215r (July 20, 1566).
253. Doubloon: a Spanish coin worth two escudo, containing 6.867 grams of gold.
254. AGS, *E* 1338 fol. 64 (October 28, 1580).
255. ASV, *SAPC*, fil. 5, c. 75r (May 2, 1551).
256. AGS, *E* 1054, fol. 173 (August 5, 1565).
257. HHStA, *Staatenabteilungen, Türkei I*, box 45, 1581 September file, fol. 31r, as told by Tobias Graf, "'I am Still Yours,'" p. 208.
258. S. Takats, *Macaristan Türk Âleminden Çizgiler*, tr. Sadrettin Karatay (Ankara: Türk Tarih Kurumu Basımevi, 2011), p. 229.
259. AGS, *E* 1527, fol. 211 (May 7, 1582).
260. AGS, *E* 1158. fol. 187.
261. Emrah Safa Gürkan, "Mediating Boundaries: Mediterranean Go-Betweens and Cross-Confessional Diplomacy in Constantinople, 1560–1600," *Journal of Early Modern History* 19 (2015): pp. 127–28.
262. Andrew Pettegree, *The Invention of News: How the World Came to Know about Itself* (New Haven and London: Yale University Press, 2014), p. 37.
263. Hugon, *Au service du Roi Catholique*, p. 508, 515.
264. Hugon, *Au service du Roi Catholique*, p. 515.
265. The first news concerning the battle reached Istanbul on March 26. However, İbrahim Pasha waited until he had received confirmation from the *bailo* of Venice on March 29 before he actually informed the sultan. Infelise, "From Merchants' Letters," p. 38; Infelise, *Prima dei giornali*, p. 7.

266. ASV, *SDC*, fil. 3, c. 359r (January 7, 1568, m.v.).
267. ASV, *SDC*, fil. 4, c. 70v (May 11, 1569).
268. Charrière, p. 69.
269. BOA, *MD* XVI, hk. 139, 144, 150, 154; Maria Pia Pedani, ed., *Relazioni di ambasciatori veneti al Senato tratte dalle migliori edizioni disponibili e ordinate cronologicamente, vol. XIV: Costantinopoli, relazioni inedite (1512–1789)* (Turin: Bottega d'Erasmo, 1996), pp. 165–66. According to Uluc Ali, the war broke out on H. Cemaziyelevvel 18, 979 / Greg. October 8, 1571, that is, a day later.
270. The *bailo* received the news on October 16, and the French ambassador informed Uluc Ali about it on the October 17. More detailed and reliable news was provided on October 20 by the Ragusan ambassador to Istanbul, Niccolò Prodanelli. AGS, *E* 1338, fol. 64 (October 28, 1580).
271. ASV, *SDC*, fil. 21, c. 265v (May 31, 1585).
272. ASV, *SDC*, fil. 28, c. 90v (September 9, 1588).
273. ASV, *SDC*, fil. 29, cc. 26v–26r (March 10, 1589).
274. ASV, *SDC*, fil. 30, c. 71r (September 18, 1589).
275. ASV, *SDC*, fil. 31, cc. 167r, 171r (May 12, 1590).

5

OTTOMAN COUNTERESPIONAGE

In the previous chapters, I have tried to show that the Ottomans established an effective intelligence system and that, with the help of various news sources and their spies operating out in the field, they kept abreast of military and diplomatic developments. Thus, when Ottoman commanders and strategists made decisions, they were able to draw on reliable information from a range of sources. Without a doubt, one of the key aims of Ottoman intelligence was to ensure that the Ottomans' enemies did not have such easy access to information. In this chapter, I shall analyze the measures that the Ottomans took to block the enemy's access to intelligence, in other words, Ottoman counterintelligence or counterespionage.

MANAGING THE BORDERS

One of the biggest challenges faced by early modern empires was keeping a watch on their borders, which could stretch for hundreds of kilometers; moreover, they had to do this with the limited military, logistical, and communication facilities available in that period. The Ottomans developed a number of tactics to overcome this challenge.

The most radical of these, and the one that was most difficult to implement, was completely shutting the border. To give one example of this, local authorities in the Ottoman territories of Ioannina and Arta refused to allow Jewish merchants returning from Venice to enter these cities. In 1572, a decree ordering the retraction of this unfortunate decision was sent out to the governors along the border and to local judges; at the same time, though, these notables were warned of the danger of Venetian spies using the opportunity to cross the border.[1] The situation was no different further north. After monks carrying letters from Yosif (of. 1560–78), the metropolitan bishop of Thessaloniki, to Poland and Moscow were captured in Wallachia, Wallachia decided to close its borders with Moldavia and Poland.[2] Even the Ottoman tributary Ragusa fell afoul of the Wallachians' suspicion, and Wallachia prohibited people entering the country from Ragusa, a nest of spies.[3] It should be remembered too that the sea was a frontier of sorts. In 1564, Istanbul noted that spies from Christian countries were arriving in Tripoli, disguised as Muslims; the palace ordered that such people should not be allowed into the city.[4]

Other than at crisis points like these, the general policy followed was to keep borders open but to make sure they were carefully monitored. Although local security forces were constantly on patrol on the lookout for enemy spies, it was still possible for people to cross the border without being noticed, as happened in 1567 with Giovanni Maria Renzo, the head of the Habsburg intelligence network in Istanbul. Ignoring the warnings of his agents in Istanbul, the audacious Renzo traveled under a different name from Ragusa to Istanbul. Following secondary roads, he managed to evade the Ottomans who were looking for him.[5]

Given the physical conditions of that period and the insufficiency of military forces, it is clear that patrols on their own were not enough to prevent incursions; it was also necessary to regulate people's travel by demanding that they carry official documents. If a person was not bearing a document that had been issued by the authorities, it was very difficult for them to enter Ottoman territory and travel around the country. Christians who were not Ottoman subjects were compelled to request a safe conduct (*aman*) from the authorities, which meant that their property and lives were placed under protection and that they had the status of *müste'min* (someone who applies for safety).[6] Licenses indicating this were only granted to subjects of states like Venice and France, which had signed a treaty with an Ottoman sultan. According to Don Garcia de Toledo, the Viceroy of Sicily, frequent patrols and new fortifications made it impossible to enter Ottoman territory without a document.[7] No exceptions were made, not even for Christian spies working for the Ottomans. Joseph Nasi assigned two Italian agents from Lucca to go to Puglia, but when these men were traveling from Istanbul to Ragusa, they could only do so under the supervision of an Ottoman marshal.[8] Another example relates to three monks bearing various kinds of letters who were stopped while trying to cross the border. These monks alleged that they had been dispatched by the Istanbul Patriarch Metrophanes III (of. 1565–72, 1579–80) in order to collect alms (*cerrâr makûlesinde olub*), but because they could not present any kind of document issued by the patriarchate, they were arrested. The fact that they were soon released on the orders of Istanbul suggests that they were not spies.[9]

Foreigners and monks were not the only people who needed documents. Muslim subjects were also expected to be able to prove their identities and to give a reason why they were traveling. In 1585, for instance, when a man by the name of Ahmed was halted while trying to cross the Straits of the Dardanelles, he let go of his horse and possessions and tried to run away and was only just caught. His testimony was full of contradictions. Ahmed contended that he was one of İbrahim Pasha's food tasters and had been sent by the pasha to collect debts owed to him. He went on to say that, because he presumed that *timar* cavalrymen would not be admitted into Anatolia, he had dressed up as a merchant, but when he was asked to show identification, he became frightened and fled. What confused his apprehenders was that in Ahmed's bag they found a copy of a document ordering the collection of the funds remaining from the fief of Grand Vizier Siyavuş Pasha. The bag also contained a number of letters on the same issue written by Ahmed Voyvoda (tax collector),[10] a notebook, and three pouches containing a considerable amount of money. When Ahmed was asked to explain what all this was, he said that the money belonged to Siyavuş Pasha. While Ahmed was escorting Ahmed Voyvoda to Istanbul, as well as taking Siyavuş Pasha's money to the same destination, Ahmed Voyvoda had fallen ill in Edirne, meaning that the other Ahmed had to continue the journey on his own. Because there were many bandits on the route between Edirne and Istanbul, Ahmed had decided to cross over from Gallipoli to Anatolia and to take the land route to Istanbul. Finding Ahmed's defense contradictory, the Imperial Council ordered that he should be sent to Istanbul.[11]

Spies who did not possess a document that could lend legitimacy to their trip had no alternative but to go in disguise. When Giovanni Maria Renzo journeyed to Istanbul in 1567, he was dressed as a French envoy.[12] Not everyone, though, was as fortunate as Renzo. In 1571, three people claiming to be associates of the French ambassador were apprehended in the village of Foča in Herzegovina, despite the fact that a Janissary had accompanied them since Ragusa. One of these men was recognized, though, as the servant of an ambassador who had returned to France, and it became clear that all three of them were trying to travel in disguise. They refused to answer questions asked about the Venetian navy and requested to be sent to Istanbul. Since Istanbul suspected them of being Venetian spies, this request was approved.[13] The same year, the Ottomans arrested a Milanese agent who claimed that he had entered the Empire in order to convey a proposal from the Spanish King Philip II for an alliance against Venice. This incident occurred just four months before the Battle of Lepanto, in which the Allied Christian fleet ended up decimating the Ottoman fleet. Given this, the claim by this agent (who insisted he was from France rather than Milan) that he was an envoy of Philip II seems quite bizarre.[14]

I have already pointed out that one method that Ottoman spies frequently used to circumvent enemy counterintelligence was to disguise themselves as clergymen. Since Christians in Ottoman territories enjoyed the freedom to live in peace and to worship as they wished, enemy spies opted to dress up like their Ottoman-Christian counterparts as well. In this way, they could move around unhindered and carry out their intelligence work. On his journey to Istanbul, for example, the famous Habsburg spy Martin de Acuña chose to stay in monasteries.[15] To give another example, in 1572 a number of spies disguised as monks were caught by the Ottomans in Kiliia, Bessarabia. They were found to be carrying letters with them.[16]

Enemy spies carried out reconnaissance missions into Ottoman territory in order to examine military fortifications and to see what kinds of defensive measures the Ottomans were taking. Understandably, commanders in the borderlands were expected to prevent such actions. In 1584, for instance, the governor-general of Bosnia came across some men transporting Turkish-Muslim soldiers who were supposed to serve as *dils* (*asâkir-i islâmdan dil*). The governor-general managed to kill these men and rescue the *dils*.[17]

In their eagerness to protect the transport network from spies, the Ottomans even forced groups whom they regarded with suspicion to travel along certain supposedly suitable routes. Shi'ite pilgrims from Iran, for example, were prevented from taking the route passing through Baghdad, Basra, and Hejaz and instead were compelled to go via Damascus, Cairo, and Yemen.[18] In December 1571, envoys from Ragusa expressed the desire to return home via the sea, but this was turned down by the Ottomans on the pretext that the navigation season was over. Presumably, the pashas' primary concern was not the safety of the envoys. Rather, they were worried that the Ragusans might bump into the Christian fleet at sea and inform the enemy about the air of panic that prevailed in Istanbul in the immediate aftermath of the defeat at Lepanto.[19]

THE FIFTH COLUMNS OF THE "WELL-PROTECTED LANDS"

From time to time, Christian subjects living in coastal areas of the Ottoman Empire or along the border displayed a willingness to collaborate with the enemy. Countless documents in the Ottoman and Spanish archives reveal that European rulers maintained close contacts with a variety of Ottoman subjects, including Orthodox nobles and clergymen and both urban and rural folk. In the extremely repetitive official records, detailed accounts are given of the steps taken by the Ottomans to maintain public security in this regard and the difficulties they faced in cutting the links between these rebels and Europe.[20]

At this point, I would warn against simplifying matters and stress that religion was not the only factor at play here. When we consider the Christian areas that were particularly active in functioning as a fifth column, such as Albania and the Mani Peninsula, we come to realize that they were also the areas whose topographical features made transportation, communication, and logistics especially complicated (see map 5.1).

The Ottoman-Venetian War over Cyprus exposed how vulnerable the Ottomans were along their borders. The Christian naval alliance under the command of Don Juan knew very well how to benefit from the cooperation of local coreligionists. The chief collaborators were members of the clergy. For example, the metropolitan bishop of Patras, who was "subject to and allied with the wretched infidel" (*küffâr-ı hâksâra tâbi' ve yek-dil ve yek-cihet*), noted that there were no troops aboard the imperial navy ships that arrived in the port, and he appealed to Don Juan to attack the Ottoman fleet. And this was not all. On Sunday October 7, the day of the Battle of Lepanto, he defied time-honored customs in opening the churches and treating the people to a feast. In the words of the Registers of Important Affairs, this amounted to "inciting the country to revolt."[21] Three months later, when it became evident that the priests of the Monastery of Saint Nicholas in Euboea were passing information to the enemy,

Istanbul called upon the governor himself to investigate the matter and asked whether there were any weapons in the monastery.[22] The following month, the Ottomans discovered that Don Juan had been sending letters to the metropolitan bishop of Rhodes and had sent a frigate to the island, together with a spy. On the orders of Don Juan, surveillance of the fortress was being carried out. A decree sent from Istanbul to Rhodes demanded the capture of those who had been involved in the delivery of this letter. The decree also stated that, if it was proven that they were guilty, it would be necessary to kill the responsible parties wherever they were hiding, even if that were a monastery (keşişhane). If the metropolitan bishop was shown to be involved, he would suffer the same fate.[23]

The Habsburgs were not the only force who took advantage of troublesome Christians disgruntled with Ottoman rule. Mention was made previously of some monks who were seized in Kiliia and accused of trying to deliver letters to Poland and Russia. They claimed that they had been assigned to do so by Yosif, the metropolitan bishop of Thessaloniki.[24] Europeans managed to find allies among the nobles of the Balkans as well. Nobles who had been exiled by Istanbul and had their land confiscated and princes who wanted to be rid of Ottoman rule regarded the Habsburgs as saviors and did not tire from offering collaboration and, of course, providing intelligence. A Wallachian prince, for example, maintained a regular correspondence with both the Venetians and the Habsburgs, offering them information about Wallachia, Moldavia, Transylvania, Podolia, Bulgaria, Bosnia, and Serbia.[25]

Ordinary people out in the boondocks, in a constant state of rebellion, took matters into their own hands and collaborated with the Habsburgs. Besides supplying the enemy with news, they planned various other schemes

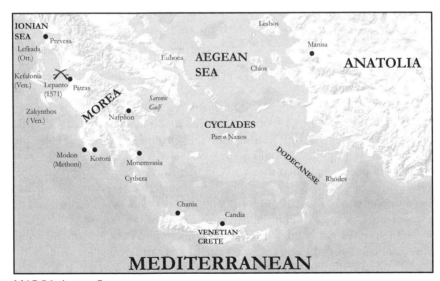

MAP 5.1. Aegean Sea

that made life difficult for Ottoman intelligence. For example, some peasants in the district of Dukagin became allies of Venice and supplied its fortress with provisions. They carried out an ambush near the castle, fighting with Ottoman forces and liberating some of the *dil*s whom the Ottomans were holding, and as if that were not enough, they also harassed the other villages in the area.[26] In some cases, the accommodation and guidance that Ottoman Christians offered enemy spies turned out to be invaluable. A striking example of this is the services that a man named Duli provided to Habsburg intelligence. Duli was the leader of the villages close to Bastia, situated facing Corfu. An Albanian noble, Duli was well-trusted by the governors of both Delvinë and Vlorë, who assigned him important duties and shared military secrets with him. Nonetheless, from 1546 onward, he assisted and housed Habsburg agents who were on their way to Istanbul. Without Duli's help, it would have been impossible for these spies to evade the Ottomans and cross over from Corfu to Ottoman territory, especially if Istanbul had sent an order (*commissario*) to interrogate everyone going into and out of the port, with an eye for capturing agents. Duli did more than just assist spies with entering and exiting; he provided them with a place to stay. In addition, he ensured that there was a regular flow of information via Corfu and Otranto. The Habsburg secret service calculated that this versatile Albanian spy, with his five thousand associates, would be very handy in the case of a "Greek[27] campaign.[28]"

The Ottomans faced a similar fifth column problem on their eastern frontier. The Ottoman-Safavid War of 1577–1590 offers us numerous examples. Shi'ism, which had effectively become a propaganda tool of the Safavid state, gained considerable traction among certain Turkmen groups in Anatolia who were dissatisfied with Ottoman rule. This created a major security risk and got Istanbul worrying. Despite their victories against the Safavids, the Ottomans struggled to eliminate the sympathy for Shi'ism in Anatolia and to prevent Safavid agents (known as caliphs) from spreading pro-shah propaganda. Besides collecting alms from Ottoman subjects, these caliphs also conducted espionage on behalf of Tabriz. In the Registers of Important Affairs, one can find several decrees commanding local authorities to put an end to the caliphs, who were quite a headache.[29]

To get rid of the caliphs, the Ottomans resorted to underhanded methods. In 1568, for instance, a plan was hatched to "disappear" the Safavid vizier Masum Bey when he was passing through Ottoman territory on the pilgrimage to Mecca. The Ottomans were obligated to grant pilgrims passage in times of peace, but when they realized that Masum Bey had appointed an Ottoman subject as a Safavid caliph, they arranged an assassination. It had become something of a custom for Bedouin Arabs to harass pilgrims, and an attack by this group would be sufficient to get rid of the Safavid vizier and to solve the problem at hand.[30] Just like the Roman governor Pontius Pilate, all the Ottomans needed to do was wash their hands and deny all responsibility. Another decree dispatched to Amasya in the same year noted that a Safavid caliph, Süleyman Fakih, had encouraged unbelievers who backed the shah to join up with agitators and had stirred up the local population; the order went out to drown Süleyman surreptitiously in the Kızılırmak River. If news got out that Süleyman had been executed, the explanation would be given that he had committed the crimes of theft and waylaying.[31]

Some of these caliphs were members of the Ottoman population who had emigrated to Iran but returned as Safavid agents. To give one example, a man referred to as Little Ali from the village of Hisarcık in the Çankırı province was alleged to have traveled to Iran and returned a Shi'ite, after which he led other people astray. He was accused of assembling people's "wives and daughters" and carrying out propaganda. Since he refused to renounce his Qizilbash beliefs, his murder was deemed to be crucial.[32] Although the Treaty of Amasya signed between Istanbul and Tabriz in 1555 ordained that Ottoman subjects who sought sanctuary in Iran should be returned to the Empire, this agreement was not really applied.[33] In a nutshell, the Ottomans were unable to prevent their subjects from traveling to Iran. For such people, who are referred to in the Ottoman documents as *râfizî*, it was easy to cross the Ottoman-Safavid border disguised as merchants, after which they were able to maintain links with the Safavids.[34] Another security problem was posed by places like Hoy, which had been conquered only recently and whose population was Shi'ite; people there remained loyal to the Safavid Shah and were forever sending news to Iran.[35]

At this point, I would emphasize that fifth columnists were not found solely in border areas or by the coast; even in the capital, members of the Ottoman administration would sometimes be overwhelmed with suspicion. In 1616, for instance, the Ottoman government was seized by the hunch that twenty thousand Catholics, who mostly lived in Pera, across from the historical heart of Istanbul, would ally with the Greeks and stage an insurrection. As a result, the government forbade Catholics from traveling back and forth between Istanbul and Pera and reinstituted laws stipulating that members of every religious community should be dressed in their customary attire.[36] At the same time, the Catholic clergy in the city were prosecuted. During a raid on the Cathedral of St. Francis,[37] one of the priests was found to be in possession of suspicious-looking letters. In response, the authorities went so far as to tie up the priest and throw him into the sea, as well as searching all the Christian homes in the area.[38] What is more, the judge of Galata and the chief of police (*subaşı*) in the same area cooked up a ridiculous charge that six Jesuits in the Church of St. Benoit in Karaköy were in cahoots with the Habsburg emperor and the Cossacks, Orthodox raiders who had recently created shockwaves through Istanbul by pillaging the villages along the Bosphorus; the Jesuits were arrested and their rooms searched. This charge was followed soon after by more serious and more logical allegations, namely that the Jesuits were spying for the Spaniards, granting absolution to converts, baptizing Muslims, and hiding slaves who had escaped, prior to sending them clandestinely to Europe. When government officials moved on to the Church of Santa Maria Draperis, situated in Pera, they caught the papal representative Giovanni Battista de Montebarocchio red-handed trying to hide some documents. Montebarocchio was found guilty of treason and strangled to death. Thanks to the determined efforts of the French ambassador de Sancy for a full two months, the Jesuits were spared, although they were forced to leave Istanbul immediately.[39]

At moments of intense conflict, the Ottomans did not hesitate to deport from war zones groups whose loyalty they did not trust. In 1532, when the Genoese admiral Andrea Doria, the commander of the Habsburg fleet, besieged Modon, he learned from the Greeks and Albanians who came to his assistance that, prior to the siege, the Ottomans had driven the city's Christians out of town.[40] In 1570, that is, at the time of another war, Uluc Ali Pasha, the governor-general of Algeria, prevented the Christian ships in the port from leaving. His aim in doing this was to inhibit Europe from finding out that, with his fleet of corsairs, he was about to set sail into the Eastern Mediterranean and join forces with the Ottoman navy.[41] Immediately after the debacle at Lepanto, the Ottomans were informed by Muslim slaves who had managed to escape from the enemy that the Christians of Ioannina had formed a secret alliance with the Venetians on Corfu. How dangerous this was becomes all the clearer when we consider that the fortress at Ioannina was crammed with Christians, whereas the Muslim population was limited to the castle warden, the chamberlain, an *imam* (the religious official leading Muslim prayers), and a handful of foot soldiers. Sensing the possibility of great harm, the Ottomans ordered the removal of the Christians from the fortress and their replacement with Muslims.[42] In a similar incident, in 1572 the Ottomans recaptured Split, having lost it to the Venetians the year before, and forced out of the city five thousand Albanians, whom they suspected of having collaborated with the enemy.[43] In 1575, it became apparent that the guard of the fortress at Paramythia/Aydonat had been infiltrated by "outsiders" (*ecnebi*), whereupon Istanbul immediately instructed the governor and the castle warden of Delvinë to do whatever was necessary.[44]

When the Ottomans conquered a region, they tried to counterbalance the number of Christians living inside the fortresses of the region by importing Muslims from Ottoman territories. According to Pierre Belon du Mans, by the middle of the sixteenth century, only a few Christian villages were left on the island of Kos.[45] In Rhodes, however, the situation was different. While the inhabitants of the island were almost entirely Greek, the population of the citadel consisted of Muslims. Christians were permitted to enter the town of Rhodes as much as they wanted, but because the Ottomans were afraid that the Christians might rebel or get involved in some kind of conspiracy, they were forbidden from staying overnight in the town.[46] After the fall of Nicosia and Famagusta, the removal of Christians from these two cities became a priority.[47]

The Ottomans also had to take precautions against enemy propaganda. The greatest threat was perceived to be the Safavids' attempt to spread Shi'ism in Anatolia. In 1576, in the village of Ortapare in Çorum, a Safavid agent by the name of Veli Fakih was found to have smuggled in thirty-four bound books from Iran, which were intended for distribution among the Ottoman community. He had passed them on to another man called Menaş Fakih. When Menaş was captured and interrogated by the authorities, he claimed that the books had been left to him when Veli died. After that, though, he had supposedly passed them on to a third person called Selim Fakih. Selim gave them to a certain Yunus, and he in turn passed them on to a fifth person, called Gülâbi. Istanbul ordered that these books, circulating from person to person, should be tracked down and that the people distributing them should be captured in an unobtrusive manner.[48] A subsequent decree called for the books to be sent to Istanbul.[49]

ENEMY AGENTS AND INFORMANTS WITHIN THE OTTOMAN ADMINISTRATION AND MILITARY

Enemy spies who managed to infiltrate Ottoman fortresses and garrisons constituted a major security problem. In 1544, for example, a monk from Split by the name of Pedro confided in the famous Spanish poet, novelist, and historian Diego Hurtado de Mendoza, who served as an ambassador in Venice, that he was secretly in contact with informants in the Ottoman garrison in the fortress at Klis. He had forged these links on the orders of the pope and of Ferdinand of Austria. The Ottomans became aware of this network just in time and were able to capture Pedro's collaborators. This did not deter Pedro himself, though, and he managed to make contact with no less than seventeen soldiers, including one man who actually held the keys to the gates of the fortress.[50] Twenty-seven years later, at a time when there was considerable activity near the borders because of the outbreak of the war over Cyprus, three castle wardens in the fortress at Nafplion were suspected of collaborating with the Venetians, and the Ottoman authorities ordered their dismissal and their replacement with "competent individuals" (*yarar kimesneler*).[51] Another method besides actually expelling people was to ban them from leaving the garrison's fortress, thereby preventing informants inside a castle from contacting the enemy fleet.[52] There were also cases in the eastern frontier of people collaborating with the enemy. There were rumors, for example, in recently conquered Tiflis, that a regimental scribe named Veli (*sol bölük katibi*) was in "union and alliance" (*ittihâd ü ittifâk*) with the Georgian prince Simon. The Ottomans decided that, if these rumors were found to be true, Veli should be expelled from the castle and sent to the capital.[53]

When the Ottomans found themselves faced with cases of treason like this, which carried obvious security risks, they tended to also prosecute the relatives and friends of the suspects. As a case in point, the "siblings and some associates" of Ali bin Osman, a guard at the castle of Lefkada/Ayamavra were ejected from the castle, the reason being that earlier on Ali's father had treacherously surrendered the castle to the enemy without putting up a fight.[54] In a similar example, after the Çepni tribe of Canik region had surrendered the castle at Erciş to the Safavids, his entourage was thrown out of the castle. Some, however, managed to return and once more enter the service of the Ottomans. A decree sent to the governor-general of Van ordered the expulsion of the entire Çepni tribe from the castles at Ahlat, Erciş, Van, Bitlis, and Adilcevaz.[55]

In order to prevent Habsburg spies from carrying out reconnaissance of the Ottomans' military preparations and fortifications, the Ottomans tried to keep foreigners well away from their castles and fortresses. Comments made by the duke of Gandia would suggest that the Ottomans were successful in doing this. The duke complained that it was impossible to gather information about the fortifications at Algiers, as merchants and foreigners were forbidden from getting close to the city walls, whether from the inside or the outside; as a result, one had to be content with looking at the walls from the sea, and even then from quite a distance.[56]

It would be wrong to assume that enemy spies and informants were only to be found in castles; they had even infiltrated the Ottoman army itself. This would become particularly clear in the case of the wars with the Safavids. It was not unusual for *timar* cavalrymen to be members of Qizilbash groups;[57] Shah İsmail had many followers within the *akıncı* raiding section of the army. The reason why the Ottomans entered the Battle of Chaldiran (1514) with a tired army was that Treasurer Piri Mehmed Çelebi had opposed giving the army some rest before the battle. Çelebi made much of the fact that several members of the *akıncı* section, which included the famous Mihaloğlu family, were devotees of the Qizilbash (*Kızılbaşa muhibb*). For this reason, he advised that no time should be lost and that the battle should commence before the enemy had time to get organized. If this did not happen, Shah İsmail's agents would persuade the Qizilbashes within the Ottoman army to fight halfheartedly.[58] The Qizilbashes were certainly providing the enemy with intelligence; Shah İsmail appears to have been aware of the Ottomans' military tactics. Malkoçoğlu Ali and his brother Tur Ali, positioned on the left flank of the Ottoman army, commanded their forces to encircle the right flank of the Safavids. However, Shah İsmail had been informed by his agents that Malkoçoğlu's forces were not so strong, so when the Safavids attacked the Ottomans' left flank, they ended up victorious.[59]

The Ottoman navy likewise suffered at the hands of enemy spies. A considerable number of corsairs, sailors, and craftsmen serving in the imperial shipyard or the navy were either Christians or converts. In the aftermath of the Battle of Djerba, the Habsburgs ensured that the intelligence network they formed in Istanbul had plenty of eyes at the shipyard or in other positions within the navy. There were also several converts within Grand Admiral Uluc Ali's entourage. According to Emilio Sola Castaño, as of 1581, there were six of them: his chamberlain (*mayordomo*), Murad Agha; a Lombard convert, Antonio de Vale/Süleyman Agha; an English convert, Carlo Daniel/Murad Agha (*Comorat*); two Frenchmen who were Knights of St. John, that is, Maltese corsairs (*habito de San Juan*); and a Spaniard, the son of the commander of the Fortress of La Goulette.[60] Two other highly productive agents were the Englishman Robert Drever/Haydar, and the Spaniard Juan Briones/Sinan. These men would send the Habsburgs several letters containing information about the route being taken by the Ottoman navy and about the discussions going on among Ottoman grandees.[61]

Given that the majority of oarsmen were Christians, one should not underestimate the risk that, in the heat of battle, they might revolt and seize control of their galleys. Indeed, even when they were not engaged in battles, they would sometimes mutiny, take control of galleys, and try to escape to harbors in Naples and Sicily. A good example of this is Giorgio Cavalà, whom we encountered in chapter 2. When these fugitive captives reached Christian territory, they were more than happy to answer questions about the Ottoman navy, shipyard, and harbors, and they provided the Habsburgs with the very latest information.[62]

A VAST BORDERLAND: THE MEDITERRANEAN

While the Romans regarded the Mediterranean as an inland sea, referring to it as *Mare Nostrum*, that is, "Our Sea," in the sixteenth century the Mediterranean did not belong to a single empire. Even though central governments made considerable investments, they proved unable to control the borderland that the Mediterranean constituted. When empires left the stage in the seventeenth and eighteenth centuries, the sea was left at the mercy of corsairs.

One of the chief factors that determined the Ottomans' grand strategy was their attempt to gain dominance of the sea and to keep the coasts free of enemy spies and ships. Behind their decision to attack Rhodes was the fact that the Knights of St. John, who had already transformed the island into a hotbed of piracy, were constantly appealing to European rulers to launch a crusade against the Ottomans, taking it for granted that they could rely on the cooperation of the sultan's Christian subjects.[63] It could be argued that the aim of the siege of Corfu in 1537 was to prevent enemy spies from sailing over from this Venetian-run island to the Ottoman coast, from which they could infiltrate Ottoman territory. The conquest of Chios and the Dodecanese in 1566 was motivated by the same concerns. According to the rumors awash in Venice a year before the conquest, the sultan had ordered the beheading of the duke of Naxos, Giovanni Crispo IV, and of sixteen or eighteen other men for allegedly sending Malta news regarding the Ottoman fleet.[64] Writing in the seventeenth century, Kâtib Çelebi claimed that the reason for the Ottomans' conquest of Chios was that the islanders had constantly been feeding Europe with news about the Ottoman Empire and about the size and movements of the Ottoman navy. The islanders did not abstain "from maintaining friendships with the infidel enemy and reporting what was going on in the Ottoman lands and how many ships were to leave the port and in which direction, thereby paving the way to damage to the Muslim ships."[65] According to the testimony of a captive who had managed to escape from Istanbul, there was a possibility that the Ottomans would launch an attack on Ragusa and Monte Sant'Angelo in Naples, the aim of which was to prevent the enemy from receiving intelligence.[66]

One of the objectives of the Cyprus campaign, which entailed a number of risks, was to stem enemy intelligence. Far away from the city of Venice and deep within Ottoman waters, Cyprus was a sanctuary for both Christian corsairs and spies. From as far back as the Mamluk era, the spies of Venice had come to use Cyprus as a stepping stone from which they traveled to the coast of Syria and then on into the interior of Iran. In 1508, for instance, the Venetian consul in Damascus, Pietro Zen, sent two Iranian agents to Venice via Cyprus.[67] On their next voyage, when they were being accompanied by the Cypriot Nicolò Soro and various Venetian merchants, the agents and their companions were arrested by the Mamluks. In his testimony, Soro did not hide the fact that he had been sent from Cyprus.[68] In 1531, a Venetian by the name of Andrea Moresini was arrested in Aleppo. He was accused of smuggling into Ottoman territory a Spanish envoy who was on his way to Iran and also of arranging a guide to take the envoy up to the Taurus Mountains. In the end, a guide was arrested and Moresini was executed, both of which the Ottomans held the Venetians responsible for.[69]

The Ottomans' conquest of the islands near the Ottoman coast only partly solved the problem, since logistic realities and the era's limited military technology meant that it was not possible to maintain full control of the Mediterranean, a sea synonymous with piracy. All the same, the fact that central governments were willing to invest in such campaigns shows how concerned they were about possible infiltration by spies.

From time to time, searches were carried out of foreign ships. In 1569, the Ottomans arrested two Spaniards they found in a Venetian ship and subsequently warned the *bailo*, Marc'Antonio Barbaro, in no uncertain terms: the sultan's friends should not be transporting subjects of the enemy.[70] Ships anchored in harbors could also be the object of suspicion and criminal investigations. In 1565, for example, the agha of the imperial gate (*Kapu Ağası*)[71] himself sailed to the harbor and personally interrogated the crew who had brought tribute from Chios. When a member of the crew let on that the ship contained some letters that had been brought for the people of Pera—who, like the population of Chios, were Catholics of Genoese origin—the Ottomans promptly confiscated these letters. Thankfully for the people of Chios, there was nothing in the letters that could have got them into trouble.[72]

In their struggle with infiltration from the sea, the Ottomans made maximum use of semiofficial forces like corsairs. The Ottomans had limited influence in the Adriatic Sea, which was dominated more by the Venetians. Here, therefore, the job of patrolling the sea and combating enemy intelligence was done by corsairs, who were given an official title and integrated into the administration. These corsairs took on a range of tasks, including intercepting frigates[73] that were carrying letters from Venice as well as enemy galleys that were involved in intelligence and dealing in illicit materials (i.e., smuggling). In 1540, for example, they managed to seize letters that the viceroy of Sicily had written to Naples, as well as a frigate that was concealing a Spanish spy by the name of Pedro Secula. What makes the letters that were found on Secula's person so significant is that they exemplify the detailed instructions that could be given to spies and demonstrate the threat that spies coming from the sea could pose. Secula's main duty was to travel in secret to the Straits of Corfu and then to enter Ottoman territory. If he did not manage to find his way into the Empire, he was going to throw the letters into the sea and move on to Heraklion, from where he would dispatch intelligence concerning the Ottoman navy. After Heraklion, Secula was supposed to be traveling to Napflion, a well-fortified Ottoman port in the Peloponnese. There, he would make contact with the rebellious Christian community and offer to send them arms, soldiers, and provisions. There was no happy ending to Secula's story, though, and he was eventually executed in Istanbul.[74]

In 1574, a volunteer captain, that is, a corsair working for the state, named Cafer, who was returning from a mission to bring back some *dil*s, managed to seize a galiot belonging to the Habsburg admiral Don Juan. He freed the *dil*s and had the whole crew transporting them killed.[75] As this example shows, Ottoman corsairs were effective in preventing local representatives of the Habsburg regime from communicating with one another and also with the Habsburgs' agents. In 1573, for instance, a Habsburg spy in Ragusa called Luis de Portillo complained that he was having to pay fifty écus for the frigate that he dispatched to Barletta. He added, "No one wants to move out of here, because they're afraid of the frigates" (*fuste*, meaning corsairs). The Habsburg authorities appealed to their counterparts in Ragusa to provide Portillo with messengers should that be necessary.[76] When a letter written by the viceroy of Sicily and dated June 24, 1574, fell into the hands of corsairs, it provoked a disgruntled response from Philip II. The solution that the viceroy of Sicily came up with was to send a copy of all letters via Naples.[77]

Even in periods when the local population was not collaborating with the enemy, enemy ships were able to embark on reconnaissance operations and gather information. To offset this, local authorities were forced to take precautions along the coast. During the Ottoman-Venetian War, for example, two galleys and three galiots entered the harbor of Tripoli in Lebanon, disguised as Muslim ships, and seized a Muslim merchant ship loaded with soap. This prompted Istanbul to request the local authorities "to ensure that the coast was protected effectively" (*yalıları onat vechile hıfz u hırâset ittirmeleri*). However, there were not sufficient ships in the area to deal with these five galleys, so it is doubtful how effectively this protection could have been carried out. Istanbul called upon local regiments to prevent the enemy from coming onto land and warned local populations not to graze animals close to the shore.[78]

In fact, the problem of coastal defense was dealt with in a more systematic way. Every year, a fleet of between twelve and sixteen ships would set sail from Istanbul and patrol the coast, providing what was then termed "maritime protection" (*derya muhafâzâsı*).[79] This fleet had numerous responsibilities, such as maintaining the safety of maritime traffic, transporting Ottoman public officers to their positions in overseas territories like Egypt, combating smuggling, and fighting enemy ships; on top of that, they were expected to gather intelligence.

When they captured enemy seamen, they would start by interrogating them and then send them off to Istanbul.[80]

With the aim of combating piracy and deterring smuggling along the coasts and out at sea, the Ottomans established a kind of alarm system designed to mobilize their subjects. In this system, local villages had a corvée duty, which was referred to in the Statute Book (*Kânûnnâme*) for Rhodes and Kos (1650) as *bedel-i vigle* ("duty of surveillance"). What this duty meant was that in villages on islands that had a good view of the sea, one person would keep watch throughout the night while another would do so during the day. If they saw a ship in the sea that aroused their suspicions, these watchmen would pass on news to the neighboring village, and by this channel, news could be passed from one village to the next and, in no time at all, to the castle. Villagers whose villages were located further inland and who were therefore not in a position to serve as lookouts were obliged to come to the local castle and help with its maintenance. This program of forced labor took up twelve days a year.[81]

This system is known to have dated back at least to the sixteenth century. Pirî Reis recounts that, when the inhabitants of the island of Gökçeada (İmroz) spotted a ship, they signaled to the seamen over on the mainland. During the day, they used smoke to do this; at night they used fire. The seamen in turn shared the news with the other villages in Rumelia and, according to Pirî Reis, within just an hour news would reach Istanbul![82] Documents reveal that a similar system of surveillance functioned on the islands of Lemnos,[83] Cyprus,[84] and Rhodes.[85] In one entry in the Registers of Important Affairs, reference is made to a village dubbed as an information provider (*dilci demekle ma'rûf*) that was assigned the duty of informing about smuggler or pirate ships moored in the harbor of the Gallipoli fortress or passing down the Straits of the Dardanelles.[86]

This practical system was not an Ottoman invention; on every side of the Mediterranean, similar alarm systems had been devised to deal with the threat posed by agile and insidious pirates. It is known that, when the Venetians controlled Cyprus, villagers there were given similar duties. Along some of the coasts of Italy too, the Habsburgs set up a comparable communication system involving towers.[87]

PERSONAE NON GRATAE: EUROPEAN AMBASSADORS

As I mentioned earlier, ambassadors functioned simultaneously as intelligence chiefs. They established close relations with Ottoman bigwigs and were able to benefit from relatively large budgets and from the freedom to move around at liberty. Exploiting these advantages, they employed numerous spies and informants in the Ottoman capital, which is how they became prime suspects in the eyes of Ottoman counterespionage.

To stop ambassadors from wandering around town gathering information, the Ottomans tried to ensure that a close eye was kept on them and their associates. The first step they took was limiting the contact that foreign ambassadors had with the local population when they were on their way to Istanbul.

With this precaution, there would be less chance of ambassadors spying out the land, identifying future collaborators, and spreading dangerous religious ideas. In any case, the route that these ambassadors followed to Istanbul was determined by the Ottomans. In addition, the Ottoman rulers appointed marshals to accompany ambassadors and requested local beys and judges to provide ambassadors and their entourages with any grain, horses, or ships they might need on a journey.[88] Before European ambassadors entered Ottoman territory, they had to wait in Ragusa for a marshal or steward[89] to be sent from Istanbul. Istanbul even insisted on monitoring the routes that ambassadors from its own tributary states were taking.[90]

Given the popularity of the Qizilbash creed among the ordinary folk of Anatolia, it is undeniable that the movements of the Iranian ambassadors within the Ottoman Empire constituted an even bigger security problem. The Ottomans were wary of Safavid ambassadors coming into contact with their subjects and wished to prevent such interaction. They also wanted to stop the local population from giving these envoys the alms (*nüzûr u sadakât*) that they had collected in honor of the shah. For this reason, in 1568 the governor of Amasya and the governor-general of Rum were ordered to arrest and kill anyone found giving alms to Safavid envoys. In order to avoid a local backlash, these people would be arrested on the pretext that they were going to appear in court in front of their accusers; later, though, they were executed on charges of theft and banditry.[91]

In the same year, the governor-general of Van received an order to prevent envoys from coming into contact with the public and to ensure that the scribe the central government provided would record the names of people who supplied envoys with alms (*nüzûr u pişkeş*) and who demonstrated sympathy toward the Safavid cause (*izhâr-ı muhabbet*).[92] The Ottomans were also concerned about the Safavids distributing alms among the local population, again in the name of the shah. They were worried that, in this way, the Safavids could gain support among Ottoman subjects. According to an entry in the Registers of Important Affairs, the envoy was told that, if the shah had so much money to give away, he should distribute it among Iran's own poor.[93]

Once ambassadors arrived in Istanbul, it was easier for them to access intelligence channels. This is why their contacts in the world outside were an intense and constant source of concern for Ottoman intelligence. That said, it should be conceded that the Ottoman rulers were not alone in wanting to limit the contacts that foreign ambassadors maintained in the capital. In 1481, for instance, the Venetian Council of Ten passed a law banning all senators, and all members of the secret councils in which important decisions were made, from discussing matters of state (*de cose pertinenti al Stado*) with foreigners.[94]

Particularly when their relations with a country were at a low point, the Ottomans resorted to placing envoys under house arrest. Istanbul was generally on bad terms with the ambassadors of the Habsburg Empire, but sometimes the situation became particularly unbearable. Let us start by considering the cases of a number of ambassadors who arrived from Vienna. In 1545, an

Austrian ambassador by the name of Gerhard Veltwyck came to the Ottoman Empire to participate in peace talks, but he was not allowed to send or receive post. In fact, Rüstem Pasha had discovered that Veltwyck was receiving news from all quarters anyway. As far as Veltwyck saw it, the ban on post was a ruse to prevent him from receiving news from the front that might have strengthened his hand. By cutting off the ambassador's communication with the outside world, the Ottomans were able to manipulate the peace negotiations just as they wanted. The initial plan was to accommodate Veltwyck in a caravanserai.[95] Later on, however, this plan was abandoned, and another strategy was followed: Veltwyck was housed in the embassy, the courtyard in front of which was blocked off and the windows looking out on to the street covered over. What is more, both the ambassador and his interpreter were essentially imprisoned in their homes. Other than the official responsible for delivering provisions (*spenditore*), no one was allowed to enter or leave the embassy.[96]

Veltwyck was succeeded by Busbecq. On his second visit to Istanbul in 1556, Busbecq was kept under house arrest for a full six months, his ties to the outside world cut off entirely. Busbecq, however, proved more determined than his predecessor and refused to acquiesce. One day, when he was particularly annoyed, in protest at his mistreatment, he locked himself inside and left the marshal waiting outside. During another mission to the Ottoman capital, Busbecq wanted to watch Süleyman the Magnificent leaving the city on his way to a military campaign; he simply got someone to smash the door down so that he could go outside.[97] The security restrictions on him did not end though, and they were still in place a few years later, when his gate would be locked every day by an Ottoman marshal. Oppressive measures of this kind were intended partly to unsettle the opposing party in diplomatic negotiations and partly to prevent envoys from collecting information.

By the second half of the sixteenth century, the presence of a permanent Austrian ambassador in Istanbul meant that matters were dealt with in a more regular way. During peacetime, ambassadors were left to go about their business. This was not the case, though, with diplomats representing Spain. Madrid not only refused to recognize Istanbul's superiority but also was set against appointing an official ambassador to Istanbul. In 1581, Giovanni Margliani was one of the signatories of the ceasefire between the two empires, but he too was the object of pressures resembling those that had been imposed on Veltwyck and Busbeck. One day, he was made an interesting offer by Hürrem Bey, an interpreter at the Imperial Council. Hürrem Bey had a key role in the negotiations and also served as a mediator between the envoy Margliani and the pashas. Negotiations had reached something of a deadlock, and it was widely suspected that Margliani might try to abscond, using the excuse of taking leave. The Ottomans wanted to prevent this from happening, and they calculated that he should pay a certain amount of money (*segurta*) in order for them to not keep him under house arrest. Another mediator, the Jewish powerbroker Salomon Ashkenazi, actually offered to act as a guarantor for Margliani and to pay out no less than fifty thousand écus so that Margliani would be freed from his captivity. Margliani, though, was having nothing of this.[98] Presumably he had figured that these two political powerbrokers, who were not averse to earning a quick buck, were up to no good.

Ottoman-Venetian relations were generally maintained in a friendly and supportive manner; this did not mean, though, that the *bailo* was completely free of suspicion. In those years when resident embassies were just starting to become more common, rulers took a dim view of foreign envoys, who they thought were likely to get involved in espionage. This is why the Ottomans decided to limit the time that these permanent envoys could stay in Istanbul. Although there is no reference to such a rule in the treaty of 1482, we do know that in 1503 the maximum period during which a *bailo* could remain in Istanbul was limited to one year, this being extended to three years after 1513.[99] In addition, particularly *non gratae* "foreign guests" were sometimes deported. This was what happened, for example, to Girolamo Marcello, whose letters were confiscated in 1492 and who was found to have been engaged in supplying Venice with intelligence.[100]

In wartime, *bailo*s found themselves faced with even tougher conditions. The time that poor Marc'Antonio Barbaro and his entourage spent in Istanbul was certainly no holiday. As soon as the war got underway, an order was passed down to the judge of Galata and to Mustafa Çavuş, who had been assigned to take care of the *bailo*: Barbaro was to be placed under house arrest and forbidden from speaking and corresponding with anyone.[101] Things turned out even worse for the *bailo*'s chaplain, Arcangelo de Lyo. Under torture, a Franciscan monk named Paolo Biscotto, who had been arrested for delivering letters to the *bailo*, claimed that de Lyo had given him these letters. Unsurprisingly, de Lyo was promptly thrown into prison, but thanks to a hefty bribe by Barbaro, he was later released. This money turned out to be wasted, though, because the priest's spell in prison had been damaging for his health. Soon afterward, he had to have his leg amputated, and he died just a month after being released.

When it became clear that the *bailo* had been communicating with the outside world, his house arrest was made even stricter. Under instructions from Sokollu Mehmed Pasha, the windows of the *bailo*'s residence were bricked in, all the paper and ink in the building were confiscated, and agents were positioned close to the residence. As if it was not bad enough that Biscotto was executed, his decapitated head was paraded around by soldiers right below the windows of the embassy. To prevent embassy staff from speaking with anyone, they were accompanied by Janissaries as soon as they left the building. People entering or exiting the embassy were searched to ensure that they were not carrying any letters with them. Even the members of the *bailo*'s family faced restrictions on the way they interacted with the public at large. Because of certain medical problems he had, the *bailo*'s son Francesco was allowed to wander around the city, albeit accompanied by Janissaries. However, when an Ottoman subject approached and greeted him, the friendly local was hit with a fine of forty *akçes*.[102]

At this point, I should note that the very same Sokollu Mehmed Pasha who was behind all these measures was actually on good terms with Marc'Antonio Barbaro. Indeed, in a portrait of the *bailo* exhibited at Vienna's Belvedere Museum, Barbaro holds a piece of paper which contains the now illegible message "*I[llustrissi]mo Domino Mahomet Pacha [Imperatoris] Musulmanorum Visiario [nostro] amico optimo*," meaning "To our good friend, the vizier of the sultan of the Muslims, His Most Illustrious Highness Mehmed Pasha."[103] In other words, these precautions were not rooted in some type of personal animosity but were actually standard procedures that were followed under similar conditions. For all their stringency, the measures taken regarding the *bailo* do not appear to have done any good, because Barbaro still managed to send news to Venice. In 1572, for instance, he shared with them his thoughts on the likely targets of the Ottoman navy.[104] In one of his letters, Barbaro even revealed that the marshal who had been assigned to keep tabs on him had confessed that he found the house arrest imposed on the *bailo* inhumane.[105] This marshal's attitude leads one to suspect that the Janissaries who were supposed to be guarding him might not have been doing their job so thoroughly; this may have been out of empathy, or perhaps bribery had something to do with it.

To understand how the *bailo* actually managed to communicate with the outside world, one only needs to look at how letters from the governor of Corfu ended up in the hands of the *bailo*. When the governor's messenger arrived in Istanbul, he met up with a Venetian merchant named Marc'Antonio Stanga, and the messenger reassured Stanga that he had been sent by Costa de Athanasio "who hoed his vineyards in Pera every year" (*qua mi manda Costa de Athanasio, quello che vi suol zappar le vigne ogn'anno*). On hearing this coded message, Stanga took the letters from the messenger. He then met up in the Cathedral of St. Francis with a servant of the *bailo* who was able to leave the embassy every three days. The venue for this liaison had been deliberately chosen to shake off the Janissaries who were trailing the servant. Knowing that the Ottomans were bound to search him, the servant first had to crack the code in which the letters were written, then to memorize their content, and finally to inform Barbaro about what he could remember was in the letters. All the correspondence and codes were stored away from the *bailo*'s residence; fearing that the Ottomans would find them, one Easter holiday they were transported to another location. It is worth pointing out that no less than four messengers (sent from Corfu, Zakynthos, Kotor, and Kefalonia) were standing by in Istanbul, ready to carry the *bailo*'s letters when the need arose.[106]

As this case clearly demonstrates, Ottoman counterespionage did not only need to keep an eye on "honorary spies" like the *bailo*; surveillance of their entourages was also necessary. It became apparent, for example, that some of the employees of the Austrian ambassador, who were ostensibly bringing tribute to Istanbul, were actually engaged in spying; this led the governor-general of Buda to call for greater caution.[107] In 1663, the interpreter of the Austrian envoy to Buda was accused of being a spy and only just avoided being executed.[108] In 1570, Giovanni Battista Zeffo, chaplain to the Austrian ambassador, was kidnapped by Janissaries in broad daylight and subsequently murdered. The background for this killing, most likely, was that another dragoman working at the same embassy, Domenico Zeffo, whom the Ottomans had once driven out of Istanbul, had gotten involved in conspiratorial activities in collaboration with a certain Mihail Černović, a spy working for the Habsburgs.[109]

INTERCEPTING DIPLOMATIC CORRESPONDENCE

As modern diplomacy started to find its feet, a need arose for messengers, who delivered the reports that resident ambassadors prepared on a regular basis to the capitals. This meant that a number of foreigners would be able to move around other countries at ease, even though they were carrying letters that might contain critical information. Of course, it would have been unthinkable for the authorities to be so lenient and thereby open the door to such a security risk. For example, from 1601 onward, messengers who had previously taken letters from Spain and delivered them to the Low Countries and Italy via France were forced to hand them over to French messengers in Lyon or Bordeaux. In theory, these French messengers were not supposed to hang on to them for more than a day, but in reality, this rule remained on paper and was widely flouted. In those periods when relations between France and the Habsburgs were at a low ebb, France took advantage of its position in the midst of different Habsburg territories and, in the words of a French historian, did not shy from instigating a "war of the messengers."[110]

In line with international agreements, the Ottomans were supposed to give free rein to messengers who were working for embassies. There was a notable gap between theory and practice, though, and when it suited them, Ottoman public officials were not averse to rummaging around in messengers' bags. For instance, when it came to the letters that the Austrian ambassador was sending to Vienna, Sokollu Mehmed Pasha was not content to just have Ali Bey, a translator at the Imperial Council, read them; he also kept tabs on the messenger who was carrying them. First of all, he insisted that a cavalryman be assigned to accompany this messenger—in fact, it would be more accurate to say to keep him under surveillance. Then he ordered the governor-general of Buda to conduct a strip search of the messenger and to check whether the messenger was carrying any other letters besides the ones that Ali Bey had read.[111] The head of Habsburg intelligence in Istanbul, Giovanni Maria Renzo, declared that the messengers working the line between Istanbul and Ragusa were unreliable. This explains why, even though the Ottomans were looking for him everywhere, Renzo was prepared to take the risk of carrying the spies' letters on his person.[112]

When the Ottomans' relations with other powers soured, they made things even harder for messengers. Even before the Ottoman-Venetian War over Cyprus had been officially declared, the Ottomans started to confiscate the *bailo's* correspondence and to detain couriers working for him. In the first few months of 1570, for example, "a number of heathens from Kotor were arrested (in Skopje) while carrying letters to the *bailo* of Venice," and the letters were sent to Istanbul. Istanbul also instructed the governor of Skopje to send the messengers and to continue to arrest further messengers if they turned up in Skopje.[113] Marc'Antonio Barbaro was well aware of what was going on. Because he suspected that the Ottomans were blocking the roads, he took the precaution of sending one copy via Corfu and dispatching another with a merchant who was on his way to Narenta.[114] On February 6, 1570, the *bailo* learned that one of his messengers had been arrested and that the Janissary agha had sent letters to the grand vizier. This happened at a time when Sokollu Mehmed Pasha had informed the *bailo* that the sultan wanted to seize Cyprus, even though war had not yet been officially declared. Barbaro's cautiousness, though, appears to have paid off, and he was in a position to guarantee his government that the other messengers would be able to deliver their copies of the letters.[115] In another letter dated March 8, Barbaro complained that for the last eight months he had not received any replies to the letters he had sent to Crete;[116] the letters that the courier from Corfu was bringing were all quite dated.[117] The job of carrying the *bailo*'s letters safely was left to Alvise Buonrizzo, a former embassy scribe who was returning to Venice. On his way to Venice, Buonrizzo came across an underling of the governor of Dukakin who was on his way to Istanbul, transporting two massive sacks full of letters that had been confiscated from Venetian messengers. On the third day of his journey, while he was staying overnight in a village where messengers tended to lodge, he found out that no less than twelve messengers had been arrested in Skopje.[118] While the *bailo* took the necessary precautions to ensure that at least one copy of the letters reached Venice, what could he do to conceal the content of these letters from the Ottomans? Barbaro does not seem to have been particularly concerned about the prospect of the Ottomans actually understanding the letters, since he apparently believed that the Ottomans would be unable to crack the code in which they were written.[119]

The messengers that the *bailo* deployed tended to come from the regions of Katun and Ljubotin in Montenegro.[120] This meant that they were Ottoman subjects, so the Ottomans actually had the right to do with them as they pleased. The following two examples demonstrate how the origins of the people in question made it easier for the Ottomans to interfere, the outcome being that different kinds of captured messengers could be treated in quite different ways. In 1580, Ottoman officials intercepted a Hungarian Muslim, an Ottoman subject, who was carrying a number of letters that had been sent to the Habsburg emperor, Rudolf II. When the Ottomans sentenced him to forced labor as an oarsman, the Habsburg ambassador opted to deny all responsibility in this matter. Just a few days later, in contrast, the governor-general of Buda arrested another messenger and sent him off to Istanbul. In this case, it turned out that the messenger was not an Ottoman subject, and the ambassador resorted to a different method, asking for the messenger and the letters to be returned to him. Although the governor-general initially stood his ground, in the end the Ottomans had no choice but to set the messenger free.[121]

Being sentenced to a term as an oarsman was not the worst thing that could happen to a captured messenger. In 1583, a Muslim messenger in Macedonia was hung, having been charged with being a spy.[122] Two years on, the Ottoman government realized that between fifty and sixty people from the village of Karadağ in the district of Scutari had been deployed as messengers by the Venetians. The governor was ordered to imprison every one of them, confiscate all the letters in their possession, and send the letters to the capital.[123] In 1605, the governor of the same province made sure that numerous Venetian messengers were seized and beaten, with saddlebags containing letters being thrown into the river.[124]

In the sixteenth century, the only regular postal service operating between Istanbul and Europe was that run by the Venetians. This is why, when the Ottomans intercepted the post earmarked for the Venetian ambassador in Istanbul, they were not just confiscating the correspondence of this and other envoys; they were also getting hold of letters addressed to merchants, captives, pilgrims, and clerics, in short, everyone. People who wanted to send letters to Europe were well aware of this and made sure they took the necessary precautions. Spies used code in the letters they wrote and became masters in the art of deploying aliases.[125] They were also familiar with methods such as writing in invisible ink and deploying the technique of steganography (concealed writing). On the front page of a letter, they would write things that were unlikely to arouse suspicions, giving the impression that this was a letter from a merchant or captive to his family. The back page would consist of an intelligence report written using lemon juice, and the public officers who received this letter would know from the name of the sender or the receiver that the letter was written by a spy. All that needed to be done now was to "torture" (*tormentar*)[126] the letter by holding a flame close to the writing in lemon juice; once this was done, the writing would turn red and legible (see fig. 10).[127]

There were times, though, when such precautions proved insufficient. For example, one would search in vain for any information of intelligence value in the letters that the Spaniards and Italians captured by the Ottomans during the Battle of Djerba sent from Istanbul. Either they did not dare to include such material or they were prevented by the Ottomans from doing so.[128] As was mentioned earlier, Barbaro found himself in a state of house arrest, but this did not stop him from receiving letters that had been prepared using the methods just outlined. On the other hand, even though four messengers were waiting in Istanbul to receive word from him, he was frightened to write—hardly surprising given that, via a message to the French ambassador, the Ottomans had warned him that, should he try to write a letter, they would decapitate not just him but also his son.[129] In 1580, Margliani confessed that he could not write letters at night, out of the fear that, at any moment, the grand vizier Koca Sinan Pasha or Uluc Ali could send a marshal to check on him.[130] The Ottomans also pulled off a major coup in intercepting the traitorous correspondence that Uluc Ali's chamberlain Murad Agha had written to the Habsburgs. In 1575, Antonio Avellán (one of the envoys that Don Juan had sent to Istanbul) was shocked when Müezzinzade Ali Pasha's son Mahmud Bey drew attention to a letter that Philip II had written to Murad Agha and asked for it to be deciphered. Thankfully, Avellán kept his cool and, after providing misleading information about the content of the letter, managed to destroy it in time.[131]

As the earlier example demonstrates, it was not so easy to decipher the codes used in letters that were intercepted. People who were familiar with the ways of the embassy chancellery could be quite helpful here. When the Ottomans needed to decode the letters of the *bailo* Vettero Brigadin, their only alternative was to cozy up to Colombina, one of the "language boys" (It. *giovane di lingua*).[132] Colombina, who was a convert to Islam, was not actually an embassy clerk, but he learned about codes while helping the embassy staff, and he was always willing to share this valuable knowledge with the pashas, who were forever on the lookout for new information.[133] Colombina would continue to serve the Ottomans for many years. Indeed, when in 1578 the Ottomans went so far as to appoint this traitorous convert as the ambassador to Venice, they were met with a harsh response from the Venetians.[134]

There were several occasions, though, when the Ottomans were at a loss to solve the codes deployed in letters. In the case of the two examples mentioned in this chapter involving the messengers working for the Austrian ambassador, the Ottomans were unable to decipher the letters in question.[135] During the siege of Malta, the Ottomans managed to capture a frigate that the grand master of the Knights of St. John had dispatched to Sicily. However, they were only partly able to decipher the encoded (*in zifara*) letters that the frigate was carrying.[136]

It was probably because of failures like this that the Ottomans raised official objections to foreign ambassadors' use of codes in their letters. In 1567, Sokollu Mehmed Pasha warned the Venetian *bailo* Jacobo Soranzo on this matter. On top of this, İbrahim Bey, an interpreter at the Imperial Council who had also previously served as ambassador to Venice, revealed to Soranzo that the pasha was considering adding an article on this matter to a new agreement, a detail that got Soranzo worrying.

It is clear from the instructions issued by the Venetian Council of Ten how seriously this matter was taken. *Bailo Soranzo* and ambassador Marino Cavalli were expected to highlight what the consequences would be if their letters were seized by others, and they were also supposed to be resolute in rejecting the introduction of a new article to the Ottoman-Venetian agreement. The pasha needed to be reminded that other envoys' letters were written in code and be warned about discriminating against Venice in this way. Should Sokollu come out with the defense that the Ottomans did not employ secret codes in their own correspondence, the response should be to emphasize that the Ottomans did not have resident ambassadors in other countries anyway. The Ten also advised its representatives to point out that, in order to avoid their important correspondence from falling into enemy hands, the Ottomans did not rely on messengers to carry their letters but rather employed marshals at the palace to do so. If the Ottomans were not swayed by any of these arguments, then the Venetians would have no choice but to comply with Sokollu's demands. In this sense, those who have branded Venice the concubine of the Ottomans are not entirely wrong. On the other hand, there was no end to the methods that the Council of Ten used to try to get what they wanted. They told their diplomats to emphasize how vital it was that Venice's reputation was maintained, which was why they had to prevent the insertion of an additional article to the Ottoman-Venetian treaty. Also, the pasha should be reminded that such an act would not be in the interests of the Ottomans either. If the Venetians were forced to abandon the use of codes in their correspondence, they would no longer be able to provide the Ottomans with intelligence, and neither would they be in a position to deliver letters between the fleet and Istanbul, as they had done at the time of the Malta Campaign in 1565.[137]

When the Council of Ten learned later on that Sokollu had made similar demands of other ambassadors, they changed their tactics; now they ordered their representatives in Istanbul to cooperate with diplomats from other countries in resisting the Ottomans' demands. If this and other techniques came to nothing, then the last resort was the tried-and-tested strategy of using bribes and presents to win over the hearts and minds of the Ottoman pashas, who had a soft spot for money.[138]

The issue of ambassadors deploying codes in their correspondence came to the fore once more four years later, at a time when the Ottoman-Venetian War over Cyprus was about to start. Sokollu told *bailo* Marc'Antonio Barbaro not to deploy codes in his letters, but at the same time, in a tongue-in-cheek manner he asked the *bailo* to get someone to teach one of his own officials how to use codes. It should not come as too much of a surprise that Barbaro diplomatically rejected this request, explaining that it would take too much effort and time.[139]

The situation was no different on the Ottomans' eastern borders. In 1571, the Ottomans got word that a number of Armenians from Ankara, who were part of a caravan traveling from Edirne to Iran, had tried to smuggle some letters to Iran by concealing them amidst the silks that they were carrying in chests. Istanbul sent an order to halt the caravan so that a search could be made for the letters. If any letters were found, those responsible for carrying them should be imprisoned and the capital should be informed of the content of the letters.[140] In 1584, it transpired that a letter in Persian had been sent to Sultan Hamza by Seyyid Seccad, a Persian grandee, who had only recently aligned himself on the side of the Ottomans. In response to this, the governor-general of Baghdad was ordered to send a spy to investigate the matter further.[141]

OTTOMAN PRESSURE ON RAGUSA AND VENICE

The Ottomans were not at all happy to see that their vassal states and those allies with whom they had built up particularly close relations were sharing information with their enemies and tolerating enemy spies operating on their territory. Venice[142] and Ragusa[143] bore the lion's share of pressure from the

Ottomans, not least because they had a critical location between East and West. On the one hand, they were both centers of intelligence; on the other hand, in terms of both politics and commerce, they were more dependent on Istanbul than were other states.

In fact, in an attempt to limit the amount of espionage being carried out within the city, in 1526 the Ragusans passed a law forbidding their citizens from passing on information related to the Ottomans. The fines imposed as punishment (one hundred ducats or six months' imprisonment), however, were hardly steep. When one considers that foreign intelligence organizations did not think twice about paying people quite generously, it is clear that the law was bound to be ineffective; after all, plenty of people were prepared to take much greater risks for the sake of financial gain.[144] The upshot of this was that Istanbul adopted a more threatening stance, while Ragusa had to do what it was told. In 1547, the Ragusan authorities ordered a citizen named Marino de Zamagno to cease providing the Habsburgs with information.[145] Letters written by spies active in Istanbul were supposed to be conveyed to Naples and Messina by means of a frigate. In 1567, though, Dino Miniati and Donato Antonio Lubelo, who were responsible for sending from Dubrovnik to the port of Barleta letters that had been written by spies in Istanbul, were expelled from Ragusa. These measures were taken under pressure from the Ottomans, and the two agents were given just three days to leave the city.

The importance of the intermediary role that Ragusa played is plain to see from a report in the Spanish archives. According to this report, Habsburg agents were operating in Corfu, Kotor, Kefalonia, and Zakynthos, but none of them were able to deliver letters from Istanbul within just seventeen days, which was how long it took the spies in Ragusa. Mindful of this, the viceroy of Naples, the duke of Alcalá, decided to escalate the crisis and to intimidate Ragusa, which led him to threaten to expel every single one of the Ragusan merchants living in the kingdom.[146]

Ottoman pressure really does appear to have complicated matters for the communication channels upon which Habsburg intelligence relied. In August, for instance, Giovanni Maria Renzo opted to send copies of letters through Venice, rather than via Ragusa. Similarly, a man named Ambrosio Judice, whom Renzo had sent to Naples, needed to take another route when traveling from Venice to Istanbul.[147] Three years down the line, another spy on his way to Naples had to go via Corfu.[148]

The problem between the Ragusans and the duke of Alcalá was solved in no time at all. The small city-state of Ragusa, which got by on trade alone, decided that it made more sense to face the ire of Istanbul than to give up trading with Naples; this is why Ragusa advised the viceroy of Naples to send along more agents. The Republic of Ragusa was home to a seemingly infinite number of decision-making organs, and because state secrets were shared with a large number of elected officials, it was quite difficult to preserve their confidentiality. For this reason, the Ragusan authorities were worried that the names of the spies operating on their territory might end up being leaked to the Ottomans, so they actually requested the viceroy not to share these names with them.[149] It is worth pointing out that, in 1571, Sokollu became angry with the Ragusans for providing intelligence to the Habsburgs[150] and prohibited people from traveling to, or returning from, Ragusa.[151]

While the Ottomans were certainly enraged with the Ragusans, the Habsburgs could not be said to have been entirely satisfied with them either. An official in Naples is reported to have claimed that, because of the mistreatment that Ragusans inflicted on spies, it was actually difficult to find a quality agent operating on Ragusan soil.[152] When Don Juan complained in a letter to the Small Council (*Consilium Minus*)[153] that he was not being sent news related to the Ottomans, the response that came was that information was being supplied to the viceroy. As far as the head of Habsburg intelligence in the region was concerned, though, the Ragusans were deliberately dragging their feet when it came to conveying intelligence.[154]

The continued presence of Habsburg spies in Ragusa prompted the Ottomans to push for the expulsion of the Habsburg station chief Cesar de la Marea from the city-state, an act that led to a third crisis in 1581. Found guilty of murdering his mother, de la Marea had actually previously been exiled to Ragusa from the Kingdom of Naples, but when he was thrown out of Ragusa, the viceroy, Juan de Cuñiga, responded harshly and gave the Ragusans twenty days to retract the decision. When Dubrovnik failed to back down, the Viceroy intensified the threats that had been made fourteen years earlier, warning that he would imprison the Ragusan ambassador in Naples, together with Ragusan merchants in the city. Four months later, the bank accounts of the six richest Ragusan traders in the kingdom were seized.[155]

As the Ragusans were not particularly keen on taking on additional risks, there were occasions when they attempted to limit intelligence activities in the city, even if the Ottomans were not pressuring them to do so. In 1532, for instance, Miho Bučinčić, one of several brothers providing information to Ferdinand I, was punished with one year in prison and the permanent loss of his citizenship rights. Ferdinand defended his spy and protested against the punishment, but all this was in vain; in any case, Miho had escaped from the city long before and gone to join his brother in Vienna.[156]

Although Venice was not subordinate to the Ottoman Empire in the same way that Ragusa was, the Venetians sometimes found themselves being subjected to similar pressure. Earlier on, mention was made of the case of Andrea Moresini. Since Venice did not want to be held responsible for this episode, the authorities opted to send an experienced diplomat, Pietro Zen, to Istanbul.[157] That said, it should also be noted that, many years earlier, Zen himself had got into hot water due to espionage. During his term as Venetian consul to Damascus, two spies that he had sent to Shah İsmail were captured. This resulted in Zen being arrested and taken to the Mamluk capital Cairo for interrogation.[158]

The Venetian intelligence service was engaged in a constant struggle with foreign spies operating on its territory. In 1535, the Venetians forbade people from talking with the Ottoman spy Marco de Nicolò, who was found to be involved in underhand dealings with the Habsburg ambassador Lope de Soria; subjects to be avoided were Ottoman and Safavid affairs (*cosas del turco y sophi*), and anyone found guilty of violating these prohibitions would be faced with the death penalty (*a pena de vida*).[159] While Venice did not actually execute anyone for talking with de Nicolò, when the Ottomans realized that their agents were two-timing them, de Nicolò paid with his head.[160]

In 1539, the Venetian governor of the port of Kotor refused to assist Estefano Seguri, who had been sent by Viceroy of Naples Pedro de Toledo with the aim of monitoring the Ottoman fleet. The Venetians did not even allow the Habsburgs to employ a messenger who would deliver the letters written by their agents in Kotor to Herceg Novi, which the Habsburgs had captured from the Ottomans the previous year.[161] What is quite remarkable is that this occurred at a time when the Habsburgs and Venetians were fighting together against the Ottomans. The Venetians were clearly uncomfortable with a Habsburg fortress on their doorstep.[162] In addition, in the wake of Hayreddin Barbarossa's decisive victory at the Battle of Prevesa, the governor obviously wanted to avoid aggravating the corsair. Indeed, as a Spanish spy in Buda pointed out, the governor had sent presents to the admiral, and when Barbarossa reciprocated, this helped pave the way to a rapprochement between the two states.[163]

The Venetian authorities were eager to take on the task of monitoring the activities of Habsburg agents on the so-called Ionian islands of Corfu, Zakynthos, and Kefalonia, located close to the Ottoman coast. For example, 1541 saw the expulsion from Corfu of one Camilla Stopa, who had been caught supplying the Habsburgs with information concerning the Ottoman navy. The last thing the Venetians wanted to do was to get on the wrong side of Istanbul and to endanger the peace treaty that had been signed only a year before.[164] A year later, the Council of Ten would reprimand the governor of Corfu for having forged links with a Habsburg spy; the Council also ordered the immediate expulsion of the spy from the island.[165] In 1552, the Council was so disturbed by the activities of the Maltese and Habsburg agents on Corfu that it made a unanimous decision (28–0) to order the governor to force spies of this kind off the island. In addition, the Council suggested that, should this issue be raised with the *bailo*, an attempt should be made to allay the fears of the Ottomans.[166] In 1553, the Venetians went in hot pursuit of a Sicilian frigate that had sailed into the Adriatic, aiming to keep an eye on the Ottoman coasts. They also warned the Habsburg intelligence station chief on Corfu to avoid undertaking activities of that kind. When this warning appeared to have fallen on deaf ears, the Venetians resorted to instilling fear in the mind of the Habsburg intelligence station chief on Zakynthos, Balthasar Prototico, threatening that Venice would set fire to frigates sailing toward the Ottomans from the Neapolitan coast, whereby the crews would not be spared either.[167] These threats, though, do not seem to have had the desired effect, in that Habsburg frigates and agents continued their activities undeterred. In 1563, the governor of Corfu was instructed to expel from the island a Neapolitan named Zuan Thomas as well as the frigate with which he had sailed to Corfu with the aim of gathering intelligence.[168] Two years later, a similar order was sent to the governor of Zakynthos.[169]

In 1567, the Ottomans went so far as to try to kidnap Balthasar Prototico. However, the plan hatched by Grand Admiral Piyale Pasha backfired, and two Ottoman soldiers ended up being captured. Nevertheless, Venice opted to side with the Ottomans and to go ahead with expelling the Habsburg station chief from the island. Since Prototico was left with nowhere to run, he actually fled to Morea in Ottoman territory.[170] Immediately after that, though, he returned to Corfu and started dispatching letters once again,[171] leading the Ottomans to lodge another complaint, in 1569. As far as Istanbul saw things, the Venetian authorities had not just provided refuge for runaway oarsmen who possessed the most up-to-date information about the Ottoman navy;[172] they were also turning a blind eye to Habsburg agents on Corfu.[173] As war broke out soon after this warning was issued, the Venetians were able to get away without responding to the Ottomans' criticism for a while. When peace returned, though, the Ottomans appear to have stepped up their pressure on the Venetians, leading to a new wave of expulsions, with a Habsburg spy[174] called Ernando Dispero being deported in 1576 and Prototico suffering the same fate (again!) in 1581.[175] The Habsburgs for their part did not react in any way to the expulsion of their spies from Venetian territory. However, when a galley—one of a fleet of four—that was sailing to Sicily to pick up some *dil*s was impounded in Heraklion, the Habsburg admiral Álvaro de Bázan, the marquis of Santa Cruz, did not hold back from retaliating and seized the Venetian ships in Sicily, holding them at ransom.[176]

INVESTIGATIONS, INTERROGATIONS, AND PUNISHMENTS

Even though it was an open secret that spies were running riot in the capital, in ports and fortresses in the border areas, and even in the navy, the Ottoman authorities conducted their investigations in a meticulous manner and even during wartime went to great lengths to distinguish between the guilty and the innocent. In cases where people who had been accused of espionage were found to be innocent, this injustice was undone. In 1570, for instance, several Ragusans were thought to have been in cahoots with the enemy and were not just imprisoned by the judge of Plovdiv and by Derviş Çavuş but also had their money confiscated. However, the Dubrovnik ambassador interceded and was able to convince the Ottomans that these people were actually innocent. As a result, Istanbul ordered that those who had been imprisoned should be released and have their money reimbursed. As long as ex-prisoners possessed safe conducts granted by Istanbul, they were left to their own devices.[177] Another decree that was issued, this time in 1572, called upon the governor of Morea to launch an investigation into a case. Three Christian Ottoman subjects in the districts of Arcadia and Kalamata had been accused by several people of spying for the Venetians. According to the judges of these two districts, though, these people were "obedient and just minding their own business" and were actually victims of vilification by a group of five or six men who were working in alliance and concord with one another. With the aim of dispossessing the three Christians of their properties, these slanderers bore false witnesses to the benefit of one another; on top of that, they did not recoil from accusing the defendants of acts of immorality (*cürm-i galiza*). The decree that was sent to the governor of Morea commanded him to make the necessary inquiries and, if it was ascertained that the gang had made baseless allegations, to exile them all to Cyprus.[178]

Whenever a person was apprehended on suspicion of being a spy, they would be interrogated straightaway. The purpose of such interrogations was not just to establish the intentions and mission of the captive but also to gather additional information about the other intelligence operatives who had been deployed by the enemy. We should not forget that the Ottomans frequently deployed torture in the course of these interrogations.[179]

The punishments meted out to those proven to be spies varied according to the circumstances. We know that many of them were simply executed. Earlier on I pointed out that, when the Ottomans realized that Marco de Nicolò was a double agent, he paid with his head. In 1540, another spy from Sicily would fall victim to an Ottoman executioner.[180] In 1570, when a group of saboteurs acting on behalf of Habsburg intelligence started a small fire in the Istanbul shipyard, the Ottoman response was harsh. In fact, the fire was reminiscent of the one that had taken place in the Venice shipyard the previous year, but because the wind turned at the very last minute, this act of sabotage ended up a failure. At a time when Venice, the Habsburgs, and other Italian states had pooled their resources to form a massive Christian fleet that was on the move throughout the Mediterranean, the Ottomans could be said to have got off very lightly. The same could not be said for the saboteurs though. As soon as they were caught, they were subjected to an interrogation and subsequently skinned.[181] After the Christian fleet had smashed the Ottoman navy at Lepanto and worked up an even greater appetite for a crusade, there were obviously going to be spies all along the Ottoman coast. Months after the debacle at Lepanto, Istanbul sent orders to Morea and Rhodes, calling for the killing of anyone found sending news to the Habsburg admiral Don Juan.[182] In the following year, no less than twenty-three people confessed under torture that they were in touch with the Habsburg admiral; all of them were decapitated.[183] When the Ottomans executed another informant of Don Juan, a noble (*gentilhombre*) from Lepanto, his two sons sought refuge in Sicily and even managed to get the Habsburgs to pay them a small salary in recognition of the plight of their father.[184] In 1616, one of the Franciscan monks in the Monastery of St. Francis in Istanbul was found in possession of a number of suspicious letters. The Ottomans did not hesitate to tie up the cleric and dump him in the sea.[185] Worse than this, indeed, was the aforementioned case of Giovanni Battista de Montebarocchio, patriarchal vicar of the Catholic community in Pera, who was put to death simply because he attempted to hide a number of documents.[186]

Assassins who had been conspiring to harm the sultan had no chance whatsoever of escaping with their lives. With the defeat at the 1517 Battle of Ridaniya and the subsequent defeat at Cairo, the Mamluks lost Egypt in its entirety; however, what they had lost by the sword they tried to recover through daggers, and five assassins were sent to kill Sultan Selim I.[187] Four of them ended up being strangled to death, while the fifth is known to us from the testimony that he gave during his interrogation. Attempting to get a lighter sentence, Mustafa Cundi claimed that, as payment for killing the sultan, he had been offered property in all the cities along the banks of the River Nile. What became of him we do not know for sure, but it would be fair to presume that he was reunited with his fellow conspirators.[188]

At times, spies were not executed in broad daylight but rather disposed of discretely. In other words, they fell prey to extrajudicial killings. As was mentioned earlier, for instance, the governor of Amasya was responsible for the killing of the Safavid caliph Süleyman Fakih. The governor either ordered Süleyman to be drowned in the Kızılırmak River or deployed trumped-up charges of robbery or banditry to legitimize his murder.[189]

Sometimes, the implementation of the death penalty was used as a deterrent to scare off those who might be inclined to resort to espionage as an easy way of earning money. In 1628, for example, when two spies working for the rebellious governor-general of Erzurum, Abaza Mehmed Pasha, were captured in Istanbul, they were paraded through the streets of Istanbul, crucified with candles on their shoulders, while officials announced their crimes.[190] One of these agents was decapitated; the other was subjected to the so-called hook punishment (çengâle urulmak), which was a gruesome way to die.[191] The spy would be stripped naked and have their hands bound. Suspended on a rope, they would be lifted to the very top of a tower made of wood. Then, all of sudden, they would be left to drop. As they fell, they would be caught on the horizontal wooden pole at the very bottom of the tower, as well as on a number of hooks, the sharp ends of which faced upward. If they were lucky, they would suffer a lethal wound and die without experiencing a great deal of pain. This, though, was rarely the case. In general, the criminal would not die on the first blow but take leave of this world after several agonizing rounds.

The death penalty was not, in fact, the only punishment meted out to spies. The type of punishment an agent received depended on a number of factors. These included the type of crime committed (e.g., spying, surveillance, sabotage, bribery, agitation); whether the crime occurred in war- or peacetime; the amount of damage caused; the extent to which the Ottomans perceived a threat; the identity, wealth, and skills of the captured spy; and the kind of relations that they maintained with the Ottoman authorities.

There were in fact cases of people who were charged with espionage but were able to avoid imprisonment thanks to the effective use of bribery. As was noted earlier, Arcangelo de Lyo, the chaplain of the *bailo* Marc'Antonio Barbaro, managed to be spared imprisonment with the help of a generous bribe.[192] Another person who sacrificed a small fortune (*la gran spesa*) to avoid prison was the Genoese Cassano Giustiniano, a representative of the Habsburg intelligence network on the island of Chios.[193] Things were not so different for the Albanian Hieronimo Combi, a captain of the cavalry (*alfer di cavallo*) in the Venetian army. Taken captive during the Cyprus campaign, Combi was brought to Istanbul, where he was freed thanks to the intervention of a Greek aristocrat (*gentiluomo*), who subsequently became Combi's partner in a timber-trading business. In the meantime, Combi acquired a good knowledge of Turkish, complementing the Latin, Greek, and Albanian he knew already. When it emerged that he was in cahoots with the Habsburg agents in Istanbul, he was arrested by the Ottomans and thrown in prison. Following a three-month spell behind bars, he managed to buy his freedom by slipping four hundred écus to one of Sokollu Mehmed Pasha's men (*ministerio*). This sum was more than the annual income of an experienced spy. However, when one considers that the yearly profit from the timber business is likely to have been one thousand écus, one can speculate that it would not have been overly burdensome for Combi to pay this bribe.[194] I would also point out that Combi fled to Albania, where he continued to work for the Habsburgs located there.[195] Our final example from Istanbul comes from the seventeenth century. In 1608, the English ambassador accepted to pay the one thousand ducats required to secure the release of Andrea Rinaldi from Ancona. Given that Rinaldi worked for both the Habsburgs and the pope, the fact that the English ambassador was willing to fork out such a hefty sum raises no end of questions.[196] It should be noted too that, when our spy complained that he had been left to deal with his situation on his own, he pointed his finger not just at the Habsburgs but also at France and Venice.[197] In other words, Rinaldi seemingly maintained close relations with no fewer than five states, a stark reminder of what a hotbed of intelligence Istanbul was. It was clearly a place where whoever paid the piper called the tune!

Although the de Ansalon brothers, Scipion and Luis, connived with Habsburg intelligence to bring about the surrender of the city of Tripoli, they were not punished with imprisonment for this grievous crime. The idea of the conspiracy, in which these brothers took a leading role, was that some members of the ruling elite in Tripoli would go over to the side of the Habsburgs and hand over the city to the navy of the enemy. After the governor-general of Tunisia found out about this and informed Tripoli, in 1575 the Ansalons and their coconspirators Kaid Ferhad and Hasan were sent to prison. Ferhad, though, managed to escape and found his way to Istanbul. He would return to North Africa as the governor of Mahdia, even though he had been sentenced to prison for treason. Indeed, it was rumored that none other than Sokollu Mehmed Pasha had recommended him for the position of governor-general of Algeria! This case does not just demonstrate how thin the line was in the Early Modern Age between the legitimate and the illegitimate. It also shows that, when it came to appointments, bribery, presents, and factionalism played as big a role in the Ottoman Empire as they did in all the other countries of Europe. To start with, a payment of eight hundred écus by Kaid Hasan was enough to spare the Ansalon brothers from being tortured. Later on, Luis escaped from prison and made it to Tunis, where he pleaded to the governor-general to grant him and his brother their freedom. When Ferhad returned from Istanbul, he was carrying with him an order that the brothers should be released, meaning that there was nothing left for the governor-general to do. We do not know the full details of the Ansalon brothers' story, which probably had much to do with factionalism, and all the contradictions that came with it. What we do know is that, at the end of the story, Scipion returned to Sicily, whereas Luis stayed in Tripoli to pay off his old debts. Indeed, leopards do not change their spots, and Luis went on hatching plans with Ferhad and supplying the Habsburgs with news.[198]

Finally, let us turn to some cases demonstrating that what money could not buy was sometimes achieved by a well-connected person; even when a convicted spy was minutes away from their death, they could be saved through the intervention of the right person in the right place. In 1663, for instance, an interpreter named Marc'Antonio Mamuca della Torre, who was on his way to Vienna together with the Austrian ambassador, was accused of espionage and sentenced to death. However, just when Marc'Antonio was entering the square where the execution was supposed to take place, he was recognized by treasurer Ahmed Pasha, who stepped in to save him.[199] Marc'Antonio could not have wished for a more propitious coincidence. Further, I have already explained how, in 1616, thanks to two months of intricate diplomacy, the French ambassador was able to save the lives of six Jesuits who had been accused of spying.

Although it did not always serve its purpose, converting to Islam was occasionally a way of avoiding a punishment. In 1571, a man from Milan was arrested and brought to Istanbul, along with the Ragusan interpreter accompanying him. All of a sudden, they recognized the merits of Islam, and this helped spare them from serving as forced oarsmen on a galley, a task from which another fellow captive, a merchant from Ancona, was also exempted.[200] The situation was rather different, however, for two priests working as ransomers in 1610; since the Moriscos in Istanbul accused these men of being Habsburg spies, they were deprived the chance of becoming Muslim.[201]

When prominent people with strong ties to the palace were accused of espionage or of being informants, the tendency was to exile them. A case in point was David Passi, whom I referred to at length in chapter 4. When it emerged that Passi was collaborating with the Habsburgs and up to no good, this once popular Jewish go-between was exiled to Rhodes.[202] Although Passi did eventually return to the capital, he never regained his earlier influence. Another interesting story was that of the Albanian Bartolomeo Brutti, one of the many colorful powerbrokers within Istanbul's intelligence and diplomatic circles. Having tried his hand twice as an apprentice interpreter in the Venetian embassy, Brutti started working for the Ottomans. To negotiate the return of Ottomans who had been held captive since the Battle of Lepanto, he traveled to Italy. When he got there, though, the Habsburg bigwigs he met persuaded him to spy for them. Thus, he was spying for Madrid but officially employed by Istanbul, and when he seemed to be interfering too much in the ceasefire talks between the two powers, this enraged Grand Vizier Sokollu, who had Brutti imprisoned. However, Koca Sinan Pasha (a relative of Brutti) intervened and persuaded Sokollu to release Brutti. Sokollu laid down one condition for Brutti's freedom though: he had to leave the capital immediately and go straight to Naples to join his masters.[203] By the time Brutti came back to Istanbul, the elderly Grand Vizier Sokollu Mehmed Pasha had been assassinated and the balance of forces within the Ottoman political elite had shifted. Thus, the fortunate Albanian was permitted not just to return but also to round off his already glowing career in a new post, namely as the adviser and favorite of the voivode, that is, the most powerful man in Moldavia. The remainder of this story, however, belongs in the concluding chapter of this book.[204]

NOTES

1. BOA *MD*, XIX, hk. 165, 230.
2. BOA, *MD*, X, hk. 325, 326 (H. Ramazan 3, 979 / Greg. January 19, 1572).
3. AGS, *E* 1331, fol. 217 (March 24, 1572).
4. BOA, *MD*, V, hk. 1502, 1503 (H. Şevval 9, 973 / Greg. April 29, 1566).
5. AGS, *E* 1056, fol. 43 (April 20, 1567).
6. Halil İnalcık, "Dâr al-'Ahd," in *Encyclopedia of Islam*, 2nd ed., 2:116; Halil İnalcık, "İmtiyâzât," in *Encyclopedia of Islam*, 2nd ed., 3:1179.
7. AGS, *E* 1127, fol. 100 (July 2, 1566).
8. AGS, *E* 1058, fol. 40 (April 7, 1570).
9. BOA, *MD*, XVI, hk. 541.
10. *Voyvoda* can refer to two things: (1) a prince of Moldavia and Wallachia or (2) a provincial officer in charge of collecting revenues. Here, the term is obviously being used with the second sense.
11. BOA, *MD*, LVIII, hk. 447 (H. Cemaziyelahir 25, 993 / Greg. June 24, 1585).
12. AGS, *E* 1056, fol. 43 (April 20, 1567).
13. BOA, *MD*, XII, hk. 291 (H. Zilkade 22, 978 / Greg. April 17, 1571); XIV, hk. 1421 (H. Zilhicce 29, 978 / Greg. May 24, 1571).
14. AGS, *E* 1060, fol. 140 (June 15, 1571).
15. AGS, *E* 1074, fol. 108.
16. BOA, *MD*, X, hk. 325, 326 (H. Ramazan 3, 979 / Greg. January 19, 1572).
17. BOA, *MD*, LV, hk. 78 (H. Zilkade 20, 992 / Greg. November 23, 1584).
18. Suraiya Faroqhi, *Pilgrims and Sultans: The Hajj under the Ottomans, 1517–1683* (London: I.B. Tauris, 1994), pp. 135–137; see also *MD*, XII, hk. 896, 897 (H. Rebiülevvel 7, 979 / Greg. July 30, 1571).
19. BOA, *MD*, XVIII, hk. 219 (H. Şaban 13, 979 / Greg. December 31, 1571).
20. A considerable number of records can be found in the Registers of Important Affairs (*mühimme defterleri*) volume numbers VI, X, XII, XIV, XVI, XVIII, XIX, XXIX, XXX, XXXI, XXXIII, XXXV, XXXVI, XXXIX, XL, XLVI, XLVIII, XLIX, LI, and LVIII, as well as in the Appendixes to Registers of Important Affairs, vol. V. It may be worth consulting the sections of *Papeles de Estado*'s archive devoted to *Venecia* and *Nápoles*, all of which can be found in the archives of Simancas. An indispensable work dealing with the cooperation between the Habsburgs and the Ottoman Empire's Orthodox

subjects is José M. Floristán Imízcoz's *Fuentes para la política oriental de los Austrias: La documentation griega del Archivo de Simancas (1571–1621)* (León: Universidad de Léon, 1988).

21. BOA, *MD*, X, hk. 174 (H. Şaban 28, 979 / Greg. January 15, 1572).
22. BOA, *MD*, X, hk. 299 (H. Zilkade 27, 979 / Greg. April 11, 1572).
23. BOA, *MD*, XIX, hk. 75 [duplicate] (H. Muharrem 13, 980 / Greg. May 26, 1572).
24. BOA, *MD*, X, hk. 325, 326 (H. Ramazan 3, 979 / Greg. January 19, 1572).
25. AGS, *E* 1329, fol. 78 (August 2, 1571).
26. BOA, *MD*, X, hk. 451 (H. Gurre-i Receb 979 / Greg. November 19, 1571).
27. *Empresa de Grecia*: This was the name given to a Balkan campaign that the Habsburgs planned to carry out in coordination with Orthodox nobles; nothing came of this plan, however.
28. AGS, *E* 487, Giralomo Combi Albanes, document dated April 20, 1577.
29. BOA, *MD*, XXIII, hk. 188 (H. Ramazan 14, 985 / Greg. November 25, 1577), 451 (H. Zilkade 8, 985 / Greg. January 17, 1578), 452 (H. Zilkade 8, 985 / Greg. January 17, 1578), 696 (H. Zilhicce 27, 985 / Greg. March 7, 1578).
30. Faroqhi, *Pilgrims and Sultans*, pp. 134–35.
31. BOA, *MD*, VII, hk. 2067 (H. Rebiülevvel 22, 976 / Greg. September 14, 1568); Ahmet Refik, *Onaltıncı Asırda Rafizîlik ve Bektaşilik* (Istanbul: Muallim Ahmet Halim Kitaphanesi, 1932), doc. 29.
32. BOA, *MD*, VII, hk. 2254 (H. Cemaziyelevvel 26, 976 / Greg. November 16, 1568).
33. BOA, *MD*, XXXII, hk. 78 (H. Ramazan 7, 985 / Greg. November 18, 1577).
34. BOA, *MD*, XXXIII, hk. 173 (H. Gurre-i Ramazan 985 / Greg. November 12, 1577).
35. BOA, *MD*, XLIX, hk. 56 (1583).
36. ASV, *SDC*, fil. 81, cc. 378v–79r (September 3, 1616), 396r (September 8, 1616).
37. On this Catholic church and monastery in Istanbul, which belonged to Franciscan monks, see Gualberto Matteucci, *Un glorioso convento francescano sulle rive del Bosforo: Il S. Francesco di Galata in Costantinopoli, c. 1230–1697* (Florence: Studi Francescani, 1967); Eric Dursteler, "Erken Modern Dönem İstanbulu'nda Latin Kilisesi Hıristiyanları," in *Osmanlı İstanbulu I: I. Uluslararası Osmanlı İstanbulu Sempozyumu Bildirileri, 29 Mayıs–1 Haziran 2013, Istanbul 29 Mayıs Üniversitesi*, ed. Feridun M. Emecen and Emrah Safa Gürkan (Istanbul: İstanbul 29 Mayıs Üniversitesi Yayınları, 2014), 127–35.
38. Adam Werner, *Padişahın Huzurunda: Elçilik Günlüğü, 1616–1618*, trans. Türkis Noyan (Istanbul: Kitap Yayınevi, 2011), p. 59.
39. Tijana Krstić, "Moriscos in Ottoman Galata, 1609–1620s," in *The Expulsion of the Moriscos from Spain: A Mediterranean Diaspora*, ed. Mercedes García-Arenal and Gerard Wiegers, trans. Consuelo López-Morillas and Martin Beagles (Leiden: Brill, 2014), pp. 283–84; Tijana Krstić, "Contesting Subjecthood and Sovereignty in Ottoman Galata in the Age of Confessionalization: The *Carazo* Affair, 1613–1617," *Oriento Moderno* 93 (2013): pp. 437–38.
40. AGS, *E* 1309, fol. 190 (October 13, 1532).
41. AGS, *E* 487, letter written from Algiers by Andrea Gasparo Corso, dated April 6, 1570.

42. BOA, *MD*, XII, hk. 1217 (H. Zilhicce 27, 979 / Greg. May 11, 1572).

43. AGS, *E* 1329, fol. 134 (December 16, 1571).

44. BOA, *MD*, LVIII, hk. 201 (H. Cemaziyelevvel 17, 983 / Greg. August 24, 1575).

45. Pierre Belon du Mans, *Les observations de plusieurs singularitez & choses memorable, trouvées en Grece, Asie, Indee, Egypte, Arabie & autres pays estranges* (Antwerp: Chez Iean Steelsius, 1555), vr. 156v; Vatin, *L'Ordre de Saint-Jean-de-Jérusalem, l'Empire ottoman et la Méditerranée orientale entre les deux sièges de Rhodes, 1480-1522* (Paris: Peeters, 1994), p. 366.

46. Belon du Mans, *Les observations*, 157r–57v.

47. Vera Costantini, *Il Sultano e l'isola contesa: Cipro tra eredità e potere ottomano* (Milan: UTET Libreria, 2009), p. 105.

48. BOA, *MD*, XXXVIII, hk. 883 (H. Şaban 19, 984 / Greg. November 11, 1576); Refik, doc. 47.

49. *MD*, XXVII, hk. 957 (H. Zilkade 5, 983 / Greg. February 5, 1576); Bekir Kütükoğlu, *Osmanlı-İran Siyâsî Münâsebetleri I: 1578–1590* (Istanbul: İstanbul Edebiyat Fakültesi Matbaası, 1962), 12, fn. 42.

50. AGS *E* 1497, libro *E* 66, fol. 234 (December 17, 1544).

51. BOA, *MD*, XVIII, hk. 204 (H. Şaban 13, 979 / Greg. December 31, 1571).

52. BOA, *MD*, XVI, hk. 636 (H. Cemaziyelahir 21, 979 / Greg. November 10, 1571).

53. BOA, *MZD*, V, hk. 220.

54. BOA, *MD*, V, hk. 1434 (H. Ramazan 17, 973 / Greg. April 7, 1566).

55. BOA, *MD*, VII, hk. 2281 (H. Rebiulahir 28, 976 / Greg. October 20, 1568).

56. AGS, *E* 487, letter from the duke of Gandia, dated May 31, 1573.

57. BOA, *MD*, X, hk. 279 (H. Zilkade 7, 978 / Greg. April 2, 1571).

58. "cenge el uciyle yapışmaya"; "can u gönülden ceng itmemeye"; Selâhattin Tansel, *Yavuz Sultan Selim* (Ankara: Milli Eğitim Basımevi, 1969), p. 53. As Feridun M. Emecen has pointed out, the source that Tansel was drawing on here, although he failed to name it, was Hezarfen Hüseyin Efendi's late seventeenth century work *Tenkitü't-Tevarih*. Emecen has doubts, though, concerning the authenticity of the story. Emecen, *Yavuz Sultan Selim*, p. 127.

59. Tansel, *Yavuz Sultan Selim*, pp. 57–58.

60. Sola Castaño and de la Peña, pp. 80–81.

61. AGS, *E* 490, Poliza de Sinan y Haydar (October 17, 1579). For two reports providing detailed information about the Ottoman navy's movements in the Black Sea, see *E* 1080, fol. 41 (May 14, 1579), 51 (June 1, 1579). According to Margliani, these reports were written by Sinan and Haydar. *E* 1080, fol. 58 (August 3, 1579). The viceroy Juan de Cuñiga believed the news presented in this report. *E* 1081, fol. 163 (November 14, 1580).

62. Expressions like this can be found in practically every file in the folders related to "Nápoles" (Naples) and "Sicilia" (Sicily) in the *Papeles de Estado* section of the Simancas archives.

63. On negotiations with the French king Charles VIII in 1494, see Paul Durrieu, "Délivrance de la Grèce projetée en France a la fin du quinzième siècle," *Revue d'histoire diplomatique* 26 (1912): pp. 333–51.

64. ASF, *AMP*, fil. 3079, c. 514v (April 7, 1565).

65. "Harbî küffar ile musâfât üzre olup her-bâr der-i devletde vâki' olan ahvâli yazub i'lâm etmededir ve donanma-yi humâyûn gemileri çıkdıkça kaç gemidir ve ne cânibe gidecekdir dâimâ bildirüb hurde İslâm gemilerine

zarar erişdirmeden hâlî"; Kâtib Çelebi, *Tuhfetü'l-kibâr fi esfâri'il-bihâr*, ed. İdris Bostan (Ankara: T.C. Başbakanlık Denizcilik Müsteşarlığı, 2008), vr. 66a–66b, 107.

66. The same ex-captive also revealed that among the places the Ottomans might attack were Cyprus, La Goulette, and Malta. AGS, *E* 487, document titled "Advertimientos de Turquia y otros de importancia."

67. Francesca Lucchetta, "L'Affare Zen," *Studi veneziani* 10 (1968): p. 127.

68. Lucchetta, "L'Affare Zen," pp. 148, 154.

69. AGS, *E* 1308, fol. 186 (May 5, 1531).

70. ASV, *SDC*, fil. 4, fol. 12 (May 11, 1569).

71. *Kapu Ağası*: Eunuch official in charge of the Ottoman palace.

72. ASG, *Archivio Segreto, Lettere Ministri Costantinopoli*, b. I, fil. 2169; Argenti, *Chius Vincta*, xciii.

73. ASV, *SDelC*, reg. 3, c. 51v (August 29, 1566).

74. AGS, *E* 1497, libro *E* 67, fol. 112; *E* 1316, fol. 70 (October 8, 1540).

75. BOA, *MD*, XXV, hk. 2686 (H. Cemaziyelahir 26, 982 / Greg. October 12, 1574).

76. AGS, *E* 1332, fol. 35 (March 20, 1573).

77. AGS, *E* 1141, fol. 159; *E* 1141, fol. 162 (October 6, 1574).

78. BOA, *MD*, IX, hk. 249.

79. Colin Imber, "The Navy of Süleyman the Magnificent," *Archivum Ottomanicum* 6 (1980): p. 255f; Pál Fodor, "The Organisation of Defence in the Eastern Mediterranean (end of the 16th century)," in *The Kapudan Pasha: His office and His domain: Halcyon Days in Crete IV, a symposium held in Rethymnon, 7–9 January 2000*, ed. Elizabeth A. Zachariadou (Rethymnon: Crete University Press, 2002), pp. 87–94; Şenay Özdemir, "Kıyı Nöbeti: Osmanlı Devleti'nin Akdeniz'de Kıyı Savunması," *Tarih İncelemeleri Dergisi* 23, no. 1 (July 2008): pp. 187–210.

80. BOA, *MD*, V, hk. 580 (H. Cemaziyelevvel 2, 973 / Greg. November 25, 1565); 660 (H. Cemaziyelevvel 20, 973 / Greg. December 12, 1565); 1006 (H. Receb 19, 973 / Greg. February 9, 1566).

81. Ömer Lütfi Barkan, *XV ve XVIıncı Asırlarda Osmanlı İmparatorluğunda Zirai Ekonominin Hukuki ve Malî Esasları, Birinci Cilt: Kanunlar* (Istanbul: Burhaneddin Matbaası, 1943), p. 340.

82. Pirî Reis, *Kitab-ı Bahriye / Book of Navigation* (Ankara: Republic of Turkey, Prime Ministry, Undersecretaryship of Navigation, 2002), p. 88.

83. Heath Lowry, "The Island of Limnos: A Case Study on the Continuity of Byzantine Forms under Ottoman Rule," *Continuity and Change in Late Byzantine and Early Ottoman Society*, ed. Anthony Bryer and Heath Lowry (Birmingham: University of Birmingham, Center for Byzantine Studies; Washington: Dumbarton Oaks Research Library and Collection, 1986), p. 246.

84. Benjamin Arbel and Gilles Veinstein, "La fiscalité vénéto-chypriote au miroir de la législation ottomane: le *Qânunnâme* de 1572," *Turcica* 18 (1986): p. 30.

85. Vatin, *L'Ordre de Saint-Jean-de-Jérusalem*, p. 115.

86. BOA, *MD*, XVIII, hk. 217 (H. Şaban 3, 979 / Greg. December 20, 1571).

87. Salvatore Bono, *I corsari barbareschi* (Turin: ERI-Edizioni RAI Radiotelevisione Italiana, 1964), pt. 5.

88. BOA, *MD*, VII, hk. 549, 594 (H. Selh-i Cemaziyelahir 975 / Greg. December 31, 1567), 619.

89. ASV, *SAPC*, documents no. fil. 4, 5, 8, 9.

90. Biegman, "Ragusan Spying," 143–44, docs. 69, 70. I would note, though, that this order was not actually put into effect.
91. Decree to the bey of Amasya: BOA, *MD*, VII, hk. 1835 (H. Gurre-i Rebiülevvel 976 / Greg. August 24, 1568); Decree to the governor-general of Rumelia: hk. 1984 (H. Selh-i Safer 976 / Greg. August 23, 1568).
92. BOA, *MZD*, II, hk. 215 (H. Zilhicce 27, 982 / Greg. April 9, 1585); Kütükoğlu, p. 5, fn. 18.
93. BOA, *MD*, VII, hk. 1292 (H. Şevvâl 17, 975 / Greg. April 15, 1568); Refik, doc. 24.
94. Preto, *Servizi Segreti*, p. 61.
95. The location in question was presumably the Elçi Hanı (Ambassador's Inn) in the Çemberlitaş area along the Divan Yolu.
96. Chesneau, *Le Voyage de Monsieur d'Aramon*, pp. 188–89.
97. Ogier Ghislain de Busbecq, *The Turkish Letters of Ogier Ghiselin de Busbecq: Imperial Ambassador at Constantinople, 1554–1562*, ed. E. S. Forster (Baton Rouge: University of Louisiana Press, 2005), pp. 79, 138–49.
98. AGS, *E* 1339, fol. 113 (January 3, 1581).
99. H. Theunissen, "Ottoman-Venetian Diplomatics: the 'Ahd-Names. The Historical Background and the Development of a Category of Political-Commercial Instruments together with an Annotated Edition of a Corpus of Relevant Documents," *Electronic Journal of Oriental Studies* 1, no. 2 (1998): pp. 383, 391, 397.
100. Longo, *Annali veneti*, 1:141–142.
101. BOA, *MD*, XVI, hk. 173 (H. Cemaziyelahir 9, 979 / Greg. October 29, 1571).
102. ASV, *CCX-LettRett*, b. 292, fol. 175r–77q; Lesure, "Notes et documents, I," pp. 152–55, 163.
103. Charles Yriarte, *La vie d'un patricien de Venise au XVIe siècle* (Paris: J. Rothschild, n.d.), p. 175. I cannot help but express my enormous respect for Yriarte, who clearly put great effort into trying to decipher this practically illegible inscription. The determined Yriarte managed to persuade the museum director to remove the frame from the painting. He was unable, however, to make out the words *imperatoris* and *nostro*, which have been almost entirely erased. See Eduard von Engerth, "Das Portrait des venetianischen Patriciers Marcanlonio Barbaro von P. Veronese im Belvedere zu Wien," *Zeitschrift für bildende Kunst* 10 (1875): pp. 29–31.
104. ASV, *SDC*, fil. 6E, fol. 7 (February 10, 1572, m.v.).
105. ASV, *SDC*, fil. 6, fol. 1 (March 7, 1573).
106. ASV, *CCX-LettRett*, b. 292, fol. 175r–77q; for the text, see Lesure, "Notes et documents, I," 158–64.
107. BOA, *MD*, XL, hk. 204 (H. Şaban 26, 987 / Greg. October 18, 1579).
108. Antonio Fabris, "A Description of the Ottoman Arsenal of Istanbul (1698)," *Mediterranea: richerche storiche* 34 (2015): pp. 435–44.
109. Martin Rothkegel, "Jacobus Palaeologus in Constantinople, 1554–5 and 1573," *Osmanlı İstanbulu IV: IV. Uluslararası Osmanlı İstanbulu Sempozyumu Bildirileri, 20–22 Mayıs 2016, İstanbul 29 Mayıs Üniversitesi*, ed. Feridun M. Emecen, Ali Akyıldız, and Emrah Safa Gürkan (Istanbul: İstanbul 29 Mayıs Üniversitesi Yayınları, 2016), p. 990. On Černović, see Michel Lesure, "Michel Černović 'Explorator Secretus' à Constantinople (1556–1563)," *Turcica* 15 (1983): pp. 127–54.
110. Hugon, *Au service du Roi Catholique*, pp. 22–27.

111. Ágoston, "Information, Ideology, and Limits," p. 84.
112. AGS, *E* 1056, fol. 43 (April 20, 1567).
113. BOA, *MD*, IX, hk. 97 (H. Ramazan 28, 977 / Greg. March 6, 1570).
114. ASV, *SDC*, fil. 4, c. 254r (December 20, 1569).
115. ASV, *SDC*, fil. 4, cc. 295r, 296r (February 6, 1569, m.v.).
116. ASV, *SDC*, fil. 5, c. 12v (March 8, 1570).
117. ASV, *SDC*, fil. 5, c. 1v (March 8, 1570).
118. ASV, *SDC*, fil. 4, c. 309r (February 1570).
119. ASV, *SDC*, fil. 5, c. 15r (March 8, 1570).
120. Eric R. Dursteler, "Power and Information: The Venetian Postal System in the Early Modern Mediterranean," *From Florence to the Mediterranean: Studies in Honor of Anthony Molho*, ed. Diogo Curto et al. (Florence: Olschki, 2009), p. 611.
121. AGS, *E* 1338, fol. 15 (June 30, 1580).
122. Dursteler, "Power and Information," p. 609.
123. BOA, *MD*, LV, hk. 166 (H. Zilhicce 21, 992 / Greg. December 24, 1584).
124. Dursteler, "Power and Information," p. 610.
125. Sola Castaño, *Los que van y vienen*, p. 203; Gürkan, "Espionage in the 16th Century Mediterranean," p. 269.
126. ASG, *Archivio Segreto, Lettere Ministri Costantinopoli*, b. I, fil. 2169, Giovanni Agostino Gigli al Doge e ai Governatori (January 8, 1563); the document is also presented in Bornate, "La Missione di Sampiero Corso," pp. 483–85.
127. On the letters that Habsburg agents in Istanbul wrote using invisible ink, which could only be deciphered "with the help of fire" (*de manera que se han sacado al fuego*), see AGS, *E* 1326, fol. 46–51, 53, 56, 60, 61, 64, 68, 69, 75, 80; *E* 1392, fol. 63–68, 75, 76.
128. AGS, *E* 1125, fol. 86 (June 29, 1560).
129. ASV, *CCX-LettRett*, 292, fol. 177q; Lesure, "Notes et documents, I," p. 163.
130. AGS, *E* 491 (after February 17, 1580).
131. AGS, *E* 1144, fol. 281 (June 6, 1575).
132. *Giovane di lingua* (It.): Apprentice interpreter learning Turkish under the auspices of the *bailo*'s office. For more information, see Francesca Lucchetta, "La scuola dei 'giovani di lingua' veneti nei secoli XVI e XVII," *Quaderni di studi arabici* 7 (1989): pp. 19–40.
133. ASV, *CCX-LettAmb*, b. 3, fol. 55; Villain-Gandossi, "Les Dépêches Chiffrées," *Turcica* 10 (1978): 77; Pedani, *In Nome del Gran Signore*, p. 42.
134. ASV, *CX-ParSec*, reg. 11, c. 154v, fil. 20, document dated March 24, 1578.
135. AGS, *E* 1338, fol. 15 (July 30, 1580).
136. ASG, *Archivio Segreto, Lettere Ministri Costantinopoli*, busta I, filza 2169, fol. 2r (July 2, 1565).
137. ASV, *CX-ParSec*, reg. 8, cc. 76v–77r (January 27, 1566, m.v.), 79r–80r (February 18, 1566, m.v.), 92v–93v (July 19, 1567); BOA, *MD*, VI, hk. 1424 (H. Evasıt-ı Zilhicce 972 / Greg. June 9–18, 1565).
138. ASV, *CX-ParSec*, reg. 8, cc. 93v–94r (July 19, 1567), 96r (August 20, 1567), 97r (October 2, 1567).
139. ASV, *SDC*, fil. 5, fol. 12 (April 21, 1570).
140. BOA, *MD*, XVI, hk. 593 (H. Cemaziyelahir 11, 979 / Greg. November 8, 1571).
141. BOA, *MD*, LII, hk. 539 (H. Selh-i Muharrem 992 / Greg. February 12, 1584).

142. Hans J. Kissling, "Venezia come centro di informazioni sui turchi," *Venezia centro di mediazione tra Oriente e Occidente, secoli XV–XVI: aspetti e problemi*, ed. Hans-Georg Beck et al. (Florence: L. S. Olschki, 1977), 1:97–109; Giovanni K. Hassiotis, "Venezia e i domini veneziani tramite di informazioni sui turchi per gli spagnoli," in *Venezia centro di mediazione tra Oriente e Occidente, secoli XV–XVI: aspetti e problemi*, ed. Hans-Georg Beck et al. (Florence: L. S. Olschki, 1977), 2:117–37.

143. Biegman, "Ragusan Spying."

144. Dedijer, "Ragusa Intelligence," p. 111.

145. AGS, *E* 1318, fol. 222 (August 23, 1547).

146. AGS, *E* 1056, fol. 84 (September 13, 1567).

147. AGS, *E* 1056, fol. 86 (August 2, 1567).

148. AGS, *E* 1059, fol. 56–57 (December 31, 1570).

149. AGS, *E* 1056, fol. 118 (January 8, 1568).

150. AGS, *E* 487, document titled "Advertimientos de Turquia y otros de importancia."

151. AGS, *E* 1331, fol. 217 (March 24, 1572).

152. AGS, *E* 1060, fol. 129 (May 9, 1571).

153. This was an executive council composed of elected members of the Ragusa Senate. It resembled the Venetian Council of Ten.

154. AGS, *E* 1331, fol. 220 (May 10, 1572).

155. AGS, *E* 1083, fol. 88; *E* 1084, fol. 44 (June 21, 1581).

156. Vinko Foretić, *Povijest Dubrovnika do 1808, 2. Od 1526 da 1808* (Zagreb: Nakladni zavod Matice Hrvatske 1980), pp. 19–33; Harris, *Dubrovnik*, p. 102.

157. AGS, *E* 1308, fol. 186 (May 5, 1531).

158. Lucchetta, "L'Affare Zen."

159. AGS, *E* 1311, fol. 40–42 (August 9, 1535), 45–47 (August 9, 1535), 48–51 (July 6, 1535), 60–61 (June 24, 1535), 149.

160. AGS, *E* 1312, fol. 12 (March 27, 1536).

161. AGS, *E* 1030, fol. 54.

162. AGS, *E* 1030, fol. 120 (July 4, 1539).

163. AGS, *E* 1030, fol. 55 (July 26, 1539).

164. AGS, *E* 1317, fol. 45; *E* 1497, libro *E* 67, fol. 158 (April 28, 1541); ASV, *CX-ParSec*, reg. 5, cc. 52r–52v (March 18, 1541).

165. ASV, *CX-ParSec*, reg. 5, cc. 72v–73r (August 21, 1542).

166. ASV, *CX-ParSec*, reg. 6, cc. 85v–86r (May 4, 1552).

167. Sola Castaño, *Los que van y vienen*, pp. 122–23.

168. ASV, *CX- ParSec*, reg. 7, cc. 128v–29r (July 30, 1563); 134r–34v (October 7, 1563).

169. ASV, *CX-ParSec*, reg. 8, cc. 34v (April 18, 1565).

170. AGS, *E* 1056, fol. 217.

171. AGS, *E* 1056, fol. 86 (September 27, 1567).

172. ASV, *SDC*, fil. 4, fol. 43–54 (April 1569); Sola Castaño, *Los que van y vienen*, p. 212.

173. ASV, *SDC*, fil. 4, fol. 111–13 (June 11, 1569).

174. AGS, *E* 1519, fol. 84 (February 12, 1576); ASV, *CX-ParSec*, reg. 11, cc. 66v–67r (November 2, 1575), 68v–69r (December 9–10, 1575), 73v–74r (November 28, 1575), 90r (March 10, 1576).

175. AGS, *E* 1524, fol. 5 (May 10, 1581).

176. ASF, *AMP*, fil. 3082, fol. 478 (June 9, 1576).

177. BOA, *MD*, XV, hk. 1738 (H. Receb 13, 978 / Greg. December 11, 1570).
178. BOA, *MD*, XIX, hk. 309 (H. Ramazan 14, 980 / Greg. January 18, 1573).
179. AGS, *E* 487, Hieronimo Combi Schiavo; AGS, *E* 1063, fol. 55 (August 8, 1573), *E* 1344, K 1675, fol. 167b (August 15, 1592); Emecen, *Yavuz Sultan Selim*, p. 193.
180. AGS, *E* 1497, libro *E* 67, fol. 112; *E* 1316, fol. 70 (October 8, 1540).
181. AGS, *E* 1059, fol. 56–57 (December 31, 1570).
182. BOA, *MD*, X, hk. 174 (H. Şaban 28, 979 / Greg. January 15, 1572); XIX, hk. 75.
183. AGS, *E* 1063, fol. 55 (August 8, 1573).
184. AGS, *E* 1152, fol. 186.
185. Werner, *Padişahın Huzurunda*, p. 59.
186. Krstić, "Moriscos in Ottoman Galata," p. 284.
187. Three of the assassins (including Mustafa Cundi) had been commissioned by the last Mamluk sultan, Tomanbay, while the other two were sent by Ulu Mirahur and Ulu Hacib.
188. TSMA, *E* 4800. An extract from the Ottoman document can be read in modern Turkish translation in Emecen's *Yavuz Sultan Selim*, pp. 301–2.
189. BOA, *MD*, VII, hk. 2067 (H. Rebiülevvel 22, 976 / Greg. September 14, 1568); Refik, doc. 29.
190. "fermân-ı Padişahî ile dâbbeler üzere çarmıha gerilip omuzları üzre bal mumları dikilip esvak-ı Dârüssaltana'da teşhîr ve nidâ olundu."
191. Naîmâ Mustafa Efendi, *Tarih-i Naîmâ*, ed. Mehmet İpşirli (Ankara: Türk Tarih Kurumu Yayınları, 2007), 2:621.
192. Lesure, "Notes et documents, I," p. 155.
193. AGS, *E* 1163, fol. 238 (May 14, 1609).
194. AGS, *E* 487, Geronimo Combi Albanes, document dated April 20, 1577.
195. AGS, *E* 494.
196. ASV, *IS*, b. 416, document dated March 3, 1608.
197. ASV, *IS*, b. 416, document dated January 24, 1607, m.v.
198. AGS, *E* 1140, fol. 137 (July 12, 1573); *E* 1144, fol. 92 (August 8, 1575), 128 (November 24, 1575), 137 (December 3, 1575); *E* 1145, fol. 118 (November 2, 1576), 119; *E* 1147, fol. 4 (January 9, 1577); *E* 1149, fol. 9 (February 10, 1579), 13 (March 1, 1579), 18, 21.
199. Fabris, "Ottoman Arsenal of Istanbul (1698)."
200. AGS, *E* 1060, fol. 140 (June 15, 1571).
201. ASV, *IS*, b. 416, document dated June 26, 1610; also see the document dated June 13, 1610.
202. BOA, *MZD*, V, hk. 266 (H. Evail-i Ramazan 999 / Greg. June 23–July 2, 1591).
203. AGS, *E* 1080, fol. 59 (August 3, 1579), 60 (August 11, 1579), 61 (August 18, 1579).
204. On Brutti, see Noel Malcolm, *Agents of Empire*; Gennaro Varriale, "La lealtà fragile: Bartolomeo Brutti e lo spionaggio di Felipe II," in *Gli antichi stati italiani e l'Europa Centro–Orientale tra il tardo Medioevo e l'Età moderna*, ed. Cristian Luca and Gianluca Masi (Brăila–Udine: Istros Editrice–Gaspari Editore, 2016), pp. 93–128.

CONCLUSION

This book has attempted to assess the success of Ottoman intelligence and paint a picture of how this network operated; to do so, it has focused on the activities of spies in the Mediterranean area during the sixteenth century. Given that institutionalized espionage, diplomacy, and the centralized state did not exist as such at this time, it is not surprising that the adroit yet deceitful individuals who populated the world of intelligence took center stage. *Spies for the Sultan* has analyzed the methods that the nascent central bureaucracy used to acquire information, undertake covert operations, and prevent enemies from carrying out espionage. In addition, the book has drawn on archival documents to retell the stories of the various agents who moved back and forth between the different shores of the Mediterranean. That said, even when dealing with such a sensational topic as espionage, serious historiography does more than just recount a series of interesting facts. From the hodgepodge of stories that have survived out of the hundreds that must have once existed, the historian should be able to arrive at some conclusions.

The purpose of this study is, therefore, not to tell interesting stories but to highlight the interwoven nature of the Mediterranean region and to uncover the intricate network of relationships that prevailed in the borderlands. The adventures of the spies featured in this book have hopefully shown that what some have presented as the endless struggle between Islam and Christianity did not actually stand in the way of contacts between the east and west of the Mediterranean. Perhaps in no other period was the rhetoric of "Holy War" (encapsulated in terms like *gaza*, jihad, and crusade) bandied about as much as it was in the sixteenth century. Nevertheless, even though the Ottoman and Habsburg empires spent practically the entire century engaged in a struggle into which all the region's powers were sucked, the very same struggle was destined to be superseded by the flow of life and the dynamism of societies, and in the end this struggle appeared rather superficial. Central governments already had enough difficulties monitoring their territories, and military forces were trying to adapt themselves to the use of firearms. Under such circumstances, their attempts at building a wall to split the sea in two were bound to fail, whether that wall-building involved closing borders, preventing people from entering and exiting, or ascertaining who was who.

The notion of a "clash of civilizations" conflicts with the findings of critical textual analysis and is a cheap projection rooted in an approach to history that lacks any analytical methodology. When tested against the documents in the archives, moreover, the arguments born of this notion fail dismally. The documents point to a much more complex reality, which elites tried to conceal beneath the veneer of their high culture, jumping through hoops to hide the truth. Examples of this complexity abound: When Dominican monks in Calabria failed in their attempt to incite a rebellion against Spain, they fled to Istanbul. A young man from Zaragoza did not find what he was looking for among the nobles of Spain, so he too traveled to the infidel sultan's "Well-Protected Lands," where he converted; he also joined the entourage of Grand Admiral Uluc Ali, a convert like himself, and when he was thrown out of this entourage, he took the opportunity to transfer to Algiers, Fez, Spain, France, and Venice. A cavalryman from Bursa, who claimed he had learned Spanish on the streets of Istanbul, was abandoned by his Greek guide and captured in Naples while engaged in espionage; he had been advised, moreover, that if he wanted to live, he should insist that he was Turkish and not Spanish.

Family ties offer the clearest indication of the connections between the different sides of the Mediterranean. A shining example of this is the story of Uluc Ali. Born in a Calabrian fishing village, his destiny changed when he was captured by Ottoman corsairs. On countless occasions, Uluc Ali anchored off the coast of Calabria and gathered news through his acquaintances. He also took numerous fellow Calabrians and relatives (including his mother) back to Istanbul. Not only did he convert to Islam, he also integrated Calabria into Istanbul. During that period, the area around the Istanbul shipyard came to be known as *Nuova Calabria*, that is, New Calabria (today's district of Kasımpaşa).

Another interesting story is that of Cigalazade Yusuf Sinan Pasha, whom you will recall was a young man originally called Scipione from a Genoese family, the Cicalas. His father, Visconte Cicala, had settled in Sicily, where he committed piracy on behalf of the Habsburgs. His mother, Lucrezia, was actually an Ottoman subject from Herseg Novi, who had converted to Christianity (with little resistance) after she had been captured by Visconte. Together with Visconte, Scipione, the eldest of Lucrezia's three sons, was captured by Ottoman corsairs, who presented them as a gift to the sultan. Following his education in the *Enderun*, the Palace School, the young Genoese quickly rose through the ranks and reached the level of vizier when he was still young. He summoned his brother Carlo to join him and tried to convert him to Islam. Although Carlo failed to achieve his goal of obtaining the voivodeship of Wallachia or Moldavia, he did find his way into the Ottoman military class by receiving the title of duke of Naxos. Yusuf Sinan did not stop at summoning his brother to Istanbul. In the course of a naval expedition, which was supposed to be part of a Holy War, he went to see his family. In 1598, he made the Ottoman fleet anchor off Messina and, having obtained permission from the Habsburg authorities, visited his mother and siblings. Lucrezia and her children enjoyed a satisfying reunion with the much-missed Scipione and then returned to Messina, but Yusuf Sinan wanted to spend more time with his family. Carlo would spend a good many years shuttling between Chios and Sicily, where he worked for both Habsburg and Ottoman intelligence. Two Jesuit cousins of Scipione and Carlo, Antonio and Vincenzo, were sent by Pope Clement VIII as envoys to persuade him to return to "the True Religion."

Scipione, Carlo, and Visconte were neither the first nor the last members of the Cicala family to experience the highs and lows of a life led between East and West. From as far back as the fourteenth and fifteenth centuries, we find references in documents to a sizable number of Genoese with the surname Cigala living in Galata, Chios, Feodosya, and Sudak. Although we will not go into their stories here, I would just like to point out that, among the first names of these Cigalas were Visconte (Scipione's father's name), Antonio (his cousin's name), and Carlo (his brother's name).[1]

Just eleven years before Visconte was captured, a relative of his by the name of Domenico Visconte who had lived in the Ottoman Empire and whose mother tongue was actually Turkish came up with an interesting proposal: he suggested to the Habsburgs that he could travel to Istanbul to connive with the Ottomans' Christian subjects. He even said that he could move on to Iran. He recommended that the Habsburgs come to an agreement with the sultan's Christian subjects.[2] In 1579, Piero Rossi, one of Lucrezia Cicala's relatives, came to Istanbul and converted to Islam.[3]

Following the death of Cigalazade Yusuf Sinan Pasha in 1606, his family members continued to shuttle back and forth between Istanbul, Chios, and Genoa. All of these details point to the depth and durability of the links between the various branches of the Cicala family spread out across the Mediterranean, links that bound together subjects of different empires and members of different religions. Carlo appeared again in Istanbul in 1630, twenty-four years after the death of Scipione and in the very year in which Philip IV bestowed the title of prince on him. On this occasion, through the mediation of his nephew Mahmud Pasha, he requested that his son Giovanbattista be granted the voivodeship of either Wallachia or Moldavia. Scipio had another son, Hüseyin Bey, who was not as successful as Mahmud Pasha. All the same, he managed to be appointed to the position of governor of the island of Chios, a former Genoese colony with which the Cicala family already had strong ties.

If we do not count Piero, who was connected to the Cicala family through his mother, just one member of the Cicala family converted from Islam to Christianity. This was Mahmud, who turned up in Italy in the seventeenth century, purporting to be a descendant of the Cigalas. Mahmud was, in fact, something of a fraudster and staged a ceremony to mark his return to Christianity. After that, he traveled around Europe and in just a short time managed to squeeze money out of the pope, the kings of France and Spain, the Republic of

Venice, the grand duke of Tuscany, and the dukes of Bavaria and Savoy. Later, when his scam came to light, he simply vanished.

As we see then, neither Scipione nor his sons nor the other relatives left in Sicily resorted to conversion. In an era when intellectuals and religious scholars were keen to invoke the discourse of Holy War, it is remarkable that, despite being split into two along religious lines, the Cicala family kept its privileged position and was able to form a robust network of relations.[4]

Just a few weeks before Cigalazade Yusuf Sinan Pasha went to speak with his mother on the Calabrian coast, he had looted the very same coast of Christendom in the name of Holy War, and this was not the only example of his ties to the world beyond the Ottoman Empire. The fascinating story of the Bruttis and Brunis, which has been retold by Noel Malcolm and Gennaro Varriale, demonstrates how easy it is to think beyond boundaries and to find the flaws in simplistic identities that have been constructed without any recognition of the messy reality reflected in the archives. The Bruttis and Brunis were an Albanian family who, having been expelled from the district of Lezhë (then Ottoman territory), settled in Ulcinj, which was controlled by the Venetians. Our protagonist, Bartolomeo Brutti, was a Venetian subject of Albanian origin. His father, Antonio, had served in the Venetian army and fought against the Ottomans in the borderlands. Later, he became involved in trade, and the Venetian government assigned him the responsibility of procuring wheat, which was very much in need. By the end of his career, he had achieved so much that the Venetians honored him with the rank of knight of San Marco. Bartolomeo followed in his father's footsteps and placed himself at the service of Venice. When he was still young, he worked as a language boy, that is, an apprentice interpreter for the *bailo*. However, when he was not particularly successful in this job, he started to work for the Ottomans and set off on a journey to Italy. The aim of this mission was to negotiate an exchange between the Ottoman soldiers who had been captured during the Battle of Lepanto and the Christian prisoners-of-war being held by Istanbul. Meanwhile, he made contact with Habsburg officials in Naples, with whom he had cultivated good relations, offering to work for Habsburg intelligence. Bartolomeo was also a relative of Koca Sinan Pasha, one of the most powerful viziers of the era,[5] and he used his connection with him to stick his nose into the ceasefire negotiations between Madrid and Istanbul. This did not impress Sokollu Mehmed Pasha, who was a rival of Sinan Pasha, and he had Bartolomeo expelled from Istanbul. Soon after that, though, Sokollu was assassinated and Sinan Pasha was promoted to the rank of grand vizier, allowing Bartolomeo to return to Istanbul and continue his career as a much-admired associate of the voivode of Moldavia.

Other members of the Brutti and Bruni families, with their roots in an insignificant village in Albania, tried their luck in different locations across Europe. One uncle in the Brutti family, Giovanni Bruni, would rise within the Catholic Church and be appointed bishop of Bar. He even participated in and spoke at the Council of Trent, where the fundamentals of the Catholic faith were redefined in the wake of the Protestant Reformation. Another uncle,

Gasparo Bruni, likewise wanted to serve "the True Religion," but he chose to do so by the sword. He joined the order of the Knights of St. John, becoming a knight in Malta, and embarked upon a career as a corsair. When the Ottomans conquered Bar and seized both Bishop Giovanni and his nephew Nicolò, a Venetian officer, this led to one of the most unfortunate coincidences in the history of the Mediterranean region. At the Battle of Lepanto, the Maltese knight Gasparo fought on the Christian side and ended up victorious; meanwhile, not far away, his brother and nephew lost their lives while serving the Ottomans as oarsmen on a galley. Consumed by the desire to seize all the booty they could, the Spanish soldiers did not think twice about murdering the Christian slaves whom they wanted to fleece. When Giovanni cried out, "I'm a bishop, a Christian," they did not believe him and simply butchered him.[6] Gasparo was reunited with Giovanni and Antonio at Lepanto, but only with their corpses. After the war, he was sent by the pope to Avignon in the south of France to serve as a castle warden. His mission was to defend this papal property from the Protestants.

Antonio Bruni, son of Gasparo Bruni and cousin of Bartolomeo Brutti, joined the Jesuit order and completed a doctorate in civil and ecclesiastical law at the universities of Perugia and Avignon. Later on, Antonio and Gasparo moved to the town of Koper, where they eventually settled. The Istanbul branch of the family turned out to be more resilient than all the others. When Bartolomeo died in Moldavia in 1592, his brother Cristoforo took after his elder and entered the service of the *bailo*. For many years, he worked as a language boy, and for centuries after him, members of the Brutti family would provide interpreting services for foreign ambassadors in Istanbul, being one of the three main families to do so.[7]

What this example and other stories presented in the book demonstrate is this: although the written sources produced by the imperial elites propagate the image of a world order revolving around religion, the reality on the ground was much more complex. Whenever we lift up the veil shrouding the Mediterranean borderlands and peer beneath, it is impossible not to be astounded by the richness of the world that awaits us, a world that is as haphazard as it is surprising. The task of the historian is not to be astounded, to condemn, or to straighten what appears bent, in other words, to bring practice in line with theory; rather, the historian's duty is to allow the countless exceptions to break the rule.

Having said that, it is by no means easy to observe, describe, and analyze the world I have been dealing with, let alone translate such a world into words. Every day, in every corner of the Mediterranean, thousands of encounters, contacts, and exchanges took place. What has hindered all these phenomena from finding their rightful place on the stage of history is the difficulty of accessing sources related to them. This becomes even more challenging when the matter at hand is intelligence.

In short, to decipher the codes of this mysterious yet captivating world, it is not enough just to consult manuscripts or printed materials—one must also delve into archival documents. If a number of developments had not taken place over the last few years that made accessing these documents possible, I would not have been able to write this book, which draws on countless spy reports, diplomatic correspondence, and internal correspondence related to intelligence from the Ottoman and European archives. The development of facilities for digital imaging has made it much easier to produce copies of archival documents. But in addition, Turkey's rapid integration into the global economy has meant that my generation of researchers has opportunities that were simply inaccessible to our predecessors. Historians today can easily learn new languages and receive training in paleography. They can find grants to complete doctorates abroad and carry out archival research, and they can exchange ideas with their fellow historians at conferences and workshops. It is my hope that, equipped with these opportunities, young researchers and academics will produce works that will complement, correct, or confirm the claims made in this book and turn their attention to analyzing different time periods and territories.

This book has also tried to engage in a systematic analysis of Ottoman intelligence and compare it with those of its rivals. It has accentuated the non-institutionalized and decentralized nature of Ottoman information gathering at a time when Venice and Madrid were experimenting with centralized mechanisms designed for gathering and analyzing intelligence as well as supervising agents in the field. The book has also demonstrated how dissimilar levels of centralization and institutionalization placed espionage at the center of Ottoman factional politics. Leaving intelligence-related tasks to imperial households, personal networks, and provincial authorities may have created a multiplicity of information channels that regularly fed Ottoman decision-makers, but it also fueled a struggle over intelligence among factions vying for power in the Ottoman capital. These not only concealed, selectively reported, and manipulated information but also even engaged in outright fabrication, hoping to sway the balance in decision-making circles and influence the Empire's foreign policy in line with their political ambitions

Although I have drawn attention to a fundamental difference between Istanbul on the one hand and Venice and Madrid on the other, I have still evaded the teleological trap of viewing history as a constant forward march and deducing causes from their supposed effects. In other words, this book has refrained from concluding that the lack of institutionalization and centralization resulted in an overall inefficiency on behalf of the Ottomans. By focusing on the tumultuous years between 1570 and 1573, when the Empire found itself in a war against united Christian front, it has demonstrated how Ottomans managed to collect reliable and timely intelligence using a variety of sources and to draw comprehensive strategies and employ their limited resources based on the intelligence that they received. Ottomans may have chosen not to follow the example of their European counterparts, but their methods produced satisfactory results within the logic of their patrimonial system. Institutionalization and centralization, which was a discontinuous process even in Western Europe, should not be taken as the sole measure of success, whether in gathering intelligence, conducting diplomatic negotiations, or administering a vast empire.

Without a doubt, there are many more rich topics in Ottoman intelligence than could be examined in this book. For example, even though a chapter has been devoted to examining Ottoman counterespionage, Ottoman attempts at disinformation have not been scrutinized here for reasons of space.[8] In reality, because the Ottomans were unable to control espionage activities in Istanbul, a city teeming with people of different religions and ethnicities from all corners of the Mediterranean, who could do more or less as they pleased, one of the main methods the authorities used to compensate for this lack of control was to spread rumors in the hope of confusing enemy intelligence. This was not the case in other European capitals, as I have explained in two separate articles that appeared after the publication of the (Turkish) first edition of this book, in 2017.[9]

Although I did not study assassination and agitation in separate chapters, in order to prevent the manuscript from being too long, the reader will still encounter numerous cases elucidating the importance of these covert operations throughout the book. While agitation played an important role in the minds of decision-makers, always eager to fund fifth columns in the land of the enemy, assassination was one of the natural consequences of a harsh political climate of Ottoman and Habsburg capitals. People of all ranks—whether they were the sultan, like Murad I, or a grand vizier such as Sokollu Mehmed—could fall victim to the dagger of a traitorous enemy. It is also suspected that several members of the Ottoman elite, including Sultan Mehmed the Conqueror and Bayezid II, were poisoned. These are just the examples we know of; as I have repeated throughout the book, for every documented case there must have been many hundreds more that have vanished into obscurity. For the moment, though, I would just add that Ottoman spies, assassins, and agitators were active practically everywhere in Europe and the Mediterranean; I will deal with this subject in much greater detail elsewhere.

Although the available documents did not allow me to delineate in minute detail how the Ottomans deployed the intelligence they acquired,[10] this book has made it evident that intelligence was essential to Ottoman statecraft and the international relations of the sixteenth-century Mediterranean world. Although employing different techniques, the Ottomans were apt information gatherers. They did appreciate the importance of intelligence, without which they could not allocate their finite resources in the most efficient manner. In an age when central governments were constantly short of money, matériel, and other resources, no polity could do without espionage. The Ottomans, a mighty empire with numerous responsibilities and borders stretching from Central Europe to Persia, from Kipchak Steppes to the Red Sea, and from Algeria to the Caucasus, could hardly be an exception.

NOTES

1. See Matteucci, p. 73, fn. 1. The recurrence of these first names would suggest that we are dealing with the same family here. In fact, in the sixteenth century, the surname "Cicala" was written as "Cigala," and this was the form in which it found its way into Ottoman.

2. AGS, *E* 1199, fol. 51; quoted in Preto, *Servizi Segreti*, p. 119; S. Pappalardo, "Ambizione politica, commercio e diplomazia alla fine del XVI secolo: Carlo Cicala," in *Acque, terre e spazi dei mercanti: Istituzioni, gerarchie, conflitti e pratiche dello scambio dall'età antica alla modernità*, ed. Daniele Andreozzi, Loredana Panariti, and Claudio Zaccaria (Trieste: Editreg, 2009), 141–68.

3. AGS, *E* 1080, fol. 58 (August 3, 1570).

4. For more on this remarkable family, see Ilario Rinieri, *Clemente VIII e Sinan Bassà Cicala* (Rome: Civiltà Cattolica, 1898); Gaetano Oliva, "Sinan-Bassà (Scipione Cicala), celebre rinnegato del secolo XVI," in *Archivio Storico Messinese* 8-9 (1907–1908), pp. 266–303; Benzoni; Pappalardo; Domenico Montuoro, "I Cigala, una famiglia feudale tra Genova, Sicilia, Turchia e Calabria," *Mediterranea: Richerche storiche* 16 (2009): pp. 277–302; Gürkan, "Espionage in the 16th Century Mediterranean," p. 447f; Levent Kaya Ocakaçan, "Cigalazade Yusuf Sinan Pasha (c. 1545–1606)," *Mediterranea: recherche storiche* 34 (2015): pp. 325–40. Evrim Türkçelik's dissertation on the topic is another important work that aims to shed light on the last 15 years of the pasha's career. "Cigalazade Yusuf Sinan Pasha y el Mediterráneo entre 1591–1606" (unpublished PhD diss., Universidad Autonoma de Madrid, 2012).

5. For a meticulous, detailed account of the life of this important Albanian commander, see Ahmet Önal, "Koca Sinan Paşa'nın Hayatı ve Siyasî Faaliyetleri (1520–1596)" (unpublished PhD diss., Marmara University, 2012).

6. Malcolm, p. 167.

7. See E. Natalie Rothman, "Between Venice and Istanbul: Trans-imperial Subjects and Cultural Mediation in the Early Modern Mediterranean" (unpublished PhD diss., University of Michigan, 2006), appendix 13, 14.

8. For an interesting and pioneering study on this subject, see Özgür Kolçak, "'Cümle Palankaları Küffâr Aldı...': 1663–64 Osmanlı-Habsburg Savaşında Dezenformasyon, Propaganda ve Siyasî İktidar," *The Journal of Ottoman Studies / Osmanlı Araştırmaları Dergisi* 43 (2014), 165–92.

9. Emrah Safa Gürkan, "*Hile ü Hu'da*: Deception, Dissimulation and Manipulation of Information in Sixteenth Century Ottoman Empire," *Acta Orientalia Academiae Scientiarum Hungaricum* 72/4 (2019): 437–54; Emrah Safa Gürkan, "Desinformación y rumores en Estambul en el comienzo de la Guerra de Chipre (1569–1570)," in *¿Si fuera cierto? Espías y agentes en la frontera (siglos XVI–XVII)*, ed. Gennaro Varriale (Alcalá de Henares: University of Alcalá, 2018), 48–61.

10. The articles on Ottoman decision-making included in Caesar E. Farah, ed., *Decision Making and Change in the Ottoman Empire* (Kirksville, Mo.: The Thomas Jefferson University Press, 1993) actually present a very superficial view of this issue. This book certainly does not meet its expectations: it does not engage with the existing extensive literature on decision-making, which mostly emerges from the field of political science, and it fails to offer any new or interesting insight into decision-making processes. These deficiencies presumably derive from the limited number of sources on this field.

BIBLIOGRAPHY

PRIMARY SOURCES
Archival Documents

Archivo General de Simancas (AGS), Valladolid, Spain
Papeles de Estado (E)
Legajos 487, 490, 491, 494, 656, 664, 1017, 1026, 1028, 1030, 1043, 1044, 1047, 1049, 1052, 1054, 1056, 1058, 1059, 1060, 1063, 1064, 1068, 1070, 1071, 1072, 1073, 1074, 1080, 1081, 1083, 1090, 1092, 1119, 1121, 1124, 1125, 1126, 1127, 1132, 1137, 1140, 1141, 1144, 1145, 1147, 1149, 1152, 1157, 1158, 1159, 1160, 1163, 1166, 1199, 1308, 1309, 1310, 1311, 1312, 1316, 1317, 1318, 1321, 1324, 1326, 1327, 1329, 1330, 1331, 1332, 1335, 1336, 1337, 1338, 1339, 1344 K 1675, 1348 K 1677, 1367, 1417, 1497, 1499, 1517, 1519, 1524, 1527, 1531, 1532, 1533, 1534, 1535, 1537, 1538, 1539, 1541, 1547, 1885, 1887, 1893, 1894, 1928, 1929.

Haus-, Hof- und Staatsarchiv (HHStA), Vienna, Austria
Turcica
Konvolut XXI, no. 4
Staatenabteilungen
Türkei I, *karton* 45, 1581 September

İstanbul Büyükşehir Belediyesi Atatürk Kitaplığı (AK), Istanbul, Turkey
Muallim Cevdet Yazmaları
O.071

Archivio di Stato di Firenze (ASF), Florence, Italy
Archivio Mediceo del Principato (AMP)
Filze 370, 2979, 3079, 3080, 3082, 4148, 4277

Archivio di Stato di Genoa (ASG), Genoa, Italy
Archivio Segreto, Lettere Ministri Costantinopoli
Busta I, *filza* 2169.

Archivio di Stato di Venezia (ASV), Venice, Italy
Capi del consiglio di dieci, Lettere di ambasciatori (CCX-LettAmb)
Buste 3, 4, 6, 292
Capi del consiglio di dieci, Lettere di rettori et di altre cariche (CCX-LettRett)
Buste 292, 302
Documenti Turchi (DocTR)
Buste 3, 4, 5, 6
Consiglio di dieci, Parti Secrete (CX-ParSec)
Registri 4, 5, 6, 7, 8, 9, 11, 12, 13, 14
Filza 20
Inquisitori di Stato (IS)
Buste 148, 416, 433, 460
Senato, Archivio Proprio Costantinopoli (SAPC)
Filze 4, 5
Senato, Dispacci, Costantinopoli (SDC)
Filze 1, 2, 3, 4, 5, 6, 6E, 9, 21, 22, 25, 28, 29, 30, 31, 32, 81
Senato, Secreta, Deliberazioni, Costantinopoli (SDelC)
Registri 3, 7, 8

Başbakanlık Osmanlık Arşivleri (BOA), Istanbul, Turkey
Kamil Kepeci
2555
Mühimme Defterleri
I, II, III, V, VI, VII, VIII, IX, X, XII, XIII, XIV, XV, XVI, XVIII, XIX, XXI, XXII, XXIII, XXV, XXVII, XXVIII, XXIX, XXX, XXXI, XXXIII, XXXV, XXXVI, XXXVIII, XXXIX, XL, XLII, XLIV, XLV, XLVI, XLVII, XLVIII, XLIX, LI, LII, LIII, LV, LVI, LVIII, LX, LXI, LXIII, LVII, LXIX, LXX, LXXI, LXXIII
Mühimme Zeyli Defterleri
II, V

Državni Arhiv u Dubrovniku (DAD), Dubrovnik, Croatia
Acta Turcorum
A7 29a, A8 9a, A8 10, K 68, K 82, K 113
Lettere di Levante
Documents dated February 11, 1592; November 24, 1579; January 20, 1580.

Topkapı Sarayı Müzesi Arşivi (TSMA), Istanbul, Turkey
Evrak 3703/1, 3192, 5994, 6306, 4265, 4575/2, 4800, 5997, 12321

Topkapı Sarayı Müzesi Kütüphanesi (TSMK), Istanbul, Turkey
Revan 1943

Manuscripts

Anonymous. "Copey unnd lautter Abschrifft ainsi warhafftigen Sendtbrieffs / wieder Türckisch Kayser Solyman / disen sein yerzt gegen würtigen Anzug wider die Christenhait geordnet / von Constantinopel aussgezogen / und gen Kriechischen Weyssenburg ankommen ist / Wie volgt." Belgrade, July 7, 1532.

————. "Copia de una lettera de la partita del Turcho. Particolare de giornata in gìomata insino a Belgrado." Belgrade, July 7, 1532.

Granvela, Antoine Perrenot de. "Correspondencia del Cardenal Granvela, Biblioteca Nacional de España." ms. 7905.

Valle, Francesco della. "Vita di Alvise Gritti." Biblioteca Nazionale Marciana, ms. Itt., cl. 6, cod. 122 (6211).

Printed Archival Documents

Albèri, Eugenio, ed. *Le relazioni degli ambasciatori veneti al Senato durante il secolo decimosesto.* Florence: Società Editrice Firoentina, 1855.

Bacqué-Grammont, Jean-Louis. "Autour d'une correspondance entre Charles Quint et İbrahim Paşa." *Turcica* 15 (1983): 231–346.

Barkan, Ömer Lütfi. "Hicri 933–934 / Miladi 1526–1527 Yılına Ait Bir Bütçe Örneği." İktisat Fakültesi Mecmuası 15, no. 1–4 (1954): 251–329.

————. "İstanbul Saraylarına Ait Muhasebe Defterleri." *Belgeler: Türk Tarih Belgeleri Dergisi* 13 (1979): 1–380.

————. *XV ve XVIinci Asırlarda Osmanlı İmparatorluğunda Zirai Ekonominin Hukuki ve Malî Esasları, Birinci Cilt: Kanunlar.* Istanbul: Burhaneddin Matbaası, 1943.

Belon du Mans, Pierre. *Les observations de plusieurs singularitez & choses memorable, trouvées en Grece, Asie, Indee, Egypte, Arabie & autres pays estranges.* Antwerp: Chez Iean Steelsius, 1555.

Berthier, Annie. "Un Document Retrouvé: La Première Lettre de Soliman au François Ier (1526)." *Turcica* 27 (1995): 263–66.

Calendar of State Papers. *Calendar of State Papers Relating to English Affairs in the Archives of Venice,* edited by Horatio F Brown. London: Her Majesty's Stationery Office, 1894. http://www.british-history.ac.uk/cal-state-papers/venice/.

Charrière, Ernest, ed. *Négociations de la France dans le Levant, ou, correspondances, mémoires et actes diplomatiques des ambassadeurs de France à Constantinople et des ambassadeurs, envoyés ou résidents à divers titres à Venise, Raguse, Rome, Malte et Jérusalem, en Turquie, Perse, Géorgie, Crimée, Syrie, Egypte, etc., et dans les états de Tunis, d'Alger et de Maroc.* Paris: Impr. Nationale, 1853.

Douais, M. L'Abbé, ed. *Dépèches de M. de Fourquevaux ambassadeur du Roi Charles IX en Espagne, 1565–1572.* Paris: Ernest Leroux, 1896.

Karapınar, Ayşe, and Emine Erdoğan Özünlü, eds. *Mihaloğulları'na Ait 1586 Tarihli Akıncı Defteri.* Ankara: Türk Tarih Kurumu, 2015.

Longo, Francesco, ed. *Annali veneti dall'anno 1457 al 1500 del senatore Domenico Malipiero.* Florence: Gio. Pietro Viesseux, Direttore-Editore, 1843.

Masiá, Maria José Bertomeu, ed. *Cartas de un espía de Carlos V: La correspondencia de Jerónimo Bucchia con Antonio Perrenot de Granvela.* València: Universitat de València, 2006.

Pedani, Maria Pia, ed. *Relazioni di ambasciatori veneti al Senato tratte dalle migliori edizioni disponibili e ordinate cronologicamente, vol. 14, Costantinopoli, relazioni inedite (1512–1789).* Turin: Bottega d'Erasmo, 1996.

Refik, Ahmet. *Onaltıncı Asırda Rafizîlik ve Bektaşilik.* Istanbul: Muallim Ahmet Halim Kitaphanesi, 1932.

Sahillioğlu, Halil, ed. *Koca Sinan Paşa'nın Telhisleri.* Istanbul: IRCICA, 2004.

————, ed. *Topkapı Sarayı Arşivi, Mühimme Defteri E-12321.* Istanbul: IRCICA, 2002.

Sanuto, Marino. *I Diarii*, edited by Rinaldo Fulin, Federico Stefani, Niccolò Barozzi, Guglielmo Berchet, and Marco Allegri. Venice: Federico Visentini Editore, 1879–902.

Segre, Arturo, and Roberto Cessi, ed. *I Diarii di Girolamo Priuli (AA. 1494–1512)*. Città di Castello: Casa Editrice S. Lapi, 1912.

Theunissen, H. "Ottoman-Venetian Diplomatics: The 'Ahd-Names. The Historical Background and the Development of a Category of Political-Commercial Instruments Together with an Annotated Edition of a Corpus of Relevant Documents." *Electronic Journal of Oriental Studies* 1, no. 2 (1998): 1–698.

Vatin, Nicolas. *L'Ordre de Saint-Jean-de-Jérusalem, l'Empire ottoman et la Méditerranée orientale entre les deux sièges de Rhodes, 1480–1522*. Paris: Peeters, 1994.

Printed Memoirs, Travelogues, Chronicles, and Treatises

Busbecq, Ogier Ghislain de. *The Turkish Letters of Ogier Ghiselin de Busbecq: Imperial Ambassador at Constantinople, 1554–1562*, edited by E. S. Forster. Baton Rouge: University of Louisiana Press, 2005.

Callières, François de. *De la manière de négocier avec les souverains*. Amsterdam: La Compagnie, 1716.

Chesneau, Jean. *Le voyage de Monsieur d'Aramon, ambassadeur pour le Roy en Levant, escript par noble homme Jean Chesneau*, edited by Charles Schefer. Paris: Ernest Leroux, 1887.

Contarini, Tommaso. *Historia delle successe dal principio della guerra mossa da Selim Ottomano a Venetiani, fino al dì della gran giornata vittoriosa contra Turchi*. Venice: Francesco Rampazzetto, 1572.

Evliyâ Çelebi b. Derşiv Mehemmed Zıllî. *Evliyâ Çelebi Seyahatnâmesi, VI. Kitap*, edited by Seyit Ali Kahraman and Yücel Dağlı. Istanbul: Yapı Kredi Yayınları, 2002.

Feridun Ahmed Beg. *Nüzhet-i Esrâr-ü'l-Ahyâr der Ahbâr-ı Sefer-i Sigetvar*, edited by H. Ahmet Arslantürk and Günhan Börekçi. Istanbul: Zeytinburnu Belediyesi Kültür Yayınları, 2012.

Haedo, Diego de. *Topographia e Historia General de Argel, repartida en cinco tratados, do se veran casos estraños, muertes espantosas, y tormentos exquisitos, que conuiene se entiendan en la Christiandad: con mucha doctrina, y elegancia curiosa*. Valladolid: Diego Fernandez de Cordoua y Ouiedo, 1612.

Hezarfen Hüseyin Efendi. *Telhîsü'l-Beyân fi Kavânîn-i Âl-i Osmân*, edited by Sevim İlgürel. Ankara: Türk Tarih Kurumu, 1998.

Kâtib Çelebi. *Tuhfetü'l-kibâr fi esfâri'il-bihâr*, edited by İdris Bostan. Ankara: T.C. Başbakanlık Denizcilik Müsteşarlığı, 2008.

Klarwill, Victor von, ed. *The Fugger Newsletters: Being a Selection of Unpublished Letters from the Correspondents of the House of Fugger During the Years 1568–1605*. Translated by Pauline de Chary. New York and London: The Knickerbocker Press, 1926.

Lütfi Paşa. *Tevârih-i Âl-i Osman*, edited by Kayhan Atik. Ankara: T.C. Kültür Bakanlığı Yayınları, 2001.

Mans, Pierre Belon du. *Les observations de plusieurs singularitez & choses memorable, trouvées en Grece, Asie, Indee, Egypte, Arabie & autres pays estranges*. Antwerp: Chez Iean Steelsius, 1555.

Naîmâ Mustafa Efendi, *Tarih-i Naîmâ*, edited by Mehmet İpşirli. Ankara: Türk Tarih Kurumu Yayınları, 2007.

Pirî Reis. *Kitab-ı Bahriye / Book of Navigation*. Ankara: Republic of Turkey, Prime Ministry, Undersecretaryship of Navigation, 2002.

Selânikî Mustafa Efendi. *Tarih-i Selânikî*, edited by Mehmet İpşirli. Ankara: Türk Tarih Kurumu, 1999.

Sereno, Bartolomeo. *Commentari della guerra di Cipro e della lega dei principi cristiani contro il turco*. Monte Cassino: Tipi di Monte Cassino, 1845.

Seyyid Murâdi Re'îs. *Gazavât-ı Hayreddin Paşa*, edited by Mustafa Yıldız. Aachen: Verlag Shaker, 1993.

Tansel, Selâhattin. "Silahşor'un Feth-nâme-i Diyâr-ı Arab Adlı Eseri." *Tarih Vesikaları* 17 (1958): 295–320; 18 (1961): 429–54.

Valle, Francesco della. "Una breve narrazione della grandezza, virtù, valore et della infelice morte dell'Illustrissimo Signor Conte Alouise Gritti, del Serenissimo Signor Andrea Gritti, Principe di Venezia, Conte del gran Contado di Marmarus in Ongaria et General Capitano dell'esercito Regno, appresso Sulimano Imperator de Turchi, et alla Maesta del Re Giovanni Re d'Ongaria." *Magyar Történelmi Tár* 3 (1857): 9–60.

Voltaire. *Essai sur les mœurs et l'esprit des nations et sur les principaux faits de l'histoire depuis Charlemagne jusqu'à Louis XIII.* 1756.

Werner, Adam. *Padişahın Huzurunda: Elçilik Günlüğü, 1616–1618*. Translated by Türkis Noyan. Istanbul: Kitap Yayınevi, 2011.

Wratislaw, A. H. *Adventures of Baron Wenceslas Wratislaw of Mitrowitz*. London: Bell and Daldy, 1862.

SECONDARY SOURCES

Books and Articles

Acero, Beatriz Alonso. *Orán Mazalquivir, 1589–1639: Una sociedad española en la frontera de Berbería*. Madrid: Consejo Superior de Investigaciones Científicas, 2000.

Afşar, Servet. "Birinci Dünya Savaşı'nda Casusluk Okulları, Casusluk Uygulamaları ve Osmanlı Devleti'nin Casusluğu Önleme Faaliyetleri." *Stratejik ve Sosyal Araştırmalar Dergisi* 3 (2018): 1–46.

———. "Birinci Dünya Savaşı'nda Irak Cephesi'nde Aşiretler ve Casusluk Faaliyetleri." *Askerî Tarih Araştırmaları Dergisi* 52 (2002): 129–45.

Ágoston, Gábor. "Birodalom és információ: Konstantinápoly, mint a koraújkori Európa információs központja." In *Perjés Géza Emlékkönyv*, edited by Gábor Hausner and László Veszprémi. Budapest: Argumentum, 2005, 31–60.

———. "A Flexible Empire: Authority and Its Limits on the Ottoman Frontiers." *International Journal of Turkish Studies* 9, no. 1–2 (2003): 15–31.

———. "Ideologie, Propaganda und Politischer Pragmatismus: Die Auseinandersetzung der osmanichen und habsburgischen Grossmächte und die mitteleuropäische Konfrontation." In *Kaiser Ferdinand I.—Ein mitteleuropäischer Herrscher*, edited by Maria Fuchs. Münster: Aschendorff, 2005, 207–33.

———. "Információszerzés és kémkedés az Oszmán Birodalomban a 15–17. században." In *Információáármlás a magyar ès török végvári rendszerben*, edited by Tivadar Petercsák and Mátyás Berecz. Eger: Heves Megyei Múzeum, 1999, 129–54.

———. "Information, Ideology, and Limits of Imperial Policy: Ottoman Grand Strategy in the Context of Ottoman-Habsburg Rivalry." In *The Early Modern Ottomans: Remapping the Empire*, edited by Virginia H. Aksan and Daniel Goffman. Cambridge: Cambridge University Press, 2007, 78–92.

————. "The Ottomans: From Frontier Principality to Empire." In *The Practice of Strategy: From Alexander the Great to the Present*, edited by John Andreas Olsen and Colin S. Gray. Oxford and New York: Oxford University Press, 2011, 105–31.

Akkerman, Nadine. *Invisible Agents: Women and Espionage in Seventeenth-Century Britain*. Oxford: Oxford University Press, 2018.

Allen, Bruce Ware. *The Great Siege of Malta: The Epic Battle between the Ottoman Empire and the Knights of St. John*. Lebanon, NH: University Press of New England, 2015.

Anhegger, Robert. *Ein angeblicher schweizerischer Agent an der Hohen Pforte im Jahre 1581*. Istanbul: Marmara Basımevi, 1943.

————. "Martoloslar Hakkında." *Türkiyat Mecmuası* 7–8 (1942): 282–320.

Arbel, Benjamin. *Trading Nations: Jews and Venetians in the Early Modern Eastern Mediterranean*. Leiden: E. J. Brill, 1995.

Arbel, Benjamin, and Gilles Veinstein. "La fiscalité vénéto-chypriote au miroir de la législation ottomane: le *Qânunnâme* de 1572." *Turcica* 18 (1986): 7–51.

Archer, John Michael. *Sovereignty and Intelligence: Spying and Court Culture in the English Renaissance*. Stanford: Stanford University Press, 1993.

Argenti, Philip P. *Chius Vincta or the Occupation of Chios by the Turks (1566) and Their Administration of the Island (1566–1912)*. Cambridge: Cambridge University Press, 1941.

Aubin, Jean. "Une frontière face au péril ottoman: la Terre d'Otrante (1529–1532)." In *Soliman le Magnifique et son temps: Actes du colloque de Paris Galeries Nationales du Grand Palais, 7–10 Mars 1990*, edited by Gilles Veinstein. Paris: La Documentation Française, 1992, 39–49.

Babinger, Franz. *Mehmet der Eborer und seine Zeit: Weltenstürmer einer Zeitenwende*. Munich: F. Bruckmann, 1953.

Bacigalupe, Miguel Angel Echevarría. *La Diplomacia Secreta en Flandes, 1598–1643*. Leioa-Vizcaya: Argitarapen Zerbitzua Euskal Herriko Unibertsitatea, 1984.

Barbero, Alessandro. *La bataille des trois empires: Lépante, 1571*. Translated by Patricia Farazzi and Michel Valensi. Paris: Flammarion, 2012.

————. *Lepanto: La battaglia dei tre imperi*. Rome and Bari: Laterza, 2010.

Baron, Salo Wittmayer. *A Social and Religious History of the Jews, vol. 18, The Ottoman Empire, Persia, Ethiopia, India and China*, 2nd ed. New York: Columbia University Press. 1982.

Barta, Gábor. "Gritti Ludovicus'un Macar Valiliği (1531–1534)." *Belleten* 263 (2008): 251–93.

Bartl, Peter. *Der Westbalkan zwischen spanischer Monarchie und osmanischem Reich: zur Türkenkriegsproblematik an der Wende vom 16. zum 17*. Wiesbaden, Harrassowitz, 1974.

Bély, Lucien. *Espions et ambassadeurs au temps de Louis XIV*. Paris: Librairie Arthème Fayard, 1990.

Bennassar, Bartolomé, and Lucile Bennassar. *Les chrétiens d'Allah: l'histoire extraordinaire des renégats, XVIe et XVIIe siècles*. Paris: Perrin, 1989.

Benzoni, Gino. "Cicala, Scipione (Čigala-Zade Yûsuf Sinân)." *Dizionario Biografico degli Italiani* 25 (1981).

Beydilli, Kemal. "Korsika." In *Türkiye Diyanet Vakfı İslam Ansiklopedisi*.

Biegman, Nicolaas H. "Ragusan Spying for the Ottoman Empire: Some 16th-Century Documents from the State Archive at Dubrovnik." *Belleten* 26, no. 106 (1963): 237–55.

————. *The Turco-Ragusan Relationship according to the Firmāns of Murād III (1575–1595) Extant in the State Archives of Dubrovnik*. The Hague: Mouton, 1968.

Bonilla, Diego Navarra, ed. *Cartas entre espías e inteligencias secretas en el siglo de los validos, Juan de Torres Gaspar-Bonifaz, 1632–1638*. Madrid: Ministerio de Defensa, 2007.

———. "Espías honorables, espías necesarios: de la información a la inteligencia en la conducción de la política y la guerra de la monarquía hispánica." In *Ambassadeurs, apprentis espions et maîtres comploteurs: Les systèmes de renseignement en Espagne à l'époque moderne*, edited by Béatrice Perez. Paris: Presses de l'université Paris-Sorbonne, 2010, 31–47.

Bono, Salvatore. *I corsari barbareschi*. Turin: ERI-Edizioni RAI Radiotelevisione Italiana, 1964.

———. *Schiavi musulmani nell'Italia moderna: galeotti vu' cumprà, domestici*. Naples: Edizioni Scientifiche Italiane, 1999.

———. *Yeniçağ İtalya'sında Müslüman Köleler*. Istanbul: İletişim Yayınları, 2003.

Bornate, Carlo. "La Missione di Sampiero Corso a Costantinopoli." *Archivio Storico di Corsica* 15 (1939): 472–502.

Bossy, John. *Under the Molehill: An Elizabethan Spy Story*. New Haven, CT: Yale University Press, 2001.

Bostan, İdris. *Adriyatik'te Korsanlık: Osmanlılar, Uskoklar, Venedikliler, 1575–1620*. Istanbul: Timaş Yayınları, 2009.

———. *Osmanlılar ve Deniz: Deniz Politikası, Teşkilat, Gemiler*. Istanbul: Küre Yayınları, 2007.

Bozkurt, Abdurrahman. "Birinci Dünya Savaşı Başlarında Casusluk Faaliyetleri." *Osmanlı Tarihi Araştırma ve Uygulama Merkezi Dergisi* 36 (2015): 1–45.

Brandi, Karl. *Kaiser Karl V: Der Kaiser und sein Weltreich*. München: König Verlag, 1973.

Braudel, Fernand. *La Méditerranée et le monde Méditerranéen à l'époque de Philippe II*, 2nd ed. Paris: Armand Colin, 1966.

Brendecke, Arndt. *Imperium und Empirie: Funktionen des Wissens in der spanischen Kolonialherrschaft*. Köln: Böhlau, 2009.

Brummett, Palmira. *Ottoman Seapower and Levantine Diplomacy in the Age of Discovery*. Albany: State University of New York Press, 1994.

Brun, Miguel Ángel Ochoa. *Historia de la Diplomacia Española, VI: La Diplomacia de Felipe II*. Madrid: Ministerio de Asuntos Exteriores, 2000, 2003.

Budiansky, Stephen. *Her Majesty's Spymaster: Queen Elizabeth I, Sir Francis Walsingham, and the Birth of Modern Espionage*. New York: Viking, 2005.

Bunes Ibarra, Miguel Ángel de. "Avis du Levant: Le réseau d'espionnage espagnol dans l'Empire Ottoman à partir du sud de l'Italie, à la charnière des XVIe et XVIIe siècles." In *Ambassadeurs, apprentis espions et maîtres comploteurs: Les systèmes de renseignement en Espagne à l'époque moderne*, edited by Béatrice Perez. Paris: Presses de l'université Paris-Sorbonne, 2010, 223–40.

Canosa, Romano, and Isabello Colonnello. *Spionaggio a Palermo: Aspetti della guerra secreta turco-spagnola in Mediterraneno nel cinquecento*. Palermo: Sellerio Editore, 1991.

Carnicer García, Carlos J., and Javier Marcos Rivas. *Espías de Felipe II: Los servicios secretos del imperio español*. Madrid: La Esfera de Los Libros, 2005.

———. *Sebastián de Arbizu, Espía de Felipe II: La diplomacia secreta española y la intervención en Francia*. Madrid: Editorial Nerea S. A., 1998.

Carrasco, Raphaël. "L'espionnage espagnol du Levant au XVIe siècle d'après la correspondance des agents espagnols en poste à Venise." In *Ambassadeurs, apprentis espions et maîtres comploteurs: Les systèmes de renseignement en Espagne à l'époque moderne*, edited by Béatrice Perez. Paris: Presses de l'université Paris-Sorbonne, 2010, 203–22.

Casale, Giancarlo. "An Ottoman Intelligence Report from the mid-sixteenth century Indian Ocean." *Journal of Turkish Studies* 31 (2007): 181–88.

Cassen, Flora. "Philip II of Spain and His Italian Jewish Spy." *Journal of Early Modern History* 21 (2017): 318–42.

Coco, Carla. "Alvise Gritti fra Veneti, Turchi e Ungheresi." In *Studi Miscellanei Uralici e Altaici*, edited by Andrea Csillaghy. Venice: Libreria Editrice Cafoscarina, 1984, 379–96.

Comissoli, Adriano. "Bombeiros, espias e vaqueanos: agentes da comunicação política no sul da América portuguesa (Rio Grande de São Pedro, sécs. XVIII–XIX)." *Revista da Indias* 78, no. 272 (2018): 113–46.

———. "A circulação de informações e o sistema de vigilância portuguesa da fronteira do Rio da Prata (século XIX)." *Revista Eletrônica Documento/Monumento* 13, no. 1 (2014): 23–40.

———. "Soberania em território alheio: comandantes e espiões ibéricos nas fronteiras da América, séculos XVIII E XIX." *Almanack* 27 (2021): 1–46.

Cortés, Fernando. *Espionagem e contra-espionagem numa guerra peninsular 1640–1668*. Lisbon: Livros Horizonte, 1989.

Costantini, Vera. *Il Sultano e l'isola contesa: Cipro tra eredità e potere ottomano*. Milan: UTET Libreria, 2009.

Dávid, Géza. "The Mühimme Defters as a Source in Ottoman-Habsburg Rivalry in the 16th Century." *Archivum Ottomanicum* 20 (2002): 167–209.

Dávid, Géza, and Pál Fodor. "Ottoman Spy Reports from Hungary." In *Turcica et Islamica. Studi in memoria di Aldo Gallotta, I*, edited by Ugo Marazzi. Napoli: Università degli Studi di Napoli "L'Orientale," 2003, 121–31.

———, eds. *Ransom Slavery along the Ottoman Borders (Early Fifteenth–Early Eigtheenth Centuries)*. Leiden and Boston: Brill, 2007.

Davis, Robert C. *Christian Slaves, Muslim Masters: White Slavery in the Mediterranean, the Barbary Coast and Italy, 1500–1800*. New York: Palgrave Macmillan, 2003.

Decei, Aurel. "Aloisio Gritti au service de Soliman le Magnifique d'aprés des documents turcs inédits (1533–1534)." *Anatolia Moderna-Yeni Anadolu* 3 (1992): 10–60.

Dedijer, Steven. "Ragusa Intelligence and Security (1301–1806): A Model for the Twenty-First Century." *International Journal of Intelligence and Counterintelligence* 15, no. 1 (2002): 101–14.

Dehqan, Mustafa, and Vural Genç. "Kurds as Spies: Information-Gathering on the 16th-Century Ottoman-Safavid Frontier." *Acta Orientalia Academiae Scientiarum Hungaricum* 71, no. 2 (2018): 197–230.

Durrieu, Paul. "Délivrance de la Grèce projetée en France a la fin du quinzième siècle." *Revue d'histoire diplomatique* 26 (1912): 333–51.

Dursteler, Eric R. "On Bazaars and Battlefields: Recent Scholarship on Mediterranean Cultural Contacts." *Journal of Early Modern History* 15 (2011): 413–34.

———. "Erken Modern Dönem İstanbulu'nda Latin Kilisesi Hıristiyanları." In *Osmanlı İstanbulu I: I. Uluslararası Osmanlı İstanbulu Sempozyumu Bildirileri, 29 Mayıs–1 Haziran 2013, İstanbul 29 Mayıs Üniversitesi*, edited by Feridun M. Emecen and Emrah Safa Gürkan, Istanbul: İstanbul 29 Mayıs Üniversitesi Yayınları, 2014, 127–35.

———. "Power and Information: The Venetian Postal System in the Early Modern Mediterranean." In *From Florence to the Mediterranean and Beyond: Essays in*

Honor of Anthony Molho, edited by Diogo Curto, Eric R. Dursteler, Julius Kirshner, and Francesca Trivellato. Florence: Olschki, 2009, 601–23.

Ellis, John. *To Walk in the Dark: Military Intelligence during the English Civil War (1642–1646)*. Gloucestershire: Spellmount, 2011.

Emecen, Feridun M. "İbrâhim Paşa, Makbul." In *Türkiye Diyanet Vakfı İslam Ansiklopedisi*.

———. *İlk Osmanlılar ve Batı Anadolu Beylikler Dünyası*. Istanbul: Timaş Yayınları, 2012.

———. *İmparatorluk Çağının Osmanlı Sultanları–I*. Istanbul: İSAM Yayınları, 2014.

———. *Osmanlı İmparatorluğu'nun Kuruluşu ve Yükselişi, 1300–1600*. Istanbul: Türkiye İş Bankası Kültür Yayınları, 2015.

———. *Osmanlı Klasik Çağında Savaş*. Istanbul: Timaş, 2011.

———. *Yavuz Sultan Selim*. Istanbul: Kapı Yayınları, 2016.

Engerth, Eduard von. "Das Portrait des venetianischen Patriciers Marcanlonio Barbaro von P. Veronese im Belvedere zu Wien." *Zeitschrift für bildende Kunst* 10 (1875): 29–31.

Ercan, Yavuz. *Osmanlı İmparatorluğu'nda Bulgarlar ve Voynuklar*. Ankara: Türk Tarih Kurumu, 1986.

Eroğlu, Haldun. "Klasik Dönemde Osmanlı Devletinin İstihbarat Stratejileri." *Ankara Üniversitesi Tarih Araştırmaları Dergisi* 34 (2003): 11–33.

Fabris, Antonio. "A Description of the Ottoman Arsenal of Istanbul (1698)." *Mediterranea: richerche storiche* 34 (2015): 435–44.

———. "Hasan 'il Veneziano' tra Algeria e Costantinopoli." *Quaderni di Studi Arabi* 5 (1997): 51–66.

Falque, Juan R. Goberna. *Inteligencia, espionaje y servicios secretos en España*. Madrid: Ministerio de Defensa, 2007.

Farah, Caesar E. *Decision Making and Change in the Ottoman Empire*. Kirksville, MO: The Thomas Jefferson University Press, 1993.

Farge, Arlette. *Subversive Words: Public Opinion in Eighteenth-Century France*. Translated by Rosemary Morris. University Park: The Pennsylvania State University Press, 1994.

Faroqhi, Suraiya. *The Ottoman Empire and the World around It*. New York and London: I.B. Tauris, 2004.

———. *Pilgrims and Sultans: The Hajj under the Ottomans, 1517–1683*. London: I.B. Tauris, 1994.

Finlay, Robert. "Al Servizio del Sultano: Venezia, i Turchi e il mondo Cristiano, 1523–1538." In *Renovatio Urbis: Venezia nell'età di Andrea Giritti*, edited by Manfredo Tafuri. Rome: Oficina Edizioni, 1984, 78–118.

Fischer-Galati, Stephen A. *Ottoman Imperialism and German Protestantism, 1521–1555*. Cambridge, MA: Harvard University Press, 1959.

Fiume, Giovanna. *Schiavitù mediterranee: corsari, rinnegati e santi di età moderna*. Milan: Bruno Mondadori, 2009.

Fleischer, Cornell. *Bureaucrat and Intellectual in the Ottoman Empire: The Historian Mustafa Âli (1541–1600)*. Princeton: Princeton University Press, 1986.

———. "The Lawgiver as Messiah: The Making of the Imperial Image in the Reign of Süleymân." In *Soliman le magnifique et son temps*, edited by Gilles Veinstein. Paris: La Documentation Française, 1992, 159–77.

Floristán Imízcoz, José M. "Felipe II ya la empresa de Grecia tras Lepanto (1571–1578)." *Erytheia* 15 (1994): 155–90.

———. *Fuentes para la política oriental de los Austrias: La documentación griega del Archivo de Simancas (1571–1621)*. León: Universidad de Léon, 1988.

Fodor, Pál. "Between Two Continental Wars: The Ottoman Naval Preparations in 1590–1592." In *In Quest of the Golden Apple: Imperial Ideology, Politics, and Military Administration in the Ottoman Empire*, edited by Pál Fodor. Istanbul: Isis, 2000, 171–90.

———. "The Organisation of Defence in the Eastern Mediterranean (end of the 16th century)." In *The Kapudan Pasha: His Office and His Domain: Halcyon Days in Crete IV, a Symposium Held in Rethymnon, 7–9 January 2000*, edited by Elizabeth A. Zachariadou. Resmo: Crete University Press, 2002, 87–94.

Foretić, Vinko. *Povijest Dubrovnika do 1808, 2. Od 1526 da 1808*. Zagreb: Nakladni zavod Matice Hrvatske, 1980.

Fraser, Peter. *The Intelligence of the Secretaries of the State and their Monopoly of Licensed News, 1660–1688*. Cambridge: Cambridge University Press, 1956.

Friedman, Ellen G. *Spanish Captives in North Africa in the Early Modern Age*. Wisconsin: The University of Wisconsin Press, 1983.

Fusaro, Maria. "After Braudel: A Reassessment of Mediterranean History between the Northern Invasion and the *Caravane Maritime*." In *Trade and Cultural Exchange in the Early Modern Mediterranean: Braudel's Maritime Legacy*, edited by Maria Fusaro, Colin Heywood, and Mohamed-Salah Omri. London and New York: I.B. Tauris, 1–22.

Fusaro, Maria, Colin Heywood, and Mohamed-Salah Omri, eds. *Trade and Cultural Exchange in the Mediterranean: Braudel's Maritime Legacy*. London and New York: I.B. Tauris, 2010.

Galanti, Avram. *Türkler ve Yahudiler*. Istanbul: Gözlem Gazetecilik Basın ve Yayın, 1995.

Garcés, María Antonia. *Cervantes in Algiers: A Captive's Tale*. Nashville: Vanderbilt University Press, 2002.

Genêt, Stéphane. *Les espions des Lumières: Actions secrètes et espionnage militaire au temps de Louis XV*. Paris: Nouveau Monde Éditions, 2013.

Ghobrial, John-Paul. *The Whispers of Cities: Information Flows in Istanbul, London, and Paris in the Age of William Trumbull*. Oxford: Oxford University Press, 2013.

Graf, Tobias P. "Of Half-Lives and Double-Lives: 'Renegades' in the Ottoman Empire and Their Pre-Conversion Ties, ca. 1580–1610." In *Well-Connected Domains: Towards an Entangled Ottoman History*, edited by Pascal W. Firges, Tobias Graf, Christian Roth, and Gülay Tulasoğlu. Leiden: Brill, 2014, 131–49.

———. "Knowing the 'Hereditary Enemy': Austrian-Habsburg Intelligence on the Ottoman Empire in the Late Sixteenth Century." *Journal of Intelligence History* 21, no. 3 (2022): 268–88.

Graf, Tobias P., and Charlotte Backerra. "Case Studies in Early Modern European Intelligence." *Journal of Intelligence History* 21, no. 3 (2022): 237–50.

Groot, A. H. de. *The Ottoman Empire and the Dutch Republic: A History of the Earliest Diplomatic Relations, 1610–1630*. Leiden and Istanbul: Nederlands Historisch-Archaeologisch Instituut, 1978.

Guilmartin, John Francis, Jr. *Gunpowder and Galleys: Changing Technology and Mediterranean Warfare at Sea in the Sixteenth Century*. London: Cambridge University Press, 1974.

Gürkan, Emrah Safa. "Batı Akdeniz'de Osmanlı korsanlığı ve gaza meselesi." *Kebikeç: İnsan Bilimleri İçin Kaynak Araştırmaları Dergisi* 33 (2012): 173–204.

——. "Bir Diplomasi Merkezi Olarak Yeni Çağ İstanbul'u." In *Antik Çağ'dan 21.*
Yüzyıla Büyük İstanbul Tarihi: Siyaset ve Yönetim I, edited by Feridun M. Emecen
and Coşkun Yılmaz. Istanbul: İ.B.B. Kültür A.Ş., 2015, 372–99.

——. "The Centre and the Frontier: Ottoman Cooperation with the North African
Corsairs in the Sixteenth Century." *Turkish Historical Review* 1, no. 2 (2010): 125–63.

——. "Desinformación y rumores en Estambul en el comienzo de la Guerra de Chipre
(1569–1570)." In *¿Si fuera cierto? Espías y agentes en la frontera (siglos XVI–XVII)*,
edited by Gennaro Varriale. Alcalá de Henares: University of Alcalá, 2018, 48–61.

——. "Dishonorable Ambassadors: Spies and Secret Diplomacy in Ottoman Istanbul."
Archivum Ottomanicum 35 (2018): 47–61.

——. "Fitilin ucunda Tersane-yi Amire." In *Osmanlı İstanbulu: I. Uluslararası
Osmanlı İstanbulu Sempozyumu Bildirileri, 29 Mayıs–1 Haziran 2013, İstanbul 29
Mayıs Üniversitesi*, edited by Feridun M. Emecen and Emrah Safa Gürkan. Istanbul:
İstanbul 29 Mayıs Üniversitesi Yayınları, 2014, 67–69.

——. "Fooling the Sultan: Information, Decision-Making and the 'Mediterranean
Faction' (1585–1587)." *Journal of Ottoman Studies* 45 (2015): 57–96.

——. "*Hile ü Hu'da*: Deception, Dissimulation and Manipulation of Information in
Sixteenth Century Ottoman Empire." *Acta Orientalia Academiae Scientiarum
Hungaricum* 72, no. 4 (2019): 437–54.

——. "His Bailo's *Kapudan*: Conversion, Tangled Loyalties and Hasan *Veneziano*
between Istanbul and Venice (1588–1591)." *Journal of Ottoman Studies* 48 (2016):
277–319.

——. "I baili veneziani e la diplomazia d'informazione fra Venezia e Istanbul."
Θησαυρίσματα / *Thesaurismata: Bollettino dell'Istituto Ellenico di Studi Bizantini e
Postbizantini* 46 (2018): 106–11.

——. "Laying Hands on *Arcana Imperii*: Venetian Baili as Spymasters in
Sixteenth-Century Istanbul." In *Spy Chiefs, vol. 2, Intelligence Leaders in Europe,
the Middle East, and Asia*, edited by Paul Maddrell, Christopher Moran, Ioanna
Iordanou, and Mark Stout. Washington, DC: Georgetown University Press, 2018,
67–96.

——. "Mediating Boundaries: Mediterranean Go-Betweens and Cross-Confessional
Diplomacy in Constantinople, 1560–1600." *Journal of Early Modern History* 19
(2015): 107–28.

——. "My Money or Your Life: The Habsburg Hunt for Uluc Ali." *Studia Historica.
Historia Moderna* 36 (2014): 121–45.

——. "Osmanlı-Habsburg Rekabeti Çerçevesinde Osmanlılar'ın XVI. Yüzyıl'daki
Akdeniz Siyaseti." In *Osmanlı Dönemi Akdeniz Dünyası*, edited by Haydar Çoruh,
M. Yaşar Ertas, and M. Ziya Köse. Istanbul: Yeditepe Yayınevi, 2011, 11–50.

——. "An Ottoman Spy in Syracuse (1562): Constantino/Mehmed from Candia."
Archivo de la Frontera, September 24, 2015. http://www.archivodelafrontera.com/
archivos/an-ottoman-spy-in-syracuse-1562-constantinomehmed-from-candia-
o-un-espia-otomano-en-siracusa-1562-constantinomehmed-de-candia-por-emrah-
safa-gurkan/.

——. *Sultanın Korsanları: Osmanlı Akdenizi'nde Gazâ, Yağma ve Esaret, 1500–1700.*
Istanbul: Kronik, 2018.

——. "Touting for Patrons, Brokering Power and Trading Information:
Trans-Imperial Jews in Sixteenth-Century Constantinople." In *Detrás de las apariencias. Información y espionaje (siglos XVI–XVII)*, edited by Emilio Sola Castaño
and Gennaro Varriale. Alcalá de Henares: Universidad de Alcalá, 2015, 127–51.

Hadsund, Per. "The Tin-Mercury Mirror: Its Manufacturing Technique and Deterioration Processes," *Studies in Conservation* 38, no. 1 (February 1993): 12.

Halacoğlu, Yusuf. "Klasik Dönemde Osmanlılarda Haberleşme ve Yol Sistemi." In *Çağını Yakalayan Osmanlı! Osmanlı Devleti'nde Modern Haberleşme ve Ulaştırma Teknikleri*, edited by Ekmeleddin İhsanoğlu and Mustafa Kaçar. Istanbul: IRCICA, 1995, 13–21.

———. *Osmanlılarda Ulaşım ve Haberleşme: Menziller*. Ankara: PTT Genel Müdürlüğü, 2002.

Harris, J. R. *Industrial Espionage and Technology Transfer: Britain and France in the Eighteenth Century*. Aldershot: Ashgate, 1998.

Harris, Robin. *Dubrovnik. A History*. London: Saqi Books, 2003.

Hassiotis, Giovanni K. "Venezia e i domini veneziani tramite di informazioni sui turchi per gli spagnoli." In *Venezia centro di mediazione tra Oriente e Occidente, secoli XV–XVI: aspetti e problemi*, edited by Hans-Georg Beck, Manoussos Manoussacas, and Agostino Pertusi. Floransa: L. S. Olschki, 1977, 117–37.

Haswell, Jock. *The First Respectable Spy: The Life and Times of Colquhoun Grant, Wellington's Head of Intelligence*. Staplehurst: Spellmount, 2005.

Headley, John M. "Germany, the Empire and *Monarchia* in the Thought and Policy of Gattinara." In *Das römisch-deutsche Reich im politischen System Karls V*, edited by Heinrich Lutz and Elisabeth Müller Luckner. Munich: Oldenbourg, 1982, 1547.

———. "The Habsburg World Empire and the Revival of Ghibellinism." *Medieval Renaissance Studies* 7 (1975): 93–127.

Hernán, Enrique García. "Espionaje en la Batalla de Lepanto." *Historia 16* 27 (2003): 8–41.

———. "The Price of Spying at the Battle of Lepanto." *Eurasian Studies* 2, no. 2 (2003): 227–50.

Hershenzon, Daniel. "The Political Economy of Ransom in the Early Modern Mediterranean." *Past and Present* 231 (May 2016): 61–95.

Hess, Andrew C. "The Battle of Lepanto and its Place in Mediterranean History." *Past and Present* 57 (1972): 53–73.

———. *The Forgotten Frontier: A History of the Sixteenth Century Ibero-African Frontier*. Chicago: University of Chicago Press, 1978.

———. "The Moriscos: An Ottoman Fifth Column in the Sixteenth-Century Spain." *American Historical Review* 74 (October 1968): 1–25.

———. "The Ottoman Conquest of Egypt (1517) and the Beginning of the Sixteenth-Century World War." *International Journal of Middle Eastern Studies* 4, no. 1 (1973): 55–76.

Heywood, Colin. "Fernand Braudel and the Ottomans: The Emergence of an Involvement (1928–50)." *Mediterranean Historical Review* 23, no. 2 (2008), 165–84.

———. "The Ottoman Menzilhane and Ulak System in Rumeli in the Eighteenth Century." In *Türkiye'nin Sosyal ve Ekonomik Tarihi (1071–1920)*, edited by Osman Okyar and Halil İnalcık. Ankara: Meteksan, 1980, 179–86.

———. "Some Turkish Archival Sources for the History of the Menzilhane Network in Rumeli during the Eighteenth Century." *Boğaziçi Üniversitesi Dergisi, Beşeri Bilimler. Humanities* 4–5 (1976–1977): 39–54.

———. "The Via Egnatia in the Ottoman Period: The Menzilhanes of the Sol Kol in the Late 17th/Early 18th Century." In *Via Egnatia under Ottoman Rule (1380–1699)*, edited by Elizabeth Zachariadou. Rethymon: Crete University Press, 1996, 129–44.

———. *Writing Ottoman History: Documents and Interpretations*. Aldershot, Hampshire: Ashgate, 2002.

Hopper, Andrew. *Turncoats and Renegades: Changing Sides during the English Civil War*. Oxford: Oxford University Press, 2018.

Howard Carter, Charles. *The Secret Diplomacy of the Habsburgs, 1598–1625*. New York and London: Columbia University Press, 1964.

Hugon, Alain. *Au service du Roi Catholique, "honorables ambassadeurs" et "divins espions": Représentation diplomatique et service secret dans les relations hispano-françaises de 1598 à 1635*. Madrid: Casa de Velázquez, 2004.

Huntington, Samuel. *The Clash of Civilizations and the Remaking of World Order*. New York: Simon & Schuster, 1996.

Hutchinson, Robert. *Elizabeth's Spy Master: Francis Walsingham and the Secret War that Saved England*. London: Phoenix, 2007.

İlter, Aziz Samih. *Şimali Afrika'da Türkler*. Istanbul: Vakit Matbaası, 1936.

Imber, Colin. "The Navy of Süleyman the Magnificent." *Archivum Ottomanicum* 6 (1980): 211–82.

İnalcık, Halil. "Dâr al-'Ahd." *Encyclopedia of Islam*, 2nd ed.

———. *Fatih Devri Üzerine Tetkik ve Vesikalar*. Ankara: Türk Tarih Kurumu, 1954.

———. "İmtiyâzât." *Encyclopedia of Islam*, 2nd ed.

———. "Mehmed II." *Türkiye Diyanet Vakfı İslam Ansiklopedisi*.

Infelise, Mario. "From Merchants' Letters to Handwritten Political Avvisi: Notes on the Origins of Public Information." In *Cultural Exchange in Early Modern Europe, vol. 3, Correspondence and Cultural Exchange in Europe, 1400–1700*, edited by Francisco Bethencourt and Florike Egmond. Cambridge: Cambridge University Press, 2007, 33–52.

———. *Prima dei giornali: Alle origini della pubblica informazione (secoli XVI e XVII)*. Rome: Editori Laterza, 2002.

Iordanou, Ioanna. "The Professionalization of Cryptology in Sixteenth-Century Venice." *Enterprise & Society* 19, no. 4 (2018): 979–1013.

———. "The Secret Service of Renaissance Venice: Intelligence Organisation in the Sixteenth Century." *Journal of Intelligence History* 21, no. 3 (2022): 251–67.

———. "The Spy Chiefs of Renaissance Venice: Intelligence Leadership in the Early Modern World." In *Spy Chiefs, vol. 2, Intelligence Leaders in Europe, the Middle East, and Asia*, edited by Paul Maddrell, Christopher Moran, Ioanna Iordanou, and Mark Stout. Washington, DC: Georgetown University Press, 2018, 43–66.

———. *Venice's Secret Service: Organising Intelligence in the Renaissance*. Oxford: Oxford University Press, 2019.

———. "What News on the Rialto? The Trade of Information and Early Modern Venice's Centralized Intelligence Organization." *Intelligence and National Security* 31, no. 3 (2015), 1–22.

Işıksel, Güneş. *La diplomatie ottomane sous le règne de Selîm II: paramètres et périmètres de l'Empire ottoman dans le troisime quart du XVIe siècle*. Paris: Peeters, 2016.

Isom-Verhaaren, Christine. *Allies with the Infidel: The Ottoman and French Alliance in the Sixteenth Century*. London: I.B. Tauris, 2011.

———. "An Ottoman Report about Martin Luther and the Emperor: New Evidence of the Ottoman Interest in the Protestant Challenge to the Power of Charles V." *Turcica* 28 (1996): 299–318.

Jenkins, Hester Donaldson. *Ibrahim Pasha, the Grand Vizir of Suleyman the Magnificent*. New York: Columbia University Press, 1911.

Jütte, Daniel. *The Age of Secrecy: Jews, Christians, and the Economy of Secrets, 1400–1800*. New Haven and London: Yale University Press, 2015.

Kafadar, Cemal. "A Death in Venice (1575): Anatolian Muslim Merchants Trading in the Serenissima." *Journal of Turkish Studies* 10 (1986): 191–218.

Kaiser, Wolfgang, ed. *Le Commerce des Captifs: Les intermédiaires dans l'échange et le rachat des prisonniers en Méditerranée, XV–XVIII siècle*. Rome: École française de Rome, 2008.

Kemp, Percy. "An Eighteenth-Century Turkish Intelligence Report." *International Journal of Middle East Studies* 16 (1984): 497–506.

Kissling, Hans J. "Venezia come centro di informazioni sui turchi." In *Venezia centro di mediazione tra Oriente e Occidente, secoli XV–XVI: aspetti e problemi*, edited by Hans-Georg Beck, M. I. Manousakas, and Agostino Pertusi. Florence: L. S. Olschki, 1977, 97–109.

Kolçak, Özgür. "'Cümle Palankaları Küffâr Aldı . . .': 1663–64 Osmanlı-Habsburg Savaşında Dezenformasyon, Propaganda ve Siyasî İktidar." *The Journal of Ottoman Studies / Osmanlı Araştırmaları Dergisi* 43 (2014): 165–92.

Köprülü, Fuad. *Bizans Müesseselerinin Osmanlı Müesseselerine Tesiri*. Istanbul: Evkaf Matbaası, 1931.

Köse, Metin Ziya. *Doğu Akdeniz'de Casuslar ve Tacirler: Osmanlı Devleti ve Ragusa İlişkileri, 1500–1600*. Istanbul: Giza Yayınları, 2009.

Kretschmayr, Heinrich. *Ludovico Gritti: Eine Monographie*. Vienna: Gerold, 1896.

Krstić, Tijana. "Contesting Subjecthood and Sovereignty in Ottoman Galata in the Age of Confessionalization: The *Carazo* Affair, 1613–1617." *Oriento Moderno* 93 (2013): 422–53.

——. "Moriscos in Ottoman Galata, 1609–1620s." In *The Expulsion of the Moriscos from Spain: A Mediterranean Diaspora*, edited by Mercedes García-Arenal and Gerard Wiegers, translated by Consuelo López-Morillas and Martin Beagles. Leiden: Brill, 2014, 269–85.

Kunt, Metin. "A Prince Goes Forth (Perchance to Return)." In *Identity and Identity Formation in the Ottoman World: A Volume of Essays in Honour of Norman Itzkowitz*, edited by Baki Tezcan and Karl K. Barbir. Wisconsin: Wisconsin University Press, 2007, 63–71.

——. "Royal and Other Households." In *The Ottoman World*, edited by Christine Woodhead. London and New York: Routledge, 2012, 103–15.

——. *Sancaktan Eyalete: 1550–1650 Arasında Osmanlı Ümerası ve İl İdaresi*. Istanbul: Boğaziçi Üniversitesi Yayınları, 1978.

——. "Sultan, Dynasty and State in the Ottoman Empire: Political Institutions in the 16th century." *The Medieval History Journal / Special Issue on Tributary Empires* 6, no. 2 (November 2003): 217–30.

——. *The Sultan's Servants: The Transformation of Ottoman Provincial Administration, 1550–1650*. New York: Columbia University Press, 1983.

Kütükoğlu, Bekir. *Osmanlı-İran Siyâsî Münâsebetleri I: 1578–1590*. Istanbul: İstanbul Edebiyat Fakültesi Matbaası, 1962.

Lazzarini, Isabella. *Communication and Conflict: Italian Diplomacy in the Early Renaissance, 1350–1520*. Oxford: Oxford University Press, 2015.

Lesure, Michel. "Michel Černović 'Explorator Secretus' à Constantinople (1556–1563)." *Turcica* 15 (1983): 127–54.

——. "Notes et documents sur les relations véneto-ottomanes, 1570–1573, I." *Turcica* 4 (1972): 134–64.

——. "Notes et documents sur les relations véneto-ottomanes, 1570–1573, II." *Turcica* 8 (1976): 117–56.

Lewis, Bernard. "Muslim Discovery of Europe." *Bulletin of the School of Oriental and African Studies* 20, no. 1–3 (1957): 409–16.

———. *The Muslim Discovery of Europe*. New York and London: W. W. Norton & Company, 1982.

Lowry, Heath. "The Island of Limnos: A Case Study on the Continuity of Byzantine Forms under Ottoman Rule." In *Continuity and Change in Late Byzantine and Early Ottoman Society*, edited by Anthony Bryer and Heath Lowry. Birmingham: University of Birmingham, Center for Byzantine Studies; Washington: Dumbarton Oaks Research Library and Collection, 1986, 235–59.

Lucchetta, Francesca. "L'Affare Zen." *Studi veneziani* 10 (1968): 109–221.

———. "La scuola dei 'giovani di lingua' veneti nei secoli XVI e XVII." *Quaderni di studi arabici* 7 (1989): 19–40.

Malcolm, Noel. *Agents of Empire: Knights, Corsairs, Jesuits, and Spies in the Sixteenth-Century Mediterranean World*. London: Allen Lane, 2015.

Manfroni, Camillo. *Storia della marina italiana*. Roma: Forzani E C. Tipografi Del Senato, 1917.

Marshall, Alan. *Intelligence and Espionage in the Reign of Charles II, 1660–1685*. Cambridge: Cambridge University Press, 1994.

Matteucci, Gualberto. *Un glorioso convento francescano sulle rive del Bosforo: Il S. Francesco di Galata in Costantinopoli, c. 1230–1697*. Florence: Studi Francescani, 1967.

Mattingly, Garrett. *Renaissance Diplomacy*. New York: Dover Publications, 1988.

Ménage, Victor L. "The Mission of an Ottoman Secret Agent in France in 1486." *Royal Asiatic Society of Great Britain and Ireland* 97, no. 2 (1965): 112–32.

Montes, Juan Sánchez. *Franceses, Protestantes, Turcos. Los españoles ante la política internacional de Carlos V*. Granada: Universidad de Granada, 1995.

Montuoro, Domenico. "I Cigala, una famiglia feudale tra Genova, Sicilia, Turchia e Calabria." *Mediterranea: Richerche storiche* 16 (2009): 277–302.

Moral, José Maria del. *El Virrey de Napoles Don Pedro de Toledo y la guerra contra el Turco*. Madrid: Consejo Superior de Investigaciónes Cientificas, 1966.

Murphey, Rhoads. *Exploring Ottoman Sovereignty: Tradition, Image and Practice in the Ottoman Imperial Household, 1400–1800*. London: Continuum, 2008.

———. "Seyyid Murâdî's Prose Biography of Hızır ibn Yakub, alias Hayrredin Barbarossa: Ottoman Folk Narrative as an under-exploited Source for Historical Reconstruction." *Acta Orientaliae Academiae Scientiarum Hungaricae* 54, no. 4 (2001): 519–32.

Necipoğlu, Gülru. "Süleymân the Magnificent and the Representation of Power in the Context of Ottoman-Hapsburg-Papal Rivalry." In *Süleymân the Second and His Time*, edited by Halil İnalcık and Cemal Kafadar. Istanbul: The Isis Press, 1993, 163–94.

Nemeth, Gizella, and Adriano Papo. *Ludovico Gritti: Un principe-mercante del Rinascimento tra Venezia i Turchi e la corona d'Ungheria*. Friuli: Edizioni della Laguna, 2002.

Ocakaçan, Levent Kaya. "Cigalazade Yusuf Sinan Pasha (c. 1545–1606)." *Mediterranea: richerche storiche* 34 (2015): 325–40.

O'Halpin, Eunan, Robert Armstrong, and Jane Ohlmeyer, eds. *Intelligence, Statecraft and International Power—Irish Conference of Historians*. Dublin and Portland: Irish Academic Press, 2006.

Oliva, Gaetano. "Sinan-Bassà (Scipione Cicala), celebre rinnegato del secolo XVI." *Archivio Storico Messinese* 8–9 (1907–1908): 266–303.

Özcan, Abdülkadir. "Martolos." *Türkiye Diyanet Vakfı İslam Ansiklopedisi* 28 (2003): 64–66.

Özdemir, Mehmet. "Birinci Dünya Savaşı'nda Propaganda ve Casusluğa Karşı Alınan Tedbirler." *Askerî Tarih Araştırmaları Dergisi* 4 (2004): 55–74.

Özdemir, Şenay. "Kıyı Nöbeti: Osmanlı Devleti'nin Akdeniz'de Kıyı Savunması." *Tarih İncelemeleri Dergisi* 23, no. 1 (July 2008): 187–210.

Pamuk, Şevket. *İstanbul ve Diğer Kentlerde 500 Yıllık Fiyat ve Ücretler, 1469–1998*. Ankara: T.C. Başbakanlık Devlet İstatistik Enstitüsü, 2000.

Pappalardo, S. "Ambizione politica, commercio e diplomazia alla fine del XVI secolo: Carlo Cicala," In *Acque, terre e spazi dei mercanti: Istituzioni, gerarchie, conflitti e pratiche dello scambio dall'età antica alla modernità*, edited by Daniele Andreozzi, Loredana Panariti, and Claudio Zaccaria. Trieste: Editreg, 2009, 141–68.

Parker, Geoffrey. *The Grand Strategy of Philip II*. New Haven and London: Yale University Press, 1998.

Pedani, Maria Pia. *In Nome del Gran Signore: Inviati ottomani a Venezia dalla caduta di Costantinopoli alla guerra di Candia*. Venice: Deputazione Editrice, 1994.

———. *Osmanlı Padişahının Adına: İstanbul'un Fethinden Girit Savaşı'na Venedik'e Gönderilen Osmanlılar*, translated by Elis Yıldırım. Ankara: Türk Tarih Kurumu, 2011.

Petitjean, Johann. "On His Holiness' Secret Service: How Ragusa Became an Intelligence Agency after Lepanto." In *Europe and the 'Ottoman World': Exchanges and Conflicts (Sixteenth to Seventeenth Centuries)*, edited by Gábor Karman and Radu G. Păun. Istanbul: The Isis Press, 2013, 83–106.

———. *L'intelligence des choses: une histoire de l'information entre Italie et Méditerranée (XVIe–XVIIe siècles)*. Rome: École Française de Rome, 2013.

———. "Mots et pratiques de l'information: Ce que *aviser* veut dire (XVIe–XVIIe siècles)." *Mélanges de l'École française de Rome* 122, no. 1 (2010): 107–21.

Pettegree, Andrew. *The Invention of News: How the World Came to Know about Itself*. New Haven and London: Yale University Press, 2014.

Pirenne, Henri. *Mahomet et Charlemagne*. Paris: F. Alcan; Brussels: Nouvelle société d'éditions, 1937.

———. "Mahomet et Charlemagne." *Revue Belge de Philologie et d'histoire* 1 (1922): 77–86.

Pohlig, Matthias. "The Uses and Utility of Intelligence: The Case of the British Government during the War of the Spanish Succession." *Journal of Intelligence History* 21, no. 3 (2022): 289–305.

Preto, Paolo. *I Servizi Segreti di Venezia*. Milan: Il Saggiatore, 1994.

———. *Venezia e i Turchi*. Florence: G.C. Sansoni Editore, 1975.

Raffa, Angelo. "L'ultima impresa di Hayreddin (Barbarossa). La guerra marittima turco-franco-spagnola del 1543–4." In *Aspetti ed attualità del potere marittimo in Mediterraneo nei secoli XII–XVI*, edited by P. Alberini. Rome: Ufficio storico della marina militare, 1999, 397–424.

Ribera, Jean-Michel. *Diplomatie et espionnage: Les ambassadeurs du roi de France auprès de Philippe II du traité du Cateau-Cambresis (1559) à la mort de Henri III (1589)*. Paris: Honoré Champion Editeur, 2007.

Rinieri, Ilario. *Clemente VIII e Sinan Bassà Cicala*. Rome: Civiltà Cattolica, 1898.

Rivas, Javier Marcos, and Carlos J. Carnicer García. *Espionaje y traición en el reinado de Felipe II: La historia de vallisoletano Martin de Acuña*. Valladolid: Diputación Provincial de Valladolid, 2001.

Rodríguez-Salgado, M. J. *Felipe II, el "Paladín de la Cristiandad y la paz con el Turco."* Valladolid: Universidad de Valladolid, 2004.

Romano, Ruggiero. *Braudel e noi: Riflessioni sulla cultura storica del nostro tempo.* Rome: Donzelli, 1995.

Rothkegel, Martin. "Jacobus Palaeologus in Constantinople, 1554–5 and 1573." In *Osmanlı İstanbulu IV: IV. Uluslararası Osmanlı İstanbulu Sempozyumu Bildirileri, 20–22 Mayıs 2016, İstanbul 29 Mayıs Üniversitesi,* edited by Feridun M. Emecen, Ali Akyıldız, and Emrah Safa Gürkan. Istanbul: İstanbul 29 Mayıs Üniversitesi Yayınları, 2016, 977–1004.

Rothman, E. Natalie. *Brokering Empire: Trans-Imperial Subjects between Venice and Istanbul.* Ithaca: Cornell University Press, 2012.

———. "Interpreting Dragomans: Boundaries and Crossings in the Early Modern Mediterranean." *Comparative Studies in Society and History* 51, no. 4 (October 2009): 771–800.

Safi, Polat. *Eşref: Kuşçubaşı'nın Alternatif Biyografisi.* Istanbul: Kronik, 2020.

Said, Edward. "Clash of Ignorance." *The Nation,* October 22, 2001, http://www.thenation.com/article/clash-ignorance.

Salinas, David. *Espionaje y gastos secretos en la diplomacia española (1663–1683) en sus documentos.* Valladolid: Ámbito Ediciones, 1994.

Sánchez, Santiago González. "El espionaje en los reinos de la Península Ibérica a comienzos del siglo XV." *España Medieval* 38 (2015): 135–94.

Sardella, Pierre. *Nouvelles et spéculations à Venise: Au début du XVIe siècle.* Paris: Librarie Armand Colin, 1948.

Sayılır, Burhan. "Çanakkale Kara Savaşları Sırasında Casusluk Olayları ve Türklerin Aldıkları Tedbirler." *Askerî Tarih Araştırmaları Dergisi* 8 (2006): 100–8.

Seng, Yvonne J. "Fugitives and Factotums: Slaves in Early Sixteenth-Century Istanbul." *Journal of the Economic and Social History of the Orient* 39, no. 2 (1996): 136–69.

Servantie, Alain. "Charles Quint aux yeux des Ottomans." In *Carlos V: Los moriscos y el Islam,* edited by María Jesús Rubiera Mata. Madrid: Sociedad Estatal para la Conmemoración de los centanarios de Felipe II y Carlos V, 2001, 295–319.

Setton, Kenneth M. *The Papacy and the Levant (1204–1571).* Philadelphia: American Historical Society, 1984.

Skilliter, S. A. "The Hispano-Ottoman Armistice of 1581." In *Iran and Islam: In Memory of the Late Vladimir Minorsky,* edited by C. E. Bosworth. Edinburgh: Edinburgh University Press, 1971, 491–515.

———. "The Sultan's Messenger, Gabriel Defrens; an Ottoman Master Spy of the Sixteenth Century." *Wiener Zeitschrift für die Kunde des Morgenlandes* 68 (1976): 47–59.

———. *William Harborne and the Trade with Turkey, 1578–1582: A Documentary Study of the First Anglo-Ottoman Relations.* Oxford: Oxford University Press, 1977.

Snyder, Jon R. *Dissimulation and the Culture of Secrecy in Early Modern Europe.* Berkeley and Los Angeles: University of California Press, 2009.

Sobecki, Sebastian. "'A Man of Curious Enquiry': John Peyton's Grand Tour to Central Europe and Robert Cecil's Intelligence Network, 1596–601." *Renaissance Studies* 29, no. 3 (2014): 394–410.

Soucek, Svat. "The Rise of the Barbarossas in North Africa." *Turcica* 7 (1975): 238–50.

Sola Castaño, Emilio. *La conjura de Campanella.* Madrid: Turpin Editores, 2007.

———. *Los que van y vienen: Información y fronteras en el Mediterráneo clasico del siglo XVI.* Alcalá de Henares: Universidad de Alcalá, 2005.

———. *Uchalí: El Calabrés Tiñoso, o el mito del corsario muladí en la frontera.* Barcelona: Edicions Bellaterra, 2011.

Sola Castaño, Emilio, and José F. de la Peña. *Cervantes y la Berbería: Cervantes, mundo turco-berberisco y servicios secretos en la epoca de Felipe II*. Madrid: Fondo de Cultura Economica, 1995.

Soll, Jacob. "The Antiquary and the Information State: Colbert's Archives, Secret Histories, and the Affair of the *Régale*, 1663–1682." *French Historical Studies* 31, no. 1 (2008): 3–28.

———. "How to Manage an Information State: Jean-Baptiste Colbert's Archives and the Education of His Son." *Archival Science* 7, no. 4 (2007): 331–42.

———. *The Information Master: Jean-Baptiste Colbert's Secret State Intelligence System*. Ann Arbor: The University of Michigan Press, 2009.

Szakály, Ferenc. *Lodovico Gritti in Hungary: 1529–1534: A Historical Insight into the Beginnings of Turco-Habsburgian Rivalry*. Budapest: Akadémiai Kiadó, 1995.

Szechi, Daniel, ed. *The Dangerous Trade: Spies, Spymasters and the Making of Europe*. Dundee: Dundee University Press, 2010.

Şimşeker, Somer Alp. *Birinci Dünya Savaşı'nda Osmanlı İstihbaratı: İkinci Şube Tarihi*. Istanbul: Kronik, 2022.

Tadić, J. *Španija I Dubrovnik*. Belgrade: Sirpska Kraljevska Akademija, 1932.

Takats, S. *Macaristan Türk Âleminden Çizgiler*, translated by Sadrettin Karatay. Ankara: Türk Tarih Kurumu Basımevi, 2011.

Tansel, Selâhattin. *Yavuz Sultan Selim*. Ankara: Milli Eğitim Basımevi, 1969.

Thompson, James Westfall, and Saul K. Padover. *Secret Diplomacy and Cryptography, 1500–1815*. New York: Frederick Ungar Publishing Co., 1937.

Tormene, P. Augusto. "Il bailaggio a Costantinopoli di Girolamo Lippomano e la sua tragica fine." *Nuovo archivio veneto*, n.s. 4, t. 7 (1904): 83–84.

Turan, Şerafettin. *Kanuni Dönemi Taht Kavgaları*, 2nd ed. Ankara: Bilgi Yayınevi, 1997.

Urban, Mark. *The Man Who Broke Napoleon's Codes: The Story of George Scovell*. London: Faber and Faber, 2001.

Valente, Gustavo. *Vita di Occhiali*. Milan: Casa Editrice Ceschina, 1960.

Varriale, Gennaro. *Arrivano li Turchi: guerra navale e spionaggio nel Mediterraneo (1532–1582)*. Novi Ligure: Città del silenzio, 2014.

———. "La lealtà fragile: Bartolomeo Brutti e lo spionaggio di Felipe II." In *Gli antichi stati italiani e l'Europa Centro–Orientale tra il tardo Medioevo e l'Età moderna*, edited by Cristian Luca and Gianluca Masi. Brăila–Udine: Istros Editrice–Gaspari Editore, 2016, 93–128.

———, ed. *Si fuera cierto? Espías y agentes en la frontera (siglos XVI–XVII)*. Alcalá de Henares: Universidad de Alcalá, 2018.

Vatin, Nicolas. "Remarques sur l'oral et l'écrit dans l'administration ottomane au XVIe siècle." *Revue du monde musulman et de la Méditerranée* 75–76 (1995): 143–54.

Villain-Gandossi, Christiane. "Les Dépêches Chiffrées de Vettore Bragadin, Baile de Constantinople (12 Juillet 1564–15 Juin 1566)." *Turcica* 10 (1978): 52–106.

Vitkus, Daniel J., ed. *Piracy, Slavery, and Redemption: Barbary Captivity Narratives from Early Modern England*. New York: Columbia University Press, 2001.

de Vivo, Filippo. *Information and Communication in Venice: Rethinking Early Modern Politics*. Oxford: Oxford University Press, 2007.

———. *Patrizi, Informatori, Barbieri: Politica e communicazione a Venezia nella prima età moderna*. Milano: Feltrinelli, 2012

———. "Public Sphere of Communication Triangle? Information and Politics in Early Modern Europe." In *Beyond the Public Sphere: Opinions, Publics, Spaces in Early Modern Europe*, edited by Massimo Rospocher. Bologna: Il Mulino, 2012, 115–36.

Walker, Jonathan. *Pistols! Treason! Murder!: The Rise and Fall of a Master Spy*. Carlton: Melbourne University Press, 2007.

Weiss, Gillian. *Captives and Corsairs: France and Slavery in the Early Modern Mediterranean*. Stanford: Stanford University Press, 2011.

Williams, Phillip. *Empire and Holy War in the Mediterranean*. New York: I.B. Tauris, 2014.

Wilson, Derek. *Sir Francis Walsingham: A Courtier in an Age of Terror*. London: Constable, 2007.

Woods, John E. "Turco-Iranica I: An Ottoman Intelligence Report on Late Fifteenth/Ninth Century Iranian Foreign Relations." *Journal of Near Eastern Studies* 38, no. 1 (1979): 1–9.

Yıldız, Gültekin. *Osmanlı İmparatorluğu'nda Askeri İstihbarat (1864–1914)*. Istanbul: Yeditepe Yayınevi, 2019.

Yriarte, Charles. *La vie d'un patricien de Venise au XVIe siècle*. Paris: J. Rothschild.

Yüksel, Ahmet. *II. Mahmud Devrinde Osmanlı İstihbaratı*. Istanbul: Kitap Yayınevi, 2013.

———. *Rusların Kafkasya'yı İstilası ve Osmanlı İstihbarat Ağı*. Istanbul: Dergah Yayınları, 2014.

———. *Sınırdaki Casus: Osmanlı Topraklarında Bir Rus Ajanı: Kafkasyalı Mehdi Kulu Şirvanî*. Istanbul: Kronik, 2019.

Yürük, Ali Yücel. "Lütfi Paşa'nın (ö. 970/1563) Osmanlı Haberleşme ve Ulaşım Sistemine Ulak Zulmü Bağlamında Getirdiği Yenilikler." *Kitaplara Vakfedilen Bir Ömre Tuhfe: İsmail E. Erünsal'a Armağan*. Istanbul: Ülke Armağan, 2013, 1:597–626.

Zele, Walter. "Aspetti delle legazioni ottomane nei *Diarii* di Marino Sanudo." *Studi Veneziani* 18 (1989): 241–84.

Unpublished Theses and Dissertations

Afinogenov, Gregory Dmitrevich. "The Eye of the Tsar: Intelligence-Gathering and Geopolitics in Eighteenth-Century Russia." Unpublished PhD diss., Harvard University, 2016.

Coix, Stephannie Coeto. "Alexandre Testanegra: An Ottoman Spy in the New World?" Unpublished MA thesis, The University of Texas at Austin, 2018.

Fleischer, Cornell. "Gelibolulu Mustafa Âli Efendi, 1541–1600: A Study in Ottoman Historical Consciousness." Unpublished PhD diss., Princeton University, 1982.

Graf, Tobias. "'I am Still Yours': Christian-European 'Renegades' in the Ottoman Elite during the Late Sixteenth and Seventeenth Centuries." Unpublished PhD diss., Heidelberg University, 2013.

Gök, İlhan. "Atatürk Kitaplığı Mc.O.071 Numaralı 909–933/1503–1527 Tarihli İn'âmât Defteri (Transkripsiyon-Değerlendirme)." Unpublished PhD diss., Marmara University, 2014.

Gürkan, Emrah Safa. "Espionage in the 16th Century Mediterranean: Secret Diplomacy, Mediterranean Go-Betweens and the Ottoman-Habsburg Rivalry." Unpublished PhD diss., Georgetown University, 2012.

Ocakaçan, Levent Kaya. "Geç 16. ve Erken 17. Yüzyılda Osmanlı Devleti'ndeki Patronaj İlişkilerinin Gazanfer Ağa Örneği Üzerinden Venedik Belgelerine Göre İncelenmesi." Unpublished PhD diss., Marmara University, 2016.

Önal, Ahmet. "Koca Sinan Paşa'nın Hayatı ve Siyasi Faaliyetleri (1520–1596)." Unpublished PhD diss., Marmara University, 2012.

Otman, Elvin. "The Role of Alvise Gritti within the Ottoman politics in the Context of the 'Hungarian Question' (1526–1534)." Unpublished MA thesis, Bilkent University, 2009.

Rothman, E. Natalie. "Between Venice and Istanbul: Trans-imperial Subjects and Cultural Mediation in the Early Modern Mediterranean." Unpublished PhD diss., University of Michigan, 2006.

Safi, Polat. "The Ottoman Special Organization—Teşkilat-ı Mahsusa: An Inquiry into its Operational and Administrative Characteristics." Unpublished PhD diss., Bilkent University, 2012.

Smiley, Will. "'When Peace Comes, You Will Again be Free': Islamic and Treaty Law, Black Sea Conflict, and the Emergence of 'Prisoners of War' in the Ottoman Empire, 1739–1830." Unpublished PhD diss., University of Cambridge, 2012.

Sobers-Khan, Nur. "Slaves without Shackles: Forced Labour and Manumission in the Galata Court Registers, 1560–1572." Unpublished PhD diss., Pembroke College, 2012.

Resende, Vasco. "L'Orient islamique dans la culture portugaise de l'époque moderne, du voyage de Vasco de Gama à la chute d'Ormuz (1498–1622)." Unpublished PhD diss., École Pratique des Hautes Études, 2011.

Tezcan, Baki. "Searching for Osman: A Reassessment of the Deposition of Sultan Osman II (r. 1618–1622)." Unpublished PhD diss., Princeton University, 2001.

Turan, Ebru. "The Sultan's Favorite: Ibrahim Pasha and the Making of the Ottoman Universal Sovereignty in the Reign of Sultan Suleyman (1516–1526)." Unpublished PhD diss., University of Chicago, 2007.

Türkçelik, Evrim. "Cigalazade Yusuf Sinan Pasha y el Mediterráneo entre 1591–1606." Unpublished PhD diss., Universidad Autonoma de Madrid, 2012.

White, Joshua Michael. "Catch and Release: Piracy, Slavery, and Law in the Early Modern Ottoman Mediterranean." Unpublished PhD diss., University of Michigan, 2012.

Yeni, Mustafa. "Birinci Dünya Savaşı'nda Başkumdanlık Vekâleti ve Harbiye Nezareti'nin II. Şube (İstihbarat) Faaliyetleri." Unpublished PhD diss., İstanbul University, 2022.

INDEX

ABOUT THE AUTHOR AND TRANSLATORS

Emrah Safa Gürkan is a professor in the Department of Political Science and International Relations at Istanbul's 29 Mayıs University. Having completed his undergraduate studies in the Department of International Relations at Ankara's Bilkent University (2003), Emrah Safa Gürkan went on to obtain his master's from the same university, writing a thesis on Ottoman corsairs in the Western Mediterranean under the supervision of the renowned historian Professor Halil Inalcık (2006). He then studied under Gábor Ágoston at Georgetown University, gaining his doctorate in history in 2012. Gürkan's fields of specialization are the history of Early Modern Europe and the history of the Mediterranean, and he has conducted research on subjects such as intelligence, piracy, slavery, conversion, Ottoman-European relations, and border studies. This book was originally published in Turkey as *Sultanin Casuslari: 16. Yüzyılda İstihbarat, Sabotaj ve Rüşvet Ağları* (Istanbul: Kronik, 2017) and won the 2018 Award for an Original Academic Work presented by the Turkish Academy of Sciences (TÜBA). He is also the author of *Sultanın Korsanları: Osmanlı Akdenizi'nde Gazâ, Yağma ve Esaret, 1500–1700* (İstanbul: Kronik, 2018), *Cumhuriyet'in Yüz Günü: İnkilabın Ayak Sesleri* (Istanbul: Mundi, 2023), *Cumhuriyet'in 100 İsmi: Büyük Devrimin Portreleri* (Istanbul: Mundi, 2023), *Ezbere Yaşayanlar: Vazgeçemediğimiz Alışkanlıkların Kökenleri* (Istanbul: Kronik, 2022), *Bunu Herkes Bilir: Tarihte Yanlış Sorulara Doğru Cevaplar* (Istanbul: Kronik, 2020), and (with Feridun M. Emecen and Ali Akyıldız) *Osmanlı İstanbulu: Uluslararası Osmanlı İstanbulu Sempozyumu Bildirileri* (Istanbul, 2014–2019). Gürkan also won the 2018 Outstanding Young Scientist Award presented by the Turkish Academy of Sciences.

Dr. Jonathan Ross was born in London, studied German and politics at Edinburgh University, and completed his doctorate in German Literature at King's College London. He now works in the Department of Translation and Interpreting Studies at Boğaziçi University, Istanbul, where he teaches both practical and research-oriented courses. His research interests include public service interpreting, nonprofessional interpreting, and audiovisual translation. His academic work has appeared in leading journals and monographs in the field of translation and interpreting. He has also published English translations of numerous Turkish books on history, archaeology, and culture, as well as translating several Turkish films, short stories, and poems.

İdil Karacadağ is a freelance translator from Istanbul, Turkey, whose work primarily focuses on contemporary Turkish literature.